MI5 *at War* 1909–1918

How MI5 Foiled the Spies of the Kaiser in the First World War

W0007907

CHRIS NORTHCOTT

In memory of the late Robert W. Johannsen

J.G. Randall Distinguished Professor of History
University of Illinois at Urbana-Champaign, USA

In fond remembrance of our good times with 'Old Hickory'

....

Dr. Chris Northcott was born in Surrey in 1973. He is an independent scholar who received his doctorate in History, which focused on the development of MI5 between 1909-1918, from the University of Bedfordshire. He has taught Intelligence and Security Studies at the Universities of Salford and Bedfordshire and has been published in the *International Journal of Intelligence and CounterIntelligence*. He has also written book reviews for *Intelligence and National Security*.

He enjoys American Football and cycling, and lives in Buckinghamshire with his partner, Diana, and their beloved dog, Foxy. *MI5 at War 1909-1918* is his first book.

Published in Great Britain in 2015 by
Tattered Flag Press
4 Eden Court
Church Street
Ticehurst
East Sussex TN5 7AF
England

office@thetatteredflag.com
www.thetatteredflag.com

Tattered Flag Press is an imprint of Chevron Publishing Ltd.

MI5 at War 1909-1918
© Chris Northcott

Design: Mark Nelson, NSW

British Library Cataloguing in Publication Data

A Catalogue Record for this book is available from the British Library

ISBN 978-0-9576892-8-2

Printed and bound in Great Britain

For more information on books published by Tattered Flag Press visit
www.thetatteredflag.com

CONTENTS

ACKNOWLEDGEMENTS

A BOOK is very much a team effort and it is my great pleasure, and privilege, to express my gratitude to all those who have helped with this study.

My most heartfelt thanks go to Ian Beckett and Anthony Clayton, my PhD supervisors, for the exceptional commitment they have shown to me and to this project over many years.

I am exceptionally fortunate that Robert Forsyth of the Tattered Flag Press is my publisher. Robert is also an acclaimed historian himself, who has written extensively on the history of the *Luftwaffe*. Thus, Robert empathised with what I was trying to do and was the ideal partner to have in turning my thesis into a book.

A great debt is also owed to the staffs at the (UK) National Archives and all the other archives that were mined for material. Their knowledge and helpfulness turned a seemingly daunting task into a fascinating voyage of discovery.

Finally, words cannot really express how grateful I am for the rock-like support of my family; I simply would not have survived the ups and downs of this immensely stimulating, yet equally demanding project without you all by my side. Thanks to: my parents (Barry and Elaine Northcott), my sisters (Rosemary Stringer and Debbie Chaplin), my nephews and niece (Dominic Stringer, Phoebe Stringer, Joe Chaplin and Harry Chaplin), and my soulmate Diana Dziubenko and our beloved dog, Foxy.

Chris Northcott
2015

GLOSSARY

Abteilung IIIb	Military Intelligence Department of the German General Staff
AE	Aliens Enquiry [card]
AG3	Adjutant General's Department, Section 3
ARA	Aliens Restriction Act
ARO	Aliens Restriction Orders
BCI	Bureau Central Interallié
BEF	British Expeditionary Force
BL	Black List
CC	Chief Constable
CCAC	Churchill College Archives Centre, Cambridge
CGS	Chief of the General Staff [India]
CID	Committee of Imperial Defence
CID	Criminal Intelligence Department [India]
CID	[Metropolitan Police] Criminal Investigation Department
CIGS	Chief of the Imperial General Staff
CMA	Competent Military Authorities
CNA	Competent Naval Authorities
CENTO	Central Treaty Organization
CSIB	Central Special Intelligence Bureau
DAC	Deputy Assistant Censor
DCI	Director of Criminal Intelligence [India]
DIP	Director Intelligence Police
DMI	Director of Military Intelligence
DMO	Director of Military Operations
DNI	Director of Naval Intelligence
DORA	Defence of the Realm Act
DPP	Director of Public Prosecutions
DRR	Defence of the Realm Regulations
DSI	Director of Security Intelligence
DSI	Director of Special Intelligence
DSO	Defence Security Officer
EMSIB	Eastern Mediterranean Special Intelligence Bureau
FO	Foreign Office
FOPO	Foreign Office Permit Office
GHQ	General Headquarters

GHQHF	General Headquarters Home Forces
GOC	General-Officer-Commanding
GPO	General Post Office
GSO	General Staff Officer
HO	Home Office
HOPO	Home Office Permit Office
HOW	Home Office Warrant
IP	Intelligence Police
IWM	Imperial War Museum, London
JP	Justice of the Peace
LHCMA	Liddell Hart Centre for Military Archives, King's College, London
MCO	Military Control Officers
MI1	Military Intelligence, Department No.1 [Secretariat]
MI1c	Military Intelligence, Department No.1 Section C [Foreign Espionage] (designation used by the Secret Intelligence Service during the First World War)
MI5	Section 5 of the Directorate of Military Intelligence (also known today as the Security Service)
MI6	Section 6 of the Directorate of Military Intelligence (the Secret Intelligence Service has also been known as MI6 since the late-1930s)
MI6	Military Intelligence, Department No.6 [Legal and Economic]
MI7	Military Intelligence, Department No.7 [Press Control]
MI8	Military Intelligence, Department No.8 [Cable Censorship]
MI9	Military Intelligence, Department No.9 [Postal Censorship]
MMLI	Ministry of Munitions Labour Intelligence
MO5	Military Operations, Department No.5 [Secret Service] (Name used until August 1915)
MO5	Military Operations, Department No.5 [Counter-espionage] (Name used by MI5 from August 1915-January 1916)
MO5(g)	Military Operations, Department No.5 section g [Counter-espionage] (Name used by MI5 from August 1914-August 1915)
N	Nachrichten-Abteilung im Admiralstab (Naval Intelligence Department of the German Admiralty Staff)
NCCL	National Council for Civil Liberties
NEP	Neutral European Port [scheme]
NID	Naval Intelligence Division
OSA	Official Secrets Act

PMS2	Parliamentary Military Secretary, section number 2
PRO	Public Record Office
PWM	Permission to Work on Munitions [stamp]
RAMC	Royal Army Medical Corps
RMLI	Royal Marines Light Infantry
RN	Royal Navy
SB	[Metropolitan Police] Special Branch
SEATO	South-east Asia Treaty Organization
SI	Special Intelligence
SIB	Special Intelligence Bureau
SIS	Secret Intelligence Service
SLO	Security Liaison Officer
SSB	Secret Service Bureau
SWL	Special War List
TNA	The National Archives (UK)
WO	War Office
YMCA	Young Men's Christian Association

INTRODUCTION

FROM 1909 to the end of the First World War, Captain (later Major-General Sir) Vernon George Waldegrave Kell, the founding father of MI5, developed a counter-espionage strategy based upon preventive and detective controls. A 'control' is an activity that either prevents or detects a risk. When in operation it mitigates the impact of a risk materialising. Controls fall into two types: preventive controls – that are designed to prevent the risk or incident from happening; and detective controls – that detect the occurrence of a risk or incident and thus enable action to be taken. Kell's legacy is an enduring one: over one-hundred years later, MI5's strategy is still based upon these very same cardinal principles.

MI5 is Britain's security intelligence agency, countering internal threats to national security, such as terrorism, espionage, and the proliferation of weapons of mass destruction (WMD).[1] MI5 sees its work today as falling into four categories, which it outlines on its website at the time of writing:

'(1) *investigating*: collecting, collating, analyzing and assessing secret intelligence pertinent to the threat; (2) *acting*: countering the threats; (3) *advising*: keeping the government and others informed about the threats, and advising on the correct countermeasures, including protective security; and (4) *assisting*: supporting other agencies, organizations and governments.'[2]

Covert intelligence is collected by various means, most of them standard for intelligence and security services worldwide. MI5's methods of collecting secret intelligence fall into four distinct categories, which it also outlines on its website:

- 'Covert human intelligence sources (agents): an agent is a source capable of providing secret intelligence on a target being investigated.

- 'Directed surveillance: involves the covert monitoring of targets' movements, conversations, and other activities in order to obtain intelligence about their organisations and the identities of those with whom they associate.

- 'Interception of communications: involves listening to telephone calls, and opening and reading targets' letters or e-mails.

- 'Intrusive surveillance: involves covertly monitoring the speech of targets under investigation, such as eavesdropping on conversations in someone's home or car.'[3]

As this study progresses, so it will assess whether there were early signs that MI5 would eventually develop its modern-day role and methods. It is also instructive to compare MI5 as it was during the First World War era with what MI5 is today, as just described.

MI5 had two main roles during the period 1909-1918. The first was counter-espionage, which can be defined as information collected and analysed, and activities undertaken to prevent an adversary's espionage (secret intelligence from human sources) service from gaining knowledge that would give him an advantage.[4] Secondly, advising the War Office on 'military policy in dealing with the Police Authorities and the civil population, including aliens'.[5]

This book examines how MI5 foiled the spies of the Kaiser in the First World War era: paying particular attention to the preventive measures MI5 instituted to 'frustrate' espionage and how investigations to 'cure' espionage were conducted. This focus has also enabled a detailed examination of how well MI5 performed in the battle against the spies of the Kaiser. The book will also suggest that attention needs to be focused on a hitherto neglected driver of MI5's development: that MI5's evolution was influenced by preconceived ideas about how counter-espionage work should be undertaken. As well as outlining what happened and how it happened, this study will also look at why this evolution occurred as it did. In so doing, the book will consider the possible explanations that have been put forward in the literature, including: (1) that MI5's development was driven by changes in the perceived threat, (2) the influence that cases and events had on MI5's development, and (3) other factors, such as the pressures of war, fear of aliens, etc.

In theory, the existing literature covers the question of MI5's effectiveness quite extensively and it also outlines MI5's overall development. However, with the partial exception of articles by Nicholas Hiley, current works also tend to simply look at the development of MI5 as a whole and make little mention of the six individual branches that made up MI5 by the end of the First World War.[6]

Histories of the British intelligence community, most notably Christopher Andrew's magisterial *Secret Service: the Making of the British Intelligence Community*, focus on MI5 overall, its place within the wider intelligence community and its relations with the other members, particularly the Metropolitan Police's Special Branch.[7] Surveys of the development of Britain's internal security apparatus, such as those by Bernard Porter and by Richard Thurlow, also concentrate on MI5 at the macro level, its role within this apparatus and especially the division of labour between MI5 and the Special Branch.[8]

Popular accounts of MI5, such as works by John Bulloch, Sidney Felstead, Leonard Sellers and Nigel West, tend to write around MI5 itself as they cover the most newsworthy spy stories that MI5 was involved in. In so doing they reveal not only much about these spy cases, but also provide insights into how MI5 detected them.[9]

Two articles by Hiley, which cover the development of British counter-espionage and internal security from 1907-1918, do focus more closely on the development of MI5's organisational structure and examine how MI5 had developed six branches by the armistice. Understandably, in keeping within the confines of a short article, Hiley does not put each of these branches under the microscope or analyse its particular development. He simply summed up each branch's role and place within the overall organisation in only a few paragraphs.[10]

Contemporary accounts, typically uncritically, lauded MI5 as the unquestioned victor over its German foe. Sir Basil Thomson, who directed the Metropolitan Police Special Branch during the war, for example, concluded that, judging by the character of the information gathered by the spies who were arrested, the intelligence the Germans received 'cannot have been of great value'.[11] Like his boss, Thomson, Detective Inspector

Herbert Fitch, a Special Branch officer employed on counter-espionage, judged that Germany's spies were no match for MI5. It was not difficult to thwart them at all, because Britain possessed 'a perfect organization' to combat them, which had 'a very considerable amount of theoretical knowledge of the details of their methods such as would have caused something approaching heart failure in certain high quarters abroad, had we paraded it'.[12]

Similarly, Felstead, the semi–official historian of MI5 during the First World War, whose account was based on access to official sources, argued that it seemed likely that 'none of the spies who came here ever picked up much that could not have been read in our newspapers', many of which were sent to Holland and thus eventually ended up being read in German hands anyway.[13] In a review of Felstead's *German Spies at Bay*, Brigadier-General Sir James Edmonds, head of MO5, which ran the War Office's special duties section, from 1907 to 1909 and later the official historian of the First World War, concluded that the Germans desired intelligence 'which no alien spy could possibly learn'. In the early part of the war, they hoped to ascertain the destination, number and equipment of the new armies and, particularly, timely warning of the sailing of British warships for their submarines. 'Their spies gave them none of these things.' Even when they spotted a warship, 'the information reached the German Admiralty far too late for any action to be taken'.[14]

This interpretation continued well into the Cold War with Bulloch, in 1963, describing Captain Kell, first head of MI5, as a 'remarkable man who did a remarkable job'. Beginning in 1909, without any staff, records or experience, Kell developed an organisation able to 'round-up' all except one of Germany's spies in the UK in 1914. MI5 then successfully frustrated German efforts to establish new spies there throughout the war.[15] Writing as recently as 2001, Dame Stella Rimington, one of Kell's successors as Director-General of MI5, continued this interpretation, praising the round-up of German spies in August 1914 and concluding that 'Kell's tiny organisation was very effective'.[16]

The emergence of the 'British School' of Intelligence Studies in the mid-1980s heralded a more questioning approach.[17] The current academic debate is less flattering of Kell, but continues to conclude that MI5 beat its German opponent convincingly. The judgements of many of MI5's harsher critics, such as Thomas Boghardt, Hiley, Porter and Thurlow, seem to be coloured by a distaste for the secrecy within which secret services have to operate, and a certain disdain for military officers.

Andrew's *Secret Service* charts the evolution of a recognisable intelligence community from the formation of the Secret Service Bureau to the end of Second World War. He is primarily concerned with the key players and how they influenced events and organisations.[18] Andrew concludes that MI5's pre-war development was driven by the evidence of suspicious aliens compiled by Kell, which convinced the Home Office and services that there was an extensive German espionage network in Britain; even though the reality was that it was not extensive.[19] MI5's wartime expansion was driven by a massive increase in spy mania, which lasted throughout the war even after the decline of genuine espionage; a much smaller outbreak of real spying; and the gradual development of what seemed to be subversion.[20] Assessing MI5's effectiveness, Andrew concludes that:

'Though Kell exaggerated the scale of his achievements in August 1914, he had none the less totally defeated third-rate opposition. With four assistants, seven clerks, and the assistance of the Special Branch and local police forces, he had tracked down all the real German agents in Britain.'[21]

Indeed, Andrew points to how the police's assistance helped Kell 'to stretch his own limited resources'.[22] However, he puts MI5's achievement into perspective, adding that Kell's subsequent boast that this had left Germany ignorant of the British Expeditionary Force's (BEF) deployment for more than two weeks was 'wildly exaggerated'. 'The major failings of German intelligence lay not in Britain but in the battle area.'[23] Andrew also suggests that MI5 was relatively well prepared for war. MI5 had rolled up the entire German espionage organisation in the UK, before Room 40 (Naval Signals Intelligence) or the Army's Intelligence Corps had even been established.[24] It went on to detect the German agents in Britain throughout the war 'with great efficiency', albeit that it had the advantage 'of dealing with weak opposition'.[25]

MI5 celebrated its centenary in 2009 by publishing an official history, *The Defence of the Realm: the Authorized History of MI5*, written by Christopher Andrew, arguably the world's foremost intelligence historian, who was given unrestricted access to MI5's own archives. Like all of Andrew's work, it is scrupulously researched, the analysis is insightful, and it is beautifully written. It will most likely stand as the definitive history of MI5 for at least a generation. Andrew concludes that:

> 'In the less than five years since the founding of the Secret Service Bureau, Kell had transformed British counter-espionage.'[26]

Andrew also makes a most thought-provoking assertion for any study of the development of MI5:

> 'The expanded HOW system for authorizing letter checks and the data-management system of the Registry laid the foundations for MI5's future development.'[27]

Andrew assesses MI5's pre-war performance:

> 'Research in German archives demonstrates that Kell's Bureau did not succeed in identifying all the German agents present in Britain at the outbreak of war. It seems, however, to have rounded up all those that mattered. There is no evidence that in the critical early weeks of the war that any worthwhile intelligence reached Germany from Britain.'[28]

Andrew puts MI5's achievements into their proper perspective, adding:

> 'The small scale of the Bureau's resources made its achievements the more remarkable. Its staff were fewer in number than the spies whose arrest it ordered in August 1914.'[29]

Andrew also assesses MI5's performance during the First World War:

> 'Surviving MI5 archives contain details of sixty-five German agents who were arrested and convicted or imprisoned under the Aliens Restriction Act during the First World

War. German archives indicate that a total of at least 120 agents were sent to Britain at some point between 1914 and 1918. Some (perhaps a majority) of the unarrested agents appear to have been 'reconnaissance agents' visiting British ports whose access to intelligence was limited to what they could observe themselves. A probably significant minority also broke contact with German intelligence after arriving in Britain. MO5(g) counter-espionage successes and the execution of convicted spies persuaded an unknown number to follow the example of Walter Rimann in 1914 and flee the country, or else to give up espionage.'[30]

Andrew is perhaps unique in the respect that he pays due attention to the importance of MI5's preventive work, as well as its investigative work:

'MI5 attributed much of its success in dealing with German espionage to good preventive security (later called 'protective security') which had turned Britain into a hard target.'[31]

Hiley attests that MI5 'proved remarkably effective' at countering German espionage in the UK from 1911-1914 and enabled Special Branch 'to watch all the main agents and make a full evaluation of the danger'.[32] Nonetheless, he goes on to deliver a stinging criticism of Kell and MI5. MI5's main role was to provide a fair analysis of the threat posed by German agents from a great quantity of suspicious reports, 'but in this they failed completely'. Kell circulated 'alarmist reports' despite 'access to evidence which flatly contradicted them'. Notwithstanding this 'strategic failure', MI5 still managed to identify and order the arrest of all the German agents in the UK on the outbreak of war:

'…but here the main work was in fact left to the police, for it was the Special Branch that watched the suspects and handled the bulk of the investigations – and indeed discovered the main forwarding address for the agents and so ensured Kell's limited success.'

It was also the Special Branch that investigated, and proved false, the mass of spy scares in the early days of the war; engaging more than 114 personnel in such matters, when MI5 was only able to field eight officers and three detectives. Thus, Hiley suggests that, if the Special Branch had been given the task, rather than Kell, it would have done a better job, because 'their judgement would not have been clouded by the same alarmist fears of invasion'. Thus, giving the military responsibility for counter-espionage guaranteed 'the appointment of an officer hostile to Germany' such as Kell, 'an obscure junior official of limited practical experience' who was 'paranoid about invasion'. Therefore, the formation of MI5 in 1909 should 'be seen as irresponsible', because it gave strong influence and considerable autonomy to a solitary officer 'unsuited to the task', which enabled him to pass on assessments to the highest levels suggesting that Germany was committed to war and plotting sabotage by means of the large alien population in the UK. This leads Hiley to conclude that:

'Despite superficial success, the employment of military officers on specialist counter-espionage duties between 1907 and 1914 did nothing except inspire 'spy fever' and encourage distrust of Germany, and in consequence failed as miserably as it could possibly have done.'[33]

Hiley observes that the First World War saw a 'dramatic advance' in British counter-espionage, from a small, specialist apparatus to detect spies, to a huge intelligence-collecting system, with a large budget, 'collecting information on virtually anyone opposed to government policy'. This evolution followed a thorough reinterpretation of counter-espionage because in 1914 this entailed the prevention of specified illegal actions conducted for foreign powers. By 1918 'it involved any act which tended to help an enemy more than it furthered the policies of the British government – permitting the widespread investigation and infiltration of political, industrial and pacifist organizations which were attempting to change those policies, and in 1919 spawning the first official body in Britain specifically dedicated to political policing'. This increased remit 'had come without any direct political review of the matter'; being driven solely by officials of the agencies themselves.

Hiley goes on to argue that the 'shameful truth' is that MI5 and Special Branch possessed such autonomy because governments preferred to leave them alone rather than risk the 'political odium' of association with secret service.[34] He opines that this autonomy meant that the development of British internal security would be driven by the biases of its chiefs. Such that the 'devious progress' of MI5 and the Special Branch 'was simply the direct result of permitting such bodies to operate in obsessive secrecy'.[35]

Porter's *Plots and Paranoia: a History of Political Espionage in Britain 1790-1988* provides a detailed account of domestic intelligence collection. He offers a harsh critique of the intelligence and security services.[36] Porter argues that MI5's early development was driven by an underlying apprehension that a European war was looming, which eroded the 'liberal confidence that had sustained the anti-spy culture of mid-Victorian times'.[37] MI5's wartime expansion was propelled by the dynamics of war:

'When war is declared, the clouds lift. The game is really on. There can be no doubt now that the other side is playing, and in deadly earnest. No one doubts that you should be playing too. Peacetime scruples disappear, as the higher priority of national survival overrides them. Obstacles are cleared from your path, and resources are poured in. The crowd is behind you.'[38]

Porter is also critical of MI5's record:

'It is possible that Edmonds's and Kell's exaggerated view of the German spy menace actually impeded them in the task they really had on hand. Most of the genuine spies who were arrested between 1910 and 1914 would probably have been picked up anyway, without any help at all from 'K'. While Steinhauer was deploying his handful of bungling amateurs around the coasts of Britain, and alert policemen and public-spirited young ladies were rumbling them, Kell's outfit was (metaphorically speaking) miles away, busy looking into all that nonsense of Le Queux's about waiters in wigs and hairdressers with funny walks, awaiting the signal for *der Tag*.'[39]

He suggests that this could have been due to 'Edmonds's and Kell's backgrounds as Army officers':

'The Special Branch had no one (or no one prominent) with a military background. All its personnel were professional policemen, with experience of the civilian grass roots. They were solider, dourer and generally less silly than the upper-class community who ran the military side.'[40]

Thurlow's *The Secret State: British Internal Security in the Twentieth Century* concludes that the intelligence and security agencies have developed as liberal principles have had to compromise with security challenges. Although critical of the growth of these agencies, Thurlow argues that Britain has not developed a secret state that acts outside the law.[41] Thurlow suggests that the 'security revolution' that caused MI5's pre-war development was a by-product of the threat of war. MI5's wartime expansion was enabled by a reversal of the liberal disregard for security and the passage of the Defence of the Realm Act (DORA), which gave virtually unlimited power to the armed forces. MI5's eventual movement into counter-subversion was driven by a belief that the main threats to national security emanated from foreign powers, such that domestic subversion should chiefly be viewed as an agent of enemy states. Thus, the British peace movement was deemed to be a puppet controlled by the hidden hand of Germany, for example.[42]

In a review of the material in The National Archives' (TNA) record class KV1, Thurlow concludes that it gives the impression that MI5 was 'an efficient counter-intelligence organisation', which exploited Britain's island defences to deprive Germany of access to meaningful intelligence and hinder sabotage. The reports in KV1 suggest that MI5 broke up the German espionage organisation in Britain, watched and arrested a number of spies and harassed numerous individuals that it thought possessed suspect sympathies but had no concrete evidence about.[43] He adds:

'MI5 was effective in denying enemy access to Britain's secrets, in winding up the enemy agent network and preventing infiltration, establishing passport control and postal interception, and after some administrative problems efficiently regulating the movements and interning enemy aliens during hostilities. Yet there is little sign of the imaginative deception operations of World War II and the feeling persists that the counter-intelligence successes of 1914-18 owed as much to enemy incompetence as to the undoubted, if unimaginative efficiency of British counter-intelligence.'[44]

Boghardt, whose study of German naval intelligence and British counter-espionage from 1901-1918 makes extensive use of German archival sources, contends that MI5 was born out of spy fiction, rather than fact, and that the perceived threat of espionage was crucial to MI5's development: MI5 grew 'not because it tracked down and dealt with German spies, but because German espionage continued to preoccupy many an Englishman'.[45]

Nonetheless, as Boghardt observes, even quite questioning commentators uphold that MI5 still beat German espionage despite its failings.[46] He alone makes the interesting claim that:

'And while MI5 was able to arrest a handful of genuine German agents during the war, these represented but a fraction of all German operatives in Britain. After 1915 MI5 became less rather than more efficient, and the fact that a significant number of German secret agents were indeed roaming the country throughout the war, raises serious doubts as to whether they posed any danger at all.'[47]

Thus, Boghardt concludes that:

'Overall, there is very little that justifies MI5's existence during the years 1909-1919. Cable and postal censorship, the only effective weapons in the detection of German agents, were not carried out by MI5, and the police and Scotland Yard were capable of arresting any suspect on their own. Had MI5's records been released earlier, the department might already have incurred as much ridicule as its by now largely forgotten German antagonist.'[48]

However, even Boghardt concedes that there are some slight problems with the evidence on which his conclusions are based. Most tellingly, 'many messages are reproduced anonymously (e.g. 'Reliable agent reports from Bristol…')', such that it is impossible to prove if all of these supposed agents were indeed real, or imaginary.[49] Indeed, the history of espionage contains many cautionary tales of spymasters who invented imaginary agents in order to ingratiate themselves with their superiors, and agents who manufactured whole networks of bogus sub-agents in order to earn more money out of their controllers.

A second, related debate over democratic accountability questions whether MI5 operated under adequate parliamentary scrutiny. Porter, for example, holds that the years 1909-1911 'witnessed the beginnings of the "secret state" as we know it today': MI5 and MI6 were both founded; the Official Secrets Act (OSA) 1911 received assent; the D-Notice system to vet newspaper articles impinging on national security was designed; an aliens register was begun; blanket interception of particular types of post was authorised; and the Special Branch moved closer to becoming 'a proper domestic counter-subversive agency on modern lines'. 'These developments marked a crucial stage in the transformation of Britain from a relatively open liberal democracy into the far more restrictive one we have today.' It occurred 'with scarcely anyone outside a narrow circle of men even being aware that it had happened'.[50]

However, he notes that MI5 'did not venture beyond counter-espionage', since it did not have the necessary resources to do so, before the war.[51] Porter further concedes that Britain did not have a genuine political police prior to the First World War: a true political police is concerned with activities which are classed as criminal because they are political; rather than those that would be regarded as criminal anyway and are simply deemed political as they have political aims or motives.[52]

The outbreak of war altered this, with Britain soon acquiring 'a proper political police'. Because 'so far as subversion was concerned, there was the Special Branch: which if it was not quite a proper counter-subversive police force yet, had all the makings of one'.[53] Porter suggests that Basil Thomson's interest in the 'political side of police work' was primarily responsible for this evolution in the Special Branch's role.[54]

Similarly, Thurlow views the formation of MI5 as part of 'the birth of the secret state'. Kell's appointment, and the Special Branch's expansion, 'marked the beginning of an organized security presence'; which could be employed by the Government, 'but was independent from parliamentary scrutiny'.[55] He acknowledges that MI5 'was originally set up as a counter-espionage agency' but suggests that it 'rapidly developed techniques which could monitor public order and internal security'. His main concern seems to be with the secrecy under which this 'silent revolution' took place. It was concealed by OSA 1911, which prohibited making official information public without the proper sanction.[56]

Above all it has been argued that Bolshevism became a newly identified threat after 1917 and that by the armistice Basil Thomson and Special Branch had become 'the prevalent force in British domestic intelligence operations'. Concerned that Bolshevism posed a greater threat than anyone appreciated, the Government also established a Directorate of Intelligence in March 1919. Thomson, however, was chosen to lead it, not Kell.[57] The historian, Brock Millman, argues that from a modest start at the outbreak of war, an extensive and very effective system of dissent management had evolved by the armistice, while even further controls had been devised but never introduced. However, the British system of control had developed incrementally, growing in relation to the perceived level of threat to the war effort. It did not become more repressive than a majority of the population would accept. It was designed to suppress the specific kind of British anti-war sentiment. He contends that Britain's comparative success in managing domestic opposition helped enable it to outlast Germany.[58] In 1917 'surveillance was systemized and became a police responsibility'. MI5 was thus 'Denied a role in domestic surveillance', which was very much Thomson's domain.[59] This study calls into question those who have suggested that MI5's move into counter-subversion was driven by a desire to increase its territory. It reinforces Thurlow's interpretation that MI5 moved into counter-subversion precisely because subversives were deemed to be under German influence. Indeed, MI5's role in these investigations was limited to establishing if there really was any German involvement; with the domestic aspects of these investigations being left to Special Branch and other agencies. It also questions those who claim that Kell was denied the lead role in counter-subversion. This implies that Kell had coveted this role but lost out to Basil Thomson. On the contrary, this study suggests that Kell never wanted MI5 to assume a wider role in counter-subversion.

This book also suggests that the current literature does not pay enough attention to some of the key factors that help to explain why MI5's organisational structure developed into the shape that it did. Between 1909 and 1914, Kell was very much implementing a grand strategy that Edmonds, and others who had worked in counter-espionage before then, had bequeathed to him. During the war MI5 evolved in response to what it learned about changes in the threat from, and methods of, German espionage. Only Hiley shows how MI5's six branches grew out of an appreciation that counter-espionage work naturally divided into investigative and preventive work and their mutual reliance upon records.

Following the release of a mass of MI5 documents covering 1909-1945 to TNA (formerly the Public Record Office) in record classes KV1-6, it is now possible to examine MI5 at the micro level and understand the intimate workings of its six branches. KV1, which was released in 1997 and has also been published on CD-ROM, is most relevant because it covers MI5 specifically from 1909-1919.[60]

Not all of MI5's records relating to its activities between 1909 and 1918 have been released. Some may have been held back because they relate to sensitive activities. Other material has been more routinely retained or weeded before release under sections 3.4 and 5.1 of the Public Records Act, in order to safeguard the identity of individuals and national security. However, some of these records may simply have been destroyed when Wormwood Scrubs, where they were being stored, was bombed in 1940.[61]

KV1 contains original MI5 documents from the pre-war period and the Historical Branch reports produced by MI5 in 1921, which described the work of each of MI5's six branches during the First World War as part of MI5's effort to record the lessons of its wartime experiences for future instruction. The authors of these branch reports summarised original documents from the wartime period, most of which were then destroyed in order to reduce the amount of papers that MI5 had to store. For example, reports of meetings between officials from MI5 and other government departments, or their correspondence, have not survived and it is precisely this kind of material which could help to explain why MI5 evolved as it did. It is also clear that the branch reports were written by quite junior MI5 officers who, although they were able to produce fairly accurate summaries of the original records and were thus able to detail how MI5 evolved, were not so capable of explaining why MI5 evolved as it did or of offering a meaningful analysis of MI5's effectiveness. Indeed, Thurlow feels that the quality of KV1's presentation is certainly 'disappointing': it is not well organised and lacks 'a succinct summary' of MI5's wartime work and although 'there is some useful analytical and comparative material' it is 'often drowned in a sea of case histories'.[62]

MI5's branch reports share many of the problems common to official history. By its very nature, official history is predisposed to present a distorted, official viewpoint that shows its subject in a favourable light. Compilers of official histories are usually chosen because they can be trusted to produce a favourable account or have a natural mindset to do so. Even though they may have access to all the relevant material, compilers of official histories may choose not to reveal everything, or be prohibited from doing so. Thus, as 'official history', the KV1 files will have recorded what the officials wanted recorded and omitted other matters. Some evidence might have been 'spiced up' for internal reasons, and some 'evidence' could even have been fabricated. In most cases however, material simply does not exist to provide criticism. Of course, it can be argued that any intelligence history has special problems in obtaining corroboration. Some of what appear to be examples of an 'official version' are noted in the chapters that follow.

Reports written in 1921 to point to useful lessons for the future may have used the benefits of hindsight to rationalise lessons from the war, even though these lessons may not have been apparent during wartime itself, thereby confusing the issue of what MI5 actually learned during wartime and what lessons were only distilled after the war as these reports were written. Nevertheless, Thurlow concludes that, because so few of the other personal (KV2) and subject files (KV3) seem to have survived from this period, this makes KV1 'a significant historical documentary record'.[63]

It is necessary to analyse these documents and question their relevance to this study. How accurate are these reports? It seems apt to accept them as being accurate on matters of fact and detail. They do not seem a deliberate attempt to mislead. However, when it comes to their analysis of the successes and failures of MI5, they overrate the organisation's achievements by largely ignoring the third-rate standard of the German opposition that MI5 had to defeat. Similarly, a report by F Branch does not acknowledge that some useful information managed to reach Germany through society gossip and diplomatic bags even though other sources do. Objectivity may have been eroded because they were partly written to justify the case for MI5's continued survival post-war.

What are their uses and limits? They are uniquely useful, and could not really be more so, in describing the six branches of MI5 and how they developed in considerable detail. However, they also have limitations. Most crucially for this study, these reports are much more descriptive in nature than analytical, and they do not really address the related question of why MI5 developed as it did.

Were these reports written to promote MI5? Clearly, they were never meant for future public dissemination. They were conceived for the purpose of in-house training and the full branch reports were not to be seen outside MI5. However, the summaries of each branch report were prepared with the intention that they could be shown to a selected few within government. They were the decision-makers who would decide upon MI5's role, and it seems clear that the summary reports were intended as a way to convince these individuals of the continued need for MI5 in peacetime. In short, they were also part of Kell's bid to protect his empire.

Towards the end of the Second World War, MI5's Director-General, Sir David Petrie, tasked a senior officer, John 'Jack' Court Curry, to produce a report on MI5's work. The two men had differing views on the scope and role of Curry's report and the finished document differed markedly from what Petrie had intended.[64] Petrie envisaged a short summary showcasing the success story of MI5 under his leadership following the security revolution of 1940. Curry produced a much more detailed historical study which, while presenting MI5's achievements, also gave an accurate portrayal of the differences between MI5 and other government departments and analysed why this was so.[65] Owing to Curry's literary skills and the far greater analysis in his report, Curry's report is in many ways superior to MI5's First World War branch reports. It is interesting to note that MI5's historical branch reports also did not turn out quite as envisaged. The rather ambitious project was never fully finished; perhaps staff cutbacks after the war meant that MI5 did not have the personnel to devote to the task, with many reports being left in an unfinished, rough draft state, and no attempt made to perform the useful task of producing a succinct summary of MI5's aims and achievements during the 1909-1918 era.

This study has also made use of published memoirs and unpublished private papers left by those who had been involved with MI5 to supplement KV1. Although it can be hoped to find an openness and honesty that would not find its way into official reports, it must be noted that diarists – perhaps intelligencers especially, with their cloak-and-dagger backgrounds – are not always completely truthful in their accounts. They often try to put a particular point of view across, or to convey a self-constructed image of themselves. It is also possible that they may not have felt comfortable with writing about such a sensitive subject as MI5 and censored their own accounts accordingly.

Thurlow's assessment of the MI5 records that have been released to TNA applies equally well to all of the material discussed here. Despite its obvious limitations and the gaps that remain in our knowledge of MI5, this material has its uses:

> 'Still, half a loaf is very much better than no bread at all, and the declassification of such material is to be unreservedly welcomed, even if the gaps and deficiencies need to be borne in mind.'[66]

CHAPTER ONE

Humble Beginnings
1903 - March 1911

W E begin the story with two remarkable men: James Edmonds, the War Office's foremost authority on secret intelligence, and Vernon Kell, his protégé. MI5 began life most humbly as the Counter-Espionage Section of the Secret Service Bureau, comprising a solitary official, Kell (who was also able to call on the assistance of an experienced investigator, William Melville). In most of his pre-war reports and diary entries, Kell referred to the Counter-Espionage Section of the Secret Service Bureau simply as 'the Bureau' and thus it seems fitting to follow Kell's example and refer to MI5 during its pre-war years, similarly, as 'the Bureau'. I have compiled this chapter into three sections as follows:

1) An account of events leading up to the Sub-Committee on Foreign Espionage, which recommended that a Secret Service Bureau should be formed.
2) The Sub-Committee on Foreign Espionage.
3) The Bureau's first eighteen months' work to March 1911.

Until the mid-1970s, Intelligence was the 'missing dimension' in the history of international relations. This began to change following the revelations about the code-breakers of Bletchley Park, which showed that any analysis of the Second World War that did not factor in the part played by Intelligence would be incomplete. Thanks to Christopher Andrew's ground-breaking *Secret Service: The Making of the British Intelligence Community*, the subjects of the first two sections of this chapter have already been very well covered, such that there is no need to go over this ground again in too much detail.[1] Instead, these two sections focus on the areas that are crucial to an understanding of the Bureau's early development:

1) Key documents outlining the methods of counter-espionage, which Kell read and was clearly influenced by as he began to develop the Bureau.
2) Key documents in which officials outlined how they felt a secret service Bureau

should be organised, which clearly acted as a route map for Kell as he built up the Bureau from scratch.

These documents served as blueprints for Kell to follow. With the use of this evidence, this chapter will demonstrate that the Bureau developed as it did in these early days very much in accordance with these blueprints. In short, Kell was following instructions that he had been given; rather than blazing an entirely new and original trail of his own design.

EVENTS LEADING UP TO THE SUB-COMMITTEE ON FOREIGN ESPIONAGE

The British Intelligence community in 1903

At the start of 1903, the British Intelligence Community consisted of firstly, tiny and under-resourced naval and military intelligence departments, 'both with little capacity to collect secret intelligence' and secondly, the Metropolitan Police Special Branch which had been set up in 1883 to counter the threat from Fenian (Irish Republican) terrorism, 'which had moved on to small-scale investigation of other terrorist and subversive threats but had minimal expertise in counter-espionage'.

Then, during 1903, two 'diminutive departments', MO2, responsible for foreign intelligence and MO3 responsible for counter-espionage, were formed within the War Office's Directorate of Military Operations (DMO). MO3 (renamed MO5 in 1907) was the 'direct predecessor of MI5'.[2] Indeed, the Bureau's records date Melville's employment from 1903, six years before the Bureau was established. As Andrew observes, this suggests that Melville's work for the Bureau 'was seen at the time as a continuation and extension of his earlier War Office investigations'.[3]

By the time that Major Edmonds took over MO5 in 1907, 'its activities had been allowed to die down'. Edmonds' staff consisted 'only of another major whose main preoccupation was cultivating a parliamentary constituency which three years later elected him as its Conservative MP' and an investigator, Melville.[4]

In 1907, the Directorate of Military Operations had the following sections:

MO1 Imperial defence: strategy and operations.
MO2 Foreign intelligence: Europe and Near East.
MO3 Foreign intelligence: Asia and the Americas.
MO4 Topography of potential foreign theatres of operations.
MO5 Special duties (covert intelligence and counter-intelligence operations).
MO6 Medical information on foreign theatres of operation.

MO5 took the lead in intelligence operations while MO2 and MO3 were more analytical, being concerned with the 'collection, preparation and distribution of information concerning the military geography, resources and armed forces of all foreign countries.'[5]

William Melville

William Melville (known as 'M') was MI5's chief detective from 1909-1917. Born at Sneem in County Kerry, Ireland, in Smith's words, Melville was 'one of a long line of Irishmen recruited to watch their own'. Melville first came to prominence in 1892 with the capture of the Walsall Bombers. Joseph Deacon, an anarchist from Walsall, was arrested in London, having been under police surveillance for some time. Melville, then an inspector with the Special Branch, was sent to Walsall to investigate the alleged anarchist group led by Deacon. Melville found bomb-making instructions, fuses and anarchist literature. Five members of the group were arrested. Four were subsequently convicted of anarchism and received prison sentences of up to ten years. In 1893, Melville was made superintendent and head of the Special Branch.

William Melville, MI5's chief detective. Prior to joining MI5, Melville had a distinguished career with the Metropolitan Police, rising to superintendent in charge of the Special Branch.

In April 1894, he arrested the French anarchist, Theodule Meunier, at Victoria Station and became 'a popular hero for the Victorian press', which delighted in chronicling his exploits in the 'fight against anarchists and Fenians'.[6]

On 1 December 1903 Melville retired from the Special Branch with a full pension and joined the War Office to undertake special investigative missions. When he later retired from MI5 in December 1917, he wrote a brief memoir outlining his work from 1903-1909. In Melville's own words:

'My duties were rather vague, but were generally to enquire into suspicious cases which might be given to me; to report all cases of suspicious Germans which might come to my notice; the same as to Frenchmen and foreigners generally; to obtain suitable men to go abroad to obtain information; to be in touch with competent operators to keep observation on suspected persons when necessary.'

Melville's early work centred on investigating South African suspects coming to the United Kingdom. He also investigated Russian spies and police agents in Britain as well as the Poles, nihilists and other discontented Russian elements that they had come to spy on; also gun-running to Persia and Abyssinia and acquiring the French bullet '*Balle* D' for the 8 mm Lebel rifle. From 1905 onwards, he focused increasingly on German espionage in Britain, such as investigating Germans suspected of plotting to blow up railway tunnels leading to London in the event of war. In 1905, Melville looked into the activities of a German agricultural student in the United Kingdom who seemed to already know even more about farming than the farmer who was teaching him; he was suspected of being a spy who was simply pretending to be an agricultural student to provide cover. In the summer of 1907, Melville investigated three Germans who spent three months in West Hartlepool taking photographs of the coast, railway stations, railway viaducts, railway junctions, coal sidings, etc. In early 1909, he tracked two Germans who made regular yachting excursions along the Holyhead coastline taking soundings to gauge water depth, temperature, etc.[7]

Anglo-German tension and spy scares

The revolution in security that led to the Bureau's creation had been brought about by changes in foreign policy and military strategy in order to deal with the perceived threat from German espionage and not by domestic challenges to public order, such as the suffragettes or labour unrest. Historian Richard Thurlow discerns the interplay of three key factors: public opinion, which took the threat of invasion seriously and helped to induce an official security consciousness; the decline of Britain as a great power, evinced by its worrying performance in the Boer War; and increased national rivalries, embodied by Germany's challenge to Britain's naval supremacy.[8] Furthermore, alarmist invasion scares, spy fiction written by sensationalist authors such as William Le Queux, popular journalism, xenophobia, politicians who felt that they could make political capital out of attacking the Liberal Government's perceived laxity on security issues and other such scare-mongering, all nurtured a public opinion which took such threats seriously and 'pressured the authorities to adopt a less liberal security policy'.[9]

The launching of the first Dreadnought type battleship in February 1906, which made all other ships obsolete, intensified the Anglo-German naval race, because the fear that Germany might build more Dreadnoughts than Britain made a German naval victory, which would leave Britain open to invasion, at least a possibility that had to be considered. There was also the related fear of a surprise invasion – 'a bolt from the blue' – if the Royal Navy was ever caught off guard and so such fears began to be taken seriously. Previously they would have been confidently ignored as Britain lay shielded behind the unchallenged supremacy of the Royal Navy. It was this feeling of vulnerability, played upon by invasion scares and spy fiction that warned of invading armies being preceded by legions of spies and saboteurs, which made the deficiencies in Britain's intelligence system a matter for concern.[10] Andrew has signposted the key points on this journey: 'Fear of the threat from the growing High Seas Fleet encouraged the myth that it was to be used for a surprise invasion of England.' William Le Queux's 1906 best-seller, *The Invasion of 1910*, described 'how German spies were already hard at work in England, preparing the way for the invaders.' By autumn 1907, a press campaign backed by the celebrated military hero, Lord Roberts VC, and some front bench Conservative MPs 'had persuaded the Liberal government to appoint a Sub-Committee of the Committee of Imperial Defence to consider the invasion threat.' Fear of a German invasion 'was further fuelled in the autumn of 1908 by reports that Germany was secretly stepping up Dreadnought construction.' Le Queux's scare-mongering 'scaled new heights in 1909 with the publication of another best-seller, *Spies of the Kaiser: Plotting the Downfall of England*, which claimed that England was awash with "a vast army of German spies".'[11]

Major James Edward Edmonds

Major (later Brigadier-General Sir) James Edward Edmonds was commissioned into the Royal Engineers in 1881, where his intellect soon earned him the nickname

'Archimedes'. In 1898, he passed the two-year staff course at the Staff College at Camberley top of his class, showing himself to be one of the army's leading intellectuals. In 1899, he was posted to the intelligence department at the War Office. From 1901 to 1904, Edmonds gained operational intelligence experience serving as an intelligence officer in South Africa. He returned to the intelligence department at the War Office in 1904 to head the Far Eastern desk. In 1907, he was promoted to become head of MO5 and later that year he started to keep a record of reports of suspected German espionage. However, 'MO5 lacked the resources to check adequately the reports it received.' Edmonds was succeeded by Colonel (later Lieutenant-General Sir) George Macdonogh in about October 1909.[12]

Edmonds continued to rise within the General Staff and at the outbreak of war he was serving as the Chief of Staff to the Fourth Division. The strain of the retreat following the Battle of Mons was too much for Edmonds and he was replaced in September 1914. He then served as a staff officer at the BEF's GHQ for the remainder of the war. After the war, he was appointed as the army's chief historian to superintend the writing of the twenty-eight volume official *History of the Great War*. Edmonds himself also wrote eleven volumes on the history of military operations in France and Belgium.[13]

Brigadier-General Sir James Edmonds, head of MO5 from 1907-1909. Edmonds served in a number of senior staff appointments from 1909-1918. After the war, he was responsible for the compilation of the British official *History of the Great War*. (Walter Stoneman, courtesy of The National Portrait Gallery).

War Office assessment of German espionage

These fears began to permeate into officialdom in 1906 when a committee established by the War Office and Admiralty to examine emergency powers suggested toughening the laws against spying.[14] The following two reports by senior intelligence officers serve to illustrate this growing concern. Colonel (later General Sir) Fraser Davies ended a report of 21 November 1905 regarding a German suspected of espionage:

> '…the fact being established that foreigners do come here on espionage, I beg to suggest that the time has arrived to take action in the matter. An easy system of doing this would be for confidential instructions to be sent from the Home Office to the Chief Constables of all Maritime counties directing their attention to the subject and asking that a discreet look out be maintained.

> 'At present the Police and the Postal authorities are as indifferent to the espionage danger as the general public.'[15]

Similarly, in a minute to MO5 of 3 June 1907, Colonel (later Major-General) Lord Edward Gleichen of section MO2 of the Directorate of Military Operations concurred that the Official Secrets Act (OSA) 1889 should be amended as recommended in order to render it applicable in peacetime as well as in times of emergency. However, he was concerned that this would not cover the control of aliens: '*As this question of Police surveillance and control of aliens during peacetime is almost as important as a preventive measure, as the amendment of the O.S. act is as an executive measure, it is hoped that action will be taken on this*'.[16]

These two brief memos outline a number of key themes that would be central to the Bureau's early development: the conviction that the authorities and the general public were indifferent to the threat of espionage, and the feeling that action needed to be taken, particularly to involve the Police and Post Office in counter-espionage; the idea that any approach should be made through the Home Office; the focus on coastal counties; the absolute necessity of amending the OSA and the conviction that the threat was largely from aliens and the consequent need for police surveillance and the control of aliens. Three key phrases are mentioned which crop up continually throughout the Bureau's first ten years: 'preventive measure', 'executive measure', and 'control of aliens'.

A note on the 'Organization of Secret Service' prepared for the Director of Military Operations on 4 October 1908, most likely by Edmonds, is arguably one of the key documents explaining why MI5 developed as it did from 1909-1918. The note opines that '…strategic information can only be got through agents' and that France's defeat in the Franco-Prussian War of 1870-1871 '…was largely due to want of secret service.' Germany's victory was, according to this note, largely attributed to the extensive espionage system operating in France during the war which had been 'carefully prepared some years before'. The German system in 1870 was directed by Wilhelm Stieber, an ex-officer and police agent. The note recommended that Britain should follow the German example: 'It is probably best to employ a first class detective under direction of an officer to collect and work agents abroad.' The note's author expressed grave dissatisfaction with the British counter-espionage system in place at that time: '…we have only casual unofficial assistance from members of police and Post Office. It is outside police duty at present to take any notice of foreigners, unless they are criminal'. The note went on to outline the secret service system that its author felt Britain actually 'required':

' a) In Germany, based on a centre in Switzerland, Denmark and [sic] Poland [There was no independent Poland at that time. Poland was then part of the Russian Empire.], to watch army and report concentrations and deployments.

b) In England, to mark down spies and agents in peace and to remain in German lines and spy on troops if they land.'

The note also suggested that the 'registration of aliens which was enforced by Act of Parliament in 1798 and 1803 must be revived' and that an 'Official Secrets Act Amendment Bill must be pushed through: at present we cannot arrest a spy or search his habitation without consent of Attorney General which takes any time to obtain'.[17]

This note goes over much ground that had already been covered in the memos by Davies and Gleichen: amendment to OSA, the indifference of the police and the Post Office, and aliens control (although it adds the point about aliens control during the Napoleonic Wars). However, it also introduces some further ideas: the need for secret agents, the role of secret intelligence in the Franco-Prussian War, the point that the German espionage system divided countries under observation into districts, and, most interestingly, it suggests the system that Britain required. It is intriguing to compare this system with the Secret Service Bureau that is eventually founded and the identified need for stay-behind agents to spy on potential German invaders was already being mooted.

Aliens legislation, 1803

The Aliens Act of 1803 was passed to regulate the growing number of refugees fleeing to Britain to escape the French Revolution, and to address the fear that enemy spies might infiltrate Britain during the Napoleonic Wars. Aliens were required to register at their port of arrival in Britain. These declarations were forwarded to the Aliens Office in London, which coordinated police surveillance of suspects.[18] The clauses of the aliens legislation were comprehensive:

Clauses I-VIII
Enacted that captains of vessels arriving in British ports were obliged to declare whether they had any aliens on board their ships and, if so, they had to provide a list of their name, rank, occupation, etc. No alien could disembark until this declaration had been made and permission had been given to disembark. There was a penalty of £50 for each alien landed in breach of the regulations. Aliens who failed to obey proclamations ordering them to leave the country were liable to imprisonment.

IX-XI
Aliens entering or leaving Britain were obliged to inform Customs officials of where they had come from, or where they were going to.

XIII
Aliens could be ordered to land at particular ports.

XIV-XVII
No alien could leave the port without a passport. Aliens wishing to change their place of residence were also obliged to obtain a passport.

XVIII
If an alien was considered dangerous to national security they could be deported; or a warrant could be issued to detain them in custody for as long as considered necessary.

XXII-XXVI
Aliens could be ordered by proclamation to register themselves and to obtain a License of Residence. A license could be withheld in suspicious cases, and forfeited if the holder was found outside the district for which it had been granted.

XXVII
No alien could leave the Realm without a passport.

XXX–XXXII
Householders were obliged to provide the authorities with copies of the licenses/passports of all aliens lodging with them for more than twenty-four hours. They also had to provide a notice giving the description of their alien lodgers and all available information concerning them.

XXXIII
Certain specified authorities were empowered to take any alien they had cause to suspect into custody. They could be detained in custody provided that a report of the case was immediately submitted to the higher authorities.

XXXIV–XXXV
Exemptions were granted for: foreign ambassadors and their servants, children under fourteen years of age, and bona fide sailors certified as being employed in the navigation of vessels.

On 2 December 1908, Edmonds wrote a note to the DMO, General Ewart, in which he outlined further evidence of suspected German espionage in the UK. A Territorial Force officer had reported '...that a certain German officer had spoken to him of his "district" in England, and had explained to him that every German officer "had a part of England to know thoroughly".' Seemingly corroborating evidence had been provided by an English lady married to a German officer who had reported 'that her husband's "district" is part of Yorkshire.' Other 'similar reports' had been reaching Edmonds since 1900. Edmonds ended his note observing that: 'We are in the position of the French in 1870; our enemy is "training" for the conflict, we are not'. Therefore, Edmonds suggested: 'I again venture to urge the necessity of a conference with the Home Office and Post Office with a view to obtaining their assistance in marking down and tracing the German agents in England.'

Edmonds was particularly keen on the strategy of keeping enemy agents under surveillance and waiting to round them up in a paralysing blow at the outbreak of hostilities. He seems to have acquired this idea from the Japanese: 'I would refer to the measures taken by Japan in Korea and Manchuria to mark down all Russian agents in peace time. Their seizure by the Japanese completely paralysed the Russian Intelligence system at a critical time.'[19]

This note covers the German espionage system in even more detail. It also suggests the strategy of waiting to round up enemy agents until the outbreak of war and it is interesting to compare this strategy with the events of August 1914. Edmonds proposed that a conference should be organized with the Home Office and Post Office in order to get something done. In January 1909, he prepared a paper entitled '*Espionage in Time of Peace*' for the DMO in which he stressed his conviction that: 'In all ages successful generals have been at great pains, before taking to the field, to organize an efficient secret service. In some cases years were devoted to its preparation and in all cases considerable sums of money.'

He once again drew attention to the prime importance that Germany had placed historically on secret intelligence: 'In some secret instructions of Frederick the Great, published in his correspondence, he said to his generals "When Marshal Soubise goes on service he has a hundred cooks following him, when I go I send a hundred spies ahead of me." This advice as will be seen has sunk deep into the minds of the leaders of the German armies of the last half century.'

Edmonds had devoted much of his adult life to the study of the German secret service. He believed that Germany did not recruit agents through the General Staff but through a special secret service department, the *NachrichtenBureau*. Until 1900, this department had had two sections: one for France and another for Russia. Then, in 1900, a third section was added to target Britain. The head agents of the British section were thought to be based in Brussels and New York. However, Edmonds was slightly mistaken on this point – Germany actually had two departments involved in secret service work: firstly, the Admiralty Staff's Naval Intelligence Department (*Nachrichtenabteilung im Admiralstab* or 'N') and secondly, the General Staff's Military Intelligence Department (*Abteilung* IIIb). Edmonds acknowledged that his analysis was largely based on French experiences: 'Much of the foregoing has been obtained from French sources, …, it would seem fairly certain … that the principles of the system organized by the Germans in France are now applied here.'

Herein lay a potential problem for anyone at the War Office, and later at the Bureau, who might subscribe to Edmonds' analysis of the nature and scope of the threat posed by the German secret service: Edmonds never seemed to question whether the German High Command would have different designs on Britain than on France and consequently different intelligence requirements. Edmonds also observed that the '…arrangements to prevent espionage in Germany are as elaborate as those to secure information abroad.' All foreigners were required to register their arrival with the local police. The German post office kept 'an especially vigilant eye on foreign correspondence and do not hesitate to open and detain letters.' The practice of universal naval and military service in Germany converted 'the whole male population' into watchful auxiliaries of the police, eager to prevent or detect espionage and, the 'law provides for the punishment of almost every possible form of collection of military information.'[20]

This paper reiterates and expands upon many points already made: the need for secret agents, the importance Germany placed on secret intelligence, and the German espionage system. It also provides a stimulating outline of the German counter-espionage organisation: compulsory registration of all foreigners, a vigilant postal service, a population active to the threat of espionage, and tough laws to protect information.

At some time in 1909 (the exact date is not specified), Edmonds produced a guide to 'Intelligence Methods'. In it, he wrote: 'Intelligence as understood in a military sense, usually implies the collection or preparation of maps and plans, and the compilation of military and naval, i.e. warlike, value concerning other countries as a basis for plans of campaigns.' Edmonds described intelligence work as consisting of three parts:

1) The collecting and compilation of such information.
2) The prevention of the compilation of such information regarding one's own country, by finding out the means used, and the persons concerned, in procuring,

and conveying such information; by watching and if possible convicting the agents employed; and also by either intercepting such communications, or by ascertaining what is communicated; if unimportant, letting it pass, and if important and of great urgency, substituting other unimportant or misleading information for it; or in some way throwing doubt upon the bona fides of the person communicating it.

3) The misleading of other countries by the publication, or the willfully permitted leaking out (a) of incorrect data regarding one's own forces, fleet, defences or intentions, or (b) of opinions not really held regarding the forces of some other country, as if they were genuine.

Edmonds went on to discuss how intelligence systems were organized. In order to achieve the objectives just outlined, intelligence services in Continental Europe depended upon 'the closest interdependence between the diplomatic and consular services, the secret-service-agents, and the army staff... The intelligence branch of the general staff of any nation has a central Bureau at army headquarters directed by an officer of high rank, and here all the information transmitted from, or in any way connected with any country, however obtained is collated and systematically arranged.'

Edmonds goes on to examine the German intelligence system in some detail observing how it was based on an 'article of faith' that 'every thousand pounds properly spent in peace-time on the acquisition of information, will eventually save a million in time of war.'

Each of the districts of the country under observation was under the supervision of a chief agent, who employed a large number of agents who are classified in distinct categories:

(1) "Mobile agents": operating all over the district, but always pursuing some clearly defined objective.

(2) "Local agents": they do not change their location. Their role is 'observing every matter', picking up all gossip that may be of use to the army or navy, and answering questions from the chief agent of the district.

In addition, officers and other members of the armed forces would be sent to the district on special missions to gain information on 'points which require elucidation' such as highly technical military and naval equipment. Regular and reserve German officers travelling through an area, either on business or on vacation, were expected to take notes and make sketches, and to pass on anything likely to be of value to the General Staff. German consuls at British ports were expected to provide intelligence on water depth, volumes handled on the wharf and by cranes, railway facilities and coal supplies, supplies available, the port garrison; and, neighbouring defences and armament. Thereby: 'Day in, day out, the ceaseless work of getting information and throwing dust in the eyes of others goes on, and the final result of it all, as far as we are concerned, is this: that a German general landing a force in East Anglia, would know more about the country than any British General ...'[21]

This paper covers the German espionage system in much more detail: particularly on the different roles played by the various types of agent, and the coordinating role of the central Bureau at headquarters. It also provides an insightful analysis of how counter-espionage work was typically conducted: counter-espionage aims to discover 1) the means used and 2) the agents involved in (a) procuring and (b) conveying intelligence. This is usually done through surveillance and postal interception. When postal interception discovers unimportant communications, they should be passed on, so as to keep the agent in the dark about their communications being intercepted. When important communications are discovered, they should be substituted or altered; or doubt should be cast upon the credibility of the sender. Thus, counter-espionage plays into deception operations to mislead the enemy.

The Sub-Committee on Foreign Espionage

At the General Staff's request, in March 1909, the Prime Minister, Herbert Henry Asquith, appointed a Committee of Imperial Defence (CID) Sub-Committee on Foreign Espionage to consider 'the question of foreign espionage in the United Kingdom.' Its terms of reference were to 'consider such evidence as may be brought before them regarding the nature and extent of the foreign espionage that is at present taking place in this country, and the danger to which it may expose us.' The Sub-Committee was tasked to report on four questions, which are worth quoting in their entirety:

'(1) Whether it is desirable that the Admiralty and the War Office should be brought into official relations with the Police, Postal and Customs authorities, with a view to the movements of aliens suspected of being spies or secret agents being properly supervised.

(2) If such official relations are desirable, in what manner can they best be established.

(3) Whether it is desirable to increase the powers we now possess of dealing in times of emergency with persons suspected of being spies or secret service agents.

(4) Whether any alteration is desirable in the system at present in force in the Admiralty and the War Office for obtaining information from abroad.'[22]

The Sub-Committee was composed of the following members:

R. B. Haldane MP	Secretary of State for War (chair)
R. McKenna MP	First Lord of the Admiralty
H. J. Gladstone MP	Secretary of State for Home Affairs
S. Buxton MP	Postmaster-General
Viscount Esher	Member of the Committee of Imperial Defence
Sir C. Hardinge	Permanent Under-Secretary of State for Foreign Affairs
Sir G.H. Murray	Permanent Secretary to the Treasury
Rear Admiral A.E. Bethell	Director of Naval Intelligence

Major-General J.S. Ewart   Director of Military Operations
Brigadier-General A.J. Murray   Director of Military Training
Sir E.R. Henry   Commissioner of Metropolitan Police[23]

The Sub-Committee was formed at the General Staff's 'request', because of apprehension over: '…the increasing amount of German espionage that is taking place in this country, and consider it desirable that both the Admiralty and the War Office should be afforded greater facilities than are at present at their disposal for ascertaining the precise nature and scope of this movement.'

The War Office and Admiralty were invited to give evidence before the Sub-Committee '…in order to show that it is desirable for those Departments to be brought into official relations with the Police, Postal and Customs authorities, with a view to the movements of aliens suspected of being spies or secret service agents being properly supervised.'[24]

First Meeting, 30 March 1909
The meeting began with a presentation by Edmonds who detailed the various cases of alleged espionage that had been reported to the General Staff since January 1908:

	1908	Jan–Mar 1909
Cases of alleged reconnaissance	27	7
Individual Germans who have come under suspicion	16	15
Houses occupied by a succession of Germans who have come under suspicion	4	2
Totals	**47**	**24**

Cases of 'alleged reconnaissance work by Germans' included a report by a Justice of the Peace (JP) in Essex on 24 March 1908 of how, from 3-19 January 1908, the informant observed three, sometimes four, 'persons riding about and noting the topography of the country near Brightlingsea.' The informant made further enquiries, which led him to believe that they were Germans. The fourth man was a German servant 'who said he had served in a British cavalry regiment.'

Cases of 'Germans whose conduct has been reported as giving rise to suspicion' included a report from a member of the General Staff based at Aldershot on 24 January 1908 to the effect that the head waiter and most of the staff of the Queen's Hotel, Farnborough (north of Aldershot), where three generals and several officers of the garrison resided, were Germans: 'They have good opportunities of collecting information.'

Cases of houses reported 'to be occupied by a succession of Germans which it is desirable to watch', included a report from a captain in the Territorial Force of 18 May 1908, that four Germans were living in a small house near Epping: 'The men change every two or three months; they have bicycles and photographic equipment; and they are stated by the informant to have asked questions about supplies and transport'.[25] Edmonds laid particular stress upon the fact that 'none of these cases were reported by the police authorities, and that he was indebted for information regarding them to private individuals.'[26]

Viscount Esher was clearly far from convinced. Indeed, when he recorded his reflections upon this meeting in his diary, he referred to Edmonds as 'a silly witness from the WO', suggesting that, 'Spy catchers get espionage on the brain. Rats are everywhere – behind every arras.'[27] At the meeting, Esher had rather mockingly asked Edmonds, if he '…felt any apprehensions regarding the large number of German waiters in this country?' Edmonds did not rise to the provocation and calmly replied that he '…did not think that we need have any apprehensions regarding the majority of these waiters, or suspect them of being in any way organized for offensive action. He thought that men who were to carry out demolitions would probably be sent over in time of strained relations, and were not likely to be resident in the country.'

Edmonds was followed by Captain R.C. Temple, who provided the Admiralty's evidence. Temple admitted that he had to concede that the Admiralty did not have the resources to look into these matters and tended simply to pass on any leads to Edmonds at the War Office. Sir Edward Henry cited suspicious cases dealt with by the police. Haldane then told the Sub-Committee that he:

'…considered that the evidence heard by the Committee had made it quite clear that a great deal of reconnaissance work is being conducted by Germans in this country. Probably, too, though it is difficult to obtain precise information on this subject, secret agents are collecting information that would enable important demolitions and destruction to be carried out in this country on or before the outbreak of war.'[28]

Andrew suggests that Haldane was initially 'bemused' by the 'extraordinary' evidence of German spying that Edmonds presented. Haldane eventually 'yielded to Edmonds's persistence and allowed himself to be convinced of the spy menace.' However, on 'a deeper level', Haldane's 'readiness to believe such remarkable tales of German espionage reflected his enormous respect for the ability and professionalism of the German General Staff.'[29]

Second Meeting, 20 April 1909

Haldane began the meeting by telling the members of the Sub-Committee that he had just returned from a visit to Germany where he had gained the impression 'that the German Government was not deliberately collecting information regarding this country with the definite intention of invading it. There was little doubt, however, that the German General Staff is collecting information systematically in Great Britain with a view to knowing as much as possible about a conceivable theatre of war.' Therefore, Haldane felt that the Sub-Committee needed to decide 'how we could best obtain information as to what the Germans were doing in this country'. Haldane went on to make a few suggestions. He thought that the Post Office, Territorial Force and Police would be able 'to get us information'. He added that the OSA 1889 'may require amendment' in order to provide 'some power of taking swift action in time of strained relations against suspected persons.'

Sir Edward Henry stated that the police could not be of any real help until the OSA was improved:

'Under the Official Secrets Act the police must first apply for the sanction of the Attorney-General, and having secured it, must go to the Courts and apply for process. The power of search for incriminating papers is absolutely essential, but it would appear that the Courts have no power to issue a search warrant under the Act, though they have this power in even petty larceny cases.'

Sydney Buxton MP, the Postmaster-General, told those present that:

'…the opening of letters in time of peace would be much against public opinion, and it was very undesirable to shake public confidence in the security of the post. It was quite legal and feasible for the Post Office to give information that a certain person is receiving letters from abroad.'

Major-General Ewart opined that:

'We require information regarding espionage in this country so that we may keep suspicious aliens under observation, and be able to lay our hands on them in time of need.'

Ewart then read to the Sub-Committee extracts from a paper by Edmonds 'showing how stringent the regulations had been for dealing with foreigners domiciled in Great Britain during the Napoleonic Wars.' Ewart ended by asking: '…whether a small secret service Bureau could not be established which might be in touch with the various Departments?'

Haldane directed that a small group of the Sub-Committee's members – Sir George Murray, Hardinge, Bethell, Ewart and Henry – 'meet and consider the question of how a secret service Bureau could be established.'[30]

Recommendations on how to set up SSB, 28 April 1909

The 'Conclusions of the Sub-Committee requested to consider how a secret service Bureau could be established in Great Britain' is a vitally important document in terms of understanding the pre-war development of the Bureau. The sub-Sub-Committee stressed that, '…any Secret Service Bureau that may be established should be separate from any of the Departments but must at the same time be in close touch with the Admiralty, the War Office and the Home Office.'

The Secret Service Bureau's 'objects' should be:

(a) To serve as a screen between the Admiralty and War Office and foreign spies who may have information that they wish to sell to the Government.

(b) To send agents to various parts of Great Britain and keep in touch with the country police with a view to ascertaining the nature and scope of the espionage that is being carried on by foreign agents.
(c) To act as an intermediate agent between the Admiralty and the War Office and a permanent foreign agent who should be established abroad, with the view of obtaining information in foreign countries.

This was desirable because '…it is customary in foreign countries to protect the Government from being convicted of any dealings with spies by using a secret service Bureau as an intermediary.'

The report noted that the current British system for acquiring information on what was happening in foreign ports and dockyards, especially in Germany, was 'defective', and that the necessary reorganization 'can best be done by bringing it into connection with the secret Bureau.' Therefore, it recommended that the Bureau should have a permanent agent, 'at some place like Brussels', in contact with the secret service Bureau. He would be 'the medium' through whom other British agents send in their reports. The Bureau should be staffed by one retired naval officer and one retired army officer, because they 'would have sufficient technical knowledge to enable them to determine the value of the evidence that they obtained from abroad and whether it was sufficiently important to pass on to the Admiralty or the War Office'. In addition, a detective should be attached to every important naval base whose work as part of the dockyard police would be to monitor any foreign espionage that was going on in the place and inform the Admiralty and War Office about 'its extent and scope'. Additionally, before the permanent agent was established abroad the Bureau should '…send a member of the detective force to reside in Germany for a few months with a view to his getting into touch with men living at important points in that country who might possibly serve as our agents.'

It was also proposed that, in order to maintain secrecy, a firm of private detectives should be utilized to provide a cover for the Secret Service Bureau.[31]

Third Meeting, 12 July 1909

Haldane began this meeting by suggesting that the Sub-Committee had seen 'sufficient evidence' to issue a report. Haldane: He 'did not think that there was any doubt that a great deal of German espionage was being undertaken in Great Britain, with a view to making a detailed study of our resources and of the topography of this country.'

Rear-Admiral Sir Charles Ottley, Secretary to the Sub-Committee, read the report suggesting the manner in which a secret service Bureau could be established. The Sub-Committee recommended that this report should be accepted. Haldane commented that the next point to consider was how best to amend the OSA. He suggested that there was a need to amend the definition of 'espionage', that the police should be given powers to arrest 'suspected persons', and that Justices of the Peace (JPs) should be empowered to issue search warrants. In reply to a question from Haldane, Buxton said 'that he would arrange that a member of the Post Office should be put in touch with the Admiralty and War Office, who would form the regular medium of communication between the Departments.'

As the Admiralty was already in touch with the Customs authorities, Haldane thought that it was only necessary for the Sub-Committee to recommend in its report that relations should be established between the proposed Secret Service Bureau and the Customs authorities.[32]

Additional Evidence

The Sub-Committee was also presented with a number of memorandums to aid its deliberations. The most interesting of these for a study of the early development of the Bureau is a note outlining the '*Powers of the Post Office for dealing with the correspondence of persons suspected of espionage*' prepared by Sir Henry Babington Smith, the Secretary to the Post Office, dated 15 April 1909. In this document Babington Smith began by explaining the implications of section fifty-six of the Post Office Act 1908 as regards counter-espionage:

> 'It is illegal to open, detain, or delay any letter or other postal packet in the course of transmission through the post, except in obedience to an express warrant in writing under the hand of the Secretary of State.'

However, it was not illegal for the Post Office to provide information which could be derived from the outside of letters (i.e., envelopes) without detaining or delaying them.

The responsibility for deciding whether or not to issue a warrant in any individual case lay with the Secretary of State. However, the Post Office held a 'strong view' that the power to interfere with the post 'should be used as sparingly as possible', on the grounds that:

> 'It is very undesirable to shake public confidence in the security of the post; and if the power of opening letters were used to any considerable extent it would be very difficult to secure that the fact remain secret. It is seldom possible to confine to a very small number of persons the knowledge that letters are being detained.'

Babington Smith also questioned the usefulness of postal interception to counter-espionage:

> 'Moreover, in the case of spies, it appears very doubtful whether any useful results would follow from the examination of correspondence, since it is improbable that any letters of importance would be received or dispatched by a spy without the use of devices for concealment.'[33]

It is worth considering what would have happened in the contest between German espionage and British counter-espionage if the Post Office's doubts about the use of postal interception had prevailed?

Final Report, 24 July 1909

The evidence that had been presented '…left no doubt in the minds of the Sub-Committee that an extensive system of German espionage exists in this country, and that we have no organisation for keeping touch with that espionage and for accurately determining its extent or objectives.'

The Sub-Committee agreed that the current system was 'defective' and recommended the formation of a secret service Bureau, along the lines suggested by the sub-Sub-Committee. The Sub-Committee was also of the opinion that 'great need' existed for amendment of the OSA in order to make it an efficient weapon in dealing with espionage and was keenly aware that in 1908, a Bill amending the OSA had been introduced which had tended to restrict the freedom of the press:

'This Bill contained clauses relating to the publication of certain documents and information which caused it to attract a good deal of anxious attention from the press, and which resulted in the Bill not being proceeded with.'

Therefore, it was recommended that a bill to amend the OSA 'should be brought in at an early date', but that it would 'excite less opposition' if:

'…it were introduced by the Secretary of State for War than by the Home Secretary, and that this might be done on the plea of its being a measure of precaution of great importance for national defence. They consider that legislation having for its object the prevention of the publication of certain documents or information should also be undertaken, but that this subject should be dealt with in a separate Bill after negotiations with the representatives of the press have resulted in an agreement as to its provisions.'

Having taken the Post Office's views into account, the Sub-Committee considered that any fresh legislation with the object of giving more power to the Post Office with regard to opening or detaining letters was undesirable and would shake the confidence that the public placed in that department. Therefore, it was recommended that the proposed Secret Service Bureau should be brought into communication, through unofficial channels, with a designated Post Office official, and similarly through unofficial channels, with a designated Customs official. The Sub-Committee also recommended that the Home Ports Defence Committee should enquire into the guarding of magazines and other vulnerable points against sabotage.

Although some of the evidence presented to the Sub-Committee seemed rather unconvincing, Andrew concludes that:

'The case for establishing the Bureau was none the less a strong one. A German naval espionage network concentrating on naval targets *was* operating in Britain and, until the establishment of the Bureau, there was, to quote the Sub-Committee report, "no organisation for keeping in touch with that espionage and for accurately determining its extent or objectives".'[34]

Action taken following the report

On 26 August 1909, Ewart, Edmonds, Macdonogh and Temple (representing the Director of Naval Intelligence) met with Henry in his rooms at Scotland Yard 'to consider the arrangements to be made in order to give effect to the recommendations of the Sub-Committee regarding the establishment of a secret service Bureau.' The Secret Service

Sir Edward Henry, Commissioner of the
Metropolitan Police, 1903-1918.

Bureau was to commence work as soon as suitable offices could be obtained which it was hoped would be as early as October that year. Vernon Kell was proposed as the War Office's representative, and Mansfield Cumming was to represent the Admiralty. Edward Drew, the late Chief Inspector of the Criminal Investigation Department (CID), was recommended 'as a suitable private detective under cover of whose name the Bureau should be conducted.' Drew would set up a private detective agency in offices at 64 Victoria Street in central London. He would sub-let certain rooms to the Secret Service Bureau. Kell and Cumming were to 'represent themselves as in partnership with Mr Drew.' Initially, the lease on Drew's offices was to be for eighteen months, with an option for renewal after that.[35] Kell and Cumming could thus use Drew's name as a screen. Indeed, in Drew's office they were known as 'Kelly' and 'Cunningham'.[36]

As suggested by the Sub-Committee, an agent had already been employed in Germany by the Admiralty. It was proposed that Henry Dale Long, who had been working on intelligence missions for the War Office for a number of years, should be the foreign agent in Brussels, and that he would obtain a commercial agency 'to cloak his movements'. Detectives were also due to be attached to important naval bases as recommended by the Sub-Committee.[37] Thus the Secret Service Bureau was established very much along the lines that had been set out in the War Office's note on the 'Organization of Secret Service' of October 1908.

Kell wrote to Ewart on 19 September 1909 accepting this post:

'I shall be very glad to accept the billet you have been good enough to offer me, and I agree to the conditions you mentioned viz: salary of £500 in addition to my full pension; and on the understanding that I am to hold the appointment for a minimum period of two years from the date of taking it over.'[38]

Vernon Kell

Vernon Kell joined the counter-espionage section of the Secret Service Bureau, which, as already noted, was not to be designated MI5 until January 1916, as its Director on 9 October 1909 aged thirty-six years, having served with the South Staffordshire Regiment. By the time he was dismissed by Churchill in June 1940, his thirty-one years in charge of MI5 would make him the longest-serving head of a British government department during the 20th century.[39]

Kell was born on 21 November 1873. His father was an army major and his mother, later divorced, was the daughter of a Polish count. After Sandhurst, he was commissioned as a second-lieutenant in his father's regiment, the South Staffordshire Regiment, in 1894. He was promoted to lieutenant in 1896 and then captain in 1901. Kell was a gifted linguist, who went on to qualify as an army interpreter in French and German, followed by postings to Russia and then to China to learn the languages of those countries. He also spoke Italian and Polish. His favourite hobbies were lawn tennis and fishing but he possessed a retiring disposition and shunned the limelight.[40] According to Andrew, Kell's 'only known publication is a newspaper letter describing the behaviour of the lapwing.'[41]

From 1900–1903, Kell served on 'special service' with the China Expedition. His big break came in 1904, when Edmonds, then head of the Far Eastern Section, chose him as his deputy and right-hand man. From 1907–1909, Kell worked for the Historical

Major-General Sir Vernon Kell, Director of MI5 from 1909-1940. Kell was the longest serving head of any British government department during the twentieth-century.
(Jay Robert Nash Collection)

Section of the Committee of Imperial Defence, compiling a History of the Russo-Japanese War.[42] Then, in 1909, Edmonds, then head of MO5, proposed Kell as the first head of what would become MI5.[43] Edmonds informed Kell that, because the Bureau had to work in secret, he would have to resign from his army career, at least officially, and that he could never expect public recognition for his work. Thus, in taking up the post, Kell was conscious that failure risked losing not only a job, but also his career.[44] Indeed, he accepted this appointment on the understanding that it would last 'for a minimum period of two years', but with no guarantee that it would continue beyond that. Porter bluntly sums up the precariousness of the situation in which Kell found himself:

> 'So Edmonds was given his "contra-espionage" agency; but only a very tiny one, which suggests that ministers were not wholly convinced. It began with nothing but a room in Victoria Street with a desk and a filing cabinet, and of course Kell himself. He was junior enough to be expendable if there proved to be nothing for him to do.'[45]

Therefore, when he began his work in October 1909, Kell had to build up his organization from scratch.[46]

THE WORK OF THE COUNTER-ESPIONAGE SECTION OF SSB TO MARCH 1911

Formation of SSB

As mentioned, the Secret Service Bureau was formed on 9 October 1909. It comprised Captain Vernon Kell, heading the military section of the Bureau, nominated by the War Office, and Commander (later Captain Sir) Mansfield George Smith Cumming, heading the naval section, appointed by the Admiralty. They shared the espionage and counter-espionage work between them and an office at 64 Victoria Street, London.[47] The Secret Service Bureau came under MO5, whose head acted as paymaster and was responsible for directing the activities of Kell and Cumming.[48] Andrew notes that the funding for the Bureau was contained in the Secret Service Vote (usually called the 'Secret Vote'), which 'had been used to finance intelligence and other secret activities since the eighteenth century.'[49] Although the Secret Vote was put before parliament, members were not told what part of the vote was devoted to the Bureau. The government's policy towards the democratic accountability of the intelligence services at that time was conditioned by the constitutional principles that 'intelligence is

undiscussable in public' and that 'parliament surrenders all its powers in intelligence matters to the executive.'[50] As Sir Austen Chamberlain, then Foreign Secretary, told the House of Commons in November 1924:

'It is of the essence of a Secret Service that it must be secret, and if you once begin disclosure it is perfectly obvious to me as to hon. members opposite that there is no longer any Secret Service and that you must do without it.'[51]

The head of MO5 was clearly a very strict paymaster and money was especially tight in the early years. For example, on 28 February 1910, Macdonogh wrote to direct Kell to rein in the purse strings:

Lieutenant-General Sir George Macdonogh, head of MO5 from 1909-1914 and Director of Military Intelligence (DMI) from 1916-1918.

'*We are and shall be very hard up until the end of this month. Will you therefore please cut down your expenses to a minimum and not incur any travelling expenses without previous reference and then only in cases that will not wait till April.*'[52]

SSB divides into Espionage and Counter-Espionage Sections

The Sub-Committee decided that an ex-army officer and an ex-naval officer should be appointed to the Bureau, but it neglected to apportion work between the two. Nor did it say whether the army or the naval officer should head the Bureau. As a result, the early days of the Secret Service Bureau were beset with tensions between Kell and Cumming as they struggled to define their positions relative to each other. Cumming was fourteen years older than Kell and had gained the impression from Bethell that he was to be in charge of the whole Bureau, whilst Kell was just intended to be a junior colleague. On 21 October 1909, Kell and Cumming agreed a division of responsibilities between themselves: Kell was to be responsible for all home work, both military and naval, whilst Cumming was to be responsible for all foreign work, both naval and military. As Kell explained in a progress report:

> 'Soon after the formation of the Bureau in October, 1909, it was found necessary, in order to avoid over-lapping, to define the dividing line between Capt. Cumming's work and my own; and it was ultimately decided to entrust the duty of espionage abroad to Capt. Cumming. Whilst I was made responsible for counter-espionage within the British Isles.'[53]

However, Cumming remained suspicious of Kell's intentions and on 26 November he complained to Bethell that Kell was attempting to interfere in his arrangements for meeting an agent. He was resolute that he, not Cumming, should pay him. Bethell took Cumming's side and insisted that he was responsible for all foreign work and that he, not Kell, was to oversee payments to agents.

Captain Sir George Mansfield Smith Cumming, head of the Foreign Espionage Section of the Secret Service Bureau, known as MI1c during the war, from 1909-1923.

This division of duties between Kell and Cumming was confirmed at a meeting they had with Macdonogh and other senior officers from the War Office and Admiralty on 9 May 1910 at which Macdonogh began by recognising that the Foreign Espionage Section and Counter-espionage Section of the Secret Service Bureau had little in common and that the respective duties of Kell and Cumming needed to be properly defined. The meeting confirmed Kell's responsibility for all work within the United Kingdom and Cumming's for all foreign work. With their spheres of operations 'fully recognized', relations between Kell and Cumming soon improved.[54]

The site of the Victoria Street office also soon revealed problems. Its location opposite the Army and Navy Stores resulted in difficult meetings with inquisitive friends. Therefore, Cumming, who would later become known as 'C', soon stopped using this office and took a flat at Ashley Mansions, Vauxhall Bridge Road, London from where he would conduct his work.[55]

This marked the separation of the Secret Service Bureau into the counter-espionage section that would become MI5, and the espionage section that would be known as MI1c for much of the First World War, and later become MI6 or the Secret Intelligence Service (SIS). However following their separation, and for some 80 years after, proposals were put forward within the corridors of power in Whitehall for their rejoining, possibly at the same location, but none of these materialised.

Kell continued to use the office at Victoria Street until the lease expired on 21 February 1911 when he moved into an office at 3 Paper Buildings, Temple, London.[56] The Bureau left 3 Paper Buildings on 28 September 1912, and moved to the third floor of Watergate House, York Buildings, Adelphi, London.[57]

Progress: October 1909-March 1910

From October 1909 to March 1910, Kell's time was chiefly spent going through the previous history of counter-espionage as shown in the War Office files, and in getting acquainted with the various aspects of his work.[58]

In his first progress report, reviewing his work from October 1909-March 1910, Kell informed his superiors that he had come across some 'definite cases of German espionage', some cases of 'mistaken suspicions', and some cases 'in which sufficient evidence was lacking, and had in consequence to be dropped'. Kell's original report clearly set out the number of cases that fell into each of these categories. However, these figures have been redacted out from the copy that was released to The National Archives in London. All this really means for any study of the early history of the Bureau, is that it is impossible to know exactly how many cases of 'mistaken suspicions' and other tenuous leads were passed on to Kell. Kell goes on to state that he wished to concentrate his report on what he felt were the two 'most important' cases: the Rusper case and the Frant case. Kell concluded that, 'They in themselves, constitute strong supplementary and confirmatory evidence to the existence, in this country of an organised system of German espionage.'

He added:

'As in the majority of cases dealt with, there are a good many links missing in the chain of circumstances, but it does not require a very great stretch of imagination to insert connecting links of one's own forging, thus producing a pretty strong chain of evidence, all emanating from the same source viz: Germany, and ending in the same objective – "the spying out of the land".'

In January 1910, a lady 'of high social standing' living close to the Surrey-Sussex border reported the following incident to a friend who happened to be a General officer on the active list. Whilst in her local Post Office she overheard two foreigners discussing a foreign money order which they wanted to cash with the village post-master. *'Being herself a good linguist, she offered to assist them out of any difficulty'* in communicating with the post-master. She noticed that the money order was made out to a Polish-German name, the sender appeared to be Polish, and it had been sent from a town in the South of France. *'Her interest and suspicions were roused, and after making some enquiries in the neighbourhood, she discovered that these two foreigners were living a few miles from her place; also that they had no visible occupation.'* Her report was eventually passed on to Kell to investigate. Kell discovered that two Germans had arrived, with a gap of time between them, each with a recommendation to a gentleman living in the village of Rusper, near the border of Surrey and Sussex. The recommendations came from a Baroness whom the gentleman had not heard of. The Germans pretended not to know each other, but quickly built up a friendship, and it was clear that whether or not they knew each other, each had a deep knowledge of the other's affairs. In early 1910, Melville stayed in the same house as the Germans and caused them some anxiety. They questioned the landlord about him very closely, being particularly concerned to know if he spoke any foreign languages; and they were obviously relieved when the landlord assured them that Melville did not. Shortly after Melville's arrival, the two Germans argued – it was clearly contrived – and would not speak to one another for the rest of Melville's stay. They drove about the village of Rusper constantly.

In early 1910, Kell also investigated a German, using the name De Corina, who took a farm in the Frant area of Sussex. He was supposed to be a poultry farmer, but it had been noticed that his farm at Bartley Mill was a meeting place for Germans, most of whom spent much of their time motoring and cycling around the area. It was obvious that De Corina was not making a living from the farm. However, no evidence was found that would definitely link him to espionage. Nonetheless, the circumstances were suspicious and lent themselves to the conclusion that the farm was used as a centre for espionage.

Kell also drew the following conclusions from his first six months' work. First, he felt that the Secret Service Bureau had 'justified its institution'. Secondly, the 'experience gained has proved that it is essential to the effective working of the Counter-espionage Section of the Bureau, that all information coming within its province should be sent to and exclusively dealt with by the Bureau.' Thirdly, for effective counter-espionage, it was 'essential to ensure the co-operation of the Chief Constables.' Finally, he urged the necessity for changes to the inadequate counter-espionage legislation provided by the OSA 1889:

'As is well known, there is at present no power to complete one's evidence by preliminary search on suspicion, although search-warrants are freely granted in trivial cases of larceny: i.e. Under the Army Act 1881. Sect.156. Subsect.5. a magistrate may grant a search-warrant upon reasonable cause for suspicion that anyone has in his possession the property of a comrade (e.g. a blanket!), and yet in cases involving the safety of the Empire, there is no such power which the Chief Constables could avail themselves of. If a clause were added to the Official Secrets Act empowering any Magistrate to grant a search-warrant on the application of a Chief Constable showing reasonable ground for suspicion, the proper working of the Counter-espionage movement would be ensured.

'Moreover, there is no direct law dealing with cases of photographing, planning, or sketching of forts etc., and unless absolute damage has been committed, the action complained of comes merely under the civil Common Law of Trespass, in which case the punishment is practically a nominal one, amounting in most cases to a small fine, which for our purposes is useless as a deterrent.'[59]

Andrew suggests that: 'With the gift of hindsight, it may seem surprising that Kell's first progress report did not inspire greater scepticism. The Rusper and Frant cases did not in reality provide the strong evidence of "an organised system of German espionage" which Kell claimed they did. Kell, however, was preaching to the converted.'[60]

Kell's critics have often accused him of believing in all of the nonsense dreamt up by authors such as Le Queux. The following episode shows that this is clearly not the case, but rather that Kell simply felt he had to be polite when confronted with such fantasies. As Kell recorded in his office diary on 6 January 1911:

> 'When I was at the Naval and Military Club this evening, a Major Kidd told me in course of conversation that a Colonel Seton had been giving lectures on National Service in Edinburgh recently, and in one of them he had said that he had certain definite information about German waiters having their arms with them over here, and that they were practising at night time in under-ground ranges. (This is the usual yarn dished up in another form.)'[61]

J R and D Westmacott

Indeed, Kell's work must have impressed his superiors because on 14 March 1910 he was granted the assistance of a clerk, Mr J.R. Westmacott, previously a soldier clerk at the War Office, who was to become the Bureau's Chief Clerk. Then, on 16 January 1911, a second clerk joined the Bureau: Miss D. Westmacott. Not much is known about the Bureau's first female recruit. She may well have been the daughter of Mr J.R. Westmacott, but this can only be conjecture.[62]

The Helm Case

In August 1910, Lieutenant Vivien Brandon of the Admiralty Hydrographic Department and Captain R.M. Trench of the Royal Marines were arrested while on a mission for British naval intelligence. They had been tasked with reconnoitring German North Sea coastal defences at Borkum and other locations.[63] The British Government needed a riposte.

On 5 September 1910, a telegram came from the General Officer Commanding (GOC) Portsmouth defences that some of his officers had arrested a German, *Leutnant* Siegfried Helm, an officer of the 21st Nassau Pioneer Regiment, in the act of sketching Fort Widley. The following day, a Captain Bonham Carter provided all the necessary evidence about Helm's spying.[64] Helm's notebook contained nine drawings of fortifications, notes on the positions of guns and searchlights, details of distances, and diagrams showing the field of fire of defending artillery.[65] Helm had come to England ostensibly to learn English. Before his arrival however, he had written to a Miss Wodehouse, a former lover of one of his fellow officers, in the hope of meeting her. Miss Wodehouse helped Helm to find lodgings near her home in the Portsmouth area.[66] She soon began to suspect that Helm was involved in espionage. As Kell later reported, when he interviewed Miss Wodehouse, she claimed that '…she had deliberately egged Lieut. Helm on to make love to her to gain his confidence as she suspected from the outset that he was spying.'[67] As Andrew politely explains, 'since Helm was the second German officer to become her lover, Miss Wodehouse's explanation does not carry complete conviction.'[68] Miss Wodehouse soon reported Helm to the local barracks.[69] The very next day, Helm was caught in the act of making further sketches.

Helm was the first foreign spy to be charged under OSA 1889.[70] Then the unsatisfactory state of the law, under OSA 1889, came to the fore. The public prosecutor's opinion was that the required evidence was present to apply for a fiat from the Attorney-General to prosecute Helm. However, as the Attorney-General was away on the Continent, it was necessary to wire for his authority to make the arrest. Therefore, it was required to detain Helm in military custody until 7 September, by which time he was given over to the civil power. At his committal hearing, Helm claimed that he had been sketching for his own amusement, not for the purposes of espionage. It was extremely difficult to prove intent. In fact, the fort he had been drawing had long been out of date and could not possibly be of interest to Germany. Helm was thus committed for trial on a lesser charge.[71] As Andrew observes, this was the key lesson that the Bureau drew from the Helm case: 'The magistrates' court had thrown out the charge of felony alleging intention to communicate "certain sketches and plans … to a foreign State – to wit the Empire of Germany" and committed Helm for trial only on a lesser charge. Under the 1889 Act it was necessary to prove intent to obtain information illegally.'[72]

Helm pleaded guilty at his trial, but he was merely bound over and discharged. As Helm and his father took the train back to London, Kell sat unrecognised in their compartment in order to try to discover more about what lay behind Helm's activities. Unfortunately for Kell, Helm and his father did not say much to each other. However, research conducted in recent years in the German archives revealed what Kell could not have known at the time (but might well have suspected) – that Helm had been acting on his own initiative, rather than on instruction.[73]

Progress: March 1910-October 1910

In his second progress report, covering March–October 1910, Kell illustrated how the work of the Bureau had gathered pace during that period:

- Over 200 cases of alleged espionage were investigated.
- By then Kell was in touch with forty chief constables.
- Over 500 aliens had been registered.
- And Kell had been in 'constant communication' with the Admiralty, Home Office, Scotland Yard, and the Committee of Imperial Defence.

However, Kell was obviously aware that, although he had diligently investigated over 200 cases of alleged espionage, he had yet to investigate a single case of genuine espionage. Indeed, the concluding remarks to his second progress report were far less confident than those of his first progress report had been:

'*If I were asked to give my opinion on the success or otherwise of the counter-espionage section of the Bureau, I would find it exceedingly difficult to do so.*

'*I have no hesitation on saying, from my year's experience of the work, that this section of the Bureau has justified its institution. Hitherto it had been found impossible to devote the necessary time and attention to this kind of work, and in many cases important clues had been lost by not being able to follow them up at the moment of their being reported. But when we come to discuss the success of this section, we are brought face to face with two great obstacles:*

> *(1) Lack of funds, and consequently an insufficient staff.*
> *(2) Inefficiency of the present legislature.'*

Kell also offered a telling analysis of counter-espionage methods, which is worth quoting at length:

> *'Counter-espionage work in peace-time should, I think, be divided under the following heads:*
>
> *A. Passive Operations.*
> *(1). Locating of, and noting all useful details regarding known spies, and other suspected aliens and traitors.*
> *(2). Compilation of handwritings, description-returns and photographs of all suspects for immediate transmission to the G.P.O. and Police at the commencement of the Precautionary Period.*
> *(3). Collection of information in Home Ports likely to be of use during the Precautionary Period, for example:*
>
> > *(a) Getting to know certain captains of merchant ships, who could be counted upon to give reliable information about an enemy's fleet, or any unusual activity in foreign ports.*
> > *(b) The ear-marking of minor agents in important British ports, who, during the Precautionary Period, would report anything of an unusual nature.*
>
> *(4). The ear-marking (and training??) of our own spies in the coast counties, to act behind the enemy's lines in case of invasion.*
>
> *B. Active Operations.*
> *(1). Shadowing known spies or highly-suspected persons; seeing whom they associate with etc thereby getting on the track of traitors.*
> *(2). Dissemination of false or useless information at places where foreigners frequent, such as ports etc.*
> *(3). The purchase of foreign information by means of an established agency in the city. (This proposal might be considered at a later period.)'*[74]

Kell concentrates on the investigative side of counter-espionage work. The preventive side had already been covered in his previous reports when he mentioned the OSA, aliens registration, the guarding of vulnerable points, and preventing access to sensitive information in places like dockyards. And, of course, Kell was focusing on peacetime. There is much more scope for preventive work and the control of aliens during wartime. Items A1 and A2 of Kell's report show that he was already planning to round-up Germany's agents in the UK in a paralyzing blow at the outbreak of war. It is possible that he may have inherited this strategy from Edmonds, who outlined it in his note of 2 December 1908. It is equally possible that Kell may have learned of this whilst writing his History of the Russo-Japanese War for the Historical Section of the Committee of Imperial Defence, and that Edmonds may have actually learned of this from Kell! Item A3(a) appears to show Kell over-stepping his mark and trying to move into Cumming's territory. Item A3(b) demonstrates the importance placed on ports and the concern that the gravest danger from German saboteurs would come in the precautionary period just before the outbreak of war. Item A4 reiterates an idea proposed back in October 1908. In item B1, Kell outlines how counter-espionage work tends to develop as leads generate further leads. Hence, the crucial importance of making the initial break into the German espionage network in the UK. Item B2 seems to build upon the concept of deception outlined by Edmonds in his paper on intelligence methods, while item B3 appears to offer another recipe for clashes with Cumming.

In his second progress report, Kell also explained that 'lack of assistance' had made it 'impossible to strike out over much new ground'. Therefore, he applied for an assistant as well as for a merchant navy officer to collect information in home ports and to select agents there who would be of use during the 'precautionary period' on the eve of war and also in time of war.[75]

By the time of the first annual review of his work, in November 1910, Kell had 'investigated a series of leads, which save for the somewhat farcical Helm case, had so far yielded no solid evidence of German espionage …'[76]

Clarke
Captain Frederick Stanley Clarke, late of the Suffolk Regiment, joined the Bureau on 1 January 1911 as Kell's assistant.[77]

Progress: October 1910-March 1911
By the end of March 1911, the Bureau had received aliens' returns from the chief constables of eighteen Southern and Eastern coastal counties, with the result that 1,245 aliens had been registered by that time. Kell also got in touch with the remaining thirty-three county chief constables of England and Wales who were all willing to cooperate. The Bureau had also investigated and registered German miners in Kent. As part of Home Defence, the Bureau had begun to draw up a map of England and Wales showing 1) all places which require special guarding, and 2) the number of Germans residing in the vicinity of these vulnerable points (excluding London, boroughs and cities). The Bureau was also in the process of enquiring into the principal German institutions in the UK, particularly their locality, members and staff. Clarke undertook a three-week walking tour along the coast of Essex and Suffolk, but he did not make any significant discoveries.[78]

Kell was also clearly concerned that the Bureau had not yet been able to uncover more concrete proof of German espionage in the UK, and felt that something needed to be done about this. As he recorded in his office diary on 3 March 1911:

> *'I had a long interview with 'M' [Melville] at his office and impressed upon him the necessity of our being more energetic in the future, and that I expected him to think out new schemes for getting hold of intelligence.'*[79]

Pre-war cooperation with Chief Constables and other Government departments
With only very limited resources at his disposal, the key to Kell's initial counter-espionage strategy was, as Andrew points out 'to gain the assistance of chief constables around the

country'. This needed the backing of the Home Secretary and in this regard Kell was lucky that Winston Churchill occupied that position for most of 1910 and 1911; more than any other British politician, Churchill appreciated and supported the world of intelligence.

Churchill's private secretary provided Kell with a letter of introduction to the chief constables of England and Wales, and he also obtained a similar introduction from the Scottish Office to chief constables in Scotland.[80] Indeed, as shown by his progress reports detailed above, Kell spent much of his first eighteen months with the Bureau cultivating good working relations with police chief constables, many of whom were retired army officers. Thus, Kell was fairly sure of a receptive audience when he expressed his concerns to the county chief constables. In his diary, Cumming referred to the county chief constables as 'Hear Hears'.[81] By 3 March 1914, the Bureau had opened correspondence with all the county chief constables of England and Wales, twenty-three in Scotland, the Isle of Man and the Royal Irish Constabulary, and with the chief constables of fifty-two boroughs in England and Wales and eighteen in Scotland.[82]

The Bureau also arranged to cooperate with a number of other government departments, as well as the police, during the pre-war period. First, there was the GPO. Right from the start it was obvious that the GPO's help would be required in order to intercept suspects' mail. Owing to the potential of using wireless telegraphy to evade censorship in wartime, it was also essential that wireless telegraph stations were controlled. On 23 August 1910, Kell met the Inspector of Wireless Telegraphy, who offered his help and gave a list of call stations. This enabled the police to be familiarised with the whereabouts of all authorised wireless stations, information about which they needed in order to detect any unauthorised stations that had been established with hostile intent. Secondly, there were the Coastguards. On 30 August 1910, the Admiralty agreed that henceforth coastguards should pass on information directly to the Bureau, rather than via the standard official channels. A section regarding a third department has been removed from both the F Branch Report and the F Branch Summary Report, under section 5.3(4) of the Public Records Act 1958. This mysterious department may conceivably have been the Registrar-General, whose census data would have been of obvious use to the Bureau in gauging the number of enemy aliens living in the UK. Fourth, there were dockyards, arsenals and other similar locations. In May 1911, with the Admiralty having agreed to provide lists of aliens employed in government dockyards, a scheme was begun for the Bureau to gain lists of aliens engaged in private shipbuilding yards. During the summer of 1911, the Admiralty instructed that aliens working in government establishments under the Controller of the Navy should be registered and the returns from the Admiralty were registered by the Bureau before October 1911.[83]

Pre-war Aliens Registration

Kell was familiar with the German *Meldewesen* system, which enforced the compulsory registration of all foreigners visiting or residing in Germany and imposed limits upon where they could go and what they could do. He knew that such a system would not be acceptable to liberal Britain. Therefore, Kell proposed a secret register of enemy aliens.

In March 1910, the Committee of Imperial Defence founded an Aliens Sub-Committee, initially chaired by Winston Churchill, then the Home Secretary.

The Aliens Sub-Committee approved Kell's work to create a secret register of aliens from likely enemy powers such as Germany, which was founded on information supplied by local constabularies.[84]

Chief constables were asked to send in reports on individual suspects, which served as the basis of registration, and 300 aliens had been registered by October 1910. This experience taught the necessity of a standard form of report.[85] Kell broached this matter with the Home Office, and a printed Aliens Return form was put to the Home Secretary and approved.[86] Importantly, all such information requested was to be gathered confidentially. By November 1910, approximately 1,500 of these forms had been given to chief constables, primarily in the east coast counties, and in January 1911, the Bureau reported that excellent progress had been made in the unofficial registration of aliens in the country districts. By April 1911, by which time some 4,500 aliens had been registered, the Bureau found that this scheme had the following benefits: firstly, a rough estimate of the number of aliens in each county could be reached; secondly, the areas most favoured by aliens could be seen; thirdly, aliens could be divided into probably harmless and probably harmful; fourth, it provided the details of aliens working in or near government works; fifth, it showed which aliens travelled around extensively and sixth, it made it possible to prepare a list of the aliens whom it would be advisable to remove from martial law areas at the start of war.

The following key issues arose and were resolved during the compilation of the unofficial register: firstly, information concerning changes of address, arrivals and departures of aliens should be reported immediately if possible, and definitely be included in the yearly revision of the aliens return; secondly, naturalised British subjects of alien birth should be included because the Bureau felt that naturalisation counted for nothing in espionage matters and thirdly, alien returns should be sent in during the first quarter of the year and amended annually. However, it was later decided that amendments should be received at least once every quarter.

The unofficial registration of aliens progressed steadily. By January 1913, 10,320 aliens of all nationalities had been registered, including 3,574 Germans and Austrians. By April 1913, these figures had increased to 21,397 and 5,241 respectively. By July 1913, the totals stood at 28,830 and 11,100.[87] In 1914, 70,000 aliens over the age of fourteen lived in Great Britain. By the outbreak of war, all of those outside London – about half of the total – had been registered.[88]

In order to prevent potential enemies from realising the existence of the unofficial register, it was of the utmost importance that all police enquiries were carried out in a confidential and quiet manner. The police did an admirable job, with great tact, as is shown by the fact that only two complaints were received from nearly 30,000 registrations.[89]

In order to add to the value of the registration, in April 1911, Kell asked the police to send in quarterly reports, known as 'special aliens returns', on twenty-five or more possible suspects from each county selected by the Bureau. The Bureau would periodically revise these lists and send all amendments to the relevant chief constables. It was hoped that this would help to mark down particularly dangerous individuals and uncover the identities of the resident and travelling agents and possibly even the centre of the German espionage organisation in the UK. The Bureau specified the following information as especially valuable in these reports:

1. Name in full and description
2. Occupation and whether the person in question had more money at his command than his apparent occupation could bring in.
3. Where he came from and what reason he gave for settling in a particular locality.
4. Did he leave – and if so where did he go? Did he ever go to Germany? Did people come to stay with him? If so who were they? Descriptions of any visitors were considered useful.
5. Did the alien appear to know a great deal about the country around him and did he appear to take an interest in horses, supplies etc.
6. Was he of military appearance and did he ever go to Germany for periodical military training?
7. Did he correspond much with Germany? Did he receive periodical supplies of foreign money, notes etc?
8. Photographs and specimens of handwriting were always viewed as useful.[90]

The pre-war possible suspect list also served as a way of teaching the police about certain aspects of a job that was new to all concerned. This was especially the case when the forces of law and order tended to think that if an individual appeared respectable and was free from criminal suspicion, he could not be a spy.[91]

As with the aliens registration, a printed form was used, which elaborated on the above, and was given to the police in books of tear-out forms with the questions numbered on them and on the counterfoil. As a precaution against the possible leakage of information in the post, the forms themselves did not include these questions, only their numbers, and no name or address, with the individual in question being identified by the Bureau by his own serial number.[92]

Beginnings of Registry

As already noted, in March 1910, six months into the life of the Bureau, Kell was provided with a clerk to handle correspondence, file records under the names of suspects and begin a card index.[93] The card index represented the embryo of what became the centralised Registry – 'the mainspring of the DEFENCE SECURITY INTELLIGENCE BUREAU and the basis of all useful Counter-Espionage work', according to an MI5 H Branch report. 'The Registry is the essential link between the various duties coming within the province of the Defence Security Intelligence Bureau.'[94] The main duties of this embryonic Registry at that time were:

(a) The carding and noting of all useful details regarding suspect aliens.
(b) The compilation of particulars regarding handwritings.
(c) Descriptive reports and photographs of suspected persons.
(d) The collation of information received.
(e) The indexing and filing of all information received.[95]

In terms of operational procedure, it is instructive to outline the system of filing and indexing employed before the First World War. The method of filing and indexing at that time was fundamentally the one that was still being used at the end of the War.

Indeed, no definite change of principle was found necessary except that the filing of papers under the heading of the official from whom correspondence originated, specially divided into subjects, had been abandoned for the filing under subjects sub-divided by the office of origin or county concerned.

The principle by which papers were filed was that only one file should be created for a particular person and that every paper concerning him or her should be filed there, including excerpts from papers mentioning him that had to be placed in other files. The guiding principle behind these personal files was that all documents received should, if practicable, be placed in the personal file of some person; if this could not be done, whenever possible, all documents were then put into one of the official files. The official files corresponded practically to the place card index, because each one concerned a particular government or police office sub-divided into different sub-divisions. Papers that did not belong, in either a personal or official file, were homed in the subject files which were, thus, at that time, the least important of the files maintained. All the correspondence that was received was recorded in a schedule book, which noted 'the date of receipt or dispatch of any communication; its serial number; the office from which it emanated or to which it was addressed; the subject of the communication and the action taken together with a note as to by whom the paper was 'put away'. All the names of people or organisations mentioned in a report were indexed in the general card index and 'the subjects connected with the report were recorded, either on the index sheet kept in each subject-file or cross-indexed by means of a subject-card-index'.

The registry also kept an index known as the special card index, which recorded the names of all aliens or individuals of alien origin reported by the police under the unofficial aliens registration scheme. The cards were ordered by their serial number. Whenever a chief constable notified the Bureau of the presence of a new alien, a card was opened and then filed in the special card index under the name of the police district from whence the report had originated. The Bureau assigned the card a serial number, which number was then passed on to the chief constable concerned, who recorded it in his register of resident aliens.[96]

The Registry was cutting edge for its time: Kell disposed of the traditional ledger system and instead used the modern Roneo card system in which the name, nationality, date of birth, family particulars, home and business addresses, whether householder, lodger or servant, trade or occupation, and employer details were recorded on a numbered card, with additional information written on the reverse. As and when new information was received from chief constables, the card was updated. The system was enhanced by the adoption of colour codes and symbols which quickly identified potential threat levels. [97]

★ ★ ★

It seems fairly clear that liberal England would not have taken the threat of German espionage so seriously had it not been for Germany's obvious intention to develop a fleet that would be able to challenge the Royal Navy's supremacy, such that it could no longer be guaranteed beyond all possible doubt that Britain would be safe from the threat of a German invasion.

The main counter-espionage developments that the Bureau would undertake before the outbreak of war had all been under official consideration well before the Bureau's conception: an amended OSA, aliens' registration, and getting the Police and Post Office more involved in counter-espionage work.

The deliberations of the Sub-Committee on Foreign Espionage also reveal a number of key points that would come to play a role in the early development of the Bureau. The War Office was clearly the driving force, as it pushed for the formation of a secret service Bureau. The War Office also had very clear ideas about how such a Bureau should develop. The secret service Bureau was intended very much as a screen to provide the Government with a 'plausible deniability' that it did not engage in such a 'dirty' business as espionage. Indeed, the Post Office stressed that it was happy to detain and open correspondence provided that it had been expressly authorised by a warrant signed by the Secretary of State. In short, the Post Office did not object to engaging in practices that might lead to public criticism provided that it could excuse itself by showing that it had only done so at the behest of its political masters. The Government's desire to distance itself from the secret service had the potential to promote a culture of excessive secrecy and lack of democratic accountability within the secret services. But, it was very much the fault of the politicians themselves – not men like Kell.

The Bureau had very humble beginnings, comprising a solitary official, who was given minimal resources. It seems hard to imagine the head of MI5 today being told to delay operations until the next accounting period because of a lack of resources! However, even by March 1911, it is possible to discern the beginnings of some key developments that still influence MI5 today. Kell's Bureau had no executive powers. Thus, the Bureau worked by cooperating with others, such as the Police and the Post Office. The Bureau was to function as the 'brain' of counter-espionage, directing these other agencies involved in its prosecution. The key to functioning as the 'brain' that directed counter-espionage was information. Kell was adamant from the very beginning that the Bureau should function as the central clearing-house for all counter-espionage information.

By March 1911, Kell had been working on counter-espionage for eighteen months; yet he was still waiting for his first real break into the German espionage network in the UK. He was also clearly worried by this lack of demonstrable success – as shown by the 'pep talk' he gave to Melville in March 1911. Kell must have been conscious that his two-year contract would soon be up for renewal – or termination. And he had not yet produced any headline-grabbing stories of enemy spies caught red-handed and successfully prosecuted, that the Government could use to counter the allegations of official laxity in the face of the threat posed by German espionage constantly levelled against them by opposition MPs and vocal critics like Le Queux. However, it is also abundantly clear that much vital ground work had been done, despite it being handicapped by scant resources. Kell had established good working relations with many chief constables and begun an unofficial register of aliens. In short, firm foundations had been laid.

CHAPTER TWO

Breakthrough

March 1911-August 1914

Introduction

BETWEEN March 1911 and August 1914, the Bureau was transformed. This chapter focuses on the key stages in the Bureau's development during this time and shows how and why they amounted to a transformation. The Bureau's strategy to 'round up' the German network in one paralysing blow required that trials were avoided if at all possible so as to protect the secret that the 'Reimers correspondence' (exchanges to and from the German spymaster, Gustav Steinhauer, who used such a cover name) was being intercepted. Furthermore, the key developments of the OSA 1911 and HOWs (Home Office Warrants – see later in this chapter) transformed the Bureau's ability to catch spies, and represented a real transformation in the powers that liberal England was prepared to use in counter-espionage. The distribution of duties between an investigative branch and a preventive branch at the time was perhaps the key step in the organisational development of the Bureau throughout the whole 1909-1918 period.

TRIALS AND TRIBULATIONS

The Lozel Case

In 1904, the Chief Constable of Kent had Franz Heinrich Lozel, a German photographer of Beach Street in Sheerness arrested for photographing men working on the building of a new fort. He was searched but without result. In April 1911, the same Chief Constable passed on a report about Lozel to the Bureau, stating that it was his routine to visit Germany every year taking large portfolios of photographs with him. Lozel was subsequently placed on the Special War List to be searched. The Chief Constable also informed the Bureau that the German had been living in Sheerness since at least 1887, and that he had kept his German nationality and 'expressed anti-British sentiments'. He also noted that Lozel's photographic studio was situated on the

Recreation Ground at Sheerness and commanded 'an uninterrupted view of the batteries and of the entrance to the dockyard at Sheerness.'

A number of incidents involving Lozel occurred up until the outbreak of war: for example, in December 1911, the military police arrested him for photographing the defences but upon examination of his films, the subject of the photographs turned out to be a pulp ship. Lozel was released. In his interview with Melville at Scotland Yard in October 1913, a one-time German seaman and suspected agent, Karl Hentschel, claimed that Lozel was a German agent. On 4 August 1914, Lozel was arrested by a corporal of the Essex Regiment for carrying a camera on the sea wall at Sheerness. The Stipendiary Magistrate deemed that there was 'insufficient' evidence for prosecution. Therefore, Lozel was interned under the ARO, eventually being deported back to Germany in September 1919.[1]

Ohlson

On 10 May 1911, Lieutenant (later Commander) B.J. Ohlson (known as 'O' in MI5's reports), a Royal Naval Reserve officer, who had been working for the P&O shipping company, joined the Bureau 'as assistant for the collection of information in the Ports along the East Coast', beginning at the Port of London.[2] As a cover for his position, Ohlson was appointed as an Immigration Officer at the Port of London. A report written by him to accompany Kell's progress report for October 1912, gives a flavour of what his work for the Bureau involved. By this time, the Bureau was 'in touch' with a number of steamship lines whose ships traded between British and Continental ports, and also with Norway, Russia, the Black Sea, and the Mediterranean, including the Wilson Line of Hull, the Hull-Holland Steamship Company, the Goole Steam Shipping Company, the Great Central Railway Company, the Great Eastern Railway Company, and the General Steam Navigation Company. According to Ohlson:

'All these Lines are willing to assist us, and it is now suggested to ask the Masters of vessels, through the medium of their marine Superintendents, to send in general reports upon the various harbours they visit, and upon anything happening therein that may seem to be of special interest or value.'

A small remuneration would be offered for these reports, in the hope that it would induce the ships' Masters to take an intelligent interest in the work, to keep in touch with the Bureau, and to use their opportunities of obtaining information to the best advantage, such that when any special item of information was required, the Bureau would know who were the most likely men to employ for the purpose.[3]

In a progress report written on 9 April 1913, Kell stated that the 'special duties' that Ohlson had been taken on for had 'lapsed ... through changes in the system of obtaining Admiralty intelligence.' Therefore, Kell felt that the question of Ohlson's 'disposal is for consideration... His knowledge of the work and his unsparing attention to his duties render it highly desirable that his services should not be lost at the time when a considerable expansion of the work is in progress.'[4]

Kell's office diary entry for 29 June 1911 may shed some light on why Ohlson's work was eventually stopped:

' *"C" made a complaint that, through "O" and the information he was acquiring, our section of the Bureau was encroaching upon his work. It was finally agreed that with Colonel Macdonogh's approval, that information acquired by "O" should be sent through "C" to the Admiralty, reference being made to the source of the receipt of the information.'[5]

Ohlson eventually left the Bureau on 12 November 1914. However, he re-joined on 2 July 1916 and stayed until 18 July 1917.[6]

Regan and Fitzgerald

On 7 June 1911, John Regan (often referred to as 'R' in MI5's reports), a former Metropolitan policeman, joined the Bureau to assist Melville with the detective work. On 1 November 1912, Henry Fitzgerald, who had been a sergeant with the Metropolitan Police, joined the Bureau's detective staff.[7]

The Schultz Case

Max Schultz was the first German agent MI5 brought to trial. On 14 July 1911, Captain W. Matthews, of the Royal Garrison Artillery at Plymouth, informed Major Haig, GSO South Western Coast Defences, that during a local mobilization, a German named 'Dr Schultz', who had been living in Plymouth for some time and who had stayed on a house-boat called the *Egret* which lay at the mouth of the Yealm near Portsmouth, had been 'seen with sketches' and was 'well supplied with money, which he spent on treating N.C.O.s and dockyard hands.' On 15 July, Major Haig informed Kell, who then wrote to the Chief Constables of Plymouth and of Devon asking for enquiries to be made. Subsequent investigation showed that Dr Max Schultz, who was thirty-one years old and who held a PhD in Philology from Berlin University, had come to the UK in March 1911 to teach languages at Plymouth. He had also been convicted of embezzlement in Germany.[8] Schultz was known to be flamboyant and had little notion of undercover operations. According to Andrew, he had set himself up '…on a houseboat in Portsmouth, flying the German flag from the stern and throwing parties at which he attempted (unsuccessfully) to turn the conversation to naval matters. Though he quickly aroused suspicion, he acquired no useful information.'[9]

A report of 22 July by Detective Sergeant Martin of the Plymouth Police contained details of Schultz's activities.[10] Whilst he had been 'engaged in gun practice', the German had 'shot his housekeeper, Miss Sturgeon, in the arm'. After the woman sued Schultz for damages he contacted a local solicitor, Mr Hugh Duff, on 4 July.[11] Schultz then offered to employ Duff as a correspondent for a German newspaper. As such it would be Duff's job to report the latest news about military and naval matters. Schultz also asked Duff if he could obtain such news from friends in the Royal Navy and arranged a meeting between Duff and the head of the newspaper syndicate at Plymouth on 18 July. However, the meeting was postponed until 22 July, but Duff notified the police on the 18th. On the 20th, Duff signed a contract which Schultz gave him to post. Instead, Duff took it straight to the police.

Schultz was also introduced to a Mr Tarren, of the National Cash Register, by a work colleague of Tarren's who Schultz knew. When Schultz realised that Tarren's job could give him access to the dockyards, Schultz asked him to supply news for a Continental newspaper. He also asked if Tarren could get into Woolwich Arsenal. On 23 July, Tarren signed a contract and Schultz gave the contract to him to post. Tarren removed the envelope and kept it, replacing it with another in his own handwriting. The available records do not explain what Tarren did with this envelope. However, it seems highly likely that he gave it to the local police.

On 31 July, Kell took Martin's report to the Home Office and asked the dockyard police to verify the information on Schultz. They reported on 2 August. On 5 August, both reports were submitted to the Admiralty which judged that it was a 'clear case' of spying. Thus, checks were placed on Schultz's correspondence. On 6 August, Kell took over the direction of the case and in almost daily correspondence with Sergeant Martin he guided the action of the police and of the two informers. On 8 August, the evidence against Schultz was placed before a representative of the Director of Public Prosecutions, who gave his opinion of what evidence would be necessary in order to secure a conviction.

Six days earlier, Schultz had held separate meetings with both Duff and Tarren for which he dictated a list of espionage questions for both of them. These questions were passed on to Kell who provided Duff and Tarren with 'answers' on 11 August. Thus, Kell had collected the evidence required by the Director of Public Prosecutions: of asking a definite question for prejudicial purposes.

On 15 August, seemingly having received Duff's and Tarren's answers, 'Onkel' (a cover name for Steinhauer) was clearly not impressed and wrote from Ostend breaking off all connections with his 'nephew'. On 16 August, the Attorney-General granted a fiat for Schultz's arrest. Two days later, Schulz was arrested and charged with having unlawfully incited Duff to commit an offence against the OSA. On 28 August, the press announced that a British spy, Bertram Stewart, had been arrested in Germany. Therefore, Britain was keen to convict Schultz as a riposte.

Schultz was tried at the Exeter Assizes on 3 November. The defence argued that information of the kind that Schultz had collected was not detrimental to national security and had been published in newspapers which had not been prosecuted. The prosecution countered that the information supplied to Duff was 'authentic', while that published by newspapers was not. Schultz was found guilty and sentenced to twenty-one months' penal servitude. He was released after serving eighteen months. Upon his release, Schultz was kept under surveillance until he left the country.[12]

BREAKTHROUGH

Reimer's Address

In August 1911, Captain Stanley Clarke, Kell's deputy, had a 'remarkable stroke of luck' which 'transformed' the Bureau's investigations of the German Admiralty's *Nachrichten-Abteilung's* (known as 'N') operations in the UK.[13] That month, Francis L. Holstein, the German proprietor of the Peacock Hotel in Leith, received a letter from Germany asking for information about the UK's feelings concerning war with Germany and its preparations for war. Clarke claimed that he happened to be in the same railway carriage as Holstein when he overheard the German hotelier telling a friend about this letter.[14]

In fact, it is possible, but can never be confirmed, that Holstein had already been under suspicion and the overhearing of the train conversation was either no coincidence or a cover story. Whatever the truth of the matter, Steinhauer's tendency to send unsolicited letters to Germans resident in Britain requesting information meant that it would be only a matter of time before one of them was betrayed by its recipient.[15]

The Chief Constable at Leith discovered that Holstein had received two letters of a similar nature from the same source in June and August 1909, namely F. Reimers from an address at Brauerstrasse in Potsdam. Holstein had mislaid these letters, and it was only in February 1913 that he found them amongst old bills and gave them to the police. The surviving records do not indicate why Holstein did this. He was possibly afraid of what the authorities might do if he did not hand them over and then discovered his evasion. Alternatively, MI5 may have come across these letters another way, and this is another cover story. The police passed them on to the Bureau. The Bureau discovered that 'Reimers' was an alias used by Gustav Steinhauer, head of the British section of the *Nachrichten-Abteilung* (see later). A HOW was taken out for Reimers on 14 September 1911.[16]

Beginning in September 1911, Kell kept a carefully compiled, cross-referenced index of the intercepted letters between Steinhauer and his agents in Britain. The index for letters from 1911 to 1914 contained 1,189 entries. This led to the vitally important discovery of Steinhauer's use of intermediaries for communications with his agents and HOWs enabled the Bureau to penetrate much of the German network.[17]

Home Office Warrant (HOW)

The Home Office Warrant (HOW) was perhaps the most important source of detection during peacetime. The Bureau's investigative powers were greatly enhanced in August 1911, when the Home Secretary, Winston Churchill, simplified the procedure enabling the interception of suspects' mail. Previously, in a cumbersome process, Home Secretaries signed individual warrants for each item. Churchill established a modus operandi whereby Home Secretaries signed general warrants which authorised the interception of every item of correspondence of specified individuals on a list.[18]

The pre-war German espionage network in the UK

The German espionage organisation in the UK before the First World War functioned through its post boxes or intermediaries. Rather than communicating directly with its agents in the UK, the German Secret Service communicated with intermediaries, who then passed these communications on to the agents. Similarly, the agents did not communicate directly with the German Secret Service. They also communicated with the intermediaries, who then forwarded these communications on to the German Secret Service. Thus, the Germans' communications with their agents formed a kind of circle. An intermediary functioned to protect both the agent in the UK and the German Secret Service abroad. This system entailed the use of two intermediaries, one for incoming letters and pay, and another for outgoing reports. For outgoing reports posted by intermediaries, foreign addresses, for example in Denmark and Belgium, were much used. This system was designed to provide protection in two ways. Firstly, if an agent did not know the spymaster's name and address, he could not be indiscreet about it. Secondly,

Winston Churchill and Kaiser Wilhelm II. As Home
Secretary from February 1910 to October 1911, Churchill
played a key role in the early development of MI5, helping
Kell to develop close working relations with police chief
constables and simplifying the process of applying for
warrants to intercept suspects' correspondence.
(Library of Congress)

Gustav Steinhauer, head of the British
section of the German Navy's foreign
intelligence service and the man who
directed pre-war German espionage in
Great Britain. (Jay Robert Nash Collection)

if an agent in the UK wrote letters to, and received letters from, only British addresses
used by intermediaries, he would not arouse suspicion. This system had the obvious
drawback – which the Bureau exploited to the full – that once spy addresses and
intermediaries were discovered, postal interception could uncover the wider spy network
that communicated through these links. Besides posting letters and registering and
forwarding agents' pay, intermediaries' duties included keeping the Germans supplied
with British stamps and stationery, forwarding press clippings of noteworthy events and
undertaking special enquiries. These special enquiries were generally to establish the
credentials of would-be agents.[19]

This reveals a key weakness in the German espionage system in the UK: namely
that, 'the problem of conveying intelligence from Britain was never entirely solved
and led to the detection of several agents.'[20] Furthermore the Germans had too few safe
cover addresses.[21]

Gustav Steinhauer

Pre-war German espionage in the UK was directed by Gustav Steinhauer, a former naval
petty officer, whose service had included time on the Imperial yacht *Hohenzollern*, and

who was said to have spent some time in America, possibly as a detective with the Pinkerton detective agency. He then joined the German police and moved into the Secret Service.[22]

The Bureau learned much about Germany's intelligence requirements from intercepted espionage questionnaires that Steinhauer posted to his agents in the UK. The Bureau's progress report covering the period from December 1911 to 31 July 1912 described 'Specimens of information, etc, which German Secret Service Agents have been instructed to obtain', namely:

Books
1. Torpedo Manuals.
2. Annual Report of progress Torpedo School.
3. Books on Wireless Telegraphy.
4. Submarine Manuals.
5. Mining and mine laying manuals.
6. Signal Book.

Information
NAVAL
1. Exact names and titles of confidential books on Wireless Telegraphy, Torpedoes & Submarines.
2. Details of armour of newest ships.
3. Details of bulkhead construction.
4. Height of double bottom.
5. Displacement.
6. Details of torpedo tubes, number, position, etc.
7. Mine Defences, position, number of mines, where stored in peace.
8. Boom defences, construction, position and where stored in peace.
9. As to probability of formation of a new submarine station and preparations in connection therewith – possibility of its being also a destroyer base – date of its being completed.
10. Movements of warships, especially submarines.
11. Details of Naval Manoeuvres.

MILITARY
1. Details of new 4.5-in Field Howitzer, especially ammunition supply; and extent of issue of this gun to the troops.
2. Progress with regard to introduction of an Automatic Rifle.
3. Training and efficiency of Territorial Force Field Artillery.
4. Details of Army Mobilization – the likelihood of its being carried out by divisions, simultaneously or otherwise.

POLITICAL & GENERAL
1. Popular feeling towards Germany, especially in the Fleet. Opinions of high officers especially to be gathered.

2. Opinion of Officers and men of British Fleet as to chances of success in a war with Germany. Are they sure of success or not?

3. Does anyone think of converting Naval Manoeuvres into actual war with Germany?

4. Does the idea mentioned in (3) originate from responsible quarters and is it at all generally discussed?[23]

Official Secrets Act 1911

The Helm case (see Chapter One) lent further weight to those who urged that the OSA 1889 desperately needed amending. A magistrates court had rejected a charge of felony which alleged that 'sketches and plans' were being communicated to Germany and Helm was committed for trial on a lesser charge, since the terms of the OSA of 1889 stipulated intent to obtain information illegally had to be proved. At the second reading of a new Official Secrets Bill at the House of Lords in July 1911, Viscount Haldane warned that such terms were creating extreme difficulties in the prevention of espionage. Haldane told the house that when found amidst fortifications at Dover, 'an intelligent foreigner' claimed he was there merely to listen to the birds singing – and that despite the fact that it was mid-winter. [24]

Having passed through the House of Lords, the Bill to amend the OSA 1889 was introduced to the House of Commons on 17 August 1911. The Liberal MP, Sir Alpheus Morton, observed that 'it upset Magna Carta altogether'. Nevertheless, Colonel 'Jack' Sealy, the parliamentary Under-Secretary of State for War, stirred up the sense of unease, bordering on fear, during the summer of that year by claiming that the Germans' despatch of the SMS *Panther* to the Moroccan port of Agadir could spark a war in Europe. Sealy managed to push the Bill through the Commons in under an hour. [25]

The OSA 1911 played such an integral part in all of the pre-war activities of the Bureau that it is worth examining in considerable detail. Clause 1 enacted that any individual would be guilty of a felony and liable to three to seven years' penal servitude if, for any purpose prejudicial to the national security of the state, he (a) entered, approached or was in the vicinity of a prohibited place, as defined in Clause 3, (b) prepared any sketch, plan, model or note that was, or might be, of direct or indirect use to an enemy, and/or (c) obtained or communicated to any individual any sketch, plan, model, note or other document or information that was, or could prove, of direct or indirect use to an enemy. Prejudicial purpose no longer had to be demonstrated by a specific act, but could be

Richard Burdon Haldane, 1st Viscount Haldane and Secretary of State for War, 1905-1912. Haldane chaired the Committee of Imperial Defence Sub-Committee on Foreign Espionage in 1909, which recommended the establishment of MI5, and played a key role in the passage of the Official Secrets Act 1911. (George Grantham Bain Collection, Library of Congress)

established by the character or conduct of the accused, or by the circumstances of the case. The key point, and the one that really strengthened the Bureau's hand, was that the *onus probandi* was placed on the accused to satisfy the court that there was not a prejudicial purpose in his act.

In Clause 2, the guilt of a misdemeanour, liable to a fine or up to two years' hard labour, referred to those who wrongfully kept in their possession or communicated to unauthorised persons any sketch, plan or information, etc. Clause 7 applied especially to people who knowingly harboured any person who had committed, or was about to commit, an offence under OSA 1911, or who enabled individuals to meet for this purpose and who refused to provide the police with information about these people. Clause 4 dealt with incitements or attempts to encourage other people to commit offences under OSA 1911.

These four clauses dealt with offences and their punishment under OSA 1911 and they are typical of the preventive legislation initiated by the Bureau. Additionally, Clause 6 provided increased powers of arrest, because it could be carried out without a warrant, not just by a policeman, but also by any individual on any person who was reasonably suspected. Clause 8 protected the public because it limited prosecutions under OSA 1911 to those carried out by the Attorney-General or those having his consent. Clause 9 allowed search warrants to be granted by a justice of the peace (JP) on satisfactory information under oath or, in cases of great emergency, by a police superintendent. Clause 10 covered the extent of OSA 1911 which was seen as being against British subjects throughout the world and against any person in any part of the British Empire. Clause 3 increased the scope of prohibited places and provided the Home Secretary with the power to declare any area a prohibited place. The other clauses dealt with technical points and interpretation.[26]

In his sixth progress report, covering the six months ending 22 November 1911, Kell briefly noted with great satisfaction that the 'New OFFICIAL SECRETS ACT is now law, and the work of counter-espionage is thereby greatly facilitated.'[27] As one writer has commented, the passage of OSA 1911 'was also a real triumph for Kell – a vindication and acceptance of all the work of his department.'[28]

The Bureau grows

On 18 September 1911, Corporal F.S. Strong, formerly with the Royal Army Service Corps (RASC), joined the Bureau as a clerk. On 27 October 1911, Miss H.M. Newport joined the clerical staff. On 1 October 1912, Mrs Sumner joined as the Bureau's caretaker. On 27 February 1913, Miss S. Holmes joined the clerical staff. On 10 July 1913, Corporal Stanley Strong, RASC, joined as a clerk. On 7 January 1914, Miss D. Bowie joined as Kell's personal secretary.[29]

EXPANDING TORRENTS

The Kruger Case

The Bureau had noticed a Kilburn postmark on a letter to Schultz and on a letter to a German seaman, Heinrich Grosse (see The Grosse Case below). Under the HOW on Reimers, on 18 September 1911, a letter carrying the Kilburn postmark, and signed 'K', addressed to Mrs Maria Reimers was intercepted. It contained test questions that were being returned by an intermediary. On 16 November, Otto Kruger signed his name on a letter offering his nephew's services to Steinhauer. Thus, Otto Moritz Walter Kruger's address was discovered and a HOW was taken out on his correspondence on 30 November. Kruger was a hairdresser, who had been born in Demmin, Prussia in 1861, coming to London in August 1910. John Regan visited Kruger's shop twice and supplied the Bureau with a description of Kruger. A suspected agent, Frederick James Ireland, who had had contact with Kruger (see The Ireland Case) was arrested on 21 February 1912. Kruger was put under surveillance on 22 and 23 February but nothing suspicious was noted. Kruger fled to Berlin on 25 February, on the pretext of raising money for Ireland's defence from his uncle. Three letters posted in London in April 1913 addressed to guests at the Hotel Stadt Konigsberg in Potsdam and signed either 'O' or 'K', were identified as being written by Otto Kruger. Thus, the Bureau learned that Kruger had by then returned to the UK but it was unable to locate him. Eventually, Kruger was discovered by the police at Abercynon in Wales, his name having been sent in on the quarterly return of aliens in June 1914. Kruger was arrested on 5 August. By order of the Director of Public Prosecutions, he was discharged on 13 August, then immediately re-arrested and detained under the ARO awaiting deportation. His wife, Violet Kruger, who was a British subject, had not been implicated in her husband's activities, so no action was taken against her. In December 1916, Kruger was repatriated as a POW over forty-five years of age. Violet Kruger did not go to Germany with her husband, and continued to reside in Abercynon.[30]

The Schutte Case

The aliens registration of August 1911 raised concerns about a Heinrich Schutte. In 1910, Schutte's occupation had been listed as manager of a coaling hulk. However, in August 1911, he was reported as having given up regular work and had begun 'loafing in the neighbourhood of the Dockyard.' Proof of his guilt was provided by the HOW on an 'F. Reimann' (Steinhauer also used a number of other cover names, such as Reimann, many of which were similar to Reimers) of 1-2 Brauerstrasse, Potsdam. The first letter to F. Reimann of 21 September 1911, was not signed nor addressed, but it carried a Portland postmark and was immediately linked to Schutte.

Heinrich Christian Wilhelm Schutte had been born at Vilsen in Hanover in 1855. He came to the UK in 1877, settling in Portland in 1883. He married an English woman and had two sons and a daughter. He had worked in the steamer bunkering business, then with provision contracts to the Royal Navy and spent several years at sea as a canteen server and manager. The Bureau learned that one of his sons, John Schutte, worked as an assistant storeman for the Royal Navy Service Stores and as such, he was in a position to supply his father with information of value to an enemy, such as details on prospective movements of the fleet. In July 1913, Schutte (sr.) was placed on the Special War List to be arrested. Reports continued to be sent from Schutte (sr.) to F. Reimann until October 1913, by which time there were thirty-eight reports dealing with the movements of the fleet and other naval matters. Money was sent to Schutte via the German agent, August Klunder (see The Klunder Case). After October 1913, Schutte stopped this correspondence, seemingly nervous about getting caught; he wanted out. At the Bureau's suggestion, John Schutte was transferred to another job on 8 December 1913. He resigned from the dockyard the very next day. However, the Bureau never had any concrete evidence against Schutte junior. Heinrich Schutte was arrested on 8 August 1914 and interned under ARO pending deportation. He was eventually deported on 20 December 1918.[31]

The Grosse Case

On 16 November 1911, the Dockyard Police at Portsmouth informed the Bureau that a Heinrich Grosse had tried to solicit information from William Salter, a naval pensioner, who worked as a telegraph operator on HMS *Vernon* and also as an enquiry agent for which services he advertised in the *Portsmouth Evening News*. On 15 November, Salter received a postcard from a 'Captain Hugh Grant' asking him to call on Grant at the Meredith Hotel in Southsea. When Salter met Grant, he immediately noticed that Grant spoke with a strong foreign accent. Grant claimed that he was seeking information for German coal owners who were preparing to send coal to the UK. Grant wanted to know how much coal would be in the UK at Christmas, and how long it would last for warships and merchant ships if there was a national miners' strike. He also enquired how many men were in the naval barracks; whether this was more than normal, and, if so, was this because they would employ sailors in the mines in the event of a strike. Salter promised to obtain the information. He then immediately reported Grant to the dockyard authorities. The naval authorities consulted with the police. They arranged that Salter would supply Grant with information of a 'harmless nature' on 18 November. Grosse was also to be kept under observation. The facts were then reported to Kell, who agreed with the approach chosen. As planned, on 18 November, Salter handed over the information to Grant. Five days later, Kell directed that Grosse should be placed under strict surveillance and his letters checked. The Bureau learned that Grosse's correspondence formed a 'circle'. Letters from an R.H. Peterssen had been posted by Kruger in Kilburn. Grosse sent his letters to Peterssen via Wilhelm Croner, an intermediary/postman for Steinhauer.[32]

Based in Brussels, R.H. Peterssen was mentioned in several pre-war espionage cases in the UK. Operating from Belgium, where there were no legal restrictions to prevent his activities, he freely advertised in newspapers and functioned more as a clearing house rather than as a spy. Not only did he offer information that he gleaned to the highest and most interested bidder, but he received a retainer from the Germans who used his Brussels base as a cover address to where their agents could write.[33]

On 30 November 1911, Peterssen wrote a message to Grosse in which all significant words were in code, to inform him that the information that he had recently supplied was correct and enclosed further questions on naval matters. This letter was delivered to Grosse's home on 5 December. A search warrant having been authorised, Grosse was arrested later that day and charged with having obtained information for purposes prejudicial to the state. The search also revealed other letters from Peterssen and part of the decoder that Grosse used.

Heinrich Grosse had been born in Grabow, Mecklenberg, in 1868, the son of a district judge. He went to sea aged fourteen and passed his pilotage exam in 1888. He served as a leading seaman in the Germany navy from 1890-1891 and went on to join the German merchant marine as a first officer. Grosse then joined the Chinese Navy. In 1898, he was sentenced to ten years' imprisonment in Singapore, for passing forged Chinese bank notes but was released after five years. Grosse had also been divorced twice. He returned to Germany and was arrested for embezzlement and imprisoned again in September 1911. He was released after only one month and taken on by the German Secret Service. He arrived in Portsmouth on 26 October, posing as Captain Hugh Grant of the merchant marine and on 14 November he advertised himself as a teacher of languages.

Grosse was brought up before the authorities on 5 December and remanded until 12 December. His solicitor contacted Croner for information that might help at Grosse's trial. Croner stubbornly 'denied all knowledge' of Peterssen. At trial, an angry Grosse 'betrayed' Croner's name, address and his connection with Peterssen. On 9 February 1912, Grosse was found guilty and sentenced to three years' penal servitude.[34] The Home Secretary, at that time Reginald McKenna, disagreed with those in the House of Commons who suggested that Grosse should have been freed in a gesture of Anglo-German friendship. The rationale for this decision says much about the Bureau's work and why even the most incompetent of German spies were punished so severely. According to Bulloch, in this, and other cases, the Home Secretary had acted on Kell's advice that '…it was important to make examples of any spies caught, and that nothing should be allowed to change that policy, except the prospect of further catches or information.'[35]

In January 1911, Grosse met a girl called Heddy Glauer, to whom he promised marriage. But he also borrowed money from her and coaxed her to rent an apartment in Berlin on his behalf and in her name, though he did provide furniture. Their child was born on 24 November 1911. Glauer came to England in January 1912 and devoted herself to the task of securing Grosse's freedom. She succeeded in gaining the interest of Joseph King MP who, in July 1913, asked a question in Parliament calling attention to Grosse's poor health. The Home Secretary admitted that Grosse was suffering from 'some disease', but 'denied that it had been either caused or aggravated by prison life'. Glauer's fortunes seemed to have changed for the better when she befriended a Member of Parliament, at which Grosse became sullen and jealous and as a result of which, declined a possible offer of help. In turn, she reproached the German for his attitude and in December 1913, she broke off her engagement to Grosse. However, as time progressed and Grosse's release drew nearer, she grew increasingly fearful.

In April 1914, Glauer unsuccessfully petitioned the Home Office for Grosse's deportation but on 8 May 1914 he was released from prison on licence on grounds of ill-health. MI5 tried but failed to frighten Grosse out of the country. He journeyed to London determined to recover his property and threatened to prosecute Glauer for stealing his furniture, but took no action. He also immediately attempted to get back in the employment of the German Secret Service but his overtures were rebuffed. Thus, on 29 July, Grosse was placed on the Special War List for arrest. On 6 August, as part of the round-up at the outbreak of war, he was arrested. His lodgings were searched and the letter was found turning down his offer to work for the German Secret Service again. His licence was revoked and Grosse was returned to prison. Grosse was subsequently released and repatriated to Germany on 11 July 1917.[36]

In May 1915, Glauer appealed to be allowed to stay in the UK since it was where she had made her home. She was allowed to stay, provided that she was kept under supervision. In October 1915, Glauer's housekeeper gave information to the effect to the authorities that her employer had travelled more than five miles without the necessary permit. While the case against Glauer was being prepared, it was further discovered that she had embezzled money from her employers, a charge that was ultimately dropped because of insufficient proof. She was, however, found guilty of the first charge and sentenced to six months in prison. Grosse seized the opportunity for revenge. In a signed statement denouncing Glauer, he claimed that Glauer was an agent of the German Secret Service who had induced him to follow her into spying. MI5 dismissed Grosse's statement as a fabrication. Grosse also unsuccessfully appealed for the custody of his child – the greatest blow he could inflict on Glauer. Upon finishing her prison sentence, Glauer was interned on 9 March 1916. She was eventually deported in March 1918.[37]

The Ireland Case

The first mention of Kruger's nephew, Frederick Ireland, occurred in a letter of 16 November 1911, signed Otto Kruger and posted at Kilburn to 'Mr G. Steinhauer, 4 Allee Sansouci, Potsdam', whose name had been under check since late October 1911. Frederick James Ireland was a second class stoker in the Royal Navy, who had been born in Bristol in 1891. He had left school aged fourteen 'with a character for regular attendance, honesty, truthfulness and respectfulness'. Kruger stressed that his nephew wished to work alone and to write directly to Steinhauer. A HOW was taken out for all letters to Kruger's name and address on 30 November. On 2 December, a letter posted at Chatham and signed 'your loving nephew Fred' was intercepted. Ireland gave his new address as 112 Mess, N.2. Block, R.N.B. Chatham. On 23 December, Ireland wrote to Steinhauer via Kruger suggesting that they should meet at Kruger's house in early January 1912. He also offered to send information about the tests of a patent for heating torpedoes in a cold climate. Steinhauer was in England at the time, but he passed through London rapidly and went to Scotland without meeting Ireland. Ireland had been careful not to use a compromising signature, however, he was identified by clues in his letters by 28 December 1911. It was only on 11 January 1912 that his name was revealed in the post. Investigation revealed that, on 2 February 1910, Ireland became an assistant to Kruger, his uncle by marriage:

> 'Ireland was very happy with his uncle, but on the 1st July 1911, he wrote to his parents that he had joined the navy for twelve years. They were much distressed and wished to get him out of it, but KRUGER opposed this saying that the navy would be the making of the boy.'

Ireland's commanding officer, Commander Ward, reported that Ireland was '…exceptionally clever' and 'would shortly be promoted' to first class stoker.

On 11 January, an open envelope addressed Mr F.J. Ireland, Mess 2, H.M.S. Foxhound, c/o G.P.O. was sent under cover to G. Steinhauer from Kilburn. It contained a signed contract to provide information and requested a monthly salary. On 12 February, Steinhauer wrote to Ireland via Karl Gustave Ernst, a hairdresser born to German parents living in London (see The Ernst Case below) and then Kruger asking Ireland to send a report on his ship's voyage to Norway and 'all interesting details' about his ship. Steinhauer also asked for directions concerning how and when Ireland's payment was to be sent. Thus, Steinhauer had entered into direct contact with a member of the Royal Navy.

On 14 February 1912, the Admiralty notified Commander Ward that Ireland was known to be in communication with a foreign agent whose letters carried the London N.W. postmark, and that any such letters should be opened in Ireland's presence with two other officers bearing witness. If a letter contained anything incriminating, Ireland should be arrested. Ireland was eventually arrested on 21 February but it was deemed injudicious to have placed him on trial owing to the nature of the correspondence which would have to be produced in court. Ireland was dismissed from the Navy and returned to Bristol. At the time, the newspapers reported that Ireland had been arrested, having been caught in the act of making notes in code and refusing to explain their contents. It can be speculated that the newspapers were fed this story as part of a cover up of the HOW system. Ireland was kept track of (his correspondence was checked under HOW). He moved on to Swansea, where he was again suspected of working for the Germans. However, checks on his correspondence did not provide any evidence that he had actually been in communication with them.

On 24 June 1914, Ireland was placed on the Special War List to be searched an event which took place on 4 August 1914. A notebook was found containing a description of the Lee Enfield rifle, and the addresses of foreigners residing in London, including the well-known German agent, Hugo Schmidt. Thus, Ireland was arrested the day he was searched and detained as one of the twenty-one agents rounded up at the outbreak of war. However, the Director of Public Prosecutions ordered Ireland's release; Ireland was a British subject, no fresh evidence had been unearthed, and it was still deemed undesirable to produce the evidence that had resulted in Ireland's arrest back in 1912. Therefore, Ireland was released but kept under 'casual observation', which showed that his conduct gave no cause for further suspicion.[38]

Trial avoided if possible

Kell preferred to 'warn off' Steinhauer's British sources rather than prosecute them, noting in August 1912:

'Owing to the fact that it is impossible in this country to hold trials for espionage and kindred offences in camera (as is the custom in continental countries) it was considered contrary to the interests of the State to bring these men to trial, which would have entailed a disclosure of the identity of our informants and other confidential matters.'[39]

The Klare Case

On 18 November 1911, a letter from Portsmouth, signed 'W.H.' was intercepted on its way to 'Herr G.F. Steinhauer, Potsdam'. 'W.H.' offered the services of a dentist who knew many naval officers and artificers and thus had the opportunity to obtain useful information. William Klare's name and address was soon discovered on 30 December 1911. A letter from 'Richard' posted in Germany was stopped, (because the handwriting had been identified as belonging to the same person who had corresponded with George

Parrott, a German spy. [covered later in this chapter]), while on its way to 'William Clare, Dentist, 33 Osborne Street, Southsea' ('Clare' was a cover version of his name). The letter gave instructions for the transport of a patient to Ostend and a meeting at the Hotel d'Allemagne. The Bureau asked the dockyard police to identify the dentist recommended for employment by the German Secret Service. On 8 January 1912, the dockyard police reported that Klare 'did not quite tally' with W.H.'s recommendation.

By 1902, Klare was working in London as a kitchen porter and married his wife, Ellen, in 1905. He apparently lived on Ellen's 'earnings as a prostitute' and found employment as an assistant to a German dentist in Portsmouth. When his employer moved on, Klare set himself up in practice. According to declassified MI5 records, Klare's nationality 'was not identified', but when he married at Camberwell Registry Office he 'made no declaration of German nationality'.

William Klare, German spy. Klare worked as a dentist, but MI5 was not able to identify his nationality. He was detected by postal interception to a known spy address and was sentenced to five years' imprisonment in June 1913. (Jay Robert Nash Collection)

Nothing more was intercepted for seven months. Then, on 16 July 1912, 'C' – as Klare signed himself on this letter as a cover name – wrote to a contact in Berlin stating that he had not yet achieved his objective 'but the doctor's expenses had continued up to the 25th and a promise had been given to carry out the poor chap at the first opportunity', which continued Steinhauer's dentist metaphor/code about the transport of a patient to Ostend, the patient referred to being confidential documents that Steinhauer had tasked Klare to obtain.

The case subsided until 22 October, when Levi Rosenthal, a hairdresser of 71 Queen Street, Portsmouth informed the police that on 18 October a man, whose name he did not know, offered him £20 if he could obtain a confidential book on submarines from the dockyard. To draw Klare out, Rosenthal pretended to accept the offer, saying that he had done 'that kind of thing before', and asked Klare to call at his shop again on 21 October which he did on 10 January 1913, to find out if Rosenthal had seen the man and when the book would be available. The confidential book that he wanted was not actually about submarines, but rather about the working of torpedoes. It was clear to the Bureau that the only way to catch Klare was to entrap him. Kell got the Director of Public Prosecution's permission to go to Portsmouth to confer with the Admiral Commanding-in-Chief about what actions to take to lead to Klare's arrest.

On 22 January, Charles John Bishop, a pensioned naval writer then employed as office-keeper of the Admiral Commanding-in-Chief's office, was introduced to Rosenthal as a go-between. On 23 January, Rosenthal arranged for a meeting between

Klare and Bishop later that night. Klare had to put off this rendezvous because he had not received the money with which to pay Bishop. Klare and Bishop eventually met at 4.00 p.m. on 19 February in Rosenthal's shop. Bishop handed over the confidential book as agreed and Klare was arrested as he left the shop.

Klare's trial took place at the Winchester Assizes on 26 June. The issue of incitement was 'brushed aside' and Klare was found guilty of having, 'for a purpose prejudicial to England, obtained a book which would be useful to an enemy.' Klare was sentenced to five years' penal servitude. He was released in May 1918 and deported.

An MI5 report noted that Rosenthal 'plays a doubtful part'. Rosenthal claimed that he had only met Klare once, about five or six years before, whereas, Klare claimed that Rosenthal, whom he already knew, had approached him towards the end of February and 'begged to be enrolled as a German agent'. Klare 'took no risks'. Thus, the report questioned '…is it likely he would have approached a man of whose past and sentiments he knew nothing on so dangerous a business as stealing a Confidential Book?', and concluded that '…Klare, no doubt did incite Rosenthal; at the same time it seems at least probable that Rosenthal had, as he himself said, "done the things before".'[40]

The Ernst Case

The HOW on Croner, Steinhauer's intermediary, revealed that he had recruited Karl Gustave Ernst as an intermediary in 1910. Thus, a HOW was also taken out for Ernst's correspondence in November 1911. Ernst was a hairdresser of 402a Caledonian Road, London. He had been born in Shoreditch in 1871 to parents of German origins. Of all the intermediaries, Ernst 'continued longest in the service and was closest to Steinhauer'. However, according to an MI5 G Branch report, he 'was a coward'. After Ireland's arrest, Ernst refused to go near Kruger. After Graves' arrest, he suggested to Steinhauer retiring. Steinhauer calmly accepted his resignation, but proposed that he should stay on and apply for a pay rise. Ernst did so and his pay was increased although he did eventually retire from this work in January 1914. He was placed on the Special War List and arrested at the outbreak of war. As Ernst was of British nationality, he could not be handled like the others (all aliens) who had been rounded up, and had to be brought to trial. This was seen as a travesty for MO5(g). During the proceedings the whole system of the HOW was necessarily revealed in court. Ernst was found guilty and received seven years' imprisonment. His son Charles had enlisted in the Royal Field Artillery under the name Charles Ernest but enquiries about the boy's mother showed she was a German and so at the request of M.O.5. he was discharged in January 1916.[41] It is believed that Ernst was probably the most active of all of Steinhauer's 'postmen' and he gained more notoriety than any of the other intermediaries. In newspaper reports of his trial, Ernst was called the 'Kaiser's postman'.[42]

The Engel Case

Johann Engel, a ships' chandler who had been born in Germany in 1853 but who had settled in the Cornish town of Falmouth in 1900, had been under observation since September 1911 when he was placed on the Possible Suspect List. It was known that he had served in the German navy for twenty-one years retiring as a Chief Deck Officer with a pension of £80 per annum. In 1884, he married the daughter of a ship's chandler.

They had three sons and three daughters. Engel took over this business when his father-in-law, who had been born in Germany but was naturalised as a British citizen, passed away. Nothing suspicious about him was noted during his time in England until, on 23 December 1911, the HOW on Kruger proved that Engel was receiving a £40 a year subsidy from German Secret Service funds. Engel was then placed on the Special War List for arrest. Intercepted correspondence revealed that in 1903 or 1904 he had agreed to place a steamer at the disposal of the German Secret Service 'for certain purposes', although the Bureau was never able to actually establish the nature of these purposes. Steinhauer terminated this agreement in 1913. Then, in July 1914, Steinhauer wrote to enquire if Engel was still in the same place and carrying on the same business as before to which the reply was in the affirmative. Engel was rounded-up on 4 August 1914 and interned under the ARO. He was retained being among the last batch of twenty internees to be released and repatriated. Engel's eldest son, John, served in HMS *Indefatigable* and went down with her in May 1916. MO5(g) had taken action to get John dismissed from the Royal Navy, but the captain of *Indefatigable* 'refused to part' with him.[43]

The Schroeder Case

Adolf Frederick Schroeder is regarded as quite probably the most successful of all of the German spies the Bureau convicted before the war.[44] Schroeder (who often went by the alias Gould), a German publican, first came to the attention of the British intelligence department owing to letters written from Paris in 1896, although the available documentation does not reveal the nature of their content. In 1908, he became the licensee of the Queen Charlotte Hotel in Rochester, a pub situated nearer to naval or military quarters than any other in Rochester and which was much-frequented by the rank and file.

Adolf Schroeder, German spy. He claimed to be German, but everything about his background is uncertain. A publican, Schroeder was detected by postal interception to a known spy address. He was sentenced to six years' penal servitude in April 1914. (Jay Robert Nash Collection)

Schroeder came to the Bureau's attention when his letter of 13 December 1911 addressed to Steinhauer in Potsdam was intercepted. From this time on 'direct touch' with Schroeder was maintained through his correspondence. On 7 May 1912, Schroeder was placed on the Special War List for arrest. He was also placed under 'special observation'. Regan, one of the Bureau's detectives, disguised as a sailor, managed to befriend Schroeder and report 'items of interest'. The Bureau was satisfied that Schroeder was 'not obtaining valuable information'. Therefore, a prolonged investigation was undertaken because the Bureau's primary aim was to identify Schroeder's informants and thus to protect Admiralty secrets from being compromised.

On 30 April 1913, a telegram from Schroeder to his informant, James Mott, was discovered. Mott was a former torpedo coxswain who was employed in Sheerness dockyard and steps were taken to make sure that he was not employed on any more confidential work. Four months later, on 24 August, Schroeder was also found to be in touch with J.H. Pinkard of HMS *Cyclops*, a repair ship. Pinkard was kept under police observation. On 10 February 1914, the Bureau suggested that the Admiralty should remove Pinkard from his station, but unfortunately, there is no record available of what happened next.

On 30 December 1913, Schroeder moved to London and the Queen Charlotte Hotel was searched after his departure. A press copy letter-book containing letters written by Schroeder in 1903 and 1904 was found, proving that he was connected with Steinhauer by 1904 at the latest. On 9 January 1914, the Rochester police passed on to the Bureau Schroeder's letter-book containing 'damning evidence that could be produced in court'. Thus, preparations were made for Schroeder's arrest. In February 1914, an intercept revealed that Schroeder's common-law wife, Maud Sloman, was going to go to Brussels with a gunnery drill book, charts of Bergen and Spithead, and plans of cruisers. On 22 February, she was arrested on the Continental train at Charing Cross station, for placed on the seat of the railway carriage and concealed by her rug were three envelopes containing the Gunnery Drill Book, the charts of Bergen and Spithead and the cruiser drawings. That same day, Schroeder was arrested at his house and searched. The search revealed more incriminating letters, a list of espionage questions and a photograph bearing the name 'Steinhauer'.

The Schroeders were tried on 3 April. Maud pleaded not guilty and the charge was withdrawn since there was insufficient evidence to prove that she knew what she was doing. Schroeder pleaded guilty and was sentenced to six years' penal servitude. Whilst he was in prison he made a number of statements to obtain mitigation of his sentence. However, Reginald Drake, the Bureau's chief counter-espionage investigator, 'doubted his information on any point'. Schroeder claimed that he had been born in Germany to a German father and an English mother, served in the German army and then settled in England but his background is uncertain – even his parentage and the date of his birth. After his conviction, Schroeder claimed that he was first employed by Steinhauer in 1890 to spy on France and Russia.[45]

The Hentschel and Parrott Cases

In October 1909, Karl Hentschel, a former German merchant seaman, sent out a circular offering his services as a teacher of languages in Sheerness, an initiative which led to his being placed on the Possible Suspect List. On 15 December 1909, Hentschel married Patricia Riley, a shop assistant in Chatham. The Riley family had known better days: Patricia's father, John Riley, was 'a broken-down Deputy Bank Manager', who had become a traveller to a tailoring firm, had embezzled money, and disappeared, while Patricia's mother, Emily Riley, was a heavy drinker, in the habit of raising money in any way she could. Patricia was one of four attractive sisters, who had many admirers and friends among the Naval men in Chatham. Thus, through his wife and her family, Hentschel was able to tap in on a ready source of information. In January 1910 Hentschel moved to Chatham and set up a language school there at which a number of students were members of the Royal Navy. In February of that year, Patricia found out about Hentschel's activities and offered to help him. Indeed, as an MI5 report later noted,

'...Patricia worked hard for her husband'. Among her circle of contacts, Patricia knew George Parrott, then the chief gunner on HMS *Agamemnon* since 1908, from whom she had frequently borrowed small sums of money for her family. Hentschel then encouraged his wife to begin an affair with Parrott, in order to get Parrott to provide them with classified naval material.

By September Parrott had supplied at least one confidential book to Hentschel, but the two men quarrelled in February 1911 over Parrott's affair with Patricia and their relative shares of the money paid by the German Secret Service. The following month the Hentschels fled to Australia. By October 1911 the Bureau finally learned that the Hentschels had gone to Australia but by this time it had no proof against Karl Hentschel. In early December, 'Richard' (an alias used by Steinhauer) wrote, via Kruger, to 'Mrs Seymour' of '87 Alexandra Road' in Sheerness to arrange a meeting, 'Richard's' cover being that he was carrying on 'an intrigue with a married woman'. Police investigation revealed that 'Mrs Seymour' did not exist, and that 87 Alexandra Road was Parrott's address. Thus, 'Mrs Seymour' was identified with Parrott. Parrott continued 'trafficking' with the German Secret Service and then, in March 1912, the Hentschels returned to England. On the 21st, Patricia Hentschel wrote to the Chief of the German Secret Service, via Kruger, pleading with him to re-engage her husband. Further intercepted correspondence enabled the Bureau to connect the Hentschels with Parrott. On 13 July, Parrott was shadowed to Ostend where he was observed meeting with Steinhauer. On 15 July, he was confined to barracks for having left the country without having first sought permission from his superiors. Further investigations were undertaken until Parrott was eventually dismissed from the Royal Navy on 16 August.

The Bureau deduced that during the years 1910-1911, Parrot had provided the German Secret Service with twenty-three classified manuals. Nevertheless, he continued to communicate with the Germans. He was finally arrested on 17 November, tried and sentenced to four years' penal servitude on 16 January 1913. The judge commented that he gave Parrott a relatively light sentence because he felt that he had been entrapped by a woman.[46]

The Hentschel's marriage soon broke down and they separated in September 1913. Hentschel offered to provide the authorities with information about the German Secret Service in return for immunity from prosecution and employment in the British Secret Service. On 22 October, Melville interviewed Hentschel at Scotland Yard during which he further incriminated Parrott, an act for which Hentschel was paid £100. Having once again tried and failed to save his marriage, on 8 November, in a moment of despair, Hentschel went to the police and gave himself up as a spy. He was arrested and brought before Westminster police court, where he was charged with conspiring with Parrott to disclose naval secrets. This caused Kell some embarrassment. At court it was acknowledged that Hentschel had been paid by a department with connections to the police for confidential information which served to incriminate Parrott, while Hentschel had been promised immunity from prosecution provided that 'he kept his own role secret'. Therefore, the Attorney General considered it appropriate to offer no evidence and to withdraw the charges.[47]

The Klunder Case

August Wilhelm Julius Klunder was a hairdresser and tobacconist of 17 Commercial Street, East London. He had been born in Germany in 1870, but came to the UK in 1895. Wilhelm Croner wrote to Steinhauer in January 1912 suggesting Klunder for employment and he was taken on as an intermediary shortly after. Thanks to the check on Croner's correspondence, the Bureau obtained a description of Klunder on 17 January, only two days after Croner had sent Klunder's name to Steinhauer. Klunder was placed on the Special War List for arrest in January 1912 and he was arrested on 4 August 1914. A search of his lodgings revealed an insurance book that contained notes which showed that he was in touch with Hugo Schmidt, a well-known German agent. Klunder also made three voluntary statements to the police about his connection to Reimers. He was subsequently charged with having obtained information which might be useful to the enemy. However, he was dealt with under the ARO and sent to Brixton Prison to await deportation. In November 1918, MI5 reserved Klunder for the last batch of prisoners to be repatriated. Unfortunately, although available documentation does not provide the date of Klunder's deportation, it seems fair to assume that he was probably deported some time in 1919.[48]

The Rimann Case

In January 1912, the HOW on Steinhauer revealed that he employed an agent who wrote to him from Grimsby and Hull. Two reports were signed 'Germanikus'. The agent's cover was writing articles about literature and art for a well-known German periodical. On 19 and 22 February, telegrams were sent from a sender who gave his address as 24 Spring Street, Hull, to Steinhauer at Allee Sanssouci 4, Potsdam from the Beverley Road Post Office in Hull. The sender was seeking to make an appointment to meet on the following Sunday morning. 'Germanikus' had also written from Hull a few days earlier stating that he could travel on 22 February. The telegrams were attributed to a Walter Rimann and his name and address were discovered. Investigation revealed that Rimann was a teacher of languages in Hull. He had been tasked by the Germans to gather intelligence on the Humber defences, particularly to locate the minefields, the base used by the mine-sweepers, and to obtain any information about new mine-laying and mine-sweeping methods and equipment. In September, the Bureau's Lieutenant Ohlson was sent to investigate. He took German lessons with Rimann, and found him willing to discuss military and naval subjects, but 'not to be drawn into confidence'. Rimann was duly added to the Special War List for arrest. For his part, Steinhauer was particularly pleased with three of Rimann's reports in October 1913. One of them gave particulars of an exercise conducted by the British Fleet, including the names of ships forming the 'invading' squadron, details of an 'attack' on Immingham, and the disguise of repair ships and transports. However, he failed to learn anything material about the umpire's verdict. The other two reports concerned flight manoeuvres near Spurn Point and their 'intimate connection' with the Fleet's manoeuvres. On 1 August 1914, Rimann received a telegram from Germany notifying him that he had not been called up, despite the imminent outbreak of war, and that money was being sent to him. Rimann replied asking for an explanation of the telegram. However, he did not wait for a reply and left for Zeebrugge later that day. Thus, Rimann was the only one of the German agents who the Bureau intended to round up at the outbreak of war but who got away.[49]

The Graves Case

On 20 January 1912, Steinhauer notified Otto Kruger that he should soon receive letters addressed to William Lewis, 'c/o hairdressing shop, 334 High Street, Brondesbury'. They were to be posted on to a PO Box in Berlin, enclosed in envelopes provided by Steinhauer, which were stamped on the back 'Bank of Australasia, 4 Threadneedle Street, E.C.' On 27 January, a report, in two halves, signed 'Meincke' was posted from Edinburgh in two envelopes addressed to William Lewis, at the aforementioned 'hairdressing shop'. The report detailed a new drill hall at Kirkcudbright, which was to be used by a new volunteer regiment of field artillery for coastal defence, along with other military and naval matters. On 29 January, a third letter, bearing the same postmark, containing a compliment slip and two visiting cards of A.K. Graves, was sent addressed to William Lewis in Brondesbury. A HOW was taken out on Graves' correspondence and he was kept under 'casual observation' by the police. A.K. Graves had arrived in Edinburgh on 24 January 1912, claiming to be an Australian doctor born to a German father and a Scottish mother. In fact, he was a chemical engineer by training and had been born in Switzerland in 1877, but had spent most of his life in Australia and the colonies. In 1902, he had been convicted of theft in New South Wales and sentenced to eighteen months hard labour. He then worked as a doctor in Australia, before returning to Germany in 1911, where he was recruited into the German Secret Service. The Bureau concluded that Graves '…was undoubtedly a trained spy besides being a very clever man. His reports were almost singular in this respect that they gave satisfaction to his employers.'

Kell ordered Graves' arrest after intercepted correspondence revealed that he was about to return to Germany. He was arrested on 14 April, charged under the OSA 1911, and remanded in prison whilst further investigations took place. In order not to jeopardise the secret of the Reimer's correspondence, Reginald Drake instructed the prosecution only to produce original documents in court, not copies taken of intercepted letters that were then sent on. During the trial of 22 and 23 July, the prosecution presented forty-five witnesses and produced forty-six items of evidence. Graves was found guilty and sentenced to eighteen months' penal servitude, during which Kell went to interview him personally. In prison, he 'gave much information concerning German agents and the higher personnel of the Secret Service'. In return, Kell arranged for his early release on 18 December and employment by the British Secret Service Bureau. A plan was hatched to send him to Berlin to obtain a book that Graves claimed contained details of every German agent in the UK. There were, apparently, only two copies of this book, but Graves knew where one was kept. He was supplied with 'a large sum of money' and sent to Berlin on 20 January 1913. However, he absconded to the USA on a steamer and, to use the words of an MI5 report, 'played with' the Bureau. Remarkably, Graves requested – and received – money for a fare to return to the UK. However, when the money was received he simply pocketed it and failed to return to Britain. At this point, the Bureau gave up on Graves, but he caused further commotion in 1914 when he published sensational accounts of his career as a spy for both the German and British Secret Services in US newspapers. He later '…fell back upon stealing and blackmailing' and in 1917, he was arrested for being in a zone closed to enemy aliens without a permit. By this time, he was poorly dressed and clearly penniless.[50]

The Marie Croner Case

At his trial, in February 1912, Heinrich Grosse stated that he had received letters from a German agent in London, naming Wilhelm Croner of 3 Monro Terrace, Hampstead. On 7 February, the Bureau's John Regan reported that Croner had indeed lived in Hampstead for the past three years and in the City of London for eleven years before that. He was a barber who had previously worked for Kruger. Owing to Grosse's trial, Croner lost customers when negative publicity in newspaper reports of the trial carried Grosse's claim that Croner was a German agent and Steinhauer, after sending him £10, ignored his 'hints of distress'. Karl Gustave Ernst became worried by Croner's behaviour and, acting on Ernst's suggestion, Steinhauer eventually sent £20 to enable the Croner family to move to Walthamstow and change their name to 'Kronauer'. This failed to relieve Croner's distress and he committed suicide on 25 January 1913. On 4 March, Croner's wife, Marie, wrote to Steinhauer asking for help. He sent her the draft of a letter that she could use to apply to the German Secret Service to continue her late husband's work as an intermediary, and she did so. Marie Croner's correspondence was placed under check and she was added to the Special War List. She was arrested at the outbreak of war and charged in association with Ernst. Although incriminating papers were found at her lodgings, the charge was dropped and she was detained under ARO awaiting deportation. Paradoxically, her son, a British citizen by birth, served in the British army during the First World War. Marie Croner was eventually released and deported to Germany in August 1919.[51]

The Hattrick Case

On 23 March 1912, a letter was intercepted on its way from England to 'The Head, Intelligence Department, War Office, Germany'. The writer, who used an illegible signature, offered information and provided the phrasing of an advert to be inserted in the *Daily Mirror* if the proposal was accepted. In reality, it was Melville, impersonating a German agent named 'A. Pfeiffer', who had placed the advert. A Walter J. Devlin responded to Pfeiffer's advertisement from the 'Sailor's Nest in Devonport'. Melville eventually persuaded Devlin to provide his proper name and address which transpired to be John James Hattrick of Devonport. On 6 May, the Admiralty informed the Bureau that Hattrick, who had been born at the Wirral in Cheshire in 1888, had deserted from HMS *Queen* in June 1909 after seven-and-a-half years' service in the Royal Navy. He was not recalled for further service and later found employment as a canteen assistant on board Royal Navy ships, 'but tired of the work'. Melville and Hattrick met at Devonport on 16 May. Hattrick wrote out a contract promising to procure and pass on any naval or military intelligence requested by the Germans in return for a salary of £30 a year. The next day he took Pfeiffer into the dockyard, but was arrested there for attempting to communicate information to a foreign power. He argued that his aim was simply to get money from the Germans, without giving them anything in return, and then to go abroad. Hattrick was subsequently released, having been cautioned that the case was being held in abeyance dependant upon his good behaviour. According to MI5: 'The fright cured him.' Hattrick found employment in the Merchant Navy and in September 1912 his discharge papers noted that his conduct was very good. MI5 concluded: 'This is an interesting case of prevention at its very best. The affair never passed beyond these shores.

The interests of the country were protected and in all probability a citizen was saved.'
However, the organisation also noted that the drawbacks of the agent provocateur method
were such as to restrict its application to the smallest possible number of cases.[52]

Drake

The prosecutions of Schultz, Grosse and Graves greatly helped Kell in his efforts to obtain
the approval of the War Office to recruit more staff for the Bureau.[53] Captain, later
Colonel, Reginald John Drake, joined it on 1 April 1912 having served with the North
Staffordshire Regiment.[54] Lady Kell remembered him as 'a most able man and most
successful sleuth – small hope for anyone who fell into his net.'[55] On 30 November 1912,
Stanley Clarke left the Bureau to become the Deputy Chief Constable of Kent Police and
Drake took over from him as the Chief Investigator for Counter-Espionage on
1 December.[56]

Holt-Wilson

Captain (later Brigadier Sir) Eric Edward Boketon Holt-Wilson joined the Bureau on
20 December 1912 to succeed Captain Stanley Clarke, having been recommended for
the post by the former head of MO5, Major James Edmonds.[57] According to Edmonds,
Holt-Wilson chose to leave the Royal Engineers (with whom Edmonds had also once
served) and join MI5, because he did not relish the prospect of serving in the tropics
again: his wife had been ill in Singapore and the couple had lost a child there.[58] Lady Kell
remembered him as 'a man of almost genius for intricate organisation' and 'an intensely
loyal and devoted friend'.[59] Holt-Wilson became Kell's deputy during the war, a post
which he held until he was sacked along with Kell by Churchill in 1940 when 'he paid
for his loyalty by being granted a pension related solely to his rank in 1912 – just £440
per year'.[60] In a distinguished military career, the Old Harrovian and Royal Engineers
officer had been an instructor in military engineering at the Royal Military Academy at
Woolwich prior to joining the Bureau. In 1914, he published a small book on field
entrenchments which sold more than 70,000 copies. He also held the Distinguished
Service Order (DSO), having fought in some twenty actions during the Boer War.[61]
The athletic, six-foot-three-inch Holt-Wilson was also known as a formidable all-round
sportsman, who described himself as 'a champion revolver shot' and later became the
President of the Ski Club of Great Britain.[62] At age thirty-eight on the outbreak of war,
he was a loyal and first-rate deputy to Kell, with whom he shared a belief in a threat
from 'secret enemies of the Empire'.[63]

Booth, Lawrence, Brodie, and Fetherston

On 1 January 1913, Mr F.B. Booth joined the Bureau as an officer of MI5, rather than as
a clerk. At that time MI5's members of staff were either graded as officers or clerks (unless
they were detectives or caretakers). Later, he became a captain on the General List.
On 31 January 1913, Captain K.E. Lawrence, formerly of the Royal Marines Light
Infantry, joined as an officer, followed on 1 July that year by Mr (joined as a civilian; later
became a captain on the General List) Malcolm Brodie who joined the Bureau as an
officer. On 1 January 1914, Mr (joined as a civilian; later became a captain on the General
List) John Barr Fetherston joined as an officer.[64] The August 1918 list of MI5 officers and

branches included Booth, Brodie, and Fetherston as being employed by the organisation at the General Post Office and they may well have been employed with the GPO before they joined the Bureau.[65] Indeed, Brodie and Fetherston gave evidence at a number of spy trials during the First World War during which they informed the court that they were clerks in the Secretary's Office of the Post Office. At the trial of the German spy, Carl Lody (see Chapter Three), Brodie described how he had examined Lody's telegrams. At the trial of Ernest Melin, another German spy (see Chapter Four), Fetherston described how he had applied a detection process to one of Melin's letters which resulted in the appearance between the lines of secret writing of a yellow colour.[66]

Incitements to Treason

'Incitements to Treason' was the term used to describe a new type of assault by the German Secret Service which, due to postal interception, came to the Bureau's attention in 1913. Under a cover of producing a work on the 'Navies of the World' to be published by Danish, Russian or French firms, attempts were made to establish direct contact with, and procure information from, officers and men of the Royal Dockyards. Names were gathered through German agents, men later tried by court martial, and by advertisements in British papers. Various petty officers responded to the advertisements and were first asked questions of a general and harmless kind. The second series of questions attempted to procure information of a confidential or secret nature. Money was offered for satisfactory responses. The letters inciting to treason were signed with different names which were revealed to be the pseudonyms of German agents. They also came through the post to German intermediaries who were required to submit large numbers of envelopes for this work. A naval weekly order was eventually issued instructing any personnel who received such letters to hand them to their commanding officer. They were then forwarded to the Bureau and eighty names of senders were noted.[67]

The Schmidt Case

A £10 remittance sent via the German spy, August Klunder (see The Klunder Case), at the end of February 1913 led the Bureau to Heinrich Schmidt, a German waiter and storekeeper in Devonport. Intercepted correspondence to Reimers revealed that Schmidt had been recruited by a 'Herr P.' (also known as 'Paul' and 'Passarge') at Kiel and was paid a salary of £10 a month which came from Hamburg. He was sent to Rotterdam on 20 February to receive further instructions from 'Haanen', presumably a member of the German Secret Service, and arrived at Devonport on 24 February, just after Klare's arrest. Owing to Schmidt's later references to the Klare case it seems likely that he was too wary to undertake any serious spying activity.

Schmidt's actions had also aroused the suspicions of his landlady's son, a Mr Wakenham, who informed the borough police who, in turn, notified the chief constable of Devonport. However, he delayed communicating with the Bureau, which had meanwhile got on Schmidt's trail owing to the £10 remittance sent via Klunder at the end of February. The Bureau then asked the dockyard police to make enquiries and it was then discovered that the borough police were already on the case. The dockyard police subsequently took over the case and carried it through. On 10 April, they reported that Schmidt had befriended a waiter in a restaurant frequented by Royal Navy ratings.

On 14 April, Schmidt was instructed to send letters via 'Hugo Munschied, 206 Boomgardstraat, Antwerp'. His reports to Munschied were duly intercepted, but they were found to hold no content of significance. The last remittance that Schmidt received from Hamburg was sent on 26 May and his last report to Rotterdam, dated 9 July, showed great hesitation. In May, Schmidt had spent three weeks away in London and during that time, the Bureau had his possessions searched. It was discovered that Schmidt had kept a record of his letters which revealed a passage of failure; he had been unable to get into the dockyard, secure the right job, or make useful friends. A search also revealed letters from Haanen and Passarge. Drake examined them and concluded that 'although there was clear proof of Schmidt's intention, there was not sufficient evidence to secure conviction.' Thus, Schmidt was kept merely under observation. He left Plymouth on 2 May 1914 and went to Sark but was later arrested at Guernsey on 12 August that year and held as a POW. An MI5 report explains that throughout the investigation, the Bureau 'exercised the greatest caution' with Schmidt, 'preferring to forego certainty about the spy's movements rather than risk giving him the alarm.'[68]

The Fowler Case

On 5 May 1913, a letter from Otto Kruger (see The Kruger Case) to Steinhauer was intercepted in which Kruger recommended a relative, Frederick W. Fowler of Penarth, for employment by Steinhauer. In an effort to trace Kruger, on 13 November, Kell wrote to the Chief Constable of Glamorganshire asking for enquiries to be made at Penarth about Fowler. The police discovered that Fowler was a hairdresser living at 56 Glebe Street in the town. He had been living in Penarth for about ten years, but he and his wife (who was related to Frederick Ireland) were originally from Bristol. Fowler was placed on the Special War List in November 1913. On 28 July 1914, Steinhauer wrote to Fowler, via Klunder, saying that he had something to offer him. On 30 July, Fowler replied that he would happily accept the offer. Fowler had thus demonstrated that he was ready to communicate with the German Secret Service and on 31 July he was placed on the list of people to be arrested upon the outbreak of hostilities. Fowler was arrested on 4 August 1914 and charged with having communicated information calculated to be useful to an enemy. He was tried by the local magistrates and discharged with a severe caution. Fowler then enlisted in the Royal Field Artillery.[69]

Distribution of Duties, October 1913

By October 1913, the Bureau had developed an organizational shape which divided its work into two distinct, but interrelated and interdependent, spheres of activity: firstly, investigations to cure espionage and secondly, preventive measures to frustrate it. Captain Drake was in-charge of the Investigative Branch, then known as A Branch, its duties being, in the words of its own summary:

1. **Investigation of cases of Espionage**
   (a) Known agents in England.
   (b) Likely counter-agents for us to employ,
   (c) Intercepted correspondence – action on.
   (d) Important cases – précis & file.

Government Departments and Officials concerned
(a) & (b) Home Office, Scotland Yard & C.C.s of Counties and Boroughs.
(c) G.P.O.

2. Preparations for War
(a) Activities of foreign agents & measures to counteract them.
(b) Vulnerable Points in U.K. – protection against possible action by foreign agents.
(c) Protection of Army Headquarters with the expeditionary Force.

Government Departments and Officials concerned
(a) & (b) War Office, Admiralty & Commands.
(c) War Office & Scotland Yard.

Captain Holt-Wilson was in charge of the Preventive Branch, then known as B Branch. Its duties were described thus:

1. Alien Registration
(a) Alien Reports & selection of Possible Suspects.
(b) Special War Lists.
(c) Foreign Communities.
(d) Aliens residing in Prohibited Areas.

Government Departments and Officials concerned
(a) (b) (c) & (d) C.C.s of Counties and Boroughs.

2. Preparations for War
(a) Observers system & action of Civil Intelligence Service for Home Defence.
(b) Vulnerable Points & action in connection therewith (for Home Defence).

Government Departments and Officials concerned
(a) C.Cs. Coast Counties, M.T.1 (W.O.)
(b) War Office, Admiralty and C.Cs.

3. Accounts

Working under Holt-Wilson, Captain Lawrence was in-charge of a section of B Branch, its duties were:

1. Intercepted Letters
Translation, filing and custody.

2. Secretary of State's Warrants
Preparation, filing and custody.

3. Handwriting Records [arrangement and comparison]

4. Photographs and identification [arrangement and comparison]

5. Scheduling and filing correspondence

6. Indexing and Carding information[70]

Thus, by October 1913, the organisation of the Bureau 'had been put on a definite footing'.[71] Kell was promoted to major in late 1913, an endorsement of his work and a clear sign that the Bureau was now well established.[72]

Pre-War Preventive Branch

The preventive work comprised primarily in preparing the unofficial aliens register which provided the basis of the action carried out during the precautionary period in late July 1914. It required cooperating with a number of government departments, principally the police chief constables and particularly those on the east coast of Britain.[73] The legislative measures begun and developed by the Bureau in the pre-war period consisted, firstly, of the OSA 1911, and secondly, of drafts of the DORA and regulations, and other emergency measures to be enacted at the commencement of hostilities.[74] As well as the unofficial registration of aliens and the general supervision of foreign communities, the administrative work of the Preventive Branch during the pre-war period also included the development of emergency schemes to be enacted on mobilisation: (a) to protect especially vulnerable points; (b) the observers scheme, to rapidly enrol a civil intelligence service in the coastal areas; and (c) to arrest, search, or specially watch over 200 chosen enemy subjects who were felt likely to be used as spies, in addition to the twenty or so known spies who would be apprehended at the start of the precautionary period as a matter of course.[75]

Pre-War Investigative Branch

The Investigative Branch's primary role was to investigate cases of suspected espionage. This entailed the related secondary duties of detecting, arresting and bringing the offenders to justice, and preparing the cases for prosecution against those to be arrested. Surveillance of suspects and employing intelligence police personnel at headquarters also served this purpose. Classification of the methods used by enemy agents was a natural adjunct to these investigative duties. As the Bureau was not self-sufficient in every way, cooperation with the military and naval authorities and government departments was required to conduct investigations successfully, which was undertaken by the Investigative Branch. The Investigative Branch also worked with the Preventive Branch in suggesting new legislation, and amendments to existing regulations, to prevent espionage.[76]

The continuity of the pre-war German espionage attack is shown by the succession of spy cases from 1911-1914 which were linked to each other by shared properties, such as a spy address, knowledge of new developments, or a method. Indeed, as Drake observed in his MI5 paper, '*The History of German Espionage in England*', this relationship was often close enough that one case would shed light upon another. Thus, although each case was an entity in itself, it was also only one link in a long chain, and its intricacies needed to be understood and brought to mind when handling all other cases.[77] Hence, a cardinal principle emerged: successful investigation depended on mastery of detail. The corollary of this was that nobody could predict which details might not turn out to be of prime importance in one particular case or in a subsequent one. Contacts were of primary importance. Therefore, as mundane as it might appear, all contacts had to be noted.[78]

This demonstrated that espionage should be handled by one counter-espionage organisation, which would oversee the store of continuous records, methods and traditions. It was also revealed that there should be a free sharing of information between the organisation responsible for counter-espionage – the Bureau, and that handling the maintenance of peace and order – the police.[79]

The Bureau had (like MI5 still does today) no executive powers. Therefore, it could not arrest suspected spies itself, and it had only a small staff in its early years. For that reason it depended on close cooperation with the police to identify, monitor and to arrest suspected spies.[80]

A good counter-espionage investigator, it was argued, needed the following qualities:

'…mental alertness, elasticity, knowledge of men, intuition, an accurate and powerful memory combined with imagination, judgement to choose the right method of handling a case and the moment to strike.

'His attainments should include besides the special knowledge of counter-espionage legislation and preventive measures, some knowledge of law, legal procedure and the laws of evidence. He should also know one or two languages thoroughly.'[81]

The initial concern of the Investigative Branch was, of course, German espionage. Before the First World War, Germany's intelligence effort against Britain was largely the responsibility of its Admiralty Staff's naval intelligence department. The General Staff's military intelligence department focused on France and Russia.[82]

Faced with the potential German threat, initial methods of detection involved both ordinary and special machinery. Ordinary machinery consisted of other government organisations functioning in their normal way, but put into action at the investigator's behest. Special machinery involved methods peculiar to counter-espionage, but undertaken by ordinary government agencies during peacetime.[83]

A typical investigation fell into three stages, dictated by the investigator's aims, as quoted from an MI5 report:

1. To discover enemy agents.
2. To collect evidence against such persons.
3. To bring them to justice or to nullify their efforts.

Spies were classified into two main classes: (1) the foreigner, on a mission or resident, and (2) the traitor, of alien or British origins.

Detection could come via either the Bureau's actions, or it could follow on information received from an outside source. These sources varied between peacetime and wartime. The peacetime sources of detection were seen as:

Inside: 1. The Precautionary Index
     2. Home Office Warrant
     3. Spy contacts established in pursuing an investigation

Outside: 1. Private informer
     2. Military or Naval
     3. Government Offices
     4. Police
     5. Chance: a Returned Letter or a letter picked up and submitted, a conversation overheard and reported.[84]

The precautionary index of those classified as 'possibly suspect' in the Bureau's unofficial registration of aliens does not appear to have resulted in the detection of any proven spy, although it provided information that was of considerable importance during wartime. The HOW and the spy contacts established in pursuing an investigation often overlapped, and as indicated previously, the former was the most important source of detection during peacetime.[85]

MI5's notes on detective intelligence work, partly derived from lecture notes by the Investigative Branch's Major Anson, explain how the Investigative Branch depended upon the records held by the Bureau. A typical investigation began upon receiving information that an individual might be suspect, then this '…information is compared with what is already available in the Bureau's records, and unless the matter is satisfactorily explained by the light there thrown upon it, the Detective Branch makes an enquiry.'[86] Various actions were taken, depending on the type of spy and the source and nature of the information received. For example, if information against an alien or civilian came from a private individual, the first stage would probably be to verify these details through police enquiry; if the accused was a government official or in the armed forces, the enquiry would begin in the department in which he worked. If a spy's existence was known but his identity was in doubt, identification was the first step. The most successful means of identification adopted was to compare specimens of handwriting. The best way to procure a sample of handwriting was to obtain a receipt from the local Post Office signed by the suspect; however, this assumed that the investigation had reached a stage where suspicion was pointed at a particular individual. The pre-war cases of Graves, Ireland, and Schroeder all provide particularly instructive examples of such identifications. The Bureau also engaged its own investigators in this demanding work.[87]

The second investigative stage, namely collecting evidence, exhibited notable differences between peacetime and wartime. During peacetime, it could be a drawn out and painstaking process, involving the repeated surveillance of an agent and the delay of arrest until, from a series of means worked out between the Bureau, the police and the GPO, it was confirmed that particular incriminating evidence would be found on the suspect or in his lodgings.[88]

Thus, the collection of evidence involved two stages: namely, (1) prior and to justify arrest, and (2) post-arrest and to prepare the case. Both stages consisted of a series of verifications, which as quoted from an MI5 report were:

'The man's civil status, movements, business, money affairs and receipts, communications, friends and associations both in England and abroad …'

In addition to this, in all spy cases involving information that had actually been communicated to the enemy, it was necessary to verify the truth and value of this information in court.[89]

The preparation of cases was under legal direction. Secrecy was the one governing principle during peacetime. In peacetime, the trials were heard in open court and fully reported. Thus, it was vital to hide the counter-espionage methods used. For this and for reasons of evidence, much damning information against the agent could not be presented in court.

As the Germans sought improved tactics, they revealed weaknesses in Britain's counter-espionage defences. Indeed, it was part of the investigator's job to record these results and to make proposals to strengthen preventive measures to those who dealt with them, namely the Preventive Branch.[90]

Pre-War Colonial Connections

Even before the First World War, the Bureau had considered the need to establish close relations with the Colonies, a term still used at this time in respect of the Dominions as well as the colonial empire.[91] In March 1913, upon an enquiry from the Australian High Commission as to '…whether the British Government asks Foreign Representatives to keep them supplied with lists of their nationals, or whether any other steps are taken to obtain complete lists of foreigners resident in Great Britain', Kell had proposed to Sir Edward Troup of the Home Office, that it would be mutually beneficial if an occasional exchange of lists of undesirable aliens could be introduced between the Bureau and the Empire.[92] However, it seems that nothing came of this.

The Bureau's pre-war efforts were entirely focused on Germany, but it never showed any concern about Austro-Hungarian intelligence work. Yet, for example, Austria-Hungary was interested in East Africa. The Austro-Hungarian consul for the East African Protectorate in 1914 was an export-import trading company businessman, who conducted his consular work on a part-time basis. When, after the outbreak of war, he was detained and his offices searched, it was found that he was also supplying naval and military intelligence to Vienna.[93]

The Apel Case

In April 1913, the correspondence of Heinrich Schmidt at Devonport revealed the address of Hugo Munschied at 206 Boomgardstraat, Antwerp (see The Schmidt Case) to be suspect. In May, the check on this address revealed that the Germans had an agent at Barrow-in-Furness who had been recruited in Copenhagen. Enquiries concerning the then unknown German agent began on 26 May and on 8 June the Chief Constable of Barrow-in-Furness provided information which proved beyond doubt that the agent wanted was one Fredrik Apel. The available records do not provide much detail about why Apel was identified as a German agent, simply stating that, 'By means of details contained in his letters abroad, he was soon identified as Fredrik Wilhelm Henrik APEL.' The police kept him under observation, supplying the Bureau with details of any remittances he received, his movements and his correspondence. On 9 June he was placed on the Special War List for arrest.

Investigation revealed that Apel had arrived in the UK at the beginning of May 1913. He approached the German Consul at Barrow-in-Furness who directed him to the Sailor's Institute. He later received money from Germany addressed to him care of the Consul. Apel had claimed to have come to England to look for a married sister who had eloped with a British ship's engineer. He also claimed that the money from Germany came from an uncle who was helping him to find his sister. Apel drifted from house to house and lived largely on the charity of Mr Conway Milne, port missionary and head of the Sailor's Institute. Milne was eventually able to help Apel obtain work with a German pork-butcher. He left this job in March 1914 to work as a labourer at the Barrow Hematite Steel Company's Wire Works. Then, in July, he went to work for the Pilkington Paper Pulp Company.

He began sending reports in May 1913. In June, he travelled to Hamburg to meet his controllers, taking with him plans that he had photographed. On 11 July, Apel's controller wrote to him from Rotterdam refusing to send him any more money until information of value had been received. Further chastening letters followed. Then, on 30 December, an 'A.S.' wrote from Petersburg that he had given up on expecting good results from Apel and cautioned him to be careful in the use of addresses. However, he added that, if Apel 'could get the things wanted' then they would fetch a 'high price'. On 6 February 1914, Apel received a letter enclosing questions about the Royal Navy ship HMS *Emperor of India*, and instructing that answers should be sent to 'A. Samper, Brussels, Poste Restante, Bureau Centrale', as the sender had ceased connection with Munschied. On 8 March, Apel sent his reply as directed, but it was returned as undeliverable. In April, Apel wrote to Munschied again, urgently requesting an answer and money. Apel left this letter with Milne, whom he asked to enclose a note confirming his statements. Milne wrote the note and posted Apel's letter to Antwerp, having first had Apel's letter translated. On 4 April, Milne supplied a summary of Apel's letter to a contact at the Vickers company who forwarded it to the Bureau.

An MI5 report concluded that as 'an agent APEL was untrustworthy and a failure.' He had clearly been tasked to obtain work at Vickers and to gather intelligence on the work being done there for the Royal Navy, but had been rejected because of his German nationality. In order to save face with his controllers, he invented the story that he had found employment as a casual labourer at the docks and that he had made useful contacts there.

Apel was arrested on 4 August 1914. He was searched but nothing incriminating was found and his only possessions were the clothes he was standing in. Nonetheless, in the words of MI5:

'The fact that nothing was found at the search does not preclude his being in possession of valuable knowledge. This however, is mere conjecture; he may have remained incurably feckless and certainly he was destitute.'

Apel was charged with breaking the OSA, but the charge was not proceeded with. He was then interned under the ARO pending deportation. As an MI5 report pointed out, the case could not be understood unless it could be related to the 'wholesale attack' ('Incitements to Treason' as above) upon the personnel of the Royal Navy, which culminated in 1913. As it was impossible for German nationals to infiltrate the Royal Navy's dockyards, the attack upon the Royal Navy had been widened to the personnel of the dockyards and private yards. In this context, it was clearly part of Apel's mission to provide the details of British citizens who could and would provide information. Indeed, throughout 1913 such letters came into the UK in considerable quantities and signed with many different cover names and addresses as used by the German Secret Service. Of interest is the fact that during October of that year, three letters were intercepted signed Samper, because Apel had been instructed to write to Samper.

The von Weller Case

Hauptmann (Captain) Kurd von Weller was a retired German officer. The Royal Irish Constabulary reported him to the Bureau in December 1913 after he had visited Ireland. He was arrested on 10 August 1914 in possession of 'information which might be useful to an enemy' and detained under ARO. Whilst imprisoned he also attempted to convey information to the enemy. Von Weller was exchanged for a British officer POW in October 1915.[94]

The Schneider Case

Adolf Schneider was a clerk with the London firm of Greidinger and Kermann (profession not known), who resided in Dulwich. About three weeks after Ernst's resignation, Schneider accepted work for Steinhauer who tasked him with forwarding letters to agents. Surviving records do not state when or how Schneider first came to the Bureau's attention but they do mention that a HOW was taken out on Schneider's correspondence. However, it is not known when this happened or what had caused him to come to the Bureau's attention. Clearly the compilers of MI5's historical reports viewed Schneider as a minor case, which did not warrant detailed study. If anything, they seemed most interested in the fact that Schneider actually complained to the GPO about delays, clearly caused by postal interception, in delivering two letters to him. But the GPO succeeded in excusing itself by stating that one of them had been addressed incorrectly, and the other had been delayed because it had been received too late to be included in the first delivery. Schneider was arrested on 4 August 1914 and detained under the ARO pending deportation.[95]

The Brown Case

In October 1911, a W.F. Brown was discovered to be corresponding with Reimers. Nothing more was heard of him until February 1914 when he applied for a job at the Talbot-Quick Waterplane Company of London. The company was at work on the production of a seaplane and Brown was employed to make scale drawings of it. The company had taken him on having seen his advertisement looking for work in the *Evening News*. This enabled him to gain a thorough knowledge of the machine's construction, and he also had the opportunity to make copies of his drawings. After only one week's work, he left the job, stating that the aircraft was a 'hopeless failure'. However, one of his co-workers had seen Brown with a £75 cheque, and formed the opinion that he had been there to obtain secrets connected with aeroplane construction. After Brown had left, a similar advertisement to the one he had posted in the *Evening News* appeared in an engineering paper. Talbot Quick immediately informed the police about this and they identified Brown as ex-police constable William Francis Brown by his handwriting.

Brown had been born in Springwood, New South Wales, Australia in 1870 to parents of German origins, but came to live at Poplar in east London about 1890. He became a seaman and in 1895 he joined the Royal Naval Reserve. Having worked as a laundryman and then a pierman, he joined the Metropolitan Police in 1906, being dismissed in 1910 for going absent without leave.

A HOW was taken out on Brown on 28 February 1914. On 6 May, Melville reported that he was living at 147 Alderney Street, London and working for the firm of Walter Johnson. He was arrested on 7 August, but no incriminating evidence was found on him and he was discharged on 12 August. He later managed to obtain employment as chief draughtsman to Macdonald Gibbs, supervising engineer to the War Office, who rated him as 'trustworthy'.[96] It seems rather strange that someone who had been suspected of espionage should be allowed to take up such a post which clearly provided easy access to a wealth of confidential information. However, the available records do not enable further consideration of this very intriguing question.

The Rosso Case

Alberto Rosso (alias Albert Celso Rodriguez) was a teacher of languages. He arrived at Portsmouth on 26 March 1914 and immediately found employment at the Berlitz School at 12 Hampshire Terrace. On 30 March he wired the well-known Brussels-based spy agency, 'Mr Adams', announcing his change of address. The next day, the Bureau took out the necessary HOW, informed the Admiralty that there was a spy at the Berlitz School, asked the borough police to verify the address for the register of aliens, and asked the dockyard police to keep Rosso under observation. On 2 April, he received a letter from Berlin tasking him with his first assignment, to visit Maddick, an electrical fitter at Portsmouth Dockyard who had approached the German Secret Service (see The Maddick Case), in order to verify certain facts about him. On 12 July Rosso sent answers to several questions to his controller. On the 22nd, the controller 'quarrelled' with Rosso's answers, commenting that 'the only things of any interest to Berlin were the official and Confidential Books and Plans.' Rosso was placed on the Special War List in early April 1914 for arrest on the outbreak of war. However, the police jumped the gun. On 3 August 1914, the wife of the manager of the Berlitz School informed the borough police that Rosso was a spy and produced letters as proof. He was arrested at 11.15 pm that day and charged under OSA. The charges were subsequently dropped and Rosso was dealt with under ARO and interned. An MI5 historical report, written in 1921, referred to him as Albert Celso Rodriguez, but added that the real identity and nationality of the man who posed as a Spanish citizen under that name 'is in doubt'. It was Professor Christopher Andrew who successfully identified him as Alberto Rosso whilst researching his official history.[97]

The Heine and Heinert Cases

The HOW on Schneider called the Bureau's attention to Lina Mary Heine on 1 April

1914. Investigation revealed that Heine had been born in Holzzweiseg, Prussia in 1893. In March 1914 she journeyed to England, arriving at Portsmouth on the 13th and began working as a teacher of German about ten days later. At the end of March a Max Power Heinert also arrived in Portsmouth, ostensibly to learn English. He was Heine's husband, but they kept their connection secret and he visited her under the pretence of taking English lessons. However, despite the Bureau's best efforts, it took several months to obtain proof that Heine was a spy. Her reports were sent to a man with a Russian name (no more detail seems to be available) and addressed to hotels in different towns in Germany. She received letters, via Adolf Schneider or August Klunder (see earlier), addressed to a 'Miss Claire Fouquet' on a poste restante basis at Southampton. Special agents shadowed her from 17 to 23 April but did not observe anything suspicious and did not see her post any letters. The Bureau's Lieutenant Commander B.J. Ohlson was sent to take lessons with Heine and was able to obtain a sample of her handwriting. He also learned that a certain officer at the Royal Naval College was intending to study under her and the officer was warned accordingly. In May, she was followed going to Ostend to meet Captain Fels, a known officer of the German Secret Service. On 1 July, the HOW on 'A. Hocke' at 257 Carstensgarde in Copenhagen (which had been in operation since August 1913) revealed a letter from Heine in which she sent a sketch of the searchlights at Portsmouth and answered some spy questions from a list that she had received in April. Heine was placed on the Special War List on 7 July. She was arrested on 4 August 1914. Heinert happened to be present when she was arrested and because he could not provide a satisfactory account of himself, he was also arrested.

After her arrest Heine claimed that she had been recruited by the German Secret Service around Christmas 1913 as a result of a bogus advertisement in the *Berliner Tageblatt* which sought a lady who spoke English to teach German at a Russian school of languages in Britain. She replied to the advertisement and was persuaded to work for the Secret Service. Subsequently, both she and Heinert were interned under the ARO pending deportation. Some time between August and December 1914 (the available records are not specific) Heine confessed to her guilt but maintained that Heinert was innocent. He died suddenly on 1 December. The Home Office wished to release Heine in June 1915, however MO5(g) refused, arguing that anything short of three years was an inadequate punishment for her crimes. In February 1916, Heine appealed for repatriation to Germany, but was turned down on the grounds that if she returned to Germany she could again be sent to spy in Allied territory. In July and November 1917 the question of Heine's repatriation was raised again. Kell held to his view 'that release was impolitic'. In February 1918, she was eventually interned under Defence of the Realm Regulation (DRR) 14B, which sanctioned imposing restrictions on, or the internment of, individuals of hostile origin and associations (see Chapter Three) owing to her 'hostile origins' and her being a professional spy. On 11 December 1918, the Director of Military Intelligence (DMI) placed Heine on the list of women (eleven altogether) who were to be held during demobilisation. But as it was clear that these women were 'suffering much' from prolonged captivity, MI5 suggested that their cases should be reconsidered on the grounds that because the decision to intern them had been based on prevention, not punishment, the principle of prevention should also govern the issue of their release. The Home Office agreed and Heine was deported to Rotterdam in April 1919.

Heine's repeated attempts to obtain her release served to emphasise a weakness in the policy of interning spies without trial and conviction. An MI5 report observed that this practice led to endless petitioning and claims that the trial had been quashed because there was no proof against the individual who had been interned.[98]

The Maddick Case

On 20 April 1914, 'A. Ransom' of the Hotel Stadt, Konigsberg in Potsdam wrote to S. Maddick (none of the available documents discloses what Maddick's first name was, only that it began with an S), of 65 Byerley Road, Portsmouth in a way that indicated that Maddick had offered his services to the German Secret Service and Ransom wished to accept Maddick's offer. They arranged to meet at Ostend on 7 June. However, on 1 June Maddick, born in Westminster in 1874 and working as an electrical fitter at Portsmouth Dockyard, confessed his intentions to the dockyard police and was arrested. He claimed that he had simply intended to raise money to go abroad by peddling 'worthless' information. Maddick was charged 'with attempting to communicate information to a person other than a person to whom he was authorised to communicate it.' He was brought up before the courts on 2 June and remanded until 9 June.

Maddick's confession was reported to the Bureau, who had actually been monitoring the situation since 20 April when Rodriguez had been instructed to make enquiries about Maddick by the German Secret Service. On 1 May, the Admiralty informed the Bureau that Maddick had worked at Devonport on electrical installations on a new type of ship from March to October 1912. He then worked afloat, installing electrical leads on ships at Chatham until December. Maddick's whereabouts for the next few months were unknown. Then, in June 1913, he took up employment as an electrical fitter on ships and yard machinery in Portsmouth Dockyard, but his attendance at work, both at Chatham and Portsmouth had been somewhat irregular. In March 1914, he was absent for several days and upon his return claimed that he had been to Paris to seek employment and that he 'did not depend upon his weekly wages.' On 4 May, the Bureau wrote to Scotland Yard asking the police to arrest Maddick on his proposed journey to Ostend on 7 June, but legal difficulties arose. The magistrate declined to issue an arrest warrant because the Bureau would not include Maddick's intercepted letters in evidence and the Portsmouth Police refused to search Maddick's lodgings without a warrant. Notwithstanding, the Bureau made sure that watch was maintained all through May.

Then, on 9 June, the Bureau assumed responsibility for Maddick's case. It soon became apparent that he was not of sound mind and the case against him was abandoned. He was released and placed in a lunatic asylum on 21 June. Exactly one year later, on 21 June 1915, Maddick escaped from the asylum but was soon re-captured. His doctor decided that he was no longer insane, but that he still needed watching and therefore, he was interned under DRR14B. Maddick's case was reviewed on 11 December 1918 and he was released on 27 January the following year when he went to work on a farm at Bromley in Kent.[99]

Haldane

Captain Lawrence left the Bureau on 31 March 1914 and was succeeded on 22 April 1914 by Captain (later Lieutenant-Colonel) Maldwyn Makgill Haldane, late of the Royal

Scots, who had occasionally assisted the Bureau while working at the War Office.[100] Haldane was the first university graduate to join the Bureau, having studied at University College, London, Jesus College, Cambridge, and the University of Göttingen. He was also a good linguist, competent in French, German, and Hindustani.[101] In the words of Bulloch, the fact that Captain Haldane, a nephew of Lord Haldane, the former Secretary of State for War, 'was another recruit' provided 'a sure sign that the young department was officially accepted, and that the value of the work being done was recognized.'[102]

The Gregory and Nedjib Cases

Owing to the difficulty in bringing charges under the 1911 OSA, the Bureau sometimes employed subtler means of countering the danger presented by German spies. One such method was to have individuals moved to another job where they would not have access to confidential information, as in the case of Peter E. Gregory, or recalled to their home country through diplomatic channels, as happened with Lieutenant Ahmed Nedjib.

From the Reimers correspondence, the Bureau discovered that 'A. Kutusow, chez Mme Muller, Pacheco 81, Brussels' was a spy address, Kutusow being another cover used by Steinhauer. As part of the 'Incitements to Treason' attack on current and former Royal Navy personnel, Kutusow had been soliciting information 'under the guise of collecting articles and materials for a Russian paper which was to treat of all the Navies of all the world.' The Bureau never ascertained precisely how Kutusow got in touch with Gregory, but it seems likely it was by the distribution of a typed circular through the Inland Post. In early February 1914 letters were intercepted between Gregory and Kutusow. Peter Gregory was a former Royal Navy artificer engineer and dockyard ship-fitter of Portsmouth who had offered information on naval recruitment and training to the Germans. It was calculated, however, that he was not in a position to learn much and that he could be safely transferred to the tool shop. On 19 June 1914 he was placed on the list of men to be watched upon the outbreak of war and in October of that year the dockyard police pushed for action to be taken. MO5(g) replied that, although there was no doubt that Gregory had been corresponding with a foreign agent, it did not think that he had been able to give away any important information. In view of the difficulties of bringing a charge under the OSA, MO5(g) would submit the case for disciplinary action to the Admiralty. There is no record of the Admiralty's decision.[103]

In 1914, a Turkish officer, Ahmed Nedjib, was working for the Turkish Government as chief overseer on a Turkish battleship being built at Armstrong's of Newcastle, and also on another Turkish ship being constructed at Vickers of Barrow. He was discovered to be communicating with a German agent in Berlin. Arrangements were made, through diplomatic channels, for Nedjib's recall. He was reported to have left for the Continent on 30 March 1914. On 29 June Nedjib was placed on the Special War List to be watched if he returned to Great Britain.[104]

The Blackburn Case

Born in 1896, Robert Arthur Blackburn was employed by his father to help manage a lodging house in Liverpool. On 30 June 1914 he received a letter that had been posted via August Klunder. This led to a HOW being taken out on Blackburn, which resulted in the detection of another letter on 20 July. Blackburn was arrested on 10 August 1914 and charged with sending valuable information to an enemy. Further investigation revealed that Blackburn had written initially to the German Embassy in London offering his services and MO5(g) noted that Blackburn '...seems to have been an impressionable youth, who excited his imagination with reading.' It was this desire for adventure that had led him to contact the German Embassy and it is quite possible that he may have fuelled his imagination by reading spy thrillers written by Le Queux. A reply soon came from Berlin asking questions about shipbuilding and the defences on the Mersey River. Blackburn answered these questions and received £2 in payment. His trial began on 28 October. He pleaded guilty, described how he had entered into relations with Germany, but argued (accurately) '...that he had given them no information that was not in some way or other accessible to the public.' Blackburn was sentenced to two years' in borstal. After his release in October 1916, Blackburn joined the Royal Army Medical Corps (RAMC). MI5 was consulted on this and advised that the decision should be left to the recruiting authorities.[105]

The von Diederichs Case

A letter from a Friederich von Diederichs was intercepted on its way to 'Streckel, 38 Königin Augustastrasse, Berlin' on 27 July 1914. 'Streckel' was known to be an alias used by Captain von Prieger, head of the *Nachrichten Abteilung* and the address, known to be the private address of the same German Admiralty organisation, had been the subject of a HOW since 22 July 1914. The letter provided details of British naval mobilization, asked for certain addresses in Amsterdam and Rotterdam to be sent to von Diederichs, suggested that a simple telegraphic code could be provided for urgent communications and that arrangements should be made to send money in the event of war. A HOW was taken out for von Diederichs on 27 July. The next day, he received a letter from Berlin rebuking him for the poor quality of his reports, '...the contents of which could be read in the papers.' He was added to the Special War List on 29 July. Von Diederichs, the son of an admiral, was a fifty-five year-old pensioned Commander of the German Navy. Investigation revealed that he had come to the UK just before the outbreak of war, and had spent some time in London before settling in to the Kenilworth Hotel on 24 July. He had left there on 29 July, apparently on route for the Continent. He was arrested in London on 4 August and detained under the ARO (the available records make no mention of von Diederichs' movements between leaving the hotel on 29 July and his arrest on 4 August). All requests for von Diederichs' release were refused on the grounds that it was quite clear that he was a German naval officer who had been engaged on an espionage assignment just before the outbreak of war. He was eventually repatriated in March 1919.[106]

The Bernstein case

Major Enrico Lorenzo Bernstein had been involved in the trafficking of intelligence since before the First World War.[107] Bernstein, alias H. Laurens, was an Australian-born son of a Pole and his American wife. He claimed British nationality by virtue of his services to the crown with the West African Frontier Force, but he later served as a major in the Brazilian Army. On 5 August 1914 he approached the Admiralty, requesting an interview with the Naval Intelligence Department, in order to provide photographs and descriptions of German agents in Britain. He was arrested at the Admiralty that day and charged with espionage. Bernstein was a known intelligence mercenary, who would sell his services to the highest bidder. The Admiralty did not trust this rather suspicious character and arrested him in order to detain him so that the British secret services could look into what he had to offer. He was conveyed to Brixton Prison under a deportation order. However, in a very fortuitous turn of events for him, the deportation order was suspended and he was released on 12 August in order to work for MI1c.[108]

The Dutton Case
Harold Dutton was a former army clerk who was discovered to have copied classified documents on the Portsmouth defences. He was arrested on 15 August 1914 and admitted possessing the documents. He was sentenced to six months' hard labour for breaching the OSA.[109]

Captain John Carter
Captain (later Colonel) John Fillis Carré Carter joined the Bureau on 4 August 1914 having served with the Indian Army, leaving on 4 March 1918 for a posting in Rome.[110] He subsequently served as a Deputy Assistant Commissioner (Crime) with the Metropolitan Police.[111]

Staff who joined the Bureau before the outbreak of war
On 4 August 1914 the Bureau had twenty members of staff: nine officers, seven administrative assistants (three male clerks and four female clerical staff), three detectives, and a caretaker. It is instructive to list all of MI5's staff to that date, including when they joined and left and their designated task, because it illustrates the early growth of the Bureau and – as 'founder members' – they deserve recording (those who had left before the war are bracketed):

W. Melville, 1 Dec. 1903-18 Dec. 1917, (Chief) Detective
V.G.W. Kell, 9 Oct. 1909-June 1940, Officer (Director)
J.R. Westmacott, 14 March 1910-1921 (Chief) Clerk
(F.L.S. Clarke, 1 Jan. 1911-30 Nov. 1912, Officer)
D. Westmacott, 16 Jan. 1911-1922, Clerical Staff
B.J. Ohlson, 10 May 1911- 12 November 1914 & 2 July 1916 -18 July 1917, Officer
J. Regan, 7 June 1911-13 Aug. 1916, Detective
F.S. Strong, 18 Sept. 1911-26 July 1916, Clerk
H.M. Newport, 27 Oct. 1911-1921, Clerical Staff
R.J. Drake, 1 April 1912-1 March 1917, Officer
Mrs. Sumner, 1 Oct. 1912-4 Aug. 1916, Caretaker
H.I. Fitzgerald, 1 Nov. 1912-(No date), Detective
E.E.B. Holt-Wilson, 20 Dec. 1912-June 1940, Officer
F.B. Booth, 1 Jan. 1913-(No date), Officer
(K.E. Lawrence, 31 Jan. 1913-31 March 1914, Officer)
S. Holmes, 27 Feb. 1913-31 Dec. 1918, Clerical Staff

M. Brodie, 1 July 1913-(No date), Officer
S. Strong, 10 July 1913-(No date), Clerk
J.B. Fetherston, 1 Jan. 1914-(No date), Officer
D. Bowie, 7 Jan. 1914-(No date), Clerical Staff
M.M. Haldane, 22 April 1914-(No date), Officer
J.F.C. Carter, 4 Aug. 1914-28 Feb. 1919, Officer[112]

Pre-War MI5 Failure!

MI5's only apparent pre-war failure concerned the German success between 1909 and July 1914 in managing 'to obtain continuous access to copies of the most secret correspondence passing between Count Benckendorff, the Russian ambassador in London, and the Ministry for Foreign Affairs in St Petersburg.' In a 'spectacular triumph in classical espionage', a German agent, von Siebert, who had served in the Russian Embassy in London, had managed to gain access to this correspondence.[113] However, it is difficult to know how the Bureau could have been expected to detect him, as the documents would have been covered by diplomatic protection.

★ ★ ★

The period from October 1909 to August 1914 saw British counter-espionage undergo a transformation. The Bureau had grown from a solitary official (aided by an investigator) with inadequate resources, inadequate powers and an uncertain future, into a dedicated cadre of counter-espionage expertise – a nucleus ready for expansion in time of war. The key developments that occurred between the Bureau's formation and the outbreak of the First World War, resulting in it being well-prepared for war, were the passage of effective counter-espionage legislation with the application of OSA in 1911; improvements in the procedure for the granting of Home Office Warrants (HOW), sanctioning the interception of suspects correspondence; the development of good working relations with the police and other relevant bodies; an unofficial register of aliens residing in the UK who could thereby be classified as probably harmless or possibly suspect and worth investigating; and the preparation of emergency legislation ready for wartime, in the shape of the Defence of the Realm Act (DORA) and the Aliens Restriction Act (ARA). The Bureau had also begun to assume a shape that would influence its development for many years to come, with the division between investigative and preventive work.

The historiography has extensively covered the poor quality of the vast majority of Germany's pre-war agents in Britain, the inherent weaknesses in a system that relied on intermediaries to act as 'postmen', and the central role that HOWs played in the Bureau's pre-war work. Two points are, however, worth stressing here. Firstly, revisiting a question posed in the previous chapter, it is now quite clear that if the Post Office's view that postal interception was of little use to counter-espionage had prevailed, then the Bureau would have been deprived of arguably the key weapon in its pre-war battle against the German espionage network in the UK. Secondly, at a time when the Bureau had only a small staff and very limited resources, postal interception was a relatively cheap and straightforward way to keep track of Steinhauer's network.

CHAPTER THREE

The Outbreak of War
August 1914-December 1914

ROUND-UP AUGUST 1914

VERNON KELL had devoted nearly five years to preparing the Bureau for the 'precautionary period' – the period when war seemed imminent, and the Bureau and the police made sure that they were ready to round up the German espionage network in Britain the moment that war was declared. With the outbreak of war, his preparations would be put to the test.

Back in May 1913 all county chief constables were informed that, in case of emergency, they would be sent a warning letter which would include the names of all those in their jurisdiction who had been selected for (a) immediate arrest, (b) search, or (c) careful watch. Even if there were none in a particular county, the chief constable was still sent a warning letter to inform him that the precautionary period was being considered and to put the police on alert. In late 1913, similar information was passed on to the chief constables of all cities and boroughs containing people on the possible suspects list, but not otherwise. The warning letter had been approved by the Home Office and the Public Prosecutor, and was sent out between 29-31 July 1914. Although the letter listed the people under categories (a), (b) and (c) above, it did not request immediate action to be taken. Its intention was simply to ensure that the police had the information they needed to be ready to act at the shortest notice. Arrests and searches were to be conducted immediately upon receiving a telegram. The warning letter specified the wording of this telegram and the legal authority on which this action was to be taken. Chief constables were also required to act against anyone under (a), (b) or (c) above against whom they deemed there was sufficient evidence, and to inform MO5(g) of any action taken.[1] In the days leading up to the outbreak of war, Kell based himself at Watergate House twenty-fours hour per day, sleeping amongst the telephones and poised to order the arrest of as many as twenty-two identified German spies as soon as hostilities commenced.[2]

The aforementioned telegrams were finally sent on the afternoon of 4 August 1914, after Britain's ultimatum but prior to the actual declaration of war. Of the twenty-two

A French postcard of suspect Germans rounded up in Willesden, London in August 1914.
(Collection IM/Harbin-Tapador/British Library)

people on the list for immediate arrest, twenty-one were arrested (plus Max Power Heinert); one other, Walter Rimann, had left England a few days earlier. Fifty-six suspects were searched under category (b) above and many of them were detained and subsequently transferred to military custody as enemy aliens likely to be dangerous. Under category (c) above, 155 others were placed under special observation. A number were subsequently interned as enemy reservists.[3]

As Christopher Andrew points out, successfully rounding-up so many enemy agents simultaneously was a considerable achievement:

'But for the co-operation established by Kell with chief constables since 1910 the rounding up of the core of Steinhauer's agent network would have been impossible. Never before in British history had plans been prepared for such a large number of preferably simultaneous arrests of enemy agents at diverse locations. With a total staff of only seventeen (including the caretaker) on the eve of war, Kell depended on local police forces for much of the investigation and surveillance which preceded the arrests as well as for the arrests themselves. Nowadays hundreds of Security Service staff and police officers would be required for such a large operation. Kell, however, had neither the staff nor the modern communications systems required to remain in close and constant touch with all the police forces involved.'[4]

Perhaps not surprisingly, six police forces acted on their own initiative. The Portsmouth force arrested Alberto Ross, alias 'Rodriguez', on 3 August, the day before Britain actually went to war, while from the following day other local constabularies, acting on insubstantial evidence, arrested seven additional suspects who had not been targeted by Kell.[5]

As previously mentioned, MO5(g)'s plan for the control of suspects on the outbreak of war was based on pre-war policy, with the primary objective of paralysing the German espionage organisation in case of hostilities with one crushing blow. This policy was so successful that on 21 August 1914, two weeks into the war, the German High Command was still unaware of the British Expeditionary Force's (BEF) despatch to France.[6] Indeed, in his account of the march on Paris and the battle of the Marne, *Generaloberst* Alexander von Kluck, who commanded Germany's First Army in August 1914, revealed his total lack of knowledge of the BEF's arrival in Belgium. He asserted that it would arrive at Boulogne, Calais and Dunkerque and its lines of communication would be east-to-west, and therefore easy for him to cut. Thus, the BEF's arrival at Mons came as a great surprise to the Germans.[7]

Of course, at the time MO5(g) was not absolutely certain if the twenty-two spies constituted the entire network of German agents in Britain, although this was later shown to be the case.[8] In his memoirs, Edmonds claimed that he had designed this strategy, which suggests that MO5(g)'s strategy was influenced by those who had worked in counter-espionage in MO5 before Kell was appointed to the newly formed Secret Service Bureau:

'I was opposed to the arrest of even undoubted espionage agents: it was better to let Germany live in the fool's paradise that we had no counter-espionage system. This was accepted: the agents were marked down, and all but one (on leave) seized on declaration of war.'[9]

It was MO5(g)'s strategy that the German spy ring in the UK should be quietly dismantled and its members interned, for deportation later on, rather than brought to trial. MO5(g) desired not to bring them to trial for two reasons: firstly, evidence given in open court would reveal how British counter-espionage worked. Secondly, MO5(g) wanted to keep the Germans in the dark about the fate of their espionage network for as long as possible, since if they became aware of the British success, they would take steps to replace it. The longer that scenario could be delayed, the more time Britain would have to make preparations for war without risk of betrayal to the enemy. However, all was revealed just over a month later, when Karl Gustave Ernst was tried in an ordinary criminal court, something he had the right as a British subject.[10]

The historian David French has challenged this interpretation, commenting that if 'the government was convinced that they were spies, its subsequent behaviour towards them was certainly peculiar'. Indeed, just one of those rounded up was ever brought to trial. In October 1914, the Home Office issued a statement excusing its inaction, saying that to have tried them would have informed the Germans how MO5(g) worked. For his part, French feels that this was not a valid excuse, as the statement went on to reveal how MO5(g) worked – namely, by scrutinising foreign letters and telegrams. Later writers ignored the fact that there had only been one prosecution and argued that the government had not wanted to warn Germany that its agents had been caught by bringing them to trial. Yet *The Times* had printed the names of all those caught shortly after they were arrested. This leads French to conclude that '...the government did not prosecute because they could not find enough evidence to do so.' However, it was considered that to have admitted this, when the public was becoming hysterical about espionage and calling for tougher action against enemy aliens, 'would only have provided more ammunition for its critics, and have damaged public confidence further.'[11] However, it seems that French has missed the key point here: expediency. At a time when MO5(g) was hard-pressed to cope with a rapidly expanding workload, it was expedient to intern these enemy aliens under the ARO, because doing so saved a huge amount of work involved in bringing twenty-one cases to trial. It should also not be forgotten that they did indeed pose some threat to Britain's national security: the twenty-two individuals arrested posed differing levels of espionage risk to the country and all but one had been in contact with German intelligence.[12]

The arrests certainly achieved the desired effect of producing a grave paralysis within the *Nachrichten-Abteilung* in Berlin and Gustav Steinhauer recalled that the Kaiser was furious when informed:

> 'Apparently unable to believe his ears, [he] raved and stormed for the better part of two hours about the incompetence of his so-called intelligence officers, bellowing: "Am I surrounded by dolts? Why was I not told? Who is responsible?" and more in the same vein.'[13]

GRAND STRATEGY

Director of Special Intelligence – DSI

Following the outbreak of the First World War on 4 August 1914, the Bureau became officially recognised, having hitherto been a secret and unrecognised organisation as part of the Directorate of Military Operations, as MO5(g).[14] MO5(g)'s wartime role would be as one element of what became the Directorate of Special Intelligence, a sub-directorate of the Directorate of Military Intelligence concerned with special intelligence and led by the Director of Special Intelligence (DSI), Brigadier-General George Kynaston Cockerill.[15] Cockerill had a lifelong experience as an intelligence officer in India, and during the Boer War he had been engaged in administering the Cape Colony under martial law.[16] The Directorate of Special Intelligence was tasked with overseeing security intelligence work, namely 'all the security services designed to prevent the enemy from gaining information'.[17] The work was divided:

> 'As regards secrecy, the problem of preventing the leakage of military information may be considered from two wholly separate points of view; (a) the repression of innocent indiscretions on the part of officers and men, the public and the press; and (b) the defeat of enemy efforts to obtain information by spies and agents in his employment.'[18]

MI7 (Press Control), MI8 (Cable Censorship) and MI9 (Postal Censorship) covered the former.[19] MI5 (at that time MO5(g)) dealt with the latter, its role within the sub-directorate being seen in terms of military security, encompassing 'Counter-espionage, including measures for the Control of Aliens and suspected persons.'[20]

Elements of the Directorate of Military Intelligence were solely wartime and preventive creations. The Legal and Economic Section (MI6) dealt with the traffic in arms, with which MI5 was not greatly concerned. By contrast, MI7, MI8 and MI9 were powerful preventive weapons. MI7 supervised foreign journalists employed for propaganda purposes. MI8 and MI9 were perhaps of greater value as preventive organisations than any other single department. A considerable number of the amendments to the war legislation were calculated to make it more difficult to send or carry correspondence so as to evade this censorship.[21]

MO5(G)'s Strategy

The main problem that MO5(g) faced from the Preventive Branch's perspective once war began was protecting the government's activities against assault by possible enemy agents. The solution adopted to this problem was in an array of controls. Some of them precluded individuals from carrying or sending uncensored communications to the enemy. Others ensured that no individual whose credentials were suspect in any way would be granted access to any area of military or naval importance, or vulnerable point, whether they were inside zones of operations or not. These included arsenals and shipyards, flotilla and fleet bases, munitions factories, ports of embarkation for transports, training grounds and experimental stations, strategic railway lines and other such places where spies could gather information of use to the enemy, or create explosions and incite industrial unrest that would harm the armed forces' operations. The measures required to protect these areas against attempted espionage or sabotage varied considerably. They ranged from conducting investigations at permit offices to check the bona fides of individuals wanting to travel to zones of operations abroad, to the employment of soldiers with fixed bayonets to guard fortified positions. As the war went on, the amount of vulnerable points in the country grew considerably, and it eventually became extremely difficult to find any places where suspects who could not be interned could live without posing a threat. This meant that, as the war progressed, the actions taken during the early part of the war to remove individuals classified as potentially dangerous from vulnerable points became of ever reducing value. The value of personal restrictions on such people, regardless of where they lived, increased by a corresponding amount.

Prohibited areas were of four types. Firstly, areas that were prohibited only to enemy aliens. Secondly, special military areas, to which the commandant had the power to refuse any individual an entry permit. Thirdly, medium protected areas, government land, premises, docks, etc, to which the Competent Military Authority (CMA) could prohibit any or all people. Fourth, small protected areas to which a local or central authority could deny entry, or to adjacent ground. Theoretically, the prohibited area provided a belt around the coast from ten to forty miles deep that had been completely cleared from known enemies. British counter-espionage was thus freed to detect the enemies disguised as friendly aliens or British subjects, who might operate in this coastal zone.

Thus MO5(g)'s policy was to gain protection from enemy agents by moving enemy aliens from the protected area, and maintaining close watch on all of those who might harm national security. Registration proved valuable here, and people who seemed dangerous according to MO5(g)'s records could be interned or subjected to other personal restrictions as appropriate. Even during the Napoleonic Wars from 1803-1814 aliens were not allowed to live within ten miles of a dockyard or the coast, their homes could be searched, and they were required to possess passports and be registered.[22]

While the public was unaware of the scheme of unofficial aliens' registration, it was not hard for the police to identify an alien whose name had been given to them by MO5(g), because these individuals had not felt that there was any need to try to hide their identity. It became much more difficult, however, to identify a suspect during wartime, when controls had been constructed, such that spies would take on an assumed identity in order to avoid them.[23]

MI5 was criticised for not focusing enough on alien friends (i.e., those of what was considered to be a 'friendly' foreign nationality who, ordinarily, posed no threat) and British subjects, most tellingly by John Moylan of the Home Office Aliens Division.[24] In October 1917 the War Office informed the Home Office that as there averaged one vulnerable point to every seven square miles of the UK, each enemy alien restricted to a radius of only five miles would have access to approximately eleven vulnerable points. Therefore, further surveillance and internment were required.[25] Moylan found the War Office's evidence of the suspicious activities of aliens residing near vulnerable points unconvincing and minuted the following critique:

'Not a single instance of an alien enemy having improperly gained access to a vulnerable point is adduced nor apparently can be adduced and it is well known to MI5 that it is not amongst alien enemies now at large that the real danger from enemy agents exists but amongst alien friends and British subjects without any German blood, whether whole or half. But enemy agents are elusive and hard to find in the mass of British subjects and alien friends, while the alien enemy presents a known and easy target at which MI5 owing to the difficulty and scarceness of the other quarry, keep firing away in their natural anxiety to appear always on the qui vive.'[26]

In many respects, Moylan's views were unreasonable; in reality, MI5 had hunted down German agents in Britain quite efficiently.[27] It is also apparent that MO5(g)'s strategy did cover the entire population. For example, counter-espionage measures like DORA and censorship also applied to alien friends and British subjects. Indeed, MO5(g) seems to have caught all of the German agents who were either alien friends or British subjects.

There is some irony to the fact that Moylan himself had spied for the Home Office during the labour unrest in South Wales of 1910-1911, keeping government informed about the public order situation there.[28]

As has been noted Edmonds had a great influence on MO5(g)'s strategy, but it is interesting to consider what other influences there might have been. The Boer War of 1899-1902 saw the British employ rudimentary press, postal and cable censorship, plus the internment of more than 116,000 Boer civilians in concentration camps. Indeed, all of these measures were later introduced to Britain during the First World War. It therefore seems possible that lessons must have been learned from the Boer War, particularly as most of those involved in the formation of MO5(g) had served during that conflict. However, this can only be speculation, because no evidence has been unearthed that explicitly sets out any such link.

Additionally, Kell would almost certainly have read reports about how the intelligence services operated in other countries, such as Germany, France, Russia and India. He probably also drew on Britain's experiences in Ireland and combating Fenian bombings on mainland Britain, administering security in India and other such experiences throughout the British Empire. Indeed, a significant number of MO5(g)'s officers had served in India: in February 1917, eight of G Branch's twenty-seven officers had gained experience there.[29] The former Indian policemen who joined MO5(g) brought considerable skills with them, having successfully coped in a challenging environment surrounded 'by plots, intrigues and disturbances.'[30] Kell was also likely to have received advice from more senior officers who took a keen interest in intelligence. Doubtless, Holt-Wilson and other senior MO5(g) officers also had a notable impact. It is possible, however, that MO5(g)'s 'grand strategy' owed more to the Director of Military Intelligence (DMI) than to Kell – Kell merely applying and refining it. In a letter to Edmonds of 17 July 1942 regarding *The Times* obituary notice for Lieutenant-General Sir George Macdonough, the DMI for much of the First World War, Holt-Wilson explained Macdonough's position concerning counter-espionage, which illuminates the relative roles of Kell and the DMI:

> '*MacD. himself, (perhaps inherited in part from Edmonds), laid the foundations of the war legislation required for all Intelligence purposes, including Counter-Espionage. I took over all this legislative work from 1912 to 1940. For example, we started the last war with some 35, purely military Defence Regulations, as devised by MacD., which I saw expanded to some 250 regulations in the course of the war.*

> '*Similarly with the control of aliens, for which MacD. had sketched a tentative Order in Council. This I developed hand in hand with the Home Office on the outbreak of the war into the formidable Aliens Control legislation which has survived to the present day.*

> '*Full credit belongs however to MacD. and Edmonds for their revolutionary pre-vision in the inception of the above measures, but when we come to the actual work of spy-catching and making it difficult for enemy agents to ply their trade as spies or saboteurs, from 1909 onwards the credit must be given to K. and his staff.*'[31]

This interpretation, that Kell's superiors initially designed MO5(g)'s grand strategy while Kell applied and refined it, was endorsed by Cockerill, DSI and Kell's direct superior during the war, who described how he managed the Directorate of Special Intelligence in his memoirs:

> '[BCI – the *Bureau Central Inter-Allie* (BCI) was a clearing house used by the Allied countries to share intelligence other than that which dealt with military operations. See Chapter Four] was also authorised to communicate direct with the heads of all my sections. In this way such services as the Secret Service and counter-espionage, economic warfare, propaganda, and the Cable, Postal, and, to a great extent, the Press Censorships were all centralized in me as regards policy and general direction, and as regards administration and executive action effectively decentralized among the several sections of my Directorate of Special Intelligence.'[32]

With especial insight, Lady Kell's portrayal of her husband pointed to those who had the greatest influence on Kell's career. However, she did not, nor does any other available material, explicitly set out the precise contribution that they each made to MO5(g)'s grand strategy. According to Lady Kell, Kell 'would laughingly allude' to General Davies, who had first sought him for an intelligence post because of his linguistic abilities, 'as the father of the work, for he had backed Vernon with much enthusiasm, using his influence to help him on.' Macdonough 'became a close friend' and Kell 'was always sure of good advice and strong backing from him… But the man who always claimed to have picked Vernon out for this intensely important job which needed such careful and delicate handling, was Brigadier-General Sir James Edmonds' who '…became a great friend of ours in the years that followed.'[33]

Thus, it seems fair to conclude that Kell received considerable guidance about grand strategy from his superiors, particularly Edmonds during MO5(g)'s early years. So in matters of grand strategy, Kell was very much putting others' advice into practice, rather than taking charge of designing it himself. However, aside from a few personal examples which have already been noted, it is not possible to measure these influences on Kell more precisely owing to a lack of documentary evidence in this particular area.

Were there any debates over strategy within MO5(g)? What alternatives were put forward? There is no surviving material relating directly to this question, thus there is no evidence upon which to base a firm conclusion. For example, there are no reports from the meetings of MO5(g)'s Standing Advisory Committee, which may well have considered such things. Compared with Cumming's more personal account of MI1c, Kell's brief office diary represents '…the mere keeping of a record'. It contains little of a personal nature or Kell's responses to events and 'virtually nothing of any sort of debate with himself.'[34]

However, there was some later questioning of MO5(g)'s strategy by those outside of it, including officials from other government departments that worked with MO5(g). Moylan of the Home Office's Aliens Division felt that the department was mistakenly focusing on enemy aliens, perhaps so that it could simply be seen to be taking action, when the real threat came from British subjects and neutral aliens. By contrast, in early 1915, a number of Conservative politicians attacked Asquith's Liberal Government, particularly Reginald McKenna as Home Secretary, for being too lax regarding enemy aliens living in Britain.

Defence of the Realm Regulations (DRR)/ Aliens Restriction Orders (ARO)

The preventive side of MO5(g)'s strategy was centred on two key measures: DRRs to protect sensitive information, and AROs to control aliens.

Despite the round-up of Steinhauer's network at the outbreak of war, there were clearly continuing fears of potential German agents, notably in the opening months of hostilities, and subsequent chapters will illustrate how changes in wartime legislation arose from perceptions of the need to plug particular gaps.

Emergency legislation during the war was in the form of two Acts of Parliament and the Orders made under them, plus certain supplementary Acts and Orders. Aliens Restriction Orders (ARO) were issued under the Aliens Restriction Act (ARA) and applied to all aliens, enemy or friendly, but not to British subjects. Defence of the Realm

Regulations (DRR) were issued under DORA and applied to all individuals regardless of nationality, including British subjects. The DORA was originally designed as a code that would embody the powers of the executive in wartime for solely military purposes including firstly, counter-espionage and secondly, the measures required to defend any given area from a threatened invasion. The DORA conferred much more drastic powers for wartime use than OSA 1911 which had really been a way to cope with a threat to national security in peacetime.

Following a decision of the Committee of Imperial Defence (CID) taken more than two years before the First World War, the civil power (Home Office) was to administer the ARA, while the DORA was to be administered by a number of Competent Military Authorities (CMAs), military commanders nominated by the Army Council, each exercising his jurisdiction over a stated district. Following an agreement between the Army Council and the Admiralty, parts of the UK were administered separately by Competent Naval Authorities (CNAs). Generally, the officer commanding in each district would also be the CMA. The head of MO5(g) and several other MO5(g) officers were CMAs. However, their position differed from the district CMAs in that they had the power to act throughout the UK. The CMA organisation was conducted by instructions from the Army Council, passed through GHQ Great Britain. In certain matters, an individual district CMA could not issue an order, such as for the removal of suspects, without the approval of the Army Council, which practically meant the consent of MO5(g). Indeed, this supervision of the work done by CMAs all over Britain was a very important aspect of the Preventive Branch's work as it included the delicate task of making sure that CMAs did not misuse their powers in situations that did not really require them, or leave them unapplied when circumstances necessitated that they should be used. Part I of the ARO was administered by the aliens' officers who were sanctioned by the Home Secretary and aided by the Military Control Officers (MCO) at ports. The distinction between the regulations administered by the police and those by CMAs lay in the fact that the CMAs carried out the provisions of the DORA, namely regulations that applied to all individuals, regardless of nationality, whereas the police carried out the provisions of Part II of the ARO, rules, mainly concerned with registration, that applied to aliens as such.[35]

In the early months of the First World War, the original versions of the ARA and the DORA were expanded considerably by means of Orders in Council. The whole shape of the DORA had to be changed and a new version, the Defence of the Realm (Consolidation) Regulations 1914, was introduced on 28 November 1914. The main aim of this emergency legislation was given in the DORA Act:

> '(a) to prevent persons communicating with the enemy or obtaining information for that purpose or any purpose calculated to jeopardise the success of the operations of any of His Majesty's Forces or to assist the enemy; or –
> (b) to secure the safety of any means of communication, or of railways, docks, or harbours.'[36]

At its full development, the preventive legislation of the DORA comprised some sixty-six paragraphs and sub-paragraphs. A considerable number of them did not concern

MO5(g), some were only of minor importance, but particular ones were intimately bound up with MO5(g) and especially the Preventive Branch. MO5(g) shared the administration of some of them with other War Office sections, but MO5(g)'s role was unusual in that it represented the interests of the Directorate of Special Intelligence (MI5-9) in all DRR.

A distinction should be made between the spheres of policy and administration. It was MO5(g)'s duty, and this was especially the Preventive Branch's work, to frame the special intelligence measures in general. Thus, it was involved from the policy perspective with a number of regulations the administration of which did not concern MO5(g). For analytical purposes the original DRR can be separated into six divisions, as follows:

A. General or Interpretative Regulations.
B. Regulations prohibiting espionage and similar activities.
C. Control Regulations for Purposes concerned with Military Operations.
D. Local Restrictions for Special Intelligence purposes.
E. Personal Restrictions for Special Intelligence purposes.
F. Miscellaneous (Preservation of Morale, etc.)

MI5 was most concerned with B then D and E.[37]

Regulations 18, 18A, 19 and 19A prohibited espionage. DRR20 protected telegraph and telephone communications. Regulations 21, 21A, 22, 25, 25A and 26 related to signalling and other forms of communication. DRR22A, 22B, 24, 24A and 24B covered the evasion of postal and telegraph censorship. Regulation 23 provided powers to prevent those suspected of communicating with the enemy from embarking at ports. DRR27, 27A, 27B and 27C regulated the publication of reports, information, etc.[38]

DRR18, 18A and 19 formed a key self-contained set that could be referred to as 'the spy section'. During wartime they assumed the role of OSA 1911, being far more severe. They dealt with the civil spy, who gathered and passed on information to the enemy, not the military spy who sneaked through the enemy's lines for intelligence covertly or disguised, and thus they were counter-espionage regulations in the fullest sense. DRR18 included three main prohibitions against spying:

'1. You are not to collect etc., information of the kind specified.
2. You are not to collect etc., undefined but dangerous information.
3. You are not to have in your possession any document containing such information without lawful excuse.'[39]

It was irrelevant whether such information was true or false, and its gathering and communication could follow an indefinite pattern, such as papers and oral statements, therefore there was a very wide potential range for an offence. 18A used a very broad definition of a 'spy', and the onus was placed on the accused to prove that he did not realise, and did not have any cause to suspect, that whoever he was communicating with, or trying to communicate with, was a spy. The definition of 'communicating' was also a very wide one, because if it was proven that a spy's name or address, or information was found on an individual, or was given to him under dubious circumstances, or he was communicating with a spy address, he had to prove his innocence despite these circumstances. Lastly, a spy address referred to any person, wherever they were, used to receive enemy communications.[40]

Local restrictions for Special Intelligence (SI) purposes were provided by the following DRR, which regulated the approach and entry into places of national or military importance: 28 concerned the penalty on injury to railways, etc; 28A regarding restriction on access to railways, Government land, foreshore, docks, etc; 29 concerned the prohibition on approaching defence works, etc; 29A concerned prohibition on entering safeguarded factories; 29B regarded prohibition on entering special military areas; 29C concerned prohibition on certain individuals entering shipbuilding yards.

Personal restrictions for SI purposes were provided by the following DRR, which regulated the civil population's movements, and aided the Preventive Branch in curtailing the potential threat posed by suspicious and undesirable individuals: 14 provided power to remove suspects from specified areas; 14B sanctioned imposing restrictions on, or the internment of, individuals of hostile origin and associations; 14C prohibited embarking or landing without a passport; 14D covered restrictions on British subjects leaving the UK as crew members of neutral ships; 14E gave power to prohibit aliens from going to Ireland; 14F restricted British subjects entering enemy countries, and 14G concerned restriction on embarkation at ports in the UK. Paragraphs 14 and 14B dealt with inland controls and the others with frontier control, while sections 14 and 14B provided the power to place dangerous and disaffected individuals under personal restrictions, who were not enemy subjects and therefore could not be interned under the royal prerogative. DRR 14B was a notably powerful preventive measure, because:

> 'Under 14B, the Secretary of State can by order require a person of hostile origin or associations to remain in, or proceed to and reside in, any specified place, or to comply with any specified directions as to reporting to the police, restriction of movement, and otherwise, or to be interned in any specified place; provided that, on the recommendation of a C.N. or M.A., or of the advisory committee on internment and deportation or of a specially appointed committee, it appears to the Secretary of State that in view of the person's hostile origin or associations, it is expedient, for securing the public safety or the defence of the Realm that he or she shall be subjected to the above restrictions and obligations.'[41]

The CMAs were concerned with recommending people for restriction or internment under DRR 14B. However, in practice, following the first two cases, the Home Secretary decided only to consider the cases emanating from the MO5(g) officers who were also CMAs. It had proven impossible for the considerable number of CMAs, most lacking legal experience, to conduct a uniform system. Indeed, during the early stages of the war, MO5(g) had warned CMAs that recommendations under 14B had to be founded on strong evidence and had to be accompanied by written statements from those giving the evidence. However, the recommendations of local CMAs directly to the Home Secretary proved unsatisfactory, so it was decided that this could only be done by the MO5(g) officers who were also CMAs, including the head of the Preventive Branch, in whose branch this work fell, as a duty of Section 3. DRR 14, having power to remove suspects from specified areas, was later dealt with in a similar fashion, no order took effect before ratification by the Army Council, effectively the Preventive Branch.[42]

DRR56, 56A, 57, 57A and 58 regulated the procedure for prosecutions. The most important point for MO5(g) was that trials could take place in camera, which prevented the enemy from learning which agent had been caught, and protected the identity of witnesses and officials whom it was unadvisable to make known.

The original DORA was considerably amended and enlarged by Orders in Council of 12 August and 17 September 1914. These provisions were amalgamated with the original regulations on 28 November in the Defence of the Realm (Consolidation) Regulations, 1914. As published, the DORA (Consolidation Stage) was split into ten groups, rather than six as before:

1. General Regulations. No.1.
2. Powers of Competent Naval and Military Authorities, etc. Nos.2-17.
3. Provisions respecting the collection and communication of information &c. Nos. 18-27.
4. Provisions against injury to railways, military works, &c., Nos. 28, 29.
5. Provisions as to arms and explosives. Nos. 30-35.
6. Provisions as to Navigation. Nos. 36-39.
7. Miscellaneous Offences. Nos. 40-50.
8. Powers of Search, Arrest &c. Nos. 51-55.
9. Trial and Punishment of Offences. Nos. 56-58.
10. Supplemental. Nos. 59-63.[43]

The main amendments that the Preventive Branch was involved in were as follows: Number 16 (later 21) regarding carrier pigeons; 13A (later 54) concerning letter smuggling; 16A (later 22) for wireless telegraph apparatus; 16C (later 24) about new postal communications; 21 and 27 (later 27 and 67) regarding the prevention of reports liable to spread alarm or disaffection; 24A (later 14) concerning powers of imposing personal restrictions on suspects; and 16B (later 23) covered the prevention of the embarkation of any person suspected of attempting to leave the country in order to communicate directly or indirectly with the enemy.

The Preventive Branch's chief duties in relation to the DORA were firstly to attend inter-departmental committees and conferences to discuss amendments to regulations that impacted on MO5(g); secondly, the military examination of the resulting draft Orders in Council; thirdly, the drafting of circular letters to be issued by the Army Council and public warning notices; fourth, interpreting the regulations for administrative purposes to the relevant authorities; fifth, examining the credentials of applicants for permits to visit protected areas; sixth, examining CMAs proposals to issue restriction or removal orders under DRR14.

The most important of the amendments and additions to the original DORA made through the action of the Preventive Branch were that DRR9 gave CMAs powers to remove part, not just all, of the inhabitants of any area. DDR18 prohibited the collection or attempted collection, recording or eliciting of information on whatever subject that could be useful to the enemy. DDR19 prohibited photographing, sketching, etc, of things other than military or naval works if it was done with the intention of assisting the enemy. DDR24 prohibited non-postal communication to and from the UK, including the suppression of private and unregistered courier services. DDR 45 prohibited tampering with or forging military, naval, or police passes, etc, or impersonation of their rightful bearers, for whatever purpose.[44]

MO5(g)'s role in enforcing DORA should not be exaggerated and needs to be seen in the wider context. It has been calculated that actions brought by MO5(g) resulted in the conviction or executive action under DORA of 1,742 cases between 1914 and 1919. However, this represented only a minute fraction of the action taken under emergency legislation. Over 136,000 people were proceeded against in 1916, for example.[45] The historian, David Englander, places MO5(g)'s role in the wider context, noting that '[m]ost offences were dealt with locally, by court-martial or by the civil power, depending on the gravity of the offence and status of the offender.' When espionage, or the influence of a foreign power, was suspected the case was passed on to MO5(g).[46]

Although not changed quite so much, the ARA was also re-issued during September 1914. The ARA's aim was implicit in its full title:

'An Act to enable His Majesty in time of war or imminent national danger or great emergency by Order in Council to impose Restrictions on Aliens and make such provisions as appear necessary or expedient for carrying such restrictions into effect.'[47]

The ARA could impose restrictions for several purposes, all of which were of interest to the Preventive Branch. Firstly, it could be used to prohibit aliens from landing in the UK, either at specific places or generally, and it imposed conditions and restrictions on aliens arriving or landing at any port in the UK. Secondly, it could be used to prohibit aliens from embarking in the UK, either at specific places or generally, and imposed restrictions and conditions on aliens embarking in the UK. Thirdly, to deport aliens from the UK. Fourth, to require aliens to live and remain within specific places and districts. Fifth, it prohibited aliens from living or remaining in any areas specified in the ARA. Sixth, it required aliens living in the UK to obey such provisions over registration, change of residence, travelling, and others as made by the ARA. Seventh, to appoint officers to put the ARA into effect, and to confer on these officers and the Secretary of State such powers as were required for the purposes of the ARA. Eighth, to impose penalties on individuals who aided or abetted any contravention of the ARA, and to impose such obligations and restrictions on ships masters and all other individuals specified in the Order as appeared required to give effect to the ARA. Ninth, it conferred upon such people as were specified in the ARA such powers of arrest, detention, search of premises or persons, and otherwise, as were set out in the Order, and for any other ancillary matters for which it appeared apt to provide in order to give full effect to the Order. Tenth, and for any other matters that appeared necessary or expedient for national security.[48]

The ARA gave general powers to a Secretary of State or officials acting under his authority such as aliens' officers or registration officers. The action taken under ARO Part I – restricting aliens entering or leaving the UK – was the concern of E (Control of Ports & Frontiers) Branch. ARO Part II included nearly all of the key measures to establish a preventive system throughout the UK. The main provisions were straightforward, namely to create a zone of prohibited areas to cover all of the areas where spies were most likely to gather valuable information. The zone developed to form a belt around the coast and the Aldershot military district. The first was because the enemy's main objective was naval information, and the second was the centre of military activity. Next, all aliens living in prohibited areas, and all enemy aliens wherever they lived, were made to register with the registration officers (the police) and to inform them of any change of address. Enemy aliens were not allowed to enter or live in a prohibited area unless they possessed a permit from the police. They were also prohibited from travelling more than five miles from their home unless they had a local registration officer's permit. Aliens were not allowed to possess telephones, photographic equipment, or military or naval maps, charts, or handbooks.[49]

In terms of alien control, a number of orders and amendments were introduced to the ARA (Consolidation Stage) between the outbreak of war and the end of 1914. ARO25A was of particular importance to counter-espionage because it forbade any change of name. In one move, MO5(g) cooperated with the Registrar-General in the compilation of a central register of all Belgian refugees in the UK which was also of real value to MO5(g). Belgian refugees required a police permit to enter prohibited areas and changes of address had to be reported. MO5(g)'s expertise was of considerable value in this. The ARA (Consolidation) Order 1914 Part III included paragraphs relevant to the Preventive Branch in the penalties and restrictions imposed on aliens breaching the regulations designed to hinder their serving the enemy both directly and indirectly, particularly 26, 27, 28, 29, 30 and 33.

The ARA's powers, mainly originated by the Preventive Branch, provided a strong hold over enemy aliens and aliens, within whose midst spies were primarily looked for. The Preventive Branch's work in relation to the ARA after the advent of war rested mostly in developing amendments to meet new challenges as they arose, such as the following additions: ARO22 prohibited the possession of some additional articles to the list of dangerous articles that had been prohibited; ARO25 provided the power to close clubs frequented by enemy aliens; 25A prohibited a change of name, and ARO27 prohibited passengers refusing to answer questions from aliens' officers or giving false statements to them. MO5(g) had been involved in preparing the original list of prohibited areas, and in their expansion. The Preventive Branch co-operated with the Home Office in revising and drafting forms used under the ARA. The Preventive Branch had the unique role of assessing the bona fides of applicants for permits for prohibited areas and other prohibited districts; the Preventive Branch obtained the necessary information from the records kept by the Organisation, Administration and Records Branch. The work of providing military advice and opinion on the desirability of allowing the exemption of enemy aliens from repatriation or internment in particular cases was devolved to the Preventive Branch.[50]

The ARA went largely unchanged throughout the war. Its great use was in the expanding area over which it was applied. Particular sections of Part II were originated by the Preventive Branch and proved of great value to them, especially those regarding hotel and lodging house registration (ARO20A), identity books (18B and C), aliens employed on munitions work (22A) (later the work of A Branch), and change of name of enemy aliens (25A).[51]

During the early part of the war, between August and December 1914, the Preventive Branch was predominantly concerned, in its administrative capacity, with the ARA, rather than the DORA. Even the DORA spy regulations required only normal investigative action by the Investigative Branch, with which the Preventive Branch was not immediately concerned. Thus the wholesale internment of enemy aliens under the royal prerogative involved primarily the Adjutant General's Directorate and not that of Military Operations, which included MO5(g). This internment of enemy aliens, from whom the enemy might recruit potential spies, greatly reduced what the Preventive Branch had to protect against. The number of alien enemies interned, excluding military or naval prisoners, by 1 November 1914 was 17,283; at 1 December it stood at 18,203 and, by 1 January 1915, this figure had risen to 18,333. This demonstrates the degree to which the ARA, initially devised by the Preventive Branch, aided it in removing potential threats during the opening months of the war.[52]

In October 1914, MO5(g) found that some counties and boroughs had not forwarded any extracts from their aliens register regarding those who had served in any army, navy or police force. It seemed unlikely that there could be none in these areas and MO5(g) drew the Home Office's attention to this matter, and it was requested that returns of nil should be returned if this was actually so.

As previously stated, enemy aliens were prohibited from possessing telephones. As such, the policy was not to allow new telephones; however, because aliens could use call offices, it was considered best to leave telephones with those who already possessed them and then to tap their conversations.

During the war, the US Embassies in London and Berlin had agreed to transmit special printed enquiry forms by which means families could obtain information about their relatives who were POWs. MO5(g) realised that this could also possibly provide a means of communicating with the enemy and so the Home Office passed these forms on to MO5(g) before sending them back as it was felt on occasion that the information sent was possibly a code.

MO5(g) also impressed upon the GPO the need to issue orders that all telegrams sent should bear the sender's name and address on the back, which proposal the GPO subsequently enacted. Even though this did not automatically guarantee that the name and address were genuine, it still helped to confirm suspicions when a telegram was held up and the original sender appeared not to exist. These examples demonstrate the various matters that the Preventive Branch had to consider and legislate for during the first few months of the war.[53]

It is relevant to examine the constitutional and historical basis for preventive legislation. Two perspectives influenced the issue of obtaining emergency powers for the executive's use in wartime or an invasion, namely those of international law and the British constitution. Obviously, the British Government's duties and rights toward its own subjects were no concern of international law. Rather, the issue of concern was the wartime treatment of aliens in general, and, of course, hostile aliens. The general consensus from the point of view of international law was that the state had a right to enact the following legislation: firstly, regarding aliens in general, they could only be detained to the extent that a national subject could be legally detained. They could be tried, and, if found guilty, punished for any crime committed in the national territory. They could be deported from, or denied entry to, the national territory for cause. Secondly, hostile aliens could be made subject to special police supervision and regulation, but they could not be made prisoners of war unless they committed an offence against the laws of war.

They could nonetheless be interned if they freely overstayed the time generally granted to leave the national territory; the same applied if their conduct or position afforded reasons for special treatment, and possibly if they belonged to the enemy's armed forces. They could only be deported en bloc in very special cases. They could be removed from the theatre of war and areas open to attack. If they provided help or information to the enemy, they could be treated as prisoners of war, traitors, or spies and punished accordingly.

Indeed, regulations enacted under the DORA and ARA 1914 were constructed largely on this basis. The broad principle was that hostile aliens could be interned individually or on mass if their being at large posed a real threat to national security. However, whatever the law of nations, it did not necessarily follow that the British executive actually had these powers from a constitutional perspective. Thus, it was extremely important to the Preventive Branch to know the exact extent of the powers that it could rely on in an emergency. The powers conferred in the first version of the DORA in 1914 had been considered in 1888 and subsequently in 1895, but these measures had never actually been put to parliament before.[54]

The internment of enemy subjects did not depend upon statutory powers derived from emergency legislation. It formed part of the royal prerogative and the courts had no right to challenge it. Internment was the most drastic and useful of all the controls. The Preventive Branch in particular always pushed for all enemy subjects to be interned, on the grounds that, to be exempt, a person born in an enemy country should be made to show that not only had he done nothing to help the enemy, but that he was really hostile to the country of his birth. Enemy subjects at large were viewed as a possible threat to national security and the government accepted the principle, in theory, that all doubtful cases should be interned. However, the civil authorities tended to interpret this principle in a way that MO5(g) felt was too lenient. Although a tougher stance was taken towards the end of the war, this situation still caused considerable concern even when most male enemy aliens had been interned. Contrasted with internment, the less strict provisions of the ARA concerning registration and entry into prohibited areas were used on the relatively less dangerous remainder of enemy aliens and other aliens, the latter it was felt being in many cases no safer than Germans or Austrians.

From the mass of aliens registered by MO5(g), a few hundred were picked as possible suspects deserving particular attention because they lived near vulnerable points, and/or they had been officers in the German or Austrian armies, or for similar reasons. Reports were received periodically from the police about the connections and activities of these possible suspects, and individuals were added to, or removed from, the list as experience suggested.[55]

When it came to internment, MO5(g)'s leadership supported a hardline policy which was informed by ethnocentric prejudice as well as by the needs of preventive security. Holt-Wilson regarded 'all persons of German blood' as security risks – despite the presence in MO5(g) of the half-German, Lieutenant William Edward Hinchley Cooke, who had been born and raised in Germany to a British father and a German mother.[56] Holt-Wilson told the Aliens Sub-committee of the Committee of Imperial Defence in June 1915:

'The patriotism and discipline inherited with their blood which lifts some men beyond the fear of death will also inspire Germans gladly to risk and suffer any penalty, and to disregard all laws of honour and humanity, that they may contribute but a trifling service to their fatherland at the cost of their enemy.'

Those of German blood who had spent much of their lives in Britain were considered to be even more dangerous than recent arrivals: 'Long residence in Britain adds greatly to the mischief to be apprehended from an alien enemy.' The longer they had been in Britain, the greater their capacity to damage the war effort. MO5(g) had some reason to suspect that German intelligence had long-term 'sleepers' in Britain. Indeed, Karl Ernst, the 'Kaiser's postman', who played a key role in Steinhauer's communications with his agents, was well integrated into British life and was discovered after his arrest in August 1914 to have British nationality. Frederick Adolphus Schroeder, alias 'Gould', probably Steinhauer's most successful pre-war spy, had an English mother, spoke perfect English and established himself in the quintessentially English profession of publican. But though MO5(g)'s fears of unidentified German sleepers were reasonable, they turned out to be misplaced. The most striking characteristic of the German spies detected after the first year of the war is that most were not German.[57]

In early 1915, the government claimed that 'Every single alien enemy in this country is known and is at this present moment under constant police surveillance.' For the popular press, however, and probably for most of the public, surveillance was not enough and a 'spy mania' ensued, combined with outrage at alleged, but mostly untrue, German war crimes – factors which provoked anger at the government's reluctance to intern just a handful of enemy aliens. Thus, in May 1915, apparently against his better judgement, Asquith, then Prime Minister, conceded to public pressure and Reginald McKenna, then Home Secretary, concluded reluctantly that anti-alien sentiment ran so high that male enemy aliens might well be safer if interned. From that point, the government adopted the principle that all enemy aliens should be interned unless they could prove themselves to be harmless, although this was an inconsistent policy and was not always seen through. Thirty-two thousand individuals (mostly men of military age) were interned, another 20,000 (mostly women, children and non-combatant men) were repatriated, and the remainder subjected to numerous restrictions.[58]

FIRST CONTACT

Spy Mania

The outbreak of hostilities caused spy mania to climb to unprecedented heights. There were many reports of German agents plotting disruption who were in contact with the Fatherland by various, but unlikely, channels and all of these were false.[59] On the first day of the war, 4 August 1914, Basil Thomson, the Assistant Commissioner of the Metropolitan Police, and in charge of the CID of which Special Branch was a part (see Chapter Five), was informed that 'secret saboteurs' had blown up a culvert near Aldershot and a railway bridge in Kent but an inspection of both 'targets' carried out the next day found both to be untouched.[60] Thomson also came across numerous cases of suspected illicit signalling to the enemy, particularly at night to guide U-Boats and Zeppelins to their targets. None of these suspicions were found to be correct.[61] In Thomson's words, spy mania 'assumed a virulent epidemic form accompanied by delusions which defied treatment… It attacked all classes indiscriminately and seemed even to find its most fruitful soil in sober, stolid, and otherwise truthful people.'[62] Thomson cites an entertaining example of this spy mania, which is worth quoting at length:

'On one occasion the authorities dispatched to the Eastern Counties a car equipped with a Marconi apparatus and two skilled operators to intercept any illicit messages that might be passing over the North Sea. They left at noon; at 3 they were under lock and key in Essex. After an exchange of telegrams they were set free, but at 7 P.M. they telegraphed from the police cells in another part of the county, imploring help. When again liberated they refused to move without the escort of a Territorial Officer in uniform, but on the following morning the police of another county had got hold of them and telegraphed, "Three German spies arrested with car and complete wireless installation, one in uniform of British officer."'[63]

Spy fever was not unique to the UK. Germany, France and most other countries at war were similarly afflicted and there were also spy scares in the battle zone.[64] Similarly to the UK, none of these other countries managed to completely cure spy mania during the First World War.

Inevitably, the work of MO5(g) increased and was reflected in organisational changes. Moreover, in the prevailing atmosphere of spy mania, and owing to pre-war invasion and spy scares, it was widely believed that Germany had hundreds of agents in the UK. On 9 October 1914, the Home Office issued a statement designed to allay the public's anxiety.[65] Although the level of hysteria died down considerably as the war progressed, thanks largely to news of the successes of British counter-espionage, there continued to be constant questions about espionage in parliament throughout the war.[66] However, criticisms in parliament tended to be against the perceived laxity of the government's policy towards enemy aliens, arguing that all enemy aliens should be interned, rather than against MO5(g).[67]

The case of Stephen Horvath, the Austro-Hungarian principal of the Corona Lamp Works, in London provides one example of this spy mania and how MO5(g) handled it. On 25 February 1914, the police were informed that the children of a foreigner named Horvath attended school in Wandsworth under the name Howard. They were also reported to have been friendly with the Goulds, an alias adopted by the convicted spy, Frederick Schroeder. A check was put on Horvath's correspondence, which was found to be potentially suspicious, but also possibly genuine. The warrant was cancelled after 30 April 1914, but on 15 October 1914, MO5(g) reported Horvath to the Criminal Investigation Department (CID) as a suspicious character who should be watched. On 26 October, the police concluded that there was nothing suspicious to report. In July 1915, Horvath, who had registered as a Hungarian subject, applied for exemption from internment, which was granted. On 9 May 1917, Horvath's neighbours insisted on his internment and Wandsworth residents signed a petition to this effect. Nothing was done, because it was found that Horvath had an enemy, Mrs Clutterbuck Barnett, and a neighbour, William Jones, wrote that Horvath really was loyal.[68]

The Lody Case

The outbreak of war brought important changes to MO5(g)'s investigative methods. The second investigative stage, namely collecting evidence, exhibited notable differences between peacetime and wartime. During peacetime, it could be a drawn out and painstaking process, involving the repeated surveillance of an agent and the delay of arrest until, from a series of means worked out between MO5(g), the police and the GPO, it was confirmed that particular incriminating evidence would be found on the suspect or in his lodgings. During wartime, the agent's arrival could be known in advance; he could be invited, or taken, to Scotland Yard on landing, duly cautioned and cross-examined, and if he failed this interrogation, he could be arrested. Indeed, this questioning could be used in evidence against him.[69] In his account of Scotland Yard, Basil Thomson explained why, during wartime, a spy could be interrogated before a charge was brought against him and how this questioning could be used as evidence against him…

> '…under what are known as the "Judges Rules", which preclude the questioning of prisoners whom the police are about to charge with a serious offence. During the war these rules were held to be in abeyance in spy cases, when it was explained to the judges that unless suspected spies could be questioned about the meaning of cipher documents they were carrying, it would be impossible to bring them to justice…'[70]

Mr (later Sir) Archibald Henry Bodkin of the DPP's office led for the prosecution in every spy trial during the First World War. Born in 1862, Bodkin was called to the Bar in 1885, knighted in 1917, and served as DPP from 1920-1930. He died in 1957.[71]

Charles A. Inglis came to the UK via Denmark and Norway, where he obtained a certificate of American nationality. He arrived at Newcastle on 27 August 1914 and went straight to Edinburgh where he stayed for about a month with occasional absences of one night, during which he made trips to London and Peebles. From Edinburgh he went on to Liverpool and then crossed to Ireland. He communicated with Stockholm in a telegraphic code and sent, under cover to the same address, letters in German containing spy reports *en clair* and directed to 'Stammer, Courbierestrasse, Berlin' (See Graves case).[72] Lody has been viewed as 'easily the worst equipped' of all the spies Germany sent to the UK during the First World War. He wrote his letters to Sweden quite openly, never even using an invisible ink.[73] He signed himself 'Charles', 'Lody', and 'Nazi'.[74] Lody's use of the word 'Nazi' is an intriguing and unsolved mystery. The NSDAP was not formed until after the end of the First World War. Members of the NSDAP did not call themselves Nazis. It was a term of abuse coined by their opponents. The available documentation does not provide any clues as to what Lody meant by the term Nazi, or why he chose to sign himself by that name. It is possible he meant 'nationalist' or something along those lines. His mission appears to have been of a general nature, although he was to stay in England until the first naval battle against the German fleet took place, when he was to report British naval losses and then go on to America.

Since 4 August 1914, all post from the UK to Norway and Sweden had been brought to London and checked for letters to certain suspect addresses. Lody telegraphed to a known Stockholm spy address on 30 August 1914, and, having to sign with his name, wrote 'Charles Inglis'. His first letter, posted on 4 September 1914, was read, photographed and forwarded. Others were treated similarly in the hope of learning more. Eventually, a letter dated 8 September 1914 came through to 'Charles A. Inglis c/o Thomas Cook, Edinburgh'. However, Inglis never called to collect it. At what precise moment the traveller Inglis was connected with the writer of the letters does not appear in MI5's records. However, two long reports signed 'Nazi' of 27 and 30 September 1914 were retained and orders for Lody's arrest were issued. He was arrested on 2 October 1914 at 9.45 p.m. by District Inspector Cheesman of the Royal Irish Constabulary at the Great Southern Hotel, Killarney, Ireland, while on his way to Queenstown, the main British naval base there.[75] After he was cautioned, Inglis responded, '*What is this: me a German agent? Take care now; I am an American citizen.*' A search revealed a small notebook that contained a list of cruisers that had been sunk in the North Sea, names and addresses of people in Berlin and Hamburg, and what seemed to be the key to a code. Inside Inglis's jacket, a tailor's ticket was found sewn into the breast pocket which read 'J. Steinberg, Berlin, R.C.H. Lody 8.5.14'. Clearly, Inglis had some explaining to do![76]

Carl Lody, German spy. Born in Germany, Lody had lived in the USA and was able to pass convincingly as a US citizen. He posed as an American tourist but was detected by a telegram check on a known spy address. He was shot on 6 November 1914. (Queensferry History Group)

Interrogation revealed that Lody was thirty-nine years of age in August 1914 and had served as an officer in the German Navy between 1900–1901. He then transferred to the First Naval Reserve and found employment in the merchant navy. By 1912, he was working as a tourist agent, running excursions for the Hamburg-Amerika Line. That year he married an American lady of German descent who he met while she was on a tour of Europe and who was the daughter of a wealthy brewer in Omaha. Subsequently, Lody planned to make his life in the USA. However, the marriage was dissolved in spring 1914 following which, Lody's former father-in-law gave him $10,000 in compensation for his financial losses. Lody found himself in Berlin in July 1914 as the war clouds gathered. He applied to be released from the Second Naval Reserve because he had been unfit for active service since an illness in 1904. He was called for an interview by German Naval Intelligence in August 1914 and asked to undertake a spying mission to the UK. Although he wanted to return to the USA and to refuse to become a spy, he felt obliged to do his duty.[77]

Lody was the first spy to be tried by court-martial since the start of the First World War. He had used the cover of a genuine American emergency passport belonging to

Charles A. Inglis, who had deposited it for a visa at the Foreign Office in Berlin where it had disappeared.[78] On 2 November 1914, the court assembled to hear the closing arguments. Lody's defence counsel, Mr George Elliott KC, told the court:

> 'First of all, sir, may I say on behalf of Lieutenant Lody that it is by his own personal wish here, and as his advocate, I say, and frankly say before you, and from his point of view I say it fearlessly before you that he came into this country in the service of his country; that he came into this country as a German actuated by patriotic motives; that he came here, secondly, in obedience to suggestions of his officer superior on command; and, thirdly, that he came here absolutely voluntarily in the sense that he was not personally compelled to come and entirely at his own expense.

> 'I therefore wish to approach this case, if I may, on behalf of this man for whom I plead – as pleading in the sense which I have told you – not as a miserable coward asking for forgiveness for his offence, not as some fear-stricken wretch whom the thought of punishment reduces to a condition in which both his mental and physical faculties are destroyed, but as a man born in a land of which he is proud, whose history and traditions he cherishes. His own grandfather was a great soldier who held a fortress against Napoleon; and it is in that position that he wishes to stand before you here today, as a man who, believing it to be his duty and his noblest mission, took upon himself that which subjects him admittedly to conditions if he were detected from which he would be the last to shrink.'[79]

It was against these noble standards of patriotism and courage that all those who followed in Lody's footsteps would be judged. The courage with which Lody faced his end only added to the respect that observers had for him. He showed his decency when he wrote to thank the officer in charge of Wellington Barracks for how he was treated whilst detained there awaiting execution:

> '*Sir, I feel it my duty as a German Officer to express my sincere thanks and appreciation towards the staff of Officers and men who were in charge of my person during my confinement. Their kind and considered treatment has called my highest esteem and admiration as regards good-fellowship even towards the Enemy, and if I may be permitted I would thank you for make this known to them.*

> *I am sir, with profound respect,*
> *Carl Hans Lody, Senior Lieutenant, Imperial German Naval Res. II.D.*'[80]

Lody also wrote to his family in Germany:

> '*My DEAR ONES,*
> *I have trusted in God and He has decided. My hour has come, And I must start on the journey through the Dark Valley like so many of my comrades in this terrible War of Nations. May my life be offered as a humble offering on the altar of the Fatherland.*

A hero's death on the battlefield is certainly finer, but such is not to be my lot, and I die here in the Enemy's country silent and unknown, the consciousness that I die in the service of the Fatherland makes death easy.

The Supreme Court-Martial of London has sentenced me to death for Military Conspiracy. Tomorrow I shall be shot here in the Tower. I have had just judges, and I shall die as an Officer, not as a spy.

Farewell. God bless you,
Hans'[81]

It was suggested that Lody's death sentence should be commuted to penal servitude for life. However, Kell was wholeheartedly against this, feeling strongly that Lody should be executed as a deterrent. In Felstead's words, it 'was argued, with excellent reason, that the execution of a spy and the public announcement thereof would have a most deterrent effect on future German spies who might be thinking of coming to this country.'[82] According to Lady Kell, her husband regarded Lody as a 'really fine man' and 'felt it deeply that so brave a man should have to pay the death penalty.'[83] Thomson held up Lody as 'a good example of the patriotic spy.'[84] He was shot in the Tower of London on 6 November 1914.[85] His execution took place there partly because, in MO5(g)'s effort to deter others, it was hoped that its gruesome history would 'place a chill in the heart of a potential enemy agent and a doubt in the mind of all but the most committed spy.'[86] As he was being taken to face the firing squad, Lody said to the Assistant Provost Marshal, 'I suppose you will not shake hands with a spy?' The Assistant Provost Marshal replied, 'No, but I will shake hands with a brave man.'[87]

Through enquiries made by MI1c, the name of the agent with whom Lody communicated in Stockholm was established as 'K. Leipziger'.

Some uncorroborated evidence suggested that Lody had visited King's Lynn and received telegrams there under the names of Inglis and Sideface. As a result, special enquiries were made there about the steps taken to guard against the arrival of undesirable aliens.[88]

Reginald Drake, the counter-espionage investigator, had requested that Lody's trial be held in camera, but he was overruled because of the feeling in Whitehall that a public court martial would promote the official success in dealing with German espionage in Britain. If the trial had taken place in camera, Drake had intended to convey false information to the enemy based on their not knowing which of their agents had been caught. Thus the Lody case might have developed into a double-cross system as happened during the Second World War, with the intent of feeding disinformation to the enemy. However, Whitehall's insistence on public trials and court-martials of spies made such a double-cross system in the First World War impossible.[89] During the Second World War the Germans named a destroyer after Lody.

Control at Ports

On 5 August 1914 an attempt was made immediately after the outbreak of war to prevent undesirable aliens from entering or leaving the UK with the issue of the ARA. Alien enemies were prohibited from entering or leaving the UK without a Home Office

Counter-espionage measures at British ports in August 1914 were rather superficial. This soon prompted MI5 to post its representatives to the ports to advise the Home Office's aliens' officers about counter-espionage matters. (Preston Guardian via Lancashire Evening Post)

permit and no alien passengers were allowed to enter or leave the country apart from through specified approved ports.[90] Other ports were declared prohibited.[91] All passenger traffic was soon restricted to the approved ports because the shipping firms found that it was not profitable to keep their services at other ports open only for British subjects. Under the ARA, a Home Office alien's officer, responsible to the Home Office's Aliens Branch, was appointed at every approved port to supervise passenger traffic, and authorised to stop any suspicious individuals embarking or landing. Passengers were also supervised by customs and police officers.[92]

In reality, the control exercised by the aliens' officers at the ports in September 1914 was rather superficial.[93] Felstead notes in his 1920 study that at the outbreak of war:

'... there was no ready-made system for dealing with the large numbers of neutrals who came through our ports, and it was primarily owing to this cause that Germany was enabled to send many spies to this country, usually in the guise of a commercial traveller of South American or Dutch origin. We had no means of sifting the harmless trader from the German agent who came spying under the cloak of commerce.'[94]

In September 1914, an agent of MO5(g) was sent to Folkestone to inform MO5(g) of the measures put into effect by police and aliens officers. Passports were not stamped and '...there was practically no check whatever on passengers going in or out.'[95] This system of control had three inherent defects. Firstly, the Home Office aliens' officers were not in contact with MO5(g); secondly, they were not trained in counter-espionage work; and thirdly, owing to the considerable number of travellers, there was insufficient time for a thorough examination at the ports.[96]

In MO5(g)'s reorganisation of 1 October 1914, the newly created C Branch's duties included port control.[97] MO5(g) sent Mr W Rolph and Mr Haag to Folkestone to keep a watching brief over Belgian refugees crossing from Ostend to Folkestone and to report suspicious cases. At that time, it was C Branch's duty to deal with the reports from Rolph and Haag and circulate warnings about suspects.[98] By November 1914, these port control duties had been assumed by B Branch.[99]

In the winter of 1914-1915, MO5(g) became concerned about the particularly serious danger posed by Belgian and French nationals, mainly women, travelling from the invaded territory via Holland and England, to visit relatives serving in the Allied armed forces and then going back to their homes behind enemy lines. For example, in response to a request from a Vice Consul, Mr Farmer, for a German governess, Marie Geugenbach, to be allowed to travel from Boulogne to Flushing via Folkestone, the Home Office robustly replied on 1 September 1914 that 'there appears to be no reason why the United Kingdom should be used as a means of transit from France to Germany of a German subject as to whom nothing is known.'[100] It was felt that this traffic provided a good chance for the Germans to acquire intelligence.[101] In order to ensure that urgent intelligence carried by this route would arrive too late for it to be of great use to the Germans, a temporary arrangement was introduced that all passengers travelling from France to Holland would be delayed in the UK for a short time.[102]

Belgian refugees

The beginning of September 1914 saw an influx of Belgian refugees, as thousands who had been made homeless by the German invasion fled to Britain.[103] MO5(g) was keenly aware of the potential opportunity that this influx of Belgians offered to the enemy, suggesting that:

> '...no measure short of official registration will serve to detect the presence among genuine refugees of undesirable persons who may have come to this country for the purpose of espionage or from other improper motive.'[104]

The first party of 437 refugees arrived on 6 September 1914. In addition, by the beginning of October, it was estimated that 2,000-2,500 Polish and Russian Jews from Belgium had also settled in England.[105] The sheer number of refugees made providing them with accommodation difficult.[106] Acting in concert with the Local Government Board, sub-committees of the War Refugees Committee were formed to provide suitable accommodation for the Belgians in areas that had been selected with the approval of the local police. Areas prohibited by the ARA were declared unsuitable. However, again, due to the sheer numbers, the Local Government Board had to take accommodation wherever it was available. This was deemed undesirable for military reasons and the War Office raised the issue with the Local Government Board with whom a conference was held in November 1914, the Admiralty, Home Office and War Office being represented, which decided:

1. Where Belgian refugees were not to settle.
2. Arrangements for investigation of identity and bona fides.
3. An organisation was to be set up for the reception of refugees to ensure that undesirables should be excluded from amongst those arriving from Holland.
4. Refugees not to be employed on munitions or public works such as railways, unless properly vouched for.[107]

Exceptions regarding where Belgians could not live were granted in favour of cases where they were related to people already living in prohibited areas, employed on munitions or by government contract companies, and wounded or convalescing soldiers on leave.[108] An Order in Council promulgating these conditions was issued on 28 November 1914.[109]

The question of finding jobs for Belgian refugees came to the fore soon after they arrived. In order to avoid competition with British workers, both Belgian and British labour were to be paid at the same rate. Companies' already employing alien workers had to submit their employees' names to the War Office (MO5(g)), which sent special Belgian investigators to check their bona fides. It was also agreed that prospective workers had to be taken on via the labour exchanges and that MO5(g) would examine them. All Aliens employed on confidential work were made to clearly understand that they were not permitted to leave the UK for the duration of the war, and employers were made to supply details of the kind of work of any alien worker who applied for permission to leave the UK.[110]

The Aliens Restriction (Belgian Refugees) Order was introduced in late November 1914 to provide further control over undesirable individuals who had managed to enter the UK posing as Belgian refugees. Its two main provisions were as follows: firstly, that all Belgian refugees had to register with the police wherever they were in the UK and report all changes of residence. They were also required to state their address and occupation in Belgium, plus provide certain information about their relatives. Secondly, that every Belgian refugee entering a prohibited area had to obtain a police permit first. This was eventually applied to aliens of every nationality, such that the special Belgian registration then became unnecessary.

Empire-wide threat

As the war progressed, MO5(g) became ever more convinced that Germany's covert activities stretched across the Empire, such that it became vital that it should be equipped to acquire intelligence wherever trouble was fomenting.[111] MO5(g) was particularly concerned that, as well as trying to collect military and naval intelligence, '...it was a special feature of Germany's policy to foster and encourage any movements of unrest and sedition directed against the British Empire.' Thus, the Sinn Fein movement in Ireland and America, the Home Rule and seditionary movements in India, the Egyptian nationalist, Turkish nationalist, Pan-Islamic and Greek royalist movements, which were supported and in some instances promoted by Germany, came to be MO5(g)'s concern.[112] However, it is now fairly clear, with the added benefit of hindsight, that Germany's support for such movements was never really more than half-hearted, being much rhetoric but of little actual material assistance, such that MO5(g) had exaggerated this threat. Germany never seriously considered landing troops in Ireland to support Sinn Fein in starting a rising, for example. Moreover, it is equally important to appreciate that the above quotation provides an expression of what MO5(g) felt at the time. This perceived reality was an important influence on the eventual formation of D (Overseas Special Intelligence) Branch, even if its analysis was someway off the mark. Indeed, examining what he terms Germany's 'global strategy', historian Hew Strachan relates that Germany certainly had intentions of promoting revolt throughout the British Empire, and gave out some signals to this effect. Typical of Germany's pan-Islamic rhetoric, on 30 July 1914, the Kaiser wrote of Britain:

> '*Now this entire structure must be ruthlessly exposed and the mask of Christian peacefulness be publicly torn away… Our consuls in Turkey and India, our agents, etc., must rouse the whole Moslem world into wild rebellion against this hateful, mendacious, unprincipled nation of shopkeepers; if we are ever going to shed our blood, then England must at least lose India.*'

Helmuth von Moltke, then Chief of the German General Staff, had soon drawn up a 'shopping list' that included, as the Kaiser told Enver Pasha, the Minister of War of the Ottoman Empire, on 15 August, Asia, India, Egypt and Africa. Metaphorically speaking, however, he had no money to buy what he wanted. Primarily, the army's European commitment left few resources for other areas. Communications between Germany and the Near East were very basic. The army also lacked knowledge of the areas where it sought influence. Essentially, Moltke was depending on diplomacy to create revolutionary armies.[113] However, the hollow nature of this threat may not have seemed so clear at the time. For example, some Irish rebels did hope for, if not really expect, German troops to land in Ireland. More tangibly, Germany later tried to support the Easter Rising by unsuccessfully attempting to ship arms to Ireland aboard the *Aud* in April 1916.[114]

At the start of the war, the Germans felt that the best way to subvert the British war effort was by aiding Irish Republican efforts at ending British rule. They placed their hopes on Sir Roger Casement, a former British diplomat who sought German support for an Irish Rebellion. At this time, Britain's most valuable source of intelligence on Casement was his male lover, Adler Christensen. Christensen accompanied Casement on a journey from the USA to Germany. When they stopped in Christiania, Norway, Christensen secretly met the British Minister there, Mansfeldt de Carbonel Findlay, and passed on copies of incriminating documents that Casement was carrying, including a ciphered letter of introduction from the German ambassador in Washington to the German Chancellor. MO5(g) also kept track of Casement's plotting through the postal censorship, which detected numerous letters that he sent to well-known Irish nationalists, hinting at German support for Ireland's liberation from British rule.[115]

Organisation – October 1914

On 1 October 1914, MO5(g) was reorganised into three branches. Increased work had necessitated the creation of a registration branch separate from the preventive branch, so that C Branch grew out of the sub-section of B Branch that had been concerned with records. A Branch, under Captain Drake, conducted 'investigation of espionage and cases of suspected persons.' B Branch, under Captain Holt-Wilson, dealt with 'co-ordination of general policy of Government Departments in dealing with aliens; questions arising out of the Defence of the Realm Regulations and Aliens Restriction Act.' C Branch, under Captain Haldane, was concerned with 'records, personnel, administration and port control.'[116] MO5(g) had now grown to twenty-nine members of staff, including sixteen officers, three clerks, five clerical staff, three detectives, a chauffeur and a caretaker.[117]

Accommodation

Like many other branches of government in wartime, growth was rapid.[118] The growth in MO5(g)'s accommodation is indicative of its development. The increase in MO5(g)'s staff after mobilisation soon required increased accommodation in London. On 21 October 1914 four rooms on the second floor of Watergate House, York Buildings on the Strand were taken over, but within a few months this proved inadequate. On 13 April 1915, MO5(g) took over the top floor of Adelphi Court, an adjacent block of flats on the Strand. As the department recorded: 'Owing to the difference of levels between this floor and the stairway landing in Watergate House at which alone it was possible to obtain communication between the buildings, it became necessary to take over the third floor which was done on April 29th.'[119] Due to this level of expansion within MI5, by spring 1916 it was clear that Watergate House and Adelphi Court provided insufficient accommodation. In August 1916, MI5 took over four floors of Waterloo House, at 16 Charles Street, Haymarket, SW1, a large office with six floors.[120] For a considerable time these offices sufficed, but ultimately the further growth of the staff necessitated a yet another increase in space and '…after a great deal of trouble and much opposition the occupants next door, in Greener House, were evicted.' The Admiralty, who occupied the other two floors of Waterloo House was persuaded to give them up and on 19 June 1918 the whole of Waterloo House was taken over and MI5 concentrated in the one block.[121] Further accommodation was provided by constructing a twin-storey, temporary bungalow on a vacant plot to the west of Waterloo House known as the Annexe and later as 14a Charles Street.[122] This marked the greatest extent in the growth of MI5's offices and remained as such until the end of the war. These offices were vacated in December 1919 and MI5 moved to 73, 74 and 75 Queen's Gate in South Kensington.[123]

Preventive Branch during the First World War

On the outbreak of the First World War, the Preventive Branch's duties were:

> 'Co-ordination of general policy of Government Departments in dealing with Aliens. Registration of Aliens. Foreign Communities. Applications of Alien Enemies to leave the United Kingdom. Records of Alien soldiers, sailors and police. Records of Alien Enemies permitted to reside in Prohibited Areas. Co-ordination of Police methods in dealing with Aliens. Questions arising out of the Defence of the Realm Act and Aliens Restriction Act. Correspondence on the above subjects. Investigations connected with technical naval and military questions.'[124]

However, with the war only a few weeks old, the volume of such coordination and administrative work coming in necessitated sub-dividing the Preventive Branch into four divisions, besides the work that was undertaken by the head of the branch. A fifth division was soon formed, comprising an officer who acted as assistant and deputy to the head of the Preventive Branch. This reorganisation was completed in November 1914, and then no significant changes were made before 20 May 1915.[125]

By late 1914, and up to May 1915, the staff of the Preventive Branch (known as B Branch from October 1914 to August 1915, and then known as F Branch) comprised the head of the Branch, five other officers and four clerks. The distribution of duties and staff of B Branch were as follows: B1 – concerned with Alien Intelligence – had one officer. B1 was responsible for Black Lists, Aliens Registration, Records of Searches and Removals under Defence Regulations, Aliens Statistics and Reports of Alien Convictions, Credentials of Aliens (as referred by Government Departments) and all other questions of detail concerning aliens except those covered by the duties of B2 and B3. B2 and B3 which were involved in the prevention of military and naval espionage respectively, shared a single officer between them in the form of Major F. Hall. B2 and B3 dealt with the credentials of aliens serving in, or employed by, the Army and Navy, with alien resorts favoured by Military and Naval personnel, with lists of Vulnerable Points, (Military and Naval) '…and so forth'.

B4's duties were special measures for the supervision and control of Belgian refugees, the investigation of the credentials of Belgian residents and lists of firms employing Belgian workmen. It comprised two officers, one of whom, a Colonel in the Belgian Army, was an attached officer with the position of *Auditaire Militaire Belge*. B5 worked on general B Branch duties, including assisting the head of the Branch, and comprised one officer, Major J. Sealy Clarke, who went on to become the head of A (Aliens on War Service) Branch, and later the head of the Investigative Branch.[126] The distribution of staff illustrated that the most pressing concerns in the early part of the war were related to the surveillance of Belgian refugees in whose midst it seemed fair to suspect that some enemy agents might have entered into the UK.[127] The supervision of these Belgian refugees later became part of the work of A Branch.[128]

By August 1915, F Branch had six officers, one additional compared to the roster of late 1914. Three female clerks had been taken on alongside the four male clerks who had been there in May 1915. F Branch still comprised five sections, but the distribution of duties to them had been slightly re-organised. F4, the Belgian section, had widened the scope of its work to cover the supervision of aliens of all nationalities – no longer just Belgians – employed on munitions or in prohibited areas. F5 remained concerned with general preventive branch duties. Back in May 1915, B2 and B3 had needed only a single officer between them. By August of that year, F2 combined both the military and naval protective duties that had been allotted to F2 and F3 respectively. The work of F1, the aliens section, had been divided up between F1 and F3, both involving one officer each. F1 was responsible for black lists; for the central register of aliens, undesirables, foreign clubs, resorts and communities; and for records of aliens in government service, alien soldiers, sailors, police and other officials in the UK, British subjects employed by foreign governments, and foreign embassies and consulates and their personnel. It also examined applications for naturalisation, as passed on by the Home Office, and assessed the bona fides of those applying for passes, passports and permits to enter, leave or travel within the UK in wartime.

F3 was concerned with civil records regarding aliens, such as reports of alien cases and convictions and records of searches and removals under DORA, and aliens allowed to live in or enter prohibited areas. It also checked proposals for internment orders or restrictions under DRR14 and 14B and had responsibility for the credentials and records of alien enemies interned or proposed for release or exemption from military internment or repatriation. F3's duties also included the collection and upkeep of information regarding police personnel and distribution; as well as studying census reports, alien statistics and the distribution of the alien population. The work of F Branch in general, and that of the head of the branch, remained much the same as before.[129]

In mid-June 1916, F Branch concentrated its structure by abolishing F5, the general duties section, and cutting loose F4, the aliens section that would be transferred to the Ministry of Munitions as PMS2 and which would later return to MI5 as A Branch. F Branch's general branch duties remained much the same, except for the inclusion of the new duty of policy and details associated with the use of Intelligence Passes and Permits, Papers of Identity, and other documents purporting to establish personal bona-fides for naval and military purposes. The work of F1, F2 and F3 continued much the same as before.[130]

By February 1917, two new sub-sections had been created. F4 took on the following duties:

Measures for maintaining military registers and records of aliens and others.

Statistics relating to aliens, with special reference to enemy aliens at large or in prohibited areas, and in H.M. Service.

Collecting and filing instructions and circulars issued by Government departments concerning counter-espionage.

Intelligence records of Prohibited Areas, Special Military Areas, and competent naval and military authorities.

Liaison duties between F. and H.1., the section now responsible for compiling historical records and black lists.

Some of these duties were new, but others had been undertaken by other parts of F Branch.

Before its transfer to F Branch, as F5, the legal section had been part of the Organisation, Administration and Records Branch since October 1914. In February 1917, it was responsible for the examination of legislative drafts and measures for counter-espionage, and also the examination of draft Administrative Instructions arising out of the Defence of the Realm Regulations. It also undertook consultations with Law Officers and Draftsmen and provided legal advice. By October 1917, F5 had taken over the examination of proposals to make, or vary the Administration of Prohibited Areas, Special Military Areas, Controlled Photography and Dock Areas, and Government Lands. It also assumed the powers and jurisdiction of Competent Military Authorities for Special Intelligence purposes – all this mostly from work carried out by the head of F Branch.[131]

In October 1917, F Branch had the following distribution of duties:

M.I.5.F. Prevention of Espionage

F.1. Cooperation with the Civil Authorities regarding Personal Credentials of aliens and others.

F.2. Cooperation with the Naval & Military Authorities regarding Personal Credentials of aliens and others.

F.3. Disposal and supervision of suspects and undesirables, otherwise than by prosecution.

F.4. Records and the classification of measures for the prevention of espionage.

F.5. Legal procedure.[132]

Sometime after March 1918, and shortly before the Armistice, F4 was abolished and F5 was re-named as FL.[133] In March 1918, F Branch's personnel were distributed as follows:

Branch Staff: 1 G.S.O.2
               1 Attached officer.
               2 personal secretaries
               3 branch clerks.

F.1   1 attached officer
       1 personal secretary

F.2   1 attached officer
       1 personal secretary

F.3   1 attached official
       1 attached officer
       2 personal secretaries.

F.4   1 attached officer
       1 personal secretary

F.5   1 G.S.O.3
       2 law officers
       3 personal secretaries.[134]

However, by no means were all security measures that were suggested eventually adopted. Some were turned down as impractical – as the following example demonstrates: on 6 August 1915, the General Officer Commanding-in-Chief Southern Command proposed, in order to guard against enemy spies masquerading as naval officers, an order for all naval officers visiting Weymouth or Portland to report to the senior naval officer who would record their presence in an arrival report book.[135] The War Office informed the Admiralty that it was against the idea because of the great difficulty in establishing a truly effective system, and the inconvenience that it would cause to naval officers.[136]

Throughout the war F Branch also worked with many other preventive organisations outside MO5(g). It was F Branch's role, within the limits of its power, to co-ordinate the activities of all the preventive intelligence organisations and government departments. As these departments did not come directly under MO5(g), they could not be given orders, only cooperated with. This included such departments as Scotland Yard and the Home Office with its chief constables and their police forces, recently created sections of the Directorate of Military Intelligence, such as censorship, CMAs, and intermediate functionaries such as the Home Office aliens officers. The departments which F Branch relied on for support with its preventive work can be divided into three categories: firstly, parts of the Directorate of Military Intelligence; secondly, other military organisations; and thirdly, civilian departments.

MO5(g) was responsible for land-based counter-espionage in the UK, but once at sea such matters were entirely the responsibility of the Naval Intelligence Division (NID). However, F Branch worked with the Admiralty in initiating new legislation and schemes of control, especially regarding prohibited or special military areas or districts that were important from a purely naval perspective. Although it often provided useful information on people, and had to be consulted about matters concerning the treatment of foreigners, the Foreign Office had little to do with the administration of preventive measures in the UK.[137]

The work of F Branch, as put down in the official manual IP Book 9, which set out the duties of the various branches and sections of MO5(g), included, in general and above all else, the policy of measures for preventing espionage, the military policy in dealing with police authorities and the civil population, including aliens, and the initiation and examination of legislative proposals relating to counter-espionage, and of executive schemes and instructions for the application of measures for counter-espionage and the control of aliens and undesirable persons.[138] However, not all legislative drafts and measures were preventive – such as the punitive regulations under which spies were executed in wartime, or DRR18A that made it an offence to communicate with the enemy. Although such punishments functioned as deterrents, they were only used when there was a definite suspicion. Therefore, the task of preparing the cases to prosecute for such offences, and other similar regulations, fell to the Investigative Branch, not F Branch. Nonetheless, the legal section undertook the initiation and examination of these investigative measures. The development of these measures also illustrates the cooperation of the Preventive and Investigative Branches.[139]

The F (Preventive) and G (Investigative) Branches of MO5(g) assisted each other. The Investigative Branch decided what action to be taken in any individual case, for gathering extra information on top of that in MO5(g)'s records, and for choosing the right time to arrest the suspected spy once the chain of evidence against him had been completed. F Branch provided the Investigative Branch with all of the legislative and administrative machinery needed for effective counter-action. Thus, if the Investigative Branch uncovered a hole in the preventive legislation, this was pointed out to F Branch with an explanation of the practical needs of the case. F Branch then assumed the work of devising changes to the current regulations that would meet these requirements, to make sure that the draft amendments were legally flawless as well as practically effective (the duty of the legal section), and lastly to get these amendments approved by the authorities concerned. F Branch also put forward amendments to the more preventive regulations and orders in a like fashion.

In normal wartime conditions MO5(g) was responsible for protecting the whole of the UK, being the area under civil government and not a part of the fighting zone. However, if the UK had ever become a fighting zone, emergency conditions would have been imposed, and the executive part of the preventive work in each area affected by the fighting would have moved from the civil authorities cooperating with MO5(g) to the headquarters intelligence section of the General Staff of the forces in the field.

In theory, possessing a single preventive intelligence organisation to protect all government departments, not just the air force, army and navy, but also foreign, imperial, colonial, commercial and domestic affairs, against intelligence attacks would doubtless have been best. However, MO5(g), while providing information to all, was especially concerned with protecting the War Office, Admiralty, Air and Munitions Ministries from enemy espionage, and each of the other government departments was responsible for its own protection.[140]

MO5(g) and the other new sections of the Directorate of Military Intelligence did not operate on their own. They were strictly hedged about with a circle of constitutional safeguards, such as the necessity of obtaining a warrant from the Home Secretary before starting to censor the letters and telegrams of an individual or of a particular country's postal service. This was true above all of the preventive side of the work, because for administrative purposes MO5(g) relied very largely on existing civilian departments. Such organisations as the police and the aliens branch (both under the Home Office) were, in actual practice, almost solely charged with the detailed execution of those restrictive measures which MO5(g) had planned for the control of aliens and other special classes whose supervision appeared desirable. In the management of these organisations, MO5(g), and indeed the military authorities of whatever kind, had no direct influence at all. The most that could be done was to bring pressure to bear on the governing authority (e.g. the Home Office) from as many quarters as possible.

The British system was very different to the German system; for example, where the General Staff's wishes would obviously dominate those of any or all other government departments that held the opposite view, and where it would have been quite possible to create a single military office with the authority to give orders to all those involved in work bearing on military security. However, the British system had certain advantages over a centralised system. Firstly, it conserved energy and entailed relatively little duplication of personnel, which was vital when locked in a struggle against an enemy with greater manpower. Secondly, it reduced the need to improvise new departments. Thirdly, provided there was an attitude of close cooperation, there was less chance of friction in the British system between the various departments concerned with different parts of national policy toward a particular individual. Notwithstanding this, the British system faced a disadvantage in coordinating the various organisations for preventive purposes, and standardising administrative instructions and routine. Overall, the British system represented an acceptable and very practical compromise between the two undesirable extremes of bureaucratic absolutism or utter disorganisation.

Following the suggestion made by a branch of the War Office, that a single military authority should be in charge of the administration of the ARA, the head of F Branch examined the merits of other possible systems in a memorandum of 29 December 1915. He responded:

> 'I do not agree with the suggestion that the entire administration of the A.R.O. should have been in military hands, unless it is also suggested that the whole Police Force of the country should have been placed under the central military control. The proper organisation would have been to form a central War Police Staff for the whole country, with control of all Police, Special Constables and Aliens (Customs) Officers etc; with a general officer in executive command, and ample funds to pay for the necessary expansion of personnel. The A.R.O. and D.R.R. could then have been administered as one consolidated Defence Code.'

He concluded that since universal registration of aliens had become a routine affair, and the residue of the orders could well be absorbed into the DRR, it was no use moving in the matter until the Central War Police Staff problem had been solved. Thus, 'a miscellaneous assortment of C.M.As. would be far worse police chiefs than the present [chief constables]'.[141]

F Branch performed its duties very successfully in terms of preventing both the leakage of information, with little intelligence of any consequence reaching Germany, and sabotage, with no acts of sabotage being conducted by German agents in the UK. It played a central role in developing and refining the ARA and DORA, which Christopher Andrew describes as 'a formidable array of legislation.'[142] MO5(g) proved very successful at preventing the leakage of information of real value to the enemy if the examples of the landing of the Expeditionary Force in France, the withdrawal from Gallipoli, or the manufacture of tanks were anything to go by.[143] Eric Holt-Wilson himself examined the value of these preventive measures in a lecture:

> '… but the efficiency of the Security Service is not to be measured merely by the number of spies caught. Allowance has to be made for efficient preventive measures, and their effect in producing general "wind-up" amongst the enemy agents. The best test is the level attained by the wages paid or offered by the enemy to their agents.

> 'We know that whereas the normal payment offered to a spy to go and work in this country in the early days of the war was £10 to £25 a month, and 10/- a page for copies of secret documents, it rose in June 1916 to £100 a month, and in 1918 was as high as £180 a month… In fact in the last months of the war, a good spy could get any money he asked for. The supply of German volunteers had completely dried up. For work in France they received less than half those salaries.'[144]

F Branch developed the far-sighted and highly successful strategy of keeping known German agents under surveillance but not apprehending them until the outbreak of war, when a paralysing blow was delivered, which was a very important part of MO5(g)'s strategy. It is also widely acknowledged that, in the well-informed words of Sir George Aston, a senior intelligence officer at the time, German agents did not commit 'a single case of sabotage in the United Kingdom' during the First World War.[145] However, some commentators have claimed that four ships which sank at British ports during the First World War were the victims of sabotage.[146] This may be the case, but no definite evidence exists and it seems more likely that they sank because of innocent accidents, probably explosions in their magazines caused by unstable ammunition which can decay and become dangerous, particularly bagged cordite.

However, it was perfectly reasonable for MO5(g) to take the threat of sabotage very seriously. Documents from German archives confirm that these fears were well founded. The German military intelligence department established *Sektion* P to conduct sabotage in Allied countries, particularly to stem the flow of essential war supplies from the USA. Agents managed to place explosives on several supply ships in US ports. On 30 July 1916, *Sektion* P succeeded in blowing up a storage depot at Black Tom Pier, New Jersey, containing over two million pounds of ammunition destined for the Russians, causing four deaths and $14 million of damage. But they did not achieve any such success in British ports, a reflection of the measures put in place by Holt-Wilson, with central and local government authorities, which saw prohibited zones set up nationally at sensitive points, such as ammunition dumps.[147]

However, not all channels that conveyed information to Germany were checked completely. Sir Edward Troup, Permanent Under-Secretary at the Home Office during the First World War, suggested that such '…information as reached Germany by secret channels was carried either in the mail bags of neutral legations which could not be opened, or by the crews of neutral ships who could not be excluded.'[148] Captain Maurice (later Lord) Hankey, Secretary to the Committee of Imperial Defence (CID) during the war, considered the real danger of leakage of important information to have been 'society gossip' – something that was never checked in Britain or in any other country. He recalled a conversation that he had had at the time with Lord Kitchener, then Secretary of State for War, who told Hankey that the reason he shared so little of his plans with his Cabinet colleagues was because they were 'so leaky'. Kitchener added that if 'they will only all divorce their wives I will tell them everything.'[149]

However, protective security at MO5(g)'s headquarters was by later standards 'casual'. In 1918, the 'Muller', one of MO5(g)'s cars, was stolen from right outside the door of Waterloo House.[150]

The Investigative Branch during the First World War

With the outbreak of war in August 1914, additional detection methods became available. These were:

Internally: General checks on the transmission of money orders, telegraphic orders, cheques, drafts, telegrams, and passenger traffic at ports and certain areas, plus H.O. Warrants and special checks such as on British Intelligence Services at home and abroad as well as the Foreign Office.

Externally: Via special Departments to include Censorship, Passport Office, Military Permit Office, Allied Services, Police, and private informers, both British and foreign.[151]

The most important of these by far were the agents working for British officials in contact with MI1c.[152]

Between MI5 and the Metropolitan Police Special Branch a healthy rivalry existed over the question as to which department could claim most credit for the capture and conviction of the many spies who came to Britain. In reality, one was essential to the other, although MI5 possessed the organization which enabled it to keep in touch with most of the enemy agents. MI1c tracked the movements of German Secret Service agents abroad and were able to warn the authorities in Britain when one of them was about to depart on a spying mission. Once the suspected enemy agent arrived in England his or her subsequent movements were passed on to the Special Branch at Scotland Yard for monitoring. MI5 also had its own team of detectives, under Melville, who were employed on the most important investigations, while Special Branch undertook the routine work that did not require the specialist expertise of Melville and his team. As far as the executive side of counter-espionage was concerned, Special Branch operated the system for checking the registration and movements of foreigners in London. It was the Counter-Espionage section, which was responsible for the tracking down of spies who arrived in Britain, not Scotland Yard. The Yard's involvement came when a spy had not definitely committed himself and it became necessary to establish a case which would stand legal argument. The difference between actual evidence and hearsay was a matter for those with experience of the law of evidence. Many inquiries were needed before it was possible to detain a suspected person, and due to the delicate nature of such highly-trained Special Branch officers were frequently being utilized. When it was decided to arrest an alleged enemy agent, Scotland Yard was called upon. Hundreds of people were so detained during the First World War on suspicion of being connected with enemy espionage. The great majority were quite innocent. Interrogations were conducted at Scotland Yard under the aegis of Basil Thomson because MI5 had no accommodation for detaining anyone. For their part, agents came equipped with well-constructed cover stories. There were many instances where only skilful questioning secured the desired information – an 'onerous task': Thomson averaged four interrogations a day throughout the war. However, before any of these examinations took place Scotland Yard was supplied with a précis of the evidence against the suspected individual. Although Thomson was nominally in charge of these interrogations, a senior MI5 officer, usually Drake, was always present. In his 1922 memoirs of his time at Scotland Yard, *Queer People*, Thomson staked his claim for public recognition. MI5, on the other hand, could not publicly stake its claim.[153]

By November 1914, Major Drake, the head of the branch, was supported by Miss S. Holmes, the branch secretary, and there were four staff officers and three secretaries. The duties of the Investigative Branch (known as A Branch from October 1914 to August 1915, and then as G Branch for the rest of the war) were generally defined as the,

> 'Investigation of cases of espionage. Correspondence regarding suspected persons. Action on intercepted correspondence. Correspondence with D.P.P. and A.G.3. Activities of foreign agents and measures to counteract them.'

It became necessary, however, to further expand these duties in order to counter the wartime actions of enemy espionage so that they became:

> 'Action on intercepted cables, telegrams, and letters. Investigation of causes of espionage, including uses of homing pigeons, wireless telegraphy, signalling, aircraft, etc. Investigation of cases of outrage and sabotage. Vise of Prisoners' letters and those of Prisoners of War.'[154]

The increase in A Branch's work from April to August 1915 was demonstrated by the number of general suspects investigated each month. In April 1915, 128 general suspects were investigated; this rose to 251 during May, 449 for June, 736 in July, and it had grown to 852 in August 1915.[155]

MI5 wanted there to be a uniform procedure; instructions were given to all GOCs of the main military centres to guide officers dealing with suspects. In its twofold work of distributing information concerning espionage and investigating reported spy cases, MO5(g) established contact with the Metropolitan Police, intelligence officers, city police, Admiralty coalfields police, diplomatic and consular services (through the Foreign Office), ports and aliens officers and customs officers (through the Home Office), permit office, Admiralty, Scottish Office, Local Government Board, Board of Trade, Registrar General, Labour Exchanges, and the Belgian Relief Committees.[156] Indeed, this circulation of information regarding suspicious cases was one of the largest parts of A Branch's work. In this, MO5(g) stressed that its role was largely administrative, advisory and co-ordinative, rather than executive.[157] This great increase in the work led to the growth and some reorganisation of A Branch in May 1915. A Branch's duties were more carefully defined, which showed the growing importance attached to particular features of the work. For example, the importance of Irish affairs was demonstrated by the creation of a section to concentrate on them. A Branch's duties became defined as:

(1) The investigation of all cases of suspected espionage, sedition or treachery by individuals.
(2) Co-ordination and organisation of auxiliary action by government departments, naval and military authorities, and police for the above purposes.
(3) Preparation of the cases of persons arrested at the instance of the Bureau for prosecution by the military or civil authorities.
(4) Examination of censored or intercepted correspondence and communications as submitted by the Censorship and Investigation Branch, G.P.O., and decisions as to the disposal of such papers.
(5) Classification of the methods employed by espionage agents.
(6) Recommendations for amendments to legislation and regulations for the purpose or preventing espionage, sedition or treachery, or of impeding the activities of naval or military spies or agents.
(7) Employment of the Intelligence Police personnel and provincial agencies, except with the Expeditionary Force.
(8) Recommendations for first appointments of personnel to 'G' Branch.
(9) Semi-official correspondence and first draft official letters on the above subjects.[158]

The staff now comprised Major Drake, as head of the branch, with eight section officers and four secretaries under him, an increase of four section officers compared to November 1914. Captain Carter and Commander Henderson carried out the work of A1, dealing with cases that arose in the Metropolitan area, while A2 was re-organised, with three officers, Mr P.W. Marsh, Mr R. Nathan and Captain H.S. Gladstone, dealing with all cases in Great Britain outside the Metropolitan area. A3, under Major F. Hall, later the head of D Branch, was allocated all cases of suspected espionage, sedition or treachery in Ireland. A4, under Mr H. Hawkins Turner and Lieutenant W.E. Hinchley Cooke, was given the new duties of examining censored or intercepted correspondence. The secretarial duties were divided between Miss Holmes, Miss Haldane, Miss Robson and Miss Hodgson.[159]

G Branch's definition of duties for August 1915 showed an advance in MO5's status and closer cooperation with other departments. The following words were added to Clause 1:

'Issue of orders to police, military and other authorities for arrest, search or observation of such persons (e.g. spies and suspects) and scrutiny of their correspondence.'

A GPO official, Mr Cousins, was appointed to act as a link between G Branch and the GPO, with the position of secretary in G Branch for the special purpose of examining mail that had been stopped under HOWs. The new definition of duties also included cooperation with the GOCs, GHQ and Allied counter-espionage services in counter-espionage, and responsibility for all official and semi-official correspondence on all issues dealt with in the detection of espionage.

This expansion of work required an increased staff. Major Drake was now supported in the general branch work by two section officers, Captain Carter and 2nd Lieutenant G.C. Peevor, with four secretaries.[160] Second Lieutenant George Charles Peevor appeared as Prosecutor (assisting Archibald Bodkin, lead prosecutor at every spy trial in Britain during the war) at a number of spy trials during the First World War. Before the war, Peevor had gained considerable experience in preparing and dealing with cases for the Director of Public Prosecutions.[161] G1 comprised three officers, with three secretaries. G2 was staffed by four officers, with six secretaries. G3, under Major Hall with one secretary, added to its duties the examination of reports on enemy agents in foreign countries, apart from Scandinavia, Holland and Denmark, and enemy territory on mainland Europe. G2a was formed, with five officers, to take over the work of the preliminary investigation of cases of espionage in Great Britain outside the Metropolitan area. G2b was created, with one officer, Mr H.L. Stephenson, to deal with cases of sedition amongst Indians and Egyptians in the UK and to cooperate with police and counter-espionage services in India and Egypt in all cases falling under G1 and G2a. G2 and these two sub-sections had a clerical staff of twelve. G3 undertook similar investigations concerning Ireland, and cooperated with counter-espionage services in the overseas dominions, crown colonies and protectorates, except Egypt. A third officer went to G4, which added the duty of examining the documents of suspected persons after arrest, to the examination of intercepted correspondence. G5 assumed the duty of preparing the cases of individuals arrested at the instance of MO5(g) for prosecution by the military or civil authorities.

In October 1915, two further additions were made to the definition of duties. Firstly the investigation of all cases of suspected fomentation of strikes and sabotage, and dissemination of peace propaganda, and secondly, the recommendation for amendments to legislation and regulations for the purpose of preventing espionage, sedition or treachery, or of impeding the activities of naval and military spies and agents.[162] The first showed the increase of certain means of attack, and the second emphasised the experience that had been gained in the previous six months.

By the end of the year, after some minor reorganisation, the distribution of duties to the five sections and two sub-sections was based on the two principles of geographical areas and race. Major Drake, with one section officer and four clerical staff, maintained the general direction and dealt specially with the means of known or suspected enemy agents. G1, under Major V. Ferguson and Major H.B. Matthews with two secretaries, was given the added section dealing with the preliminary investigations of the fomentation of strikes, sabotage and peace propaganda. G2, under Mr R. Nathan, was concerned with all cases of espionage, treachery and sedition in Great Britain.[163]

This development in G Branch's organisation had been driven by growing operational needs, as is illustrated by the far greater number of spies MO5 brought to trial during 1915 than in previous years. Throughout 1915, ten German spies were shot, one was hung, another committed suicide while undergoing trial, and five were imprisoned.[164] During that year, the main sources of information that led to the arrest of these spies were checks on spy addresses, scrutiny of telegrams to the continent, scrutiny of telegraphed money orders from the Continent, postal censorship, intelligence officers, British agents and the Belgian counter-espionage service.[165]

In 1916, a further reorganisation was necessitated by cases of sedition among Indians and Egyptians. In April 1916, G2a disappeared and its duties – the preliminary investigation of cases of espionage in Great Britain – were absorbed by G2. A new section, G6, comprising two officers and six secretaries, took over the work of G2b, cases of sedition among Indians and Egyptians, etc. G2 then consisted of seven officers and seven secretaries.

By September 1916, the work in Ireland following the Easter Rising and in the Dominions had increased to such an extent that G3 was re-constituted into a separate branch labelled D Branch. G5, which dealt with the preparation of cases of individuals arrested at the instance of MI5, was absorbed by the direction of G Branch, and G6 was re-labelled as G5. In November, the photograph and handwriting books were transferred into the keeping of H2, and the work needing translation was passed on to the Military Translation Bureau (MI7c). A further sub-division took effect from 18 December, when the enquiries necessitated by intercepted correspondence, previously handled by G4, were transferred to G2a, and the remaining work of G2 was allocated to G2b.[166]

Drake left MI5 in early January 1917 and on 15 January Major Carter became head of G Branch. G5 was re-constituted into a new branch, B Branch, concerned with Oriental affairs. G2, under Major Anson, was divided into four sub-sections. G2a dealt with enquiries stemming from intercepted correspondence. G2b handled enquiries from matters referred by the port control. G2c covered enquiries that arose out of matters referred by F Branch. G2d focused on enquiries arising from any other source.[167] The Branch underwent considerable change in February 1917. The general duties laid down that recommendations to amend legislation and regulations were to be reached in cooperation with F Branch. G1's duties were restricted to the investigation of cases of sedition and peace propaganda that arose from enemy activities. G2 continued to investigate cases of suspected espionage in Great Britain. G4 took over the investigation of intercepted correspondence from G2a. (E Branch retained control of investigations of people in transit through the UK.) Three new sections were formed to deal with matters connected with secret writing and correspondence. G3 dealt with photography, chemistry and technical research. G5 handled translation. G6 worked on procedure and investigation in special questions.[168] The reasons why these changes took place are unclear from the available documentation. However, there was much alarm at this time over pacifism and pacifist movements and it can be speculated that G1's restriction to investigations arising only from enemy activities may have been due to the scandal caused by the agent provocateur tactics of PMS2 (the previous F4, the aliens section transferred to the Ministry of Munitions), Kell's desire not to spy on the British labour movement, and the fact that this was becoming Thomson's turf. The new sections concerned with secret writing and correspondence were probably a response to the increasingly sophisticated secret writing techniques that had been used by spies. The cooperation with F Branch in designing legislation seems to have been driven by a desire to more efficiently plug in gaps in legislation that spy cases had revealed.

With these changes, G Branch comprised the following personnel on 11 June 1917: the head of the branch was assisted by five secretaries; G1 consisted of four officers and three secretaries; G2 included an officer with five secretaries; G2a was made up of five officers and four secretaries; G2b employed four officers with two secretaries; G2c had four officers assisted by three secretaries; G3 comprised two secretaries; G4 consisted of an officer with two secretaries; G5 employed one officer; and G6 had four officers. Thus, G Branch had fifty-one members of staff, made up of twenty-five officers and twenty-six secretaries.[169]

Further re-organisation occurred in September and again in October 1917. G Branch's general duties remained the same, but changes were made in the sections. Photography, chemistry and technical research were removed. G2's duties were taken over by G3 and expanded under the new definition of 'Executive duties connected with investigation, arrest or trial of persons suspected of espionage'. G2 was allocated general duties related to enquiries into individuals' credentials. G4 was concerned with special duties.[170] While it is not clear why these developments occurred, it seems likely that they were only minor changes, possibly to streamline G Branch, by removing work not directly related to the investigation of espionage, so that the Branch could concentrate on this. By September 1917, H7 was conducting laboratory work, which strongly suggests that G Branch's photography, chemistry and technical research work was relocated there.

In October 1918, Captain Radcliffe of G3 was tasked to maintain liaison between MI5 and allied military missions in the UK, including military attachés. The examination of special censorship documents was transferred from G3 to H3. The collection of codes and ciphers was moved over to D5, and coordination of British special intelligence missions in allied countries was handed over to D4.[171] In November 1918 changes were made to the organization of G Branch, many due to the Armistice. However, some of them illustrated '…the progress of Bolshevism and urgency of checking its propaganda.' As such, G4 took on the duties of:

(i)   Russian, Finnish, Polish and Czecho-Slovak affairs.
(ii) Investigation of cases of persons of the above nationalities and their activities in connection with Bolshevism, espionage, strikes, Pacifism, etc in the United Kingdom.
(iii) Investigation into the bona fides of persons of the above nationalities entering or leaving the United Kingdom, or applying for permits to work on munitions; and of all persons travelling to or from Russia …'[172]

In November 1918, G4 ascertained that a Russian named 'Axelrod' who belonged to the Russian Socialist Revolutionary Party and who was 'possibly also a Bolshevik', was receiving money through Arthur Henderson, a Labour MP. Sealy Clark, who became head of G Branch on 4 March 1918 when Carter was posted to Rome, made strong representations to the Foreign Office to the effect that it '… should get rid of this dangerous party of Russians as soon as possible and should no longer sanction the issue of visas to Russians of the type.' G Branch referred all cases of refusal of visa to Kell. The DMI ordered that where strong military reasons (and Bolshevism was one) existed for refusing a visa, MI5 was to take a firm stand with the Foreign Office and, if necessary, the Foreign Secretary himself was to be consulted. What happened to Axelrod is not known.[173]

At the end of the war, the final strength of G Branch was sixty: the head of the branch was assisted by seven secretaries; G1 comprised seven officers; G2 consisted of an officer with three secretaries; G2a had four officers and six secretaries; G2b was made up of five officers and five secretaries; G3 employed four officers with five secretaries; G4 consisted of four officers assisted by four secretaries; GL had one officer; and GP comprised two officers and one secretary. Thus, of the total of sixty, twenty-nine were officers and thirty-one secretaries.[174]

G Branch had thus succeeded in its mission, but in the course of its development between 1909 and 1918 a number of changes had taken place. These had reflected how the scope of counter-espionage work had widened in response to changes in the nature of the threat posed by Germany. On the eve of the First World War, G Branch's role was limited to counter-espionage in a narrow sense – namely, investigating suspected spies. War was to serve as the engine of G Branch's growth. As its workload increased, it needed a growing staff. However, although this accounts for much of the increase in G Branch's size, the way in which it grew and its role evolved can be explained by how the perceived threat that MI5 faced changed as the war went on. By 1916, G Branch had also begun to assume an interest in industrial unrest, pacifists and others deemed subversive, because some within official circles equated opposition to the government's policies with support for Germany and thus felt that such activities should be investigated to establish if they were being directed by Germany. G Branch's development from 1917 onwards was driven by a conviction that it had defeated German espionage, such that Germany had switched its efforts to promoting subversion and other forms of unrest in order to undermine British society. However, G Branch's development was guided by the fact that it was restricted to investigating only those cases that arose from enemy activities. It was not to have a wider interest in counter-subversion.

It is widely accepted that G Branch successfully discovered all of the German agents operating in the UK between 1909 and 1918. However, Jules Crawford Silber may provide a possible exception to this rule. MI5 historian, John Bulloch in his 1963 study of MI5 makes the interesting claim that:

> 'Jules Crawford Silber is the one German spy known to have been completely successful throughout the war. There were a few others who made quick trips to Britain and managed to return to their base with scraps of information but Silber alone lived and worked in enemy territory for years, constantly sending reports of the utmost importance to Germany. He was probably one of the most consistently effective spies of all time.'

Silber was born in Silesia and as a young man worked for a German firm in South Africa. With the beginning of the Boer War in 1899, he offered his services to the British Army as an interpreter, was appointed to POW and internment camps, and was eventually sent to India to work with Boer prisoners. He spent one-and-a-half years stationed in the Punjab and became friends with a number of the junior British officers in the garrison there. After the war ended, in 1902, he migrated to the USA where he worked until 1914. When the First World War broke out, Silber decided to serve Germany by becoming an intelligence agent in Britain. He passed immigration by pretending to be a Canadian without a passport, his service in South Africa and India helping him to convince immigration. Once in Britain, he applied for a job in the postal censorship, was accepted and given a censor's job. His linguistic abilities and his record of service in South Africa and India and his genuine friendships with officers there who had provided him with testimonials, also helped him to pass the interview for this post. He learned much from the letters he censored and passed such information he gleaned on to Germany. His job enabled him to post his information: he put it into an envelope, addressed it to a suspect address that he thought would pass it on to Germany, and then sealed the envelope with his own 'opened by censor' tag, so that nobody else would open it again before it got there. Silber was stood down on 27 June 1919 and worked for film companies in England before his eventual return to Germany in 1925.[175]

A more recent writer, Thomas Boghardt, has concluded that Silber 'was not a master spy'. Rather, he 'was either an outright fraud', or a former censor 'who had waited for his files to be destroyed and now used his inside knowledge to make some money.' Indeed, as Boghardt observes, the 'files of Silber's alleged employer, the German Admiralty Staff, remain completely silent on the topic.' Boghardt reasoned that, if Silber had conducted such ingenious work, he would have left some trace in the German records.[176]

Organisation, Administration and Records Branch

Changes were introduced after the outbreak of the war, because the system that had been sufficient in peacetime was unable to meet wartime demands. Censorship and other wartime measures were in operation, and the need for quicker communications with other government departments necessitated some changes.[177] As the work increased, the subject files promptly increased in importance, and the official files eventually became 'little more than bundles of index sheets containing cross references to papers which were either in personal or subject files, that is to say that with greater experience it was found that if a paper could not be "put away" into a personal file the next best place was to try a subject file.'[178]

Shortly after the outbreak of war the amount of papers became so great that only one schedule book, which recorded when files were taken out of the central registry by particular members of MI5's staff and when they were returned (for example, a schedule book would record that Drake had custody of Lody's Personal File, to stop files getting mislaid) was no longer enough. Work was considerably delayed by having to make entries in the book and it was also necessary to open a second and then a third in November 1914, making a schedule book for each of MO5(g)'s branches. However, this process was soon shown to be inadequate and, because it was often impossible to put papers into the file where they belonged, many simply floated around the office and there was the prospect of their being mislaid.[179] A system of file jackets, or I.P. (Intelligence Police) covers as they were officially known, was instituted. An official H Branch record describes them as follows:

'Each cover contained spaces for recording its own contents; its movements; the action taken upon it and its ultimate disposal, as well as a space for minuting between Branches. These covers enabled action to be taken on any document received and for the whole of the correspondence involved in that particular transaction being kept together with a record of everything that had taken place, in a unified form. When the papers were eventually filed the front page of the cover was put away in a special box. When the paper was first put into this cover a brief record was kept in the Registrar's schedule book in order that if necessary papers might be traced firstly, by their own number, secondly, by the date of receipt or dispatch, or by the office number of the sender.'[180]

In late 1914 the *Bureau Central Interallié* (BCI) was set up in Paris – the British section being the *Mission Anglaise* – 'to exchange information between the allies in regard to suspected persons and all other matters dealt with in the Directorate of Special Intelligence.'[181] In September 1915, following the institution of the BCI, MO5 chose to standardise the ways of circulating names, to observe the same methods that had been drafted by Holt-Wilson and chosen for the central office in Paris. It was also decided that a more intelligible system of organising the details known about an individual should be instituted. Therefore, Captain W. Maxwell was recalled from his post as press censor at Gallipoli to serve as an attached officer with MO5. Maxwell's main task was to produce the MO5 black list, which developed to twenty-one consecutive volumes containing 13,524 entries.[182] The system used was broadly to give the suspect's real name and aliases, followed by an identifying number, which was the serial number of his entry on the black list. Next came letters indicating the categories of suspicion held against him, such as E (Espion) if he was suspected of espionage, or F (False) if he was suspected of using false or forged identity papers. These were followed by letters denoting the countries where the information came from, A stood for Anglais, B for Belgian, F for French and so on. Then the particulars that could not change were given, such as date of birth, age, personal appearance and such. After that, the general details of the reasons for suspicion were provided as simply as possible, distinguishing between factors that were proven or probable, and those which were only allegations.[183] Black list entries were quite detailed, as the following example demonstrates:

'LAMBERT, OLYMPE FANNY CHARLOTTE, née GUILLOT or QUILLOT or NUILLET.
(F.)   11091
    Class–AEJ.   Source–A.F.

10 Ap 18, whereabouts uncertain. French, born 6 Feb 1879 Meteren, Nord. Father, Jules GUILLOT or QUILLOT or NUILLET. Mother, Octavie née LAGACHE. Widow of Francois LAMBERT. Domiciled 29 rue de Bourg, Lausanne. Before war lived Lille, kept a dairy with her mother. Was interned Holzminden until July 1916, was then sent Switzerland as repatriée. Went Lyons, states had stationery shop there, was there Aug 1917, was expelled and sent into department of Allier, has crossed Swiss frontier several times, is reported to have escaped surveillance Mar 1918 and is believed to have gone to Switzerland to join her lover Maurice BOURGEOIS at 29 rue de Bourg, Lausanne. Photograph with M.I.5, War Office, ports and controls. Possibly identical with LAMBERT (see 984) whose description corresponds with hers.

Speaks English and Flemish fluently.

A.– 31 Mar 13, for fraud, sentenced Tribunal of Douai 10 months' imprisonment. 6 Sept 16, for fraud, sentenced Tribunal of St. Julien en Genevois, 6 months' imprisonment.

E.– 10 Ap 18, repatriated from Holzminden where she was mistress of camp Kommandant; is now mistress of Maurice BOURGEOIS, French, born 25 May 1896, Paris, formerly interned Holzminden, now in Switzerland; is also in relations with one VULLIEND, French, born 27 Oct 1889, mistress of MAUZACQ, French, born 27 Nov 1892, Bordeaux, formerly interned Limburg, now in Switzerland, and JERLY, born 25 May 1876, Pont la Ville, Fribourg, living 29 rue de Bourg, Lausanne; all above persons lodge with JERLY and are accomplices of LAMBERT. 21 May 18, was expelled from Lyons where she made constant efforts to get into relations with French and British officers; was arrested 21 Jan 18 crossing French-Swiss frontier without passport; is considered dangerous.

J.– 11 Sept 18, signalled British ports and authorities concerned for arrest.

(19 Sept 18. Reference M.I.5/T.C. 1438.)'[184]

To someone familiar with the black list classes, this informed them that Olympe Lambert was a spy (E for Espion), with a criminal record (A for Antecedents), and a wanted person (J for Junction wanted).

At first, the black list had a very limited circulation as only eight copies of the first volume were distributed. This grew rapidly and at the end of the war 115 copies of the list were issued to British officers at home and abroad. The black list was MO5's primary official notification regarding suspect individuals.[185] It was meant to comprise the names of those about whom suspicion was credible. However, unfortunately, owing to a certain 'indiscriminate use of the authority exercised by branch officers', the list became overloaded with names of persons who should not have been on it. Therefore, it was strongly recommended that in future the right to add an individual to the black list should be restricted to the director and branch heads, or officers specially chosen for this role. When subordinate officers wished to place an individual on the black list, they were to suggest the name to the relevant official who would choose whether it belonged on the black list or just on the warning circular.[186]

However, the black list was not a full record of the available information by any means. While working on the re-organisation of the duties of the Special Intelligence Mission in Rome, Captain Haldane and his assistant, Miss Matheson, concluded that the working of the military controls abroad would be made much simpler if an index of all known black lists and suspect circulars could be produced. This led to the production of a special intelligence index. It comprised the names of every individual contained in the MI5 black list, the BCI List, the Belgian *Calipan des Signales*, the Eastern Mediterranean Black List, the China Command List, the *Contre Espionage* Index Part II issued by GHQ France, and certain parts of the War Trade Black List. Nonetheless, it was not meant to be a basis for any action: it was simply a list that referred the reader to documents that he possessed or to information that he could request, which would permit him to assess what action needed to be taken. It had a wide circulation and was viewed as one of the most valuable productions issued by any of the Allies during the War.[187]

To give an example of the use of the list, Emil Brugman, a Dutch chemical engineer, had visited England on business and then returned to Holland in October 1915. The following month the BCI list reported to MO5 that Brugman associated with German agents and was also said to be passing contraband rubber into Germany. In March 1916, an MI1c agent, agent 'T', reported that Brugman was coming to England.[188] On 9 May 1916, an agent 'R', a British agent acting as a double agent in Holland, reported that he had unexpectedly seen Brugman in London. Brugman was arrested on the next day. Owing to insufficient evidence for trial, because there was no direct evidence against him, Brugman was deported to Holland on 15 July 1916.[189]

On mobilisation, MO5(g) did not have any messengers. Letters were taken to the War Office and other offices by MO5(g) officers who often went there. This was unsatisfactory, so arrangements were made for the Brigade of Guards to provide a staff of orderlies.[190] However, they were fully employed with external messages, and so arrangements had to be made for the internal transit of papers because it was considered wasteful to use clerical staff for such a task. Accordingly, Boy Scouts were engaged from 29 October 1914 to 4 September 1915, but they were 'found to be very troublesome… The considerable periods of inactivity which fell to their share usually resulted in their getting into mischief.' Therefore, when the Admiralty began to employ boys as coast watchers, they 'were advised to take up this work; outdoor work being much more fitted to their energy.'[191]

The Boy Scouts were then replaced with Girl Guides and the results were judged to be 'most satisfactory.' The girls proved more amenable and their methods of getting into mischief were on the whole less distressing to those who had to deal with them than were those of the boys. A Miss Roubaud looked after the Guides for a considerable time. Following her departure for Paris, she was succeeded by a Miss Enid Balance. When she was urgently needed elsewhere, on 23 January 1917, Miss A.D. Campbell Tiley, a captain of a troop of Girl Guides took charge. She remained in charge of them until 21 October 1918, when she resigned due to ill health. She was succeeded by one Miss Evelyn Erskine Hill, who stayed until 1 November 1919.[192]

The orderlies provided by the Brigade of Guards continued to work as outdoor messengers for a long time, although changes were made so as to meet the need for soldiers to serve in the field. The following example shows the high calibre of these men. In his book *Most Secret War*, Professor R.V. Jones, Britain's Assistant Director Intelligence (Science) during the Second World War, mentioned that his father had served as a guard at MI5 headquarters during the First World War. Jones' father was a career soldier and sergeant in the Grenadier Guards. He was recommended for the Victoria Cross in March 1915, and then seriously wounded in May 1915. After spending about a year convalescing, he became a guard at MI5 headquarters, then a drill sergeant at Aldershot.[193] Once the Guardsmen were withdrawn, they were replaced with men from a labour battalion. When they were then removed, their places were filled by discharged soldiers engaged as War Office messengers.[194] There does not seem to have been any form of vetting procedure.

Soon after the outbreak of war, it became clear that a substantial addition to the staff would be required and further reform in the way that papers were handled. MO5(g) decided to appoint a man who had experience of registry work and approached a Mr Pedley who was in charge of a department within the War Office. Pedley maintained that his staff was so busy that it was not possible to spare anyone to help MO5(g). MO5(g) then sought assistance in the commercial world and Kell acquired, from a friend in business, the name of a man seeking employment whom he felt was qualified to register correspondence. Mr A.G. Brown joined MO5(g) but he survived for only a week. Apparently 'the system already employed proved itself too much for his comprehension' and Brown departed declaring that he had never been in a place where things were 'in such a muddle.' A Mr Campbell of the Foreign Office recommended a Miss Lily Steuart as a trustworthy individual looking for Government employment. Captain Haldane interviewed Miss Steuart at the Foreign Office and she was taken on to be the head of the Registry that was due to be established. On 4 November 1914, Miss Steuart and two or three others were placed in a back room in Watergate House with all of the index cards and files which constituted the germ of the Registry.[195]

Despite these moves, the need for yet more staff was soon felt. The pattern for MO5(g)'s recruitment policy was set in the early years when Kell personally interviewed all candidates. He maintained very high standards of reliability within his staff, which tended to mean that his officers and secretarial staff were drawn from his own social circle, typically having a military and county background. This policy has been attacked as arrogant and snobbish, but in reality its basis was financial. Kell's officers were very badly paid and his secretaries fared even worse. Therefore, as a matter of simple expediency, he was compelled to employ those of independent means who could afford to take such relatively low salaries.[196] Moreover, during wartime, in order to save manpower for active service at the front, MO5(g) was not permitted to recruit officers who were medically fit for general service, apart from in exceptional circumstances. It was also to employ female rather than male clerks whenever possible.[197]

With the need to expand rapidly, however, MO5(g) first turned to – in the words of H Branch – 'an organisation in Grosvenor Gardens under Miss Beaves.' However, applications came in rather slowly. Therefore, Miss C. Spurgeon, of the professorial staff at Bedford College, was asked if she could recommend any ladies from there, and Miss Lilian Clapham, of the Labour Department of the Board of Trade, also agreed to look for suitable people. A certain number was forthcoming. However, it was necessary to look further afield and following the advice of Miss M.E. Haldane, Miss Will's secretarial Bureau in Victoria Street, London was approached.[198]

As the staff grew, affairs started to grow progressively better. However, it was felt that, despite all of her qualifications, Miss Steuart did not possess the experience to manage a large staff satisfactorily and she was accordingly transferred to M.I.9. where she did excellent work in the Code Branch. She was succeeded on 20 February 1915 by Miss E.A. Lomax, who also brought Miss E.L. Harrison with her.[199] On 1 January 1918, Miss Lomax was awarded an MBE. Then, on 1 January 1920, she was also awarded an OBE, and Miss Harrison was awarded an MBE. Miss Harrison and four other ladies were mentioned in *The London Gazette* of 2 September 1918, and a further ten ladies were mentioned on 18 August 1919 (unfortunately, the H Branch Report does not record specifically why they received these awards).[200] Sometime after her arrival, Miss Lomax was asked what she thought the maximum number of staff needed in the Registry would be and she concluded that fifteen would probably be enough. This was passed in about two months.[201]

Due to a lack of accommodation it was not possible to find enough room to employ an adequate staff in the Registry. Therefore, a night shift was introduced and the daytime staff was split into two shifts. The first shift worked from 9 a.m. to 5 p.m., the second shift worked from 2 p.m. to 10 p.m., when the night shift came on and worked until 7 a.m. the next morning.[202] The night shift was expensive and inconvenient and it was abandoned shortly after the move to Charles Street, as the more spacious accommodation allowed the night staff to be added to the daytime staff. However, two day shifts were maintained, partially as many of the executive staff continued working past normal hours and also because the greater quiet in the evenings allowed that shift to process much more routine work, which had proven prone to interruption in normal working hours.[203] It was decided that something more than the normal shorthand typist was required and so it was that MO5(g) sought to employ well-educated ladies and preferred those who had attended the larger public schools or colleges, although the salaries on offer were not good enough to attract many university graduates. This resulted in the majority hailing from public schools. In early 1915, MO5(g) chose not to engage ladies older than forty because the system used in the Registry 'threw a very considerable strain on those whose minds were not elastic enough to adapt themselves to new methods.' Within a year this limit was lowered to thirty, apart from very exceptional cases. This age limit helped in recruiting a teachable and adaptable workforce. However, it did have the disadvantage that comparatively few 'women of the world' were engaged and when recruiting a staff to compile the black list and write historical records, it was decided to abandon the age limit and to recruit, rather than reject, more mature candidates.[204]

In the distribution of duties for 5 August 1914, the administrative duties were directed by the Preventive Branch. As part of the Preventive Branch, Captain Haldane worked on duties at the War Office.[205] As noted earlier, on 1 October 1914, MO5(g) was reorganised and the Organisation, Administration and Records Branch (known as C Branch from October 1914 to August 1915, and then known as H Branch) was born. Its duties were 'records, personnel, administration and port control'. The growth of MO5(g)'s workload had necessitated the creation of a registration branch, separate from the Preventive Branch. Captain Haldane, who had been in charge of some of the Preventive Branch's duties, became the head of the new branch, under which these duties had become grouped.

From late 1914 onwards, C Branch grew to be far larger than any other branch contained entirely within the Bureau itself. It soon began to divide itself into sections, and inside one week of its formation, its distribution of duties and staff had developed considerably.[206] By February 1915, C Branch had divided into the following four sub-sections. C1 dealt with general office procedures and with the male clerical establishment together with orderlies and messengers; C2 was responsible for recording the transit of registered papers; C3 was responsible for the receipt, registration and distribution of documents; and C4 recorded documents passing between the Bureau and the War Office.[207] By May 1915, a fifth sub-section had been formed to provide legal advice, in the charge of W.H. Moresby as its section officer.[208] Kell's cousin, Walter Moresby, a barrister and the son of Admiral John Moresby, had joined MO5(g) on 9 October 1914 as its legal adviser.[209] The Registry's Transit Division was born on 31 May 1915.[210]

In May 1915, a new branch, E Branch, was formed for the control of ports and frontiers. Although controlled by E Branch, the system was administered by C Branch.[211] Thus, C Branch assumed the complete administration of MO5(g)'s four branches.[212]

On 11 August 1915, C Branch changed its designation to H Branch by which time a sixth section, H6, had been added to deal with work at the War Office.[213] In the distribution of duties to sections, H1 drafted official War Office letters, compiled MI5's historical records, and had custody of official War Office documents. H2 handled the registration and transit of documents, indexing, filing and custody of MO5's correspondence and records, and was custodian of official War Office documents under instruction from C1 (War Office). H3 was responsible for the receipt of correspondence, providing and maintaining office premises and equipment, and the interior economy of MO5. H4 controlled office procedure, issued office instructions, and undertook printing, and estimates, accounts and payments. H5 provided legal advice, and prepared draft bills, orders and regulations. H6 conducted work at the War Office.[214]

At that time, H Branch had sixty-seven members of staff, including eight officers and fifty-nine other staff, comprising one assistant director as head of the branch, seven section officers (including Miss Lomax of H2, who was also superintendent of the card room), nine clerical staff, also one deputy superintendent (Miss Harrison) and forty-six other staff in the card room, and one assistant superintendent (Miss A. Bliss) and two other staff in the Transit Section.[215] Since its new designation as H Branch in August 1915, H Branch continued to grow, not just into sections but also these into sub-sections, such that by the end of the war designations such as H6c or H7d could be seen, each performing distinctive duties.[216] On 18 December 1915, a seventh sub-section, H7, was added to distribute information and prepare records.[217] H7 had four section officers and six clerical staff.[218] By February 1916, the detailed duties of H7 were the circulation of useful information to all counter-espionage organisations of the British and Allied armies, maintaining MI5's black list and its accompanying special card index, compiling the monthly report of MI5's work, and the preparation of précis and summaries for record or circulation.[219]

H7 underwent some changes in May 1916, and the inter-working of the E and H Branches is illustrated by office instruction number 192 of 19 May 1916, signed by Major Haldane. From this point, information concerning counter-espionage was to be distributed by E Branch or H7 as follows: E Branch was to circulate information needed by the controls under MI5's orders or directly associated with it, while H7 was tasked to communicate information to Allied counter-espionage services and other organisations.[220]

In June 1916, MI5 produced the first book of office instructions (I.P. Book 9), which set out the distribution of duties of MI5 and its branches. H1 produced historical reports and statistics, compiled, held and issued the black list, examined newspapers and prepared extracts, summarised and made précis of documents, produced and distributed records of important decisions, and compiled and issued counter-espionage reports from abroad. H2 handled the registration and transit of documents, indexed, filed and had custody of documents, assumed temporary custodianship of documents possessed by other departments, and destroyed obsolete documents. H3 received and distributed correspondence, issued money, and maintained and held the service records of MI5's staff. H4 was responsible for estimates, accounts and contracts. H5 handled legal questions. H6 conducted interviews and work at the War Office. H7 dealt with MI5's interior economy, allocated rooms, stationery, furniture and office equipment and despatched correspondence.[221] H Branch also carried out other editorial work. In the summer of 1916 the volume of material collected through the working of the ARA was put into an intelligible format.[222] Captain Maxwell's section (H7 and later H1) also wrote up MI5's monthly reports. This had been neglected from mobilisation until April 1915, when Mr R Nathan produced a report.[223] Reports were subsequently produced every month. They were first edited by Mr R.E.A. Elliot, then by Captain Maxwell and lastly by Lieutenant-Colonel Jervis. According to H Branch,

> 'They gave a very good history of the principal cases dealt with by the Service during the War and still more so of the legislation for which the office was responsible. With the exception of the statistical tables, which are of the greatest value, they do not contain very much of interest as regards the administrative working of the Bureau.'[224]

H1 compiled or edited all reference books produced by MI5, such as the 'Notes on the German Espionage Methods' and the 'Port Officers' Guide'.[225]

In July 1916, the duties of H7 were taken over by H1.[226] In August 1916, H6 was expanded considerably to become a secretarial section, having an officer from each branch on attachment. The secretarial section was formed to ensure that War Office documents were handled speedily by the relevant branch or branches; miscellaneous questions were fielded within a decent time; and telephone requests for information and papers were noted and passed on to the branch involved to respond. The officers seconded were at the disposal of their branch heads. Their special duties were drafting official letters on standard lines according to War Office procedure and following the branch heads' instructions; replying to requests for information on issues related to the branch's work; and taking charge of War Office documents in temporary custody of the branch.[227]

Office instruction 236d of 14 September 1916 set out the reformation of H7 with new duties. All matters of interior economy, stationery and office equipment were to be handled by H7 to whom all requisitions were to be sent. H7 was also responsible for the despatch of correspondence and all questions relating to male clerks, orderlies, lift attendants, 'charwomen' and cleaners, as well the messing arrangements. The staff comprised one officer, Major G. Pepper, and three clerks, Mr Westmacott, Mr C.G. Riley and Miss D. Westmacott.[228] In December 1916, H Branch had 134 staff, comprising eighteen officers and 116 other staff.[229]

MI5's distribution of duties for February 1917 showed some changes in the work of H Branch. The main difference was the attachment of H Branch officers to MI5's branches in agreement with the branches affected. The legal work undertaken by H Branch was transferred to F Branch, becoming F5, and H5 was disbanded.[230] H1 assumed the additional duties of compiling and issuing counter-espionage reports from abroad; and, printing indexes and lists of those of interest to MI5. H2's duties remained as they had done in June 1916. H3 took on special censorship. H4 added the duties of pay and allowances that did not arise from the Royal Warrant for Pay and Allowance Regulations. H6 continued with the same duties as before. H7 added the duties of catering; travel expenses; and, allowances and pay questions that arose from the Allowance Regulations and Royal Warrant for Pay.[231] Slight modifications occurred in September 1917, when H5 was recreated to deal with the control, selection and discipline of all women employed on executive and clerical duties as well as general control of the work of the Registry and branch clerical staffs.[232]

The head of H Branch also became the adjutant to the Director Intelligence Police (DIP), and the duties of sections H1 to H7 were rearranged as follows: H1 and H2 continued to perform the same duties that they had done in February 1917. H3 dealt with office premises, equipment, stores and supplies, stationery, telephones, passes and keys, interior economy, duty rosters, catering, cleaning, waste paper, posts, receipt of documents, address books, motor cars, laundry, male clerks, orderlies, menials, car drivers, and Girl Guides. H4's duties showed no change from February 1917. H5 performed the duties set out above. H6 had the same duties as in February 1917. H7's duties were cash, laboratory, office routine, correspondence, office instructions, circular memoranda, advisory committee, instructional courses, returns, officers, agents, military ports police, telephonists, and records of service.[233]

By October 1917, H Branch had 164 members of staff, including eighteen officers and 146 other staff. The head of the branch was assisted by one other member of staff. H1 had eight officers and twelve other staff. H2 comprised two officers and 112 other staff. H3 included three officers and three other staff. H4 was made up of one officer and two other staff. H5 comprised one officer and two other staff. H6 had one officer and one other member of staff. H7 was made up of one officer and three other staff. H Branch also included seven printers and three telephone operators.[234] From 21 January 1918, it was further enlarged to ten sections, and the duties of the three new sections were as follows: H8 compiled counter-espionage black lists and produced printed indexes and lists of individuals of interest to MI5. H9 was responsible for printing and compiling a so-called 'grey list' – presumably some kind of list of suspects. H10 dealt with action in cases of seditious speeches in the UK and the collection of information concerning pacifist organisations and propaganda.[235] In February 1918, H7 was relieved of the duty of 'Maintenance and custody of all records of service, other than those of women actually serving' which was transferred to H4. H4 also gained the duties of 'Preparation of Office Gazette' and 'Preparation of Lists of staff for Office use.'[236]

In March 1918, H8 was divided into the following three sub-sections: H8a compiled MI5's black list. H8b produced the military intelligence index, which comprised the names of all those mentioned in the Allied black lists. H8c prepared and compiled I.P. Forms 94c, 95c and 96c. It was considered vital that these identity forms should be processed uniformly, so H8c was made the only authority for handling them from that point on.[237] In May 1918, H10's duties were taken over by F4, and H10 ceased to exist.[238]

In September 1918, H7 was divided, its general duties being office routine, correspondence, preparing office instructions and circular memoranda, officer personnel, compiling minutes of MI5's weekly conference, preparing lists and books for MI5's use, and administration related to Special Intelligence Missions in Allied countries. The distribution of specific duties to sub-sections was as follows: H7a handled photography and MI5's laboratory work. H7b conducted interviews and work at the War Office. H7c was tasked with printing and supervising the grey list.[239]

By this late stage in the war, Lieutenant-Colonel Gunn was in charge of H7. Miss Dallas was in charge of H7a, Major Peebles was in charge of H7b, and Captain H.S. Gladstone and Captain Duguid were in charge of H7c.[240]

H Branch ran MI5's own printing press. It was begun by Mr Riley, who purchased a small 'Arab' machine plus second-hand letter blocks, which enabled him to perform minor printing jobs for MI5. This worked so well that MI5 decided to acquire more equipment and engage professional printers. Consequently, Misses M. and G. Ewen were engaged and the personnel was increased. The extra accommodation provided by the annexe allowed further growth to take place. Captain Gladstone was placed in charge of the printing press, the staff was increased, and a Lanston Monotype outfit was brought. The press grew until the printing staff comprised four men, eight women and two girls, working two Lanston Monotypes, two Cylinder machines and two small platen machines. MI5's printing press not only did much work for MI5, but also for other sections of the intelligence directorate and government departments that needed emergency printing undertaken.[241]

The total number of papers registered and unregistered by H Branch to 31 December 1918 was 383,346; 67,445 files were opened and 358,964 letters were posted.[242]

The H Branch Report urged that,

'It is most essential that on a future mobilisation both H.1. and H.6. should be among the first sections to be created… Had the machinery existed at the beginning for producing black lists, for writing up periodical reports of the work of the Service and for the weeding out of the useless from the useful files, much time and labour would have been saved; the records would have been kept to more manageable dimensions, and the search for names mentioned in new papers would have been greatly facilitated. As it is, the enormous bulk of the personal files will entail work for a very long time before any end can be reached in the process of elimination and the consolidation of useful material. Much has been done, but far more yet remains to be done.'[243]

The report closed with a section on notes and lessons. Firstly, with respect to 'Lists of personnel', it was stated that 'Complete lists showing the composition of the various branches and sections, should be issued at definite intervals', and notable changes should be embodied in a circular memoranda, so as to keep all concerned informed of these changes as they occur. Any reorganisation of duty should also be notified in this way. Secondly, in terms of 'Movements of personnel', records of the monthly returns of the staff were considered useful, and it was suggested that something akin to an office gazette should be produced every month. Thirdly, under 'Preparation before war', it was recommended that 'At the beginning of a war, people are as a rule too much occupied with the urgent matters of the moment to attend to the necessary routine; but it should not be overlooked or the omission will sooner or later be regretted.' Therefore, an adequate staff to maintain returns of individuals and distribution of duties was viewed as necessary from the very beginning. The report opined that, 'Even if current work in other directions is falling behind, it is sheer folly to neglect the details of administration; and the remedy is to be sought not in cutting down the administrative branches but in re-inforcing the executive branches with new recruits.' Fourth, it was considered that 'Time after mobilisation' was very important. Clearly the first few months after mobilisation would always be a period of considerable disorganisation and almost disorder, and although officers would have their specific duties allotted to them the enormous influx of work necessitated almost everyone lending a hand. This was particularly the case with regard to the enquiries which arose from the innumerable letters which came pouring in from every kind of source, regarding persons suspected of being German agents. Probably the worst month of all in this regard was November 1914.[244]

The system was, however, not above criticism. Historian Richard Thurlow's colourfully expressed assessment is fairly typical of those who have criticised what he calls 'the infamous Registry of MI5':

'…the file index of unchecked information, gossip, rumour and innuendo which was collected by British counter-intelligence and which originally related to aliens but extended to so-called subversives in the latter stages of the First World War. The list was to prove invaluable to the authorities during the roundup and internment of aliens in 1915. It was to ensure a meal ticket for Kell until he was sacked as director-general of MI5 in 1940, and gave employment to an ever expanding number of upper class female clerks, or 'queens', as they became jocularly known, in what was to become the hub of British counter-intelligence.'[245]

Thurlow did not cite the sources upon which his criticisms were based, which makes it more difficult to judge their accuracy. This problem is compounded because too few examples of the material stored in MI5's Registry have survived to allow any meaningful analysis of its contents. Furthermore, it should also be acknowledged that it was the Registry's role to store all the information that was passed on to it, even that which seemed frankly laughable, just in case it might turn out to have relevance in future. Thus, the Registry may have retained some quite ludicrous reports. As Macdonough, DMI during the First World War, explained in a lecture, the intelligence department's results were produced by,

'...hard work, great diligence, and untiring watchfulness, and the painstaking collection and collation of every possible form of information. Nothing is too small to be unworthy of the attention of the I.D., and no problem too big for it. Even the most unlikely rumours should be forwarded by intelligence agents to Headquarters, for it is there alone that their worth can be apprised.'[246]

In terms of the checks on the quality of the information stored by the Registry, it can be noted that the evidence MI5 provided for spy trials had to stand up to proper scrutiny in court and court martial proceedings. Therefore, the pertinent question is not really of the quality of the information stored in the Registry, but of how well this information was analysed and assessed. Was the true information correctly sifted from the false? Then other questions of how well this information was managed arise, such as, was it then stored and indexed so as to be easily retrievable for use and cross-referencing with other information, for example?

Information scientists, Alistair Black and Rodney Brunt, present another seemingly more fruitful and objective way of judging the information stored by MI5, by analysing the quality of the information management procedures practised by MI5. By comparison to Thurlow, Black and Brunt acknowledge the use of some of the most advanced information management techniques available at that time, such as the Roneo carding system:

'Established in 1909, MI5 was immediately faced with the huge task of organising the mass of disparate information which its investigations generated. In response to problems thrown up by both the period of international tension which preceded the First World War and the war itself, MI5 developed a relatively efficient, labour-intensive information management infrastructure.'[247]

This provides an instructive example of MI5's readiness to acknowledge problems with its performance, proactively implement changes to overcome them and successfully improve effectiveness.

The Registry functioned very much as the heart of MI5, enabling it to fulfil its role as the central clearing house for all counter-espionage information. Information was perceived as the life-blood of counter-espionage work and the Registry was the essential artery which ensured that it circulated between the different branches, which were all united by a shared reliance on information. Indeed, the great volume of information about undesirable aliens stored in the Registry, which could be used to monitor the activities of Russians and their supporters in Britain, plus the expertise MI5 had shown as an efficient clearing-house for information may well have been the keys to MI5's survival after the war, when it assumed the role of defence security intelligence and checking the spread of Bolshevism within the military.

Statistics

Declassified MI5 reports reveal statistics concerning the volume of MI5's work for most of the First World War. Unfortunately, it has not been possible to locate statistics concerning the period 4 August 1914 to 31 December 1914. It seems likely that MO5(g)'s staff was too small and over-worked to keep such statistics at that time. Nonetheless, it is clear that during the first six months of the war, MO5(g) was deluged with a mass of reports of suspected enemy activity borne of spy mania. However, an available MI5 report does recount MO5(g)'s assessment of the threat at that time. According to this report, by December 1914, it:

> '...became known that Germany expected to maintain easy communication by post with her spies in the United Kingdom; ...commerce destroyers would keep in touch with German residents in the United States by means of wireless. Floating mines would be laid to prevent food supplies from reaching our shores and missionaries would stir up sedition among the natives.'[248]

★ ★ ★

The round-up of enemy agents on the outbreak of war was well conceived and well executed. Especially so, given MO5(g)'s limited resources and the communications technology available at that time. The key was cooperation. MO5(g) was the conductor of the counter-espionage orchestra, as well as the composer of the 'music' played.

A knock-out blow had been delivered. But MO5(g) could not let up. It had to be on its guard against further attacks. At this point, MO5(g) was still fairly convinced that the threat came from agents of German (enemy alien) origins. MO5(g)'s wartime grand strategy shows that it appreciated that the primary task of counter-espionage is to protect, and control access to, sensitive information. Spy-catching is only one part of the overall strategy. MO5(g) had its first wartime contact with the enemy, the Lody case, and acquitted itself very well. In evaluating MO5(g)'s grand strategy, the key question seems to be: Was MO5(g)'s grand strategy too focused on enemy aliens, to the neglect of other threats? This question would be answered when MO5(g) faced enemy agents of neutral, Allied or British origins.

The first autumn of the war reveals much about the 'drivers' of MO5(g)'s wartime development, most notably during this period, the great influence of the perceived (perceptions are key here) threat from enemy aliens. The demands of war had an obvious impact on MO5(g)'s development, necessitating rapid growth to deal with an exponentially increased workload as it became deluged with reports of suspicious activity borne out of spy mania. The particular directions that this growth took are telling. The development of a dedicated organization, administration and records branch further underlines MO5(g)'s sense that its role was very much as the central clearing-house for all counter-espionage information. MO5(g)'s concerns that enemy agents might try to hide amongst the influx of Belgian refugees, and the deployment of MO5(g) officers to evaluate the control at ports, clearly demonstrates that it developed in response to changes in the perceived threat. In short, development was influenced by a desire to plug any gaps revealed in its defences.

CHAPTER FOUR

The Year of the Spy

1915

A S 1915 began MO5(g) fully expected Germany to send more agents to the UK and that these agents would communicate with their controllers through the post. This chapter will examine the threat posed by German espionage and how MO5(g) responded to it.

CONTROL OF PORTS AND FRONTIERS: PART 1

Port Control: January-May 1915

A means of control was introduced by MO5(g) which still operates even today. From New Year's Day 1915, passports became compulsory for those travelling from France or Holland to the UK. According to an E Branch Report from 1921 on the control of ports and frontiers:

'From this small beginning there was developed that world-wide system of consular control, which was afterwards strengthened by the appointment of Military Control Officers throughout Europe and the United States of America.'[1]

In light of these experiences, Field Marshal Sir John French, Commander-in-Chief of the BEF, proposed a conference between the British, French and Belgian services to coordinate and improve means for combating espionage, particularly 'to ensure that every possible suspect was thoroughly searched at one place on the through journey, instead of partially at several.'[2] On 4 January 1915, an inter-Allied conference met at Boulogne to discuss what could be done to stop undesirables entering Northern France, particularly the areas under military occupation.[3] The conference decided upon a number of measures that were brought into effect on 1 March that year. They included appointing British agents to help a specially formed control staff at French channel ports, French agents at the ports of call in England, and regulations to make Red Cross organizations responsible for the bona fides of their members working in the Army Zone.[4] A tighter control over passengers between England and France was also introduced in which all travellers from England to France required a French consular visa, a police visa was necessary for all travellers from France to England, and letter-carrying between the two countries was prohibited.[5] In order to strengthen the French consular control of passengers from England, which had proven unsatisfactory, an officer representing the counter-espionage section of the French General Staff was attached to the consular staff in London. This indirectly led to the formation of the British Military Permit Office next to the French Consulate General in Bedford Square, London.[6]

At the beginning of March 1915, the control of the aliens' officers over passengers from France and Holland to the UK was supplemented with the control of the consular authorities. In the opposite direction, a French consular visa was required for passengers from England to France; however, there was no increase in the aliens officers control on travellers from England to Holland, save for the brief delay put on those in transit from France. Apart from the agents who had been sent to aid the control staff at French channel ports, there was no British military control over passengers, and on other routes, apart from those to Holland and France, the aliens officers maintained their role as the sole control authorities.[7] On 3 March, the Home Office Permit Office (HOPO) was opened in London to issue permits for travellers to Holland. Between March 1915 and February 1919, the HOPOs, except for the zone of the armies in France, handled 228,234 applications for permits, of which 224,187 were granted and 4,047 refused.[8]

Owing to delays caused by postal censorship, firms began to send their mail abroad by using a clerk who regularly travelled there and back. On 21 March 1915, an officer at the port of Tilbury, Mr A. Barker, 'reported that an immense traffic of this kind was in progress and that one carrier would carry as many as one hundred letters.' The influx of undesirables and persistent illegal carrying of letters caused MO5(g) to send a senior officer to conduct a tour of the principal ports in May 1915.[9] The decision was then reached to post permanent representatives of MO5(g) to assist and advise the aliens' officers at the approved ports, where 'shortage of staff and the lack of time and accommodation combined to make the control ineffective.'[10]

At this time, attention was still largely focused on traffic between the UK and France or Holland. From 25 April 1915 all aliens and British subjects coming from France or Holland, or going to France or Belgium, were required to possess passports in order to land or embark in the UK.[11] However, it was soon discovered advisable to extend the Permit Office system. In July 1915, it was found that certain individuals were leaving the UK for Scandinavia, thence moving on to Germany or Holland via Copenhagen. Accordingly, the Home Office permit became necessary for all people leaving the UK for Norway, Sweden and Denmark.[12] The Boulogne route to France was also closed to normal passenger traffic, thus restricting the cross-Channel services to Folkestone-Dieppe and Southampton-Le Havre.[13]

Until July 1915 there were few restrictions on alien seamen. Thus there was no check on their movements while ashore and they enjoyed obvious opportunities to gather information and to communicate with others.[14] The Aliens Restriction (Seamen's) Order was issued on 28 July 1915 which required that all alien seamen had to be registered and to carry passports or other identification documents with photographs attached, to be produced on landing at the request of an alien's officer.[15]

The Sampson Case

The case of Private Barry Sampson demonstrates that MO5(g) did not always press for the draconian punishment of German agents. Sampson, a former sergeant in the Royal Marines Light Infantry (RMLI), had been reduced to the ranks and had deserted. He opened correspondence with a German department and was investigated by the police for a time, who then lost sight of him when he left home unobserved. A conversation overheard by chance in the Lansdowne Hotel, Cardiff enabled MO5(g) to pick him up on 6 January 1915. By this time, Sampson had enlisted in the Gloucestershire Regiment, having admitted that he was a deserter, for which he was given twenty-eight days in the cells. He told MO5(g)'s detective that he had received money from Germany as the result, he claimed, of a bluff. His officers were informed of this and nothing was done to him because he had been honest on re-enlistment and to the detective.[16]

The Kupferle Case

Anton Kupferle, a US citizen of German birth, operated as a German spy under cover as an importer of woollen goods. Detected by postal interception to a known spy address, Kupferle committed suicide on 20 May 1915 during his trial. (The British Library Board)

The first winter of the war was the most active period for German espionage in Britain. Germany's intelligence efforts against Britain were no longer limited to those of 'N'. Following the outbreak of war, German military intelligence (*Abteilung* IIIb) also began to target Britain, although its main priorities remained France and Russia.[17]

On 26 January 1915, a Belgian refugee living in Rotterdam wrote to the War Office claiming that Frans Leibacher (or Laibacher and Laybaker) of 12 Waanensteeg in Rotterdam was a German agent who received letters containing messages in secret ink and forwarded them on 'to their proper quarters.' During February 1915, three men (Kupferle, Muller and Hahn) were found to be communicating with this address.

On 17 and 18 February, two letters were intercepted addressed to Leibacher on the headed paper of 'A. Kupferle & Co, Importer of Woolens, 1665 de Kalb Avenue, Brooklyn, N.Y.' These letters contained messages in secret ink. They suggested that the writer had been in Liverpool on 15 February, Dublin on 16 February, and was expected to be in Queenstown on 18 February.

MO5(g) telegraphed the Dublin and Liverpool police to arrest Kupferle. Dublin replied, giving a description of Kupferle, and advising that he had left Kingstown for Holyhead on 17 February, apparently intending to return to the USA from Liverpool. However, the police report did not agree with Kupferle's letters and MO5(g) thought that he might still be in Ireland. Search was also made of hotels in the Euston area of London. It was discovered that Kupferle had stayed in one of them on the night of 17 February and left for Victoria on the morning of 18 February. That day boats for Flushing were held up due to the German blockade, and on the 19th a letter was intercepted revealing that Kupferle was waiting for further money at the Wilton Hotel in London. He was arrested there later that day.

Anton Kupferle was born in Germany on 11 June 1883, but was educated in the USA and became a naturalized US citizen in 1912. He had worked as a woollen draper in New York. Under questioning, he confessed that he had served in the German army at the front. On 14 January 1915, he had received $100 from Franz von Papen of the German Embassy in Washington DC and was also issued an American passport on 25 January. On 4 February he set sail for Liverpool. Following his arrest, evidence of Kupferle's connection with Leibacher and material for secret writing was found in Dublin and London. His movements were traced and the information he had sent abroad 'was found to be mostly incorrect.' His defence was that an American, named Reihly (real name Ruehle), had asked him to collect information for the press and forward it to Leibacher. Kupferle's trial began on 18 May 1915. He committed suicide on 20 May before the trial was completed, after leaving behind a written confession that he had been a German spy.[18] Kupferle also wrote a letter to another spy awaiting trial, which was confiscated by the authorities and in which he commented:

'... The [mustard] gas must have a great effect and be distasteful to the English. In any case, it is a stupefying death and makes them first vomit, like sea-sickness. It is an easy death, and if the war lasts for some time many more will be killed by it.'

Basil Thomson felt that this showed that Kupferle 'had the true Prussian mentality.'[19]

The Hahn and Muller Cases

Meanwhile, under the check on Frans Leibacher letters of 3 and 4 February, posted in the W.C. postal district of London, had been intercepted containing secret messages about military matters which had been written between the lines. They were signed 'A.E.111' which appeared to confirm previous reports received by MO5(g) of a book containing the record of German agents targeted against the UK wherein every agent was entered by a number relating to the order of his recruitment. After the first letter was intercepted, enquiries were made at the address given in the *en clair* message, but without any results. Then, the second letter giving a different name and address was intercepted. On 15 February 1915, Commander Richard Tinsley, head of MI1c's Rotterdam station, informed MO5(g) that Karl Frederick Muller was a spy for the German GOC Brussels. He was said to be receiving letters in London, either to a PO Box or poste restante, to the name of 'Leidec'. Once the message indicting Muller had been received, the police were instructed to call at Guildford Street where he was known to be living. Muller was interviewed on 16 February without any results. The name Leidec was put under check which led to the interception of two letters dated 20 and 21 February addressed to

'Mr Lybecq, postbox 447, Rotterdam' and posted in the W.C. district. They both contained a secret message signed 'A.E.111' written on the back of the letter.

Then came a letter dated 24 February written on the same kind of notepaper as the fourth letter (later discovered to be from Muller), posted in Deptford and containing a secret message '*In the absence of A.E.111*' and signed 'Hahn.' MO5(g) referred to the aliens' register and came across John Hahn. Hahn's shop was raided and evidence connecting Hahn with the writing of the last two letters was found. He was arrested on 24 February and made a reference to Muller. On 25 February Hahn's wife called at Scotland Yard, gave Muller's address and suggested that he might be connected with this trouble.

John Hahn was a British subject, the son of a German father, who had been naturalized as a British subject in 1897. He spent the years 1901 to 1903 in Germany learning his trade as a baker and confectioner. From 1903 to 1910, he worked as a baker in Dublin and London and in September 1910, he brought a bakery at 111 High Street, Deptford. In May 1912, Hahn married Christine Dorst, the daughter of Richard Dorst, a German living at 4 Osy Straat in Antwerp. The bakery was raided by a local British 'mob' which attacked Germans and German businesses in Britain as part of anti-German hysteria fuelled by spy mania, in November 1914 and, as a business, 'failed utterly in consequence of the war.' This left Hahn with financial difficulties and a sense of grievance.

In May, Hahn made a valuable written confession. Muller had received two week's training at Antwerp. His primary objective was to gather precise details of Kitchener's armies. Muller got Hahn to write two letters so that his own handwriting would not appear too often. He also offered Hahn a position in the German Secret Service.[20] In Thomson's estimation, Hahn was merely a 'tool' and his 'object, no doubt was mercenary.' Muller's charisma enabled him to entrap Hahn 'by the promise of partnership in profitable speculations.'[21]

Karl Frederick Muller was a Russian, born at Libau, of German parents. He was fifty-eight years old in 1915, having been born on 21 February 1857. He went to sea at the age of sixteen and married a Norwegian girl in 1881. He began working as a beer retailer in Hamburg and in 1886 he moved to Antwerp where he opened a boarding house. In 1900 he became a cargo superintendent in the Belgian port city, but all of his business interests and occupations stopped on the outbreak of war.

Muller had met Hahn in Antwerp on 12 May 1912 at Hahn's wedding to Christine Dorst, the daughter of Muller's landlord, Richard Dorst. Muller made a grave mistake in involving Hahn, for Hahn 'was not a spy by nature and was out of his depth.' Rather Hahn has been described as an unsettled and simple individual who had been informed that Muller might be able to set him up with a new livelihood somewhere. He therefore decided to write one more letter, which he happened to sign with his own name.[22]

Before the German siege of Antwerp during the autumn of 1914, Richard Dorst and his family left for Holland. Muller stayed there and took charge of Dorst's property. Muller had a daughter who was said to have lived in Hamburg and Bremen and who was married to a German sailor who had died in the battle of the Falklands. Muller arrived at Sunderland on 12 January 1915. He carried Russian papers stating that he had recently been released from a German prison where he claimed he had suffered harsh treatment.

He called at the home of some English acquaintances but at that time Sunderland was prohibited to all aliens. He was thus expelled by the police. On 13 January he arrived at 38 Guildford Street, London W.C., and contacted Hahn. Then, between 17 January and 13 February, he made three trips to Holland and back.

The letter of 21 February was written on a peculiar kind of paper and the *en clair* message was in another's handwriting. MO5(g) deduced that 'A.E.111' probably resided in the Bloomsbury district of London, as he always used a 2½d stamp and stamps of this value issued to a branch office were specially marked. Then came the letter dated 24 February signed 'Hahn.' Muller was arrested the next day and four of the specially marked stamps were found on him. MO5(g) learned that the information that Muller had sent abroad had been generally correct.

Thus three German agents had been arrested within six days but the issue of how to try these men caused problems. Kupferle's American nationality caused political problems and Hahn's British nationality caused judicial problems. Muller's case could not be separated from Hahn's and it was not possible to try Kupferle and Hahn by court martial. In March 1915, the case of treachery of a British subject (Hahn) caused DRR56 to be re-drafted in order to uphold the rights of British citizens. It was amended to enable a British citizen to claim trial by judge and jury in the civil court, as opposed to a court martial, and to give the civil court powers to inflict the same punishment as a court martial. When an individual was tried in a civil court, it was obligatory to publish the sentence, whereas following a court martial, such publication was not required.

Following the arrests of Kupferle, Muller and Hahn, on 23 March 1915, DRR24A was issued prohibiting the use of secret means of communication.[23] On 23 March 1915, DRR56A was issued to give the civil court power to inflict such punishment as might have been inflicted by a court martial, and to recognize a British subject's right to trial by jury. The three defendants were thus treated as British subjects and tried in the civil court under DRR56A. They were all charged with attempting to communicate information with a view to helping the enemy. Some of the evidence was heard in camera, but the cases were generally tried and the sentences were passed in open court. Muller and Hahn were tried on 2 June 1915. Hahn was sentenced to seven years' imprisonment. Muller was condemned to death by firing squad. The names of the prisoners and their fates were soon published in the British and American press. However, with Muller being a very common name, it was possible that he was not identified by the Germans, because at least one attempt was made from the USA to find out which 'Muller' had received the death penalty.[24]

On 10 June 1915, DRR22A was promulgated: restricting the use and possessions of codes and ciphers. In July 1915, DRR18A was issued: prohibiting communication with a spy.[25]

The *Kriegsnachrichtenstelle* (KNSt or War Intelligence Centre) in Antwerp did not know of Muller's arrest and continued to despatch messages to the agent. This provided Reginald Drake with an opportunity to send fabricated reports from Muller to Antwerp, most of them written in secret ink. The *Kriegsnachrichtenstelle* duly responded by sending money and requests for further information. Muller's 'messages' duped the *Kriegsnachrichtenstelle* until the end of May 1915, when the Germans first began to have doubts about their credibility – doubts which had been prompted largely by Muller's claim that 80,000 additional British troops had been sent to France, a number that was contradicted by other sources of intelligence.

MO5(g) finally gave up on this deception when the *Kriegsnachrichtenstelle* summoned Muller back to Rotterdam to receive further instructions. For his part, Kell was unable to maintain secrecy over the arrest and trial of German spies in Britain, especially since the British government was keen to demonstrate to a doubting public that it *was* catching spies. Muller's execution also ended any continuation of credible disinformation generated in his name and, unlike British Intelligence during the Second World War, MO5(g) did not enjoy regular SIGINT with which it could monitor the extent of its deception efforts.[26]

By the time they realised that Muller's information was bogus, the Germans had paid MO5(g) about £400 for it.[27] MO5(g) used the proceeds to buy a car, which, with a delightfully dark sense of humour, was christened 'The Muller'.[28]

The Melin Case

On 16 March 1915, MO5(g) was informed that one E.W. Melin of 25 Upper Parkway, Hampstead was attached to the German Secret Service – however, the available documents do not give any indication of who informed MO5(g) about Melin, or how the informant came to discover that he was a German spy. On 15 April, the censor intercepted a cheque from Schwedersky and Co – a fake front company used by Schwedersky, a known German agent – to Melin. On 10 June, two envelopes containing three letters signed 'Kate' and addressed to Melin were intercepted. Between the lines of an affectionate family letter were questions about British ships in secret writing. Melin was arrested on 14 June. Search revealed spy equipment, and between the pages of an English–Swedish dictionary there was found a slip of paper bearing the names of regiments and other military terms. At interrogation, Melin was shown the three letters containing secret writing and he immediately confessed his connection to the German Secret Service. Between 2 March and 12 June, Melin sent off twenty-nine reports, made on the fifth page of a newspaper. He was paid by cheques forwarded by Schwedersky and Co and drawn on the Union of London Bank and Smith's Bank.[29] Interrogation and further enquiries revealed that Melin was a forty-nine year old Swedish citizen, and that he had arrived in London on 26 February. His father had been a Swedish MP for over thirty years and owned a shipping business. Melin worked for his father's company but was an alcoholic and a drug addict, and when his health gave way in 1906, it became impossible to employ him. His father helped him financially for a number of years while he sought to cure his health problems. Eventually, he secured a job as a clerk in a shipbroker's office in Nikolaieff in Russia, but as a result of the war, the firm closed down in August 1914 and Melin found himself once more in financial difficulties. His father was by now eighty-one years old and refused to help him any further. In desperation, Melin went to Germany, where he had friends, to look for work. An acquaintance introduced Melin to a recruiter from the German Secret Service, who were always on the lookout for English-speaking neutrals. With seemingly no other way of supporting himself, Melin reluctantly agreed to become a German agent.[30] He was found guilty at trial by court martial on 21 August and shot on 10 September.[31]

It is interesting to note that Melin was tried under DRR18 – with an act preparatory to the commission of a prohibited act – plus three other regulations, which had been added to the original DRR in order to plug gaps that had been revealed in Britain's counter-espionage defences. DRR24A made it an offence to send any document from the UK containing anything written in any medium that was not visible unless subjected to heat or some other treatment. DRR4 forbade being in possession of a code. DRR22A provided that anyone possessing any code, cipher or other means that could be adapted to secretly communicating naval or military information was guilty of an offence unless he proved that it was intended solely for commercial or other legitimate purposes.[32]

THE GERMAN ESPIONAGE SYSTEM

German Espionage Centres in Belgium and The Netherlands

In August 1914, all German officials withdrew from Allied territory and direct contact between Germany and the UK ceased. Both the British and German Secret Services concentrated on neutral countries as bases from which to collect intelligence on the enemy. The Germans used the Netherlands, the USA and the Scandinavian countries as portals from which to launch missions into the UK. The Germans also set up *Kriegsnachrichtenstellen* (KNSts or War Intelligence Centres) just inside Germany's borders or in occupied territory. The KNSts were run by military or naval officers who gathered information on the enemy by analyzing foreign newspapers and other such openly available sources. They also recruited and trained agents and sent them on missions in enemy territory.

Germany's intelligence effort against the UK was carried out by spy centres in Brussels, Wesel on the German-Dutch border, and Antwerp which were all connected to German Secret Service officials operating in the Netherlands. The centre at Brussels, under *Oberleutnant* Burmann, played a relatively minor role. Burmann's main task was collecting intelligence on the Dutch armed forces, but the centre was disbanded in April 1917 and its remaining personnel transferred to Antwerp. Antwerp, directed by *Hauptmann* Kefer, was the largest of these three western KNSts. Kefer was assisted by Heinrich Grund, a German who had resided in Antwerp before the war. The Antwerp centre ran a spy school that trained agents for missions in the UK, as well as providing them with secret codes and invisible inks. This centre reached its height in November 1916, and then began to decline in importance. It was disbanded in spring 1918, and the staff was transferred to Lorrach on the German-Swiss border.

Like the other two KNSts, the Wesel centre was founded by *Abteilung* IIIb. However, as it focused entirely on the UK, in early 1915, it was transferred to the *Admiralstab* which oversaw operations conducted against Britain. The Wesel centre was first directed by *Kapitän zur See* Kroeger, who was succeeded by *Korvettenkapitän* Walther Freyer and it posted a liaison officer to the Antwerp centre to coordinate its activities.

The German Consul in Rotterdam, Carl Gneist (he later changed his cover to that of commercial attaché), played a central role in the German intelligence system. Gneist was closely connected to Freyer, Kefer and the intelligence chiefs in Berlin, but did not actually recruit agents himself. He left this to his contacts, mostly Germans or Dutch.

His most important contact, however, was Hilmar Dierks, an NCO who had fought in the opening campaign on the Western Front before being chosen for intelligence work and assigned to assist Gneist in recruiting agents. Dierks employed sub-agents in Rotterdam, Flushing and The Hague.[33]

On 9 February 1915, some Dutch post-boxes used by German agents in England were reported to MO5(g), namely one operated by Richard Sanderson (alias Dierks, alias de Boer), at Post-box 417 in Rotterdam and by Dr Brandt in Dordrecht. They were put on check that same day.

During the second quarter of 1915, MO5(g) learned more about the existence of Dierks' recruiting agencies in Rotterdam and The Hague. Direct enquiry established that he and his organisation 'had no genuine business, or concurrently that they were in direct contact with Germans.' Even more was learned about Dierks' activities through spy cases and 'the treachery of some of the Dutch agents employed.' Melin's confession revealed the existence of the spy centre at Wesel that acted independently of Dierks.[34]

On 28 May 1915, Ernest Maxse, the British consul-general at Rotterdam, forwarded to the Foreign Office a report supplied by the French military attaché which coupled Sanderson, of 72 Provenierstraat, Rotterdam, with W Muller, of the Hotel Weber, Antwerp; M Blanken of 7b Wolfshoek, Rotterdam, and Brandwicjk & Co, of 106a Bingley Straat, Rotterdam. Sanderson represented Bjarks & Leming, a firm of tea merchants engaging young Dutch men to become travelling tea salesmen in London, Cardiff and Southampton. According to the report, wires were to be sent in code, while letters were to be addressed to Blanken and to Brandwijk. Brandwijk's connection with Sanderson, at an address at 166Y, Locaduinschekade, The Hague, was confirmed by a Dutch sailor named Hoogendyk on 10 June 1915 who provided the following an address at Ipers Schiedamschedyk 33 as the post-box for letters.[35]

In June 1915, DRR18 was made 'absolute' by forbidding 'the collection etc. of any information for communication to the enemy.'

A spate of spy convictions in mid-1915 roused the Dutch Government 'to take action to protect its subjects from the machinations of German recruiting agents.' Arrests were made and the Dierks gang was broken up.[36]

Commander Richard Tinsley

MO5(g) learned much about the German espionage organization in Belgium and the Netherlands from Commander Richard Tinsley (often referred to as 'T' in MI5's reports), who was the head of MI1c's Rotterdam station. Tinsley was a former naval officer and shipping manager. Intelligence from Tinsley led to MO5(g)'s detection of four German agents in 1915 and one in 1916.[37] Tinsley, who used a fake business, The Uranium Steamship Company, as cover, was tasked with tracking down German agents operating in The Netherlands. The Rotterdam station also paid particular attention to the arrival and departure dates of German trains in Belgium. Such information was crucial, since it gave conclusive evidence of German troop movements and possible military initiatives in France. During the last two years of the war, Tinsley's organization comprised over 2,000 agents with wide-ranging tasks.[38]

The Buschman Case

Fernando Buschman was a Brazilian subject and a mechanical engineer of German origin, who had been born in Paris on 16 August 1890. He had designed an aeroplane in 1911 and built two aircraft, but his aviation venture was a failure. Buschman then went into a business partnership with his cousin, but left after a disagreement.[39] He landed at Folkestone on 14 April 1915 claiming to be a businessman who dealt in picric acid, rifles and cloth, and went to London. On 5 May, he travelled to Rotterdam, returning to London on 16 May. Immediately after his first landing in the UK, Buschman entered into telegraphic communication with H. Flores (Dierks' partner in Rotterdam), whom he wired repeatedly for money. On 4 June, a telegram from Dierks asking Buschman to return to Holland and confer with Flores was intercepted. Buschman was arrested. Subsequent investigation showed that he had not concluded any business in England and that he was well equipped to act as a spy. His papers, newspapers and music were covered with minute figures in secret ink, and on a telegraph form there was a microscopic map in

Fernando Buschman, German spy. A Brazilian subject of German origins, Buschman posed as a businessman. He was detected by a telegram check on a known spy address. Buschman was shot on 19 October 1915. (The British Library Board)

secret ink showing the positions of the headquarters of British armies, corps and divisions in France during April 1915. Buschman was tried by court martial on 28 September 1915. He was found guilty and shot on 19 October 1915.[40] Thomson 'felt most sorry' for Buschman. He had been married to the daughter of a rich soap manufacturer in Dresden, 'who had kept him liberally supplied with funds for his studies in aviation.' He had also been a talented violinist.[41]

ORGANISATIONAL DEVELOPMENT, 1915

MO5(G)'s coordinating role

MO5(g) quickly came to appreciate that its wartime role was twofold: as the central clearing house for all counter-espionage information, and as the central coordinator of all those departments involved in counter-espionage. MO5(g)'s monthly report for April 1915 stressed the fact,

> '...that although the Special Intelligence Bureau employed a certain number of persons on direct enquiry, yet, on the whole, its functions were administrative, advisory and co-ordinative rather than executive. It gathers information from all sources on subjects bearing on espionage, sees that this information is placed at the disposal of the executive authorities concerned, and supervises enquiries and their results.'[42]

ORGANISATIONAL CHANGES, 1915

As related in the previous chapter, a fourth branch, later to be labeled E, was formed in May 1915 to take over the fast developing work of organising and administering the control of ports and frontiers.[43] Following the formation of this new sub-division it was decided to reorganise MI5, so that on 11 August 1915 MO5(g) became known as MO5, with four branches labeled E, F, G and H. The preventive branch became known as the F Branch, the investigative branch was thenceforth called G Branch, and the administration and records branch acquired the title H Branch (see Chapter Three).[44]

Despite changing its designation from MO5(g) to MO5, MO5 continued to use the former name until January 1916, because as Kell wrote to A.L. Dixon, of the Home Office, on 10 September 1915, '*we are better known to the Police under this "nom de guerre"*.'[45]

CONTROL OF PORTS AND FRONTIERS, PART 2

E (Control of Ports and Frontiers) Branch during the First World War

Spies travelling to the UK had to pass through three 'fences' – and at each of these points a record would be kept which E Branch had access to. Firstly, the work of MI1c and consular officials at foreign ports, where a visa had to be obtained as a preliminary step in coming to the UK, acted as an outer frontier. Secondly, the permit system (people could not leave the UK without stating where they were going, on what business, to what address, and without satisfying the authorities of their bona fides) provided a check on outward traffic from the UK. Thirdly, the controls at the ports, which had been developed by E Branch, collected information on all travellers, and acted as the link between MO5(g) and the Permit Office and also between MO5(g) and British consuls. Incoming suspects could be searched and sent to Scotland Yard.[46]

The wartime control of the UK's frontiers as a way of defending against the attacks of the enemy's intelligence service was theoretically the Preventive Branch's concern. But this vital work needed so large an organisation that it was considered necessary to form a distinct branch to focus on the policy and administration of the control of ports and frontiers.[47] This new branch, later to be labelled MO5E, was formed as a separate branch to the Preventive Branch in May 1915, and its duties were described as: 'Military policy connected with the control of civilian passenger traffic to and from the United Kingdom. Passes and permits for the Zone des Armees. Port Intelligence.'[48]

The measures instituted to control passengers and seamen leaving or entering the UK and civilians wishing to enter the Army Zone were, firstly, appointing MCOs to assist and advise aliens officers at approved ports and, secondly, the establishment of permit offices to issue permits and passports. It was the role of E Branch to supervise the MCOs and the Military Permit Office. E Branch was also involved with the drafting and administration of the regulations regarding the Military Permit Office, the control of passengers and seamen at the ports, plus developing and extending the permit office system in the UK and overseas.

The control of civilians travelling to the Army Zones, which was handled by the Military Permit Office, differed from the normal frontier control. The Military Permit Office functioned as the London bureau of the intelligence sections of the General Staffs in the various Army Zones. The Commanders in the Army Zones obviously held the final say about the admission of civilians into the areas occupied by their troops, and in theory it was the role of the Military Permit Office to transmit particulars about applicants for Army Zone permits to the authorities there. Nonetheless, in practice, the Military Permit Office found that its advice concerning the grant or refusal of a visa was usually taken. However, the key point here is that the ultimate decision lay with the armies in the Field, and the policy and methods used to control Army Zone traffic did not fall strictly within MO5(g)'s domain.[49]

MO5(g) did, however, hold a key position within the system of control. It established close relations both with the HOPO and the FOPO, it had direct authority over the Military Permit Office, the Paris Permit Office, and MCOs at the British ports, and it also cooperated closely with MI1c in directing the work of MCOs abroad. The information that MO5(g) alone possessed regarding enemy agents and suspects worldwide was made available to the control authorities by the black list and supplementary circulars. Owing to its understanding of enemy methods, MO5(g) was not only able to provide answers to enquiries, but also to supply constant warnings against both specific individuals and the many subterfuges they had been shown to employ. Besides the detail work, due to its expertise in counter-espionage, MO5(g) was also able to propose policy initiatives and legislative measures in response to the results of methods employed and the wider context of the counter-espionage system as a whole. It was for these reasons that, as soon as proper passenger control had been achieved, a scheme to improve the control of alien seamen was suggested by MO5(g), mainly through E Branch's efforts.[50]

The reason for military rather than civilian control was that the system existed to prevent the enemy's acquisition of military and naval intelligence, which required that it should not be under exclusively civilian control. It was also felt that the guiding principles of the control should be set by MO5(g), as the counter-espionage agency. Additionally, the unique nature of counter-espionage, and the secretive character of the papers routinely used in a Permit Office, made it appropriate that the staff should be chosen and trained by those with experience of this kind of work. Lastly, the records that every Permit Office needed could only be provided by MO5(g).[51]

Geography affected the British system of traffic control in two particularly important ways. Firstly, because the UK is an island, the authorities had no land frontier to control. This made the system relatively simple to enforce, because ships could be concentrated at a few ports, which were much easier to guard than a whole land frontier.[52] As *Oberstleutnant* Walter Nicolai, head of Germany's military secret service, *Abteilung* IIIb, ruefully recounted, 'England and America were all but completely protected by the sea against the penetration of our espionage. For the same reason both countries could reduce the leakage of news to a minimum.'[53] Secondly, owing to the concentration of all railway and steamer routes in Northern and Western Europe upon London and because of the war, London became the hub for passenger traffic between Allied and neutral European countries and even many non-European ones, particularly the USA and Canada.[54]

In June 1915, representatives of MO5(g) (who would later become known as MCOs) were assigned to assist the aliens officers at Hull, Newcastle, Southampton and Folkestone.[55] The author S. T. Felstead recounts in his book of 1920 how 'one of the first things insisted upon by the officer in charge was that he should have a representative of his own at every port, and thus have a direct check on people passing to and fro.'[56]

An MCO's duties were very demanding. They involved examining passengers and crews, limiting and controlling the individuals permitted at the arrival and departure of vessels, supervising alien seamen aboard and off their vessels, collecting information about passengers and seamen, and searching ships and crews. The MCO was also responsible for censoring mail to seamen on out-going ships, maintaining office records and transmitting reports to MO5(g). He was additionally supposed to propose ideas to MO5(g) for discussion with the Home Office, liaise between the civil, military and naval authorities at the port, swap information and discuss problems with them, and encourage the cooperation of the local railway, dock and shipping companies and businessmen when their help was needed. In short, as E Branch described it, the Military Control Officer at a Port was 'a kind of axle' to 'the wheel of counter-espionage.'[57]

Initially, MCOs carried a notebook containing lists of suspects and other details, which was replaced with the Port Officers' Guide which included,

'…descriptions of suspects, lists of suspect addresses, suspect firms, suspect hotels, suspect seamen and suspect ships, followed by a list of private letter-carriers. There were also lists of books, and publications which were either to be confiscated, detained or destroyed. The whole was compiled with a view to ready reference and the book was liberally interleaved to allow of additions.'[58]

The MCOs also received suspect lists from:

'M.I.5., Scotland Yard, the Home Office, the Home Office Permit Office, G.H.Q Home Forces (through the Local Commands) as and when they were issued. They also received the Liste des Suspects of the Bureau Central Interallie, the Suspect List of the Eastern Mediterranean Special Intelligence Bureau, Cairo, the War Trade Intelligence Department's Black List and Supplements and other publications.'[59]

On 1 July 1915, the Military Permit Office was opened in Bedford Square in London to examine the bona fides of those applying for permits to travel to the Army Zone, passing applications on to GHQ and obtaining the required passes for those involved.[60]

In August of that year, the head of E Branch was Major (later Colonel Sir) Claude E.M. Dansey, Assistant Director and Inspector of Port Intelligence.[61] Dansey, who had been given a wartime commission in the Monmouthshire Territorial Force Regiment, joined MO5(g) on 14 December 1914.[62] As previously mentioned, following the entry of the United States into the war, Dansey was chosen to serve on an intelligence liaison mission to the USA between 12 April and 11 July 1917. He then left MI5 on 19 August 1917 having been posted to MI1c to reorganise the Secret Service in Holland.[63] As the culmination of a most successful career in intelligence, Dansey went on to become Assistant Chief of SIS during the Second World War.[64]

E Branch now had fourteen members of staff, including two officers (Dansey himself and a section officer) as well as three clerical staff at MO5's headquarters, one military permit officer and two examiners (graded as assistant military permit officers) at the

Military Permit Office, and six port officers of the Port Intelligence Service. E Branch's duties were military policy connected with traffic to and from the United Kingdom, policy connected with the grant of passes and permits for the 'zone des armies', control of port intelligence service, control of Military Permit Office, distribution of counter-espionage reports and circulars and the examination of reports on enemy agents in Scandinavia, Denmark and Holland and in belligerent territory in Europe.[65] As an example of the kind of circular issued by E Branch, on 6 December 1917, it warned that:

> 'Information has been received that the Germans are giving agents, employed for sabotage, pencils which have the appearance of being ordinary large blue or red pencils. In the interior of these is a glass tube containing chemicals, the extremity of the tube being finished off with blue lead. When the pencil is cut, the tube is exposed and the end removed. The contents coming into contact with the air, after a period varying from 15 to 20 minutes, produce a powerful flame, which lasts 90 seconds. The German Service is likely to employ these pencils to produce fires on quays and ships.'[66]

In late August 1915, an inter-Allied conference met in Paris to consider how to improve the control over people entering the Army Zone. It resulted in the introduction of new passport regulations for the Army Zone in February 1916, known as the French carnet regulations. However, the French carnet system was soon found to be cumbersome and changes were later introduced at the suggestion of the Military Permit Office.[67]

The initial measures to improve the control at ports were not a complete success. The MCOs were beset with many problems; one of the main ones was their want of authority, which placed them at a disadvantage with the aliens' officers. This was partly overcome in October 1915, when MCOs received the extra title and status of military advisers to the Home Office, and were officially recognised as military advisers to the aliens' officers at ports in matters relating to counter-espionage.[68]

Until this time, the control exercised by the permit offices was only over outward traffic to certain countries, and it was becoming ever clearer that more checks were needed to deter non-essential travel and to hinder the movements of suspicious individuals. On 30 November 1915, as noted earlier, passports were made obligatory for all travellers by an Order in Council that made passports compulsory for all individuals, of any nationality, leaving or entering the UK.[69] MO5 was responsible for the restrictions which made travel to and from the Continent so difficult. Understandably, travel was discouraged as much as possible and it was not desirous either for MO5 or Britain's allies to create further trouble by permitting more or less unrestricted movement.[70]

In autumn 1915, it was discovered that German agents were being sent to Britain as seamen, discharging themselves on arrival, and then returning to Germany by passenger ship, having probably most likely acquired a considerable amount of useful information during their stay in England.[71] On 16 August 1915 Dansey sent a circular letter to the Home Office for issue to port officers, advising them to be on the look-out for enemy agents coming to the UK on tramp steamers from Holland and Scandinavia.[72] Therefore, from 15 March 1916, alien seamen on short-voyage ships from Holland and Scandinavia were not allowed to take their discharge; however, long-voyage ships were not felt to pose a threat.[73]

In autumn 1915, Sir John French suggested that the permit office system should be extended to inward traffic, because it was superior to the granting of visas by individual consuls. The results of permit office control of outward passenger traffic led to the same system being adopted for the control of individuals wanting to travel from Allied and neutral countries to the UK.[74] This prompted the opening of a permit office, under military control, at Berne on 15 November 1915. A passport control officer was appointed for Athens, and the Paris Permit Office opened on 1 March 1916. The aims of the permit office system in Allied and neutral countries were summed up in a memorandum on the working of the Paris Permit Office:

'(a) To prevent suspects travelling to the United Kingdom except in certain cases when it is desired to get them here for arrest; to give facilities to persons who are travelling on bona-fide business; and to refuse visas to those who cannot show an adequate reason for travelling.
(b) To curtail examination at ports as far as possible and to indicate passengers who should be especially watched or searched in the United Kingdom.
(c) To forward information which may be of use to Contre-Espionage and Trading with Enemy organisations.'[75]

Together the Military Permit Office in London and the Permit Office in Paris provided an efficient check on cross-Channel traffic.[76] The controls abroad were soon extended as British MCOs were sent to Petrograd, Christiania, Stockholm, Copenhagen, Madrid and Lisbon. In July 1916, a permit office was opened in Rome and an MCO was sent to work at the Consulate General in New York. In November 1916, an MCO was appointed at Bucharest.[77]

Two cardinal principles were universally applied. Only certain consuls had the authority to issue visas, and, no matter what route he was taking, a traveller was required to have his passport endorsed in the country where his travels began by an official of the country that was his final destination.[78] MCOs stationed abroad placed a secret symbol on the passports of suspicious individuals to alert port control officers when they reached the UK. However, the visa of an MCO or British Consul was not a definite guarantee of entry into the UK. The aliens' officer at the port of arrival had the final say. Nonetheless, it was an unwritten rule that British subjects should not be stopped from disembarking in their own country.[79]

The experience of MCOs at British ports had demonstrated that it was not possible to perform searches of passengers and maintain security of the docks without sufficient personnel.[80] In June 1916, the Military Foot Police (Port Section) was formed to work under the MCOs and to assist the aliens' officers at the various ports. Its original establishment was 200, but in September 1917 a full establishment of 300 was approved.[81] In October 1917, there were 227 ports police, but this figure had risen to 230 by December 1917, and on 11 November 1918 it stood at 255.[82]

The Germans tried to exploit all the gaps in this system. Before the issue of DRR14D in May 1916, passports or other identifying documents were not necessary for British seamen. Hence, it had become a well known ruse of German agents to adopt this guise and DRR14D failed to put an end to this threat. Therefore, attempts were made to provide British seamen with proof of identity. However, it was not until July 1918 that a satisfactory system was adopted.[83] The insistence upon identity papers was not an effective deterrent, because traffic in both genuine and false seamen's papers was a typical enemy tactic. Other means were needed to render these efforts to evade the control unsuccessful.[84] Provision of Military Foot Police at ports, and additional aliens officers, improved the physical control at ports and effectively tightened the control over alien seamen. This made it possible to impose effective physical restrictions and introduce more systematic and thorough ways of searching people and baggage.[85]

MI5's list of staff for 11 December 1916 names E Branch's staff at MI5's headquarters, but does not mention its staff at places away from headquarters. E Branch had sixteen members of staff at MI5's headquarters, including seven officers and nine clerical staff. Three officers and eight clerical staff were assigned to E Branch (but not to a particular section), with section E1 comprising two officers, and E2 consisting of two officers and one member of clerical staff.[86]

Following Dansey's transfer to MI1c, Major H.E. Spencer, OBE, late Captain in the 13th Hussars, Reserve of Officers, succeeded him as head of E Branch in August 1917. Spencer had joined MO5(g) on 27 May 1915 and had served with E Branch, interrupted by a brief stint as head of A Branch from 16 July to 26 August 1917, before returning to take over E Branch, and finally leaving on 8 September 1919.[87] As in December 1916, MI5's list of staff for 22 October 1917 lists E Branch's staff at MI5's headquarters, but again does not include its staff posted away from headquarters. E Branch had twenty members of staff at MI5's headquarters, including nine officers and eleven clerical staff. Three officers and three clerical staff were assigned to E Branch (but not to a particular section); section E1 consisted of four officers and four clerical staff, and E2 comprised two officers and four clerical staff.[88]

An MI5 report concluded that the '…control system in force at the end of the War approximated very closely to the ideal.' Although not absolute, permit office control over outward and inward passengers covered all routes between Britain and the continent of Europe, and inward traffic from the USA and Japan. Turning to seamen, 'it is hard to see how the methods developed at British ports in the last year or so of the war could have been improved.' There was a division of authority between MI5 and the Home Office Aliens Branch, 'but cooperation between these two departments remained at all times so close and so friendly that the practical disadvantages of dual control were reduced absolutely to the minimum.'[89]

MI5's list of officers and branches in which they were employed for August 1918 is very revealing. E Branch now had twelve officers at MI5's headquarters, including four who were assigned to E Branch (but not to a specific section), six in E1 and two in E2. The Military Permit Office comprised six officers. There were twenty-two MCOs in the UK assigned to Aberdeen, Folkestone, Glasgow, Gravesend, London Docks, Hull, Liverpool, Newcastle, Plymouth, Southampton and the South Wales ports. There were also twenty-one MCOs abroad: in Paris, Rome, Milan, Genoa, Turin, I(B.)G.H.Q Italy, Washington, New York, Tokyo and Malta.[90] A further MI5 list of staff for 20 September 1918 shows that E Branch had twenty-three members of staff at MI5's headquarters, including ten officers and thirteen clerical staff. Of these, three officers and six clerical staff were assigned to E Branch (but not to a given section), E1 consisted of five officers and four clerical staff, and E2 comprised two officers and three clerical staff.[91]

The eventual system of control that evolved was not MI5's ideal choice, although it was still very pleased with it. In fact, there were alternatives to the scheme of control that was actually chosen. Every permit office could have been directly subordinated to MI5, which would have supplied it with its trained personnel and its records, and with which it could be in constant communication. It was not possible, however, to carry out this ideal programme. Nevertheless, both in theory, and practice, the system which was gradually developed did not fall far short of the ideal.[92]

One example of how E Branch was positioned to contribute to the catching of spies by either detaining suspects when they attempted to enter the UK, notifying the authorities of their arrival so that they could be placed under surveillance, or stopping them as they attempted to leave the UK, is the Rosenthal case, which is examined later in this chapter. Interestingly, none of the spies caught by MI5 was actually detected initially by passport checks or baggage searches at the ports. Nonetheless, a number of spies who were initially detected by other means were subsequently discovered to have used false passports, particularly American ones, which added tellingly to the evidence against them, and to the desire for a thorough examination at the ports.[93]

The case of Sopher illustrates how effective the vetting for travel permits could be. Sopher [the surviving record refers only to this name], an Indian who had worked as a dresser and a clerk at the Indian Hospital in Brighton, and who had aroused suspicion for wearing his uniform after he had been discharged, applied for a permit to visit a 'Mrs D'Aumont' at The Hague in February 1916. At interview he first lied that 'D'Aumont' was a journalist but, on being shown his error, he dropped all pretence and admitted a brief acquaintance with D'Aumont and 'De Regals', aliases used by known spies. He was interned under DRR14B, on the grounds of his hostile associations and attempts to renew a dangerous connection.[94]

It is believed that no more than a small number of enemy agents were able to evade the system of control at the ports.[95] Indeed, once MI5 was given the opportunity of checking the ingress and egress of 'neutrals' by keeping its own staff at British ports, the threat from, and activity of, German spies receded.[96] On 14 November 1918, Kell wrote to Sir John Pedder, the Principal Assistant Secretary at the Home Office, expressing his appreciation of the great value of this work:

'*The efficiency of the control at the Ports of all movements to and from this country has undoubtedly been one of the decisive factors in defeating the enemy's endeavours to communicate prejudicial naval and military information to their forces and has been of incalculable military value as a factor in our great victory.*'[97]

Pedder's reply of 16 November 1918 also acknowledged,

'*…the value to us in carrying out our powers and duties of having a call on your special sources of information and points of view. The results of the co-operation of our two Departments in safeguarding the national interests need not, I am confident, fear the most searching examination.*'[98]

The available evidence suggests that E Branch accomplished the task that it was set up to achieve and should thus be rated as having been very successful. It performed its preventive role and provided leads for investigation and intelligence on the methods used by German agents, it managed to run the system to control ports and frontiers, and as a result of its activities, German spies were caught. Furthermore, an analysis of the system developed and supervised by E Branch leads to the conclusion that it was effective, notably thorough and quite sophisticated for its time. It did not take too many staff to impose this system, nor cause overly great disruption to trade and passenger traffic considering the wartime circumstances. No system can be perfect and, considering the technology available at that time, E Branch did about as good a job as could legitimately be expected.

The Rosenthal Case

Robert Rosenthal, a German, made three journeys to the UK on behalf of the German Admiralty Secret Service in Berlin: from November to December 1914, again during January 1915, and lastly from mid-April until his arrest as a result of a stroke of luck in May 1915. Rosenthal was detected by a 'happy accident.' On 8 April 1915, he wrote a letter from the Hotel Bristol in Copenhagen to 'Franz Kulbe, Berlin, Schoneberg, Beizigerstrasse 10' containing a secret message stating that he was 'going to start work in England' under the pretext of selling a patent gas lighter and signed it Robert Rosenthal. Due to a postal sorting error the letter came to England where the censor detected the secret message. The letter was passed on to MO5(g) on 3 May. MO5(g) already knew that Kulbe's address was really that of Captain von Prieger, the chief of the German Admiralty Secret Service in Berlin. As a result, MO5(g) ordered the arrest of any travelling salesman dealing in a patent gas lighter.[99] In an exceptionally accurate circular of 4 May 1915, MO5(g) alerted the ports:

> '*From information received it is likely that a GERMAN Agent (or agents) posing as a traveller in patent gas lighters, may attempt to enter the UNITED KINGDOM, most probably from COPENHAGEN. Any such persons should be closely questioned as to the name of their employer, and should they give the name as ROSENTHAL, they should be arrested…*'[100]

On 11 May, Rosenthal was arrested at Newcastle whilst embarking for Bergen. During interrogation he was confronted with his letter and immediately confessed his true nationality and mission. He possessed spy equipment, a copy of Jane's *Fighting Ships 1914-15*, eau de Cologne and violet powder. Investigation revealed that as a boy Rosenthal had been apprenticed to a baker in Cassell. He disliked the work and at only fifteen years of age was imprisoned for three months for forgery. Upon his release from prison in 1908, he left Germany for the USA, but returned in November 1913.[101] Although he was German, Rosenthal had managed to procure an American passport that had been issued at Washington DC on 26 January 1915, but there is no record as to how he was able to obtain it. Five of Rosenthal's telegrams were produced in evidence and proved to contain substantially accurate information. He was found guilty at court martial on 6 July and hanged on the 16th.[102] It is believed that Rosenthal was the youngest spy to be executed in the UK during the First World War, with one writer observing that he was 'a typical

Robert Rosenthal was a German citizen who had lived in America. As a spy he posed as an American travelling salesman selling gas lighters. He was detected by postal interception to a known spy address. Rosenthal was hanged on 16 July 1915.
(The British Library Board)

specimen of the ne'er-do-well, drugging himself with cocaine…'[103]

Rosenthal provided MO5(g) with key insights into German methods and how they were evolving. He revealed that rather than recruiting German nationals as spies, use was made of agents from neutral countries who would be disguised, like himself, as commercial travellers. Acting on Rosenthal's revelations, Kell ordered rigorous censorship of letters and cables from Britain to neutral countries.[104] Rosenthal readily offered his services as a double-agent, also providing information on secret inks, codes and the methods of passport forgery used by German intelligence. But Kell turned Rosenthal down, likely because of the events of the Graves Case which took place before the war (see Chapter Two). As Christopher Andrew has observed, 'Kell thought it safer for MO5(g) to impersonate a dead German agent than to turn a living one.'[105] Of course, the very fact that Rosenthal was caught on his third mission to the UK, after two successful attempts at entering and leaving the country, clearly illustrates that the control at ports and frontiers was not absolutely infallible.

Experience from recent spy cases led MO5 to issue a circular on 10 August 1915 advising that '…all commercial travellers coming into England for the first time since the war were to be looked upon with suspicion.'[106]

SECRET WRITING

Testing for Secret Writing

In 1915 the discovery that German agents were using invisible ink led Kell to enlist the help of Henry Aird Briscoe, an inorganic chemist from Imperial College at the University of London. Briscoe and his laboratory developed a method for detecting invisible ink in letters and the increasingly sophisticated chemicals used in secret writing.[107]

According to an MI5 report:

'Physical disturbances due to writing on paper with a dry point or with any liquid medium or secret ink can be detected by a number of simple methods known as General Developers. These depend for their action on physical principles rather than chemical reactions …' It was found that the best general developers were iodine vapour and iodine solution. However, general developers will not develop any writing if the paper is afterwards damped, as this has the effect of producing a uniform surface and so rendering the general developers ineffective. Paper was damped after writing to 'remove the surface effects (caused by writing) which can be revealed by iodine solution.' Damping involved wiping 'the paper lightly with cotton wool moistened with water or dilute ammonia, after writing the secret message.' After damping 'the secret writing will only develop legibly with the specific reagent for the ink employed.' In order to develop secret writing that has been damped, 'specific developers which react chemically with the correct ink material are necessary.' Choosing the correct mix of chemicals to develop a particular secret ink 'is a matter of extreme difficulty and is dependent on a knowledge of what ink the enemy has actually used and also what he would be likely to use, ...' In short, it was vital to acquire a sample of the secret ink that had been used.[108]

In the early days of the war, German agents such as Lody, Kupferle, de Rysbach and de Bournonville used secret inks of a relatively simple nature such as lemon juice, cobalt chloride, alum, and potassium ferrocyanide, and they did not yet take the precaution of damping. Thus their secret messages were easily revealed by iodine vapour or iodine solution.

'Unless therefore, some means are adopted for overcoming this effect [of the disturbance of the paper produced in writing] there is no object whatever in using a secret ink of a recondite nature.' Therefore, German agents were instructed 'to adopt precautions for reducing the physical disturbances produced in writing to a minimum', by using a suitable pen and paper, and then damping the paper after writing. [109]

German agents were instructed to use ballpoint steel pens and to apply very little pressure when writing in order to avoid scratches. Indentations could be avoided by placing the paper on a hard surface, such as a mirror. Unglazed paper of a good quality was to be used, because highly glazed paper showed the writing on it.

In May and June 1916, information was obtained that German agents were using two inks known as 'F' and 'P' which were of an entirely different nature from those previously described. At this time, German agents were also instructed to damp the paper after writing, in order to render impossible the development by iodine and other general developers. These inks were first carried in liquid form and disguised as scent, gargle, mouth wash, and similar substances. Later, these same inks were impregnated into various articles of clothing such as soft collars, ties, and handkerchiefs. The secret ink was prepared by soaking these articles in water. The nature of 'F' ink was deduced by examining the contents of a scent bottle used by Leopold Vieyra, a German spy (see Chapter Six). When Vieyra was arrested his lodgings were searched as a result of which it was discovered that he possessed secret writing equipment: ammonia, cotton wool, ballpointed pens, and a scent bottle containing an unknown liquid. Tests revealed this unknown liquid to be secret ink F. 'P' ink was found to be a solution of Protargol, a substance used for medical treatment, as were similar compounds known as Collargol and Argyrol. Until it became known that they could be used as secret inks, they could be carried without suspicion under the pretence that they were being used for medical treatment. A report on the work of the Testing Department during the First World War (known as MI9c by the end of the conflict), observes that, 'Numerous cases have been met with in which articles of clothing, impregnated with this substance, have been taken from enemy agents.' For example, George Vaux Bacon, an American journalist and German spy (see Chapter Six), carried it in his socks and buttons. Four other inks, 'Rg', 'Q', 'J' and 'D', were also known to have been used by the enemy. The composition of all these inks was determined and a number of investigations were carried out on them. Declassified reports do not reveal any more than that about these four secret inks.

In a report by MI9c in 1919, it was noted that, 'For communication with their agents in this country the enemy spy masters have used substances which could be developed by comparatively simple methods requiring chemicals which could readily be brought in this country.' 'E' ink was developed by dipping the letter into a solution of potassium permanganate followed by washing, while 'G' ink was developed by means of a solution of potassium iodide in water acidified with vinegar. Alfred Hagn, a Norwegian journalist and German spy (see Chapter Seven), carried tablets of Burroughs Wellcome's potassium iodide for the purpose of developing letters from his spy master.[110]

The Jappe Case

The bungling of the case of Abdon Jappe, a Danish electrician, by detectives of the Plymouth garrison, who employed unsuitable agent provocateur tactics, provides a telling contrast with MO5(g)'s methods. Around 20 May 1915, a Detective-Sergeant Bellinger of the intelligence office, Plymouth garrison, posing as the manager of a timber and copper company that dealt with the dockyard, established contact with Jappe. By pretending to be considering illegal traffic in copper to Germany, he induced Jappe to show his hand. Unfortunately, the available records do not provide any indication as to why the detective chose to target Jappe with this sting. However, Jappe replied that he could smuggle the copper across the Danish frontier if the manager – in reality Bellinger – would ship it to Copenhagen. Jappe then proposed that the manager/Bellinger, being frequently in the dockyard, might send information about ships' movements to him in Copenhagen. When the manager enquired how this intelligence was to be conveyed by telegram, Jappe at once explained two secret codes.[111] He was arrested on 29 May 1915 by order of the CMA and caught in possession of the two codes. On 2 November 1915, he was sentenced to three years' penal servitude. The detective's action had forestalled MO5(g) and the improper agent provocateur methods of investigation employed meant that evidence of hostile association could not be procured. Thus, when the Home Office decided to reduce his sentence, Jappe could not be interned under DRR14B. He seems to have been subsequently deported.[112]

The Janssen and Roos Cases

Haicke Marinus Petrus Janssen was born in Kamper, Holland in 1885 and later worked as a merchant seaman.[113] He had had been granted a life-saving medal, by the UK's Board of Trade in 1913 after his ship had responded to the SOS call from a vessel that was burning at sea and saved 500 lives.[114] On 13 May 1915, Janssen arrived in the British east coast port of Hull and wired Hilmar Dierks asking for money. He then went on to

Southampton, where he sent five telegrams to Dierks & Co, a known spy address operating as a fake front company run by Hilmar Dierks of the German secret service, between 24-28 May, purportedly ordering different kinds of cigars, as part of his cover as a cigar merchant for the company. In reality, they conveyed information about ships' movements.

Wilhelm Johannes Roos was a sailor who had served in the Dutch Navy. He landed at Tilbury on 14 May 1915 and went to Edinburgh, from where he wired to Dierks & Co on 17, 18 and 25 May, for whom, like Janssen, he purported to be a cigar merchant. He moved on to London and was traced and arrested there on 2 June.[115] Thomson recalled that as Roos was being taken back to Canon Row police station after interrogation at Scotland Yard, he smashed the panes of a glass door and tried to kill himself by slashing his wrists on the fragments of broken glass. He was put on suicide watch.[116]

Wilhelm Roos, a Dutch citizen who spied for Germany. He posed as a cigar merchant, but was detected by a telegram check on a known spy address. Roos was shot on 30 July 1915. (The British Library Board)

Search of telegraphic money orders showed that Dierks & Co had remitted money to Janssen on 19 and 27 May and to Roos on 25 May. Search of Janssen's lodgings revealed spy equipment, telegrams to and from Dierks & Co, a copy of *Jane's Fighting Ships 1915*, and a price list of cigars supplied by Dierks & Co which contained some figures and letters that were interpreted as a code. Search of Roos' lodgings also revealed spy equipment, a communication from Janssen giving the address of the hotel he had been staying in at Hull, and a copy of *Pearson's Magazine, May 1915* containing an article by F.T. Jane, illustrated with photographs of different types of British warships, and the name of several Royal Navy ships written in pencil on the margin. He had a few cigars, but no samples of different brands. It was ascertained that neither of them had called on any tobacconists, or in any other ways even attempted to conduct any genuine business. Roos admitted knowing Janssen whereas Janssen denied knowing Roos.

Chemical experts tested the cigar price lists and brought up secret writing by using scent with talc powder as a fixative. Cigar trade specialists told the court that Dierks & Co's price lists were 'unintelligible or at least unusual.' Furthermore, expert naval evidence proved that the information that they had sent abroad was 'approximately correct and most valuable to the enemy.' Both were found guilty and shot on 30 July 1915.[117] Although Roos had been confined as a lunatic between February 1909 and January 1913, MO5(g) investigated his medical history, but found nothing that called for mitigation of his sentence.[118] After the court martial, but before sentence was confirmed, Janssen tried to buy his freedom by providing information about German spy methods. Unfortunately for him, MO5(g) already knew of all the spy addresses that he gave them.[119]

The Breckow and Wertheim Cases

George Breckow, German spy.
A naturalised US citizen of German birth,
Breckow posed as a businessman.
He was detected by a telegram check on
a known spy address. He was shot on
26 October 1915.
(The British Library Board)

George Breckow (alias Reginald Rowland, alias Parker) had been born at Stettin in Germany in 1884, the son of a failed Russian landowner who became naturalized as a German citizen. Breckow's father later worked in the piano trade and George went into the family business. In 1908 he emigrated to the USA, eventually becoming a US citizen and worked exporting pianos. Following his father's death, Breckow returned to Germany in May 1914 to see his family. He found work in a German bank. By February 1915 he had decided that life was too tough in Germany and decided to return to the USA. However, he could not afford to do this. He thus applied to the German Bureau of Foreign Affairs for work as a courier carrying despatches to the USA. In March 1915, he was approached by Naval Intelligence, who promised to enable him to return to the USA if he would spy for them in Britain first.[120] Breckow carried a forged passport in the name of Reginald Rowland and was also told to sign his letters 'George T. Parker'. Dierks gave him papers and business cards for the firm of Norton B. Smith of New York.

'Reginald Rowland' landed at Tilbury on 11 May 1915. The check on Dierks & Co revealed a telegram from Holland on 30 May, announcing the dispatch to 'Reginald Rowland, c/o Societe General, Regent Street, London' of £50 on account of Norton B. Smith & Co of New York. Rowland was arrested on 4 June. Search revealed the receipt for a registered letter to 'L. Wertheim' of Inverness. Suspicious possessions included Jane's *Fighting Ships 1914-15*, a phial of lemon juice, pens, a tin of talc powder, and a code resembling that used by Janssen and Roos.

The postal censor submitted to MO5(g) two letters of 25 May and 2 June because they seemed to be from a German who wished to reside by the coast and take photographs, and they were signed 'George T. Parker'. After Rowland's arrest, his handwriting was checked, and they were found to have been written by him. Tests revealed that they contained naval and military information, references to a female accomplice and references to 'Lizzie' in secret writing. It was on 9 June 1915, that 'Lizzie' was eventually connected with L. Wertheim.

Louise Emily Klitschke had been born a German Pole, but she became a British subject by marriage.[121] She came to England in 1901 and in 1902 she married Bruno Wertheim, a man she had met in Berlin, and the son of a Russian who was later naturalized as a British citizen. Bruno Wertheim worked as an accountant for an Austrian bank in London and his marriage was not a happy one. In May 1913 the Wertheims took out a deed of separation. Lizzie Wertheim was awarded an allowance of £518 per annum from her former husband. However, Bruno Wertheim was a great spendthrift, who soon found himself in financial difficulties and unable to pay Lizzie her allowance.[122]

Lizzie Wertheim was arrested on 9 June 1915. While the police were searching her room, she tore up a letter from 'George T. Parker' and threw it out of the window. The police also found an envelope addressed to 'R. Rowland', a bottle of scent and tins of talc powder, letters of 7 and 16 May written in the handwriting of Dr Brandt, the address of Brandt's wife, Netta, at Loosduinsche-Kade, and Rowland's visiting card. The examination of telegrams showed that on 1 May Lizzie had sent a 'conventional message' to a known spy address in Holland.

Eventually Breckow 'made some sort of confession.' Breckow and Wertheim were tried together in the civil court, because Wertheim claimed her rights as a British subject.[123] At trial, Breckow admitted to having had a love affair with 'Mrs Wertheim'.[124] Both were found guilty. Breckow was shot on 26 October 1915 and Wertheim was sentenced to ten years' penal servitude.[125] She was sent to Aylesbury women's prison, but in January 1918, she was certified insane with 'chronic persecutory delirium' and sent to Broadmoor criminal lunatic asylum. She apparently became very suspicious of her food and could be seen smelling each spoonful when under covert observation. She died of pulmonary tuberculosis on 29 July 1920, aged thirty-six years.[126]

The Zender Case

Ludovic Hurwitz Y Zender was born in 1878 of Peruvian nationality, although his father was Scandinavian. Zender was a genuine commercial traveller, representing several European firms in Peru. In early-June 1915, MO5(g) ordered that all telegrams sent from certain UK ports in May were to be scrutinized. Five telegrams from Ludovic Hurwitz in Glasgow sent between 15-24 May to one August Brockner (or Brochner) at 11 Todboldgatan, Christiania in Norway attracted the notice of code experts. They purported to be orders for different kinds of tinned fish goods, but the wording of the messages varied suspiciously and in a way that resembled the code that had been used by Janssen and Roos. The chief constable of Glasgow informed MO5(g) that Hurwitz Y Zender had left the United Kingdom intending to return soon. His description was signalled to the ports with orders to arrest and search him. He was arrested as he landed at Newcastle on 2 July 1915 and sent to Scotland Yard.[127] Thomson interrogated Zender and concluded that he had been tempted by the 'high pay' offered by the German Secret Service.[128] MO5(g) sent an agent to Christiania to make inquiries about Brockner. He was seen visiting the German Ambassador and said to be organizing German counter-espionage in Christiania. Zender's correspondence with Brockner was submitted to the 'destructive criticism' of an expert in the fish trade, for Zender was ordering and Brockner was transmitting orders for fish out of season, in wrong quantities and packaging. Zender was found guilty at court martial and shot on 11 April 1916.[129]

The Roggen Case

Alfredo Augusto Roggen was a Uruguayan citizen, who had been born in Montevideo, Uruguay in 1881. His father was a German naturalized in Uruguay and Roggen married a German woman. He became a farmer, but did not own his own farm. In March 1914

Alfredo Roggen, German spy.
A Uruguayan citizen of German ancestry,
Roggen's cover was as a farmer looking
to buy agricultural machinery. He was
detected by postal interception to a
known spy address and was shot on
17 August 1915.
(The British Library Board)

he travelled to Germany but there is no indication as to why he went there or how he was recruited by the German Secret Service. [130] He then arrived at Gravesend on 30 May 1915 and travelled to Edinburgh, then on to the Tarbet Hotel on Loch Lomond. As a farmer, he claimed he had visited the UK to buy agricultural machinery.

On 8 June, he posted two cards: one to '[H.] Flores', who worked for the German secret service in Rotterdam in partnership with Hilmar Dierks, and the other to 'H. Grund, c/o Ivers and von Stad, 17 Glashoven, Rotterdam'. Grund was known to work with Flores. The card to Grund gave Roggen's address at the Tarbet Hotel but it was intercepted and Roggen was arrested. When he was interviewed he gave an unsatisfactory account of his relations with Flores, whom he described as a friend of his business partner in South America.

Roggen's notebook contained a spy address – 'Ivers & von Stad, 17 Glashaven' and a piece of blotting paper which contained a partly legible name taken to be 'G. Breck(o)w'. However, no connection between Roggen and Breckow was ever established. Secret writing was developed on several of his papers. Most importantly, a map of the North Sea on which some minute characters, words and figures were detected. He was found guilty at trial by court martial and shot in the Tower of London on 17 September 1915. [131]

The Stad and Den Braber Cases

On 9 June 1915, the British Consul General at Rotterdam reported that David Stad had come over on 1 June and that Cornelis Marinus den Braber would soon be on his way over to London. He eventually arrived on 18 June 1915. They were both Dutch seamen who claimed to be representatives of the firm of von Brandwijk and Co selling custard powder. Orders were issued that they should be watched. Having departed Rotterdam, they were subsequently traced to Lindley Street in London. Stad and den Braber were both arrested on 23 June 1915 'for having neglected to give proper particulars to their landlords.' Search revealed dummy cases of custard powder, no samples and the fact that neither had conducted any genuine business. Stad had wired to Brandwijk for money and £7 was sent to den Braber by 'Ipers', most likely a spy address, on 26 June 1915. The charges failed on a 'technical point' and they were freed on 14 July. There was, however, no doubt that they had come over to spy and they were interned under DRR14B on 16 July 1915. Den Braber was eventually deported in October 1919. There is no record of what happened to Stad, but he was probably also deported in 1919. The landlords of both men were also arrested for not having maintained a proper record of their guests. Stad's landlord, Liebfreund, was sentenced to six months' hard labour, and Braber's landlord, Carlishe, was fined £5.[132]

The Marks Case

On 21 June 1915, Josef Marks, a civil engineer, went to the American Legation at The Hague, with the object of coming to England. The American Minister at The Hague believed that Marks' American passport was actually a forgery and warned the British Consulate there. On 25 June, the British Consulate signalled MO5(g) that Marks was coming to England as an independent spy sent by GHQ Berlin. Orders were issued to the ports to arrest Marks upon his arrival and convey him to Scotland Yard. On 15 July, the British Consulate signalled MO5(g) that Marks was on his way. As soon as his boat docked, Marks was recognized and challenged on board by a police constable. Marks immediately asked to see an intelligence officer to whom he would give important information. At various interviews, Marks said that he was coming to the UK to find out about munitions for the German Secret Service.[133] In Basil Thomson's well-considered opinion, Marks was the 'most absurd person employed by the Germans.' A 'positive mountain of flesh', Marks stood at over six feet tall and weighed at least sixteen stone. When Thomson interrogated him, Marks claimed that while living in Aix-la-Chapelle, the Germans accused him of being a French agent and, in Thomson's words, 'told him that he could clear himself from suspicion only by proceeding to England to obtain naval information for them. He preferred to take his chance of escaping discovery in England to being shot as a French spy by his own people.'[134] Before he was challenged by the constable, he had made up his mind to give information to the British authorities and on the way over wrote a letter to the Minister of Munitions. The letter was written on the ship's notepaper and was offered up by Marks himself. MO5(g) learned that Marks had been born in Munich but educated in the USA. He had become a US citizen, but returned to Germany and allowed his US citizenship to lapse. MO5(g) identified him as Multerer, 'the former fraudulent managing director of the Safety Chemical Co, who had lived in England as a German subject from 1911 to about June 1913 and had left owing many debts.' Whilst living in the UK, Multerer had business notepaper printed for his wife under the name Marks. Marks was charged under DRR 18 and 48 with an act preparatory to committing an offence – for example, travelling to Tilbury in the ship with the intention to spy. The question for the court, however, was at what precise moment he abandoned that intention and whether he was sincere in his confession. Marks was tried by court martial on 28 September, found guilty, and sentenced to five years' penal servitude. He was eventually deported in December 1919.[135]

The Marks case was one of a number of cases (including Rosenthal, Stad and den Braber) '…where no overt act in this country could be proved against the agent, although it was certain he had come to spy.' In response, MO5(g) requested the passage of DRR 18A, which was issued on 28 July 1915, making it an offence to communicate with a spy.[136] As all of the recently caught spies had carried Jane's *Fighting Ships 1914-15*, on 14 August 1915, DRR 18 was also amended to order that recent editions of naval annuals were to be withheld from sale.[137]

The Meyer Case

On 29 June 1915, the censor 'took exception' to a letter posted from London to Mrs Goedhardt at 147 von Blankenbergestraat, The Hague. He ironed the back of the letter and uncovered a secret message about the Thames defences and Chatham Dockyard. Thus, on 2 July, this address was put on check. A typewritten letter, headed 1 Margaret Street 'and begging for a remittance of £50', signed 'Tommy', was intercepted addressed to 'Niendiker' at the aforementioned address in The Hague. The police searched 1 Margaret Street and identified the handwriting on a label as that of the writer of the letters. The two occupants – husband and wife, Albert and Katherine Meyer – were arrested on 30 August. Albert Meyer was a German who had come to the UK in June 1914.[138] He was twenty-two years old and worked as a cook and waiter. He married on 20 May 1915 and lived off the immoral earnings of his prostitute wife.[139] On 5 November he was charged with having attempted to communicate information of use to an enemy, having used secret ink, and having attempted to communicate with a spy. At trial, the prosecution proved that the information that Meyer had attempted to send was correct, that he had used lemon juice as a secret ink, and that 'Niendiker' was in touch with the German Secret Service. Meyer was found guilty on all three charges and shot on 2 December.[140] In Thomson's opinion, 'the spy who made the worst impression was Albert Meyer… with a very mean history. He was one of those young scoundrels who live upon women, defraud their landladies, and cheat their employers.' Meyer moved from one lodging house to another, promising his landladies that he would pay them as soon as he received money from his parents abroad. He also cheated the German Secret Service since his communications apparently 'contained a mass of fictitious information.'[141]

There was 'no evidence' against Ketherine Meyer. However, she was 'a woman of bad morals' and MO5(g) thought that her husband 'had obtained some of his information through her associations.' She was released from prison before her husband's trial, but as she failed to notify her change of address she was again arrested and sentenced to three weeks' imprisonment on 27 October. She was interned in January 1916, eventually being removed to a lunatic asylum.[142]

The De Rysbach Case

Kurt Herlot de Rysbach, the son of a naturalized Austrian, was a British subject and a music-hall performer who came to England via Switzerland and France on 27 June 1915. He set himself up in rooms with an Englishwoman who was a trick cyclist and who was due to perform from 2 August

Kurt de Rysbach, German spy. A British subject of Austrian ancestry, he used the cover of a music hall performer. He was detected by postal interception to a known spy address and sentenced to penal servitude for life in October 1915. (The British Library Board)

at a music hall in Glasgow. On 9 July 1915, de Rysbach wrote to Mr J. Cords at the spy address used by Zender. A secret message claimed that he had a brother on HMS *Commonwealth* who would provide information and that he himself would soon gain employment as an interpreter in the War Office. A check on the handwriting on letters to crew members of HMS *Commonwealth* led to the identification of the writer's brother. The brother was exonerated. De Rysbach, who had given various pseudonyms, was traced by a letter to his brother in which he gave his address, photograph and stage name.

De Rysbach was arrested on 26 July 1915. Secret writing equipment was found in his room. He had also sent sheets of music abroad covered with invisible ink, as well as twenty-four newspapers, eight letters and two telegrams. At his first trial, in the civil court on 20 September 1915, de Rysbach claimed that 'he came to England and promised to serve the Germans in order to obtain his liberty [from internment], and he had no intention to assist the enemy.' This defence carried some weight with the jury. The jury ultimately disagreed on the verdict and de Rysbach was remanded. At his second trial however, in October 1915, the jury found him guilty and sentenced him to penal servitude for life.[143]

The Slager and Ulrich Cases

The threat from some German agents was removed by the less drastic measure of having them leave the UK with a no return permit, of which the case of Pauline Slager and Georgine Ulrich provides an example. On 16 July 1915, Rotterdam signalled that Slager and Ulrich (or Ulricht or Ullrich) were spies. They arrived at Tilbury on 29 July where they were searched and their passports taken from them. They were also ordered to call at Scotland Yard. They were informed that their passports would be returned to them as soon as they notified the authorities of their permanent address. At interview, they claimed that they had come to England to work as music hall entertainers. Without informing the police, they moved on to Glasgow and then Edinburgh on 14 August. As a result, they were arrested in Edinburgh for entering a prohibited area without the required identity papers. They left the UK on 25 August with a no return permit.[144]

IMPERIAL DIMENSIONS – 1915

Establishing connections with the Colonies

MO5(g) had observed the grave consequences of the want of an Empire-wide counter-espionage system. In some cases the need of a definite organisation had serious repercussions. The trouble that had arisen among the native troops of the Malay States Guides in December 1914 and the mutiny of the 5th (Native) Indian Light Infantry at Singapore in February 1915 were thought to have been due to German influence.[145] Analysing the mutiny at Singapore, which led to the deaths of thirty-two Europeans and the public execution of thirty-seven mutineers, historian Ian Beckett concludes that:

'In reality, while rumours of the regiment's impending despatch to fight in Mesopotamia provided the trigger, internal divisions between Indian officers and men lay at the root of the mutiny. The situation was compounded by poor rations and the strained relationship between the commanding officer and the other British officers.'[146]

A comprehensive system of German espionage had been discovered in British East Africa that had been totally unsuspected owing to the lack of a central clearing house for information. It was suggested that better intelligence might have been provided if an organisation had been established there before the war.[147] As MO5(g)'s Irish work grew, in May 1915, a section (A3) was formed in the Investigative Branch to deal entirely with Irish affairs, viewed as being 'all cases of suspected espionage, sedition or treachery in Ireland.'[148]

When MO5(g) raised the question of establishing relations with the Colonies with the Colonial Office in July 1915, India was the only part of the Empire that was already in personal communication with MO5(g). Links had been established with India's Criminal Intelligence Department (CID) in the same way as relations with the police chief constables in the UK had been maintained, correspondence being carried on with the Director of Criminal Intelligence (DCI) through his representative in London, Major J.A. Wallinger. However, although the DCI kept MO5(g) fully supplied with information concerning Indian seditionists, it was found that very few reports on the subject of European suspects were forthcoming.[149]

The first real origins of D Branch are to be found at the beginning of July 1915 when the officers of MO5(g) discussed the question of establishing closer relations with the Colonies regarding counter-espionage. This had been under consideration even before the war, having only been deferred due to the huge amount of work in other areas that had to be dealt with.[150] On 15 July 1915, Kell and Hall of MO5(g) discussed this with Sir Maurice Hankey, Secretary to the Committee of Imperial Defence (CID). Hankey favoured an opening by personal letter from the DMO to the military staffs at Colonial bases, but suggested consulting Henry Lambert, Assistant Under-Secretary at the Colonial Office. Later that day, Kell and Hall called on Lambert, finding him entirely in agreement with the scheme. On 1 August 1915 the approval of Sir John Anderson, Under-Secretary of State at the Colonial Office, was obtained.[151]

Appreciating the need, which MO5(g) had suggested, of establishing direct communication with the Self-Governing Dominions and Colonies in order to facilitate cooperation in counter-espionage, the Colonial Office issued a secret circular memorandum (discussed later in the text), the draft of which had been prepared by Drake, Holt-Wilson and Hall, to Governors-General, Governors and Administrators of all the Self-Governing Dominions and Colonies. The intention was that if MO5(g) could establish relations with the Colonies, it could be a clearing house for the whole of the Empire and a rapid interchange of counter-espionage intelligence would result. In such a way a watch could be kept on the movements of suspects, and means could be taken to prevent the entry of any undesirables into the UK.[152]

Regrettably, most of the Colonial Office's correspondence with the Colonies concerning counter-espionage seems to have been destroyed. For example, the Colonial Office's register of secret correspondence covering the years 1914 to 1927 contains many intriguing references to letters under the subject heading 'Counter-espionage' that have been stamped 'DESTROYED UNDER STATUTE'.[153]

Little has been said about what actually happened on the ground in the Colonies themselves, because this was the work of the local counter-espionage officials there and thus outside the work of MO5(g). Indeed, at that time, MO5(g) knew little of events in the Colonies. It only received occasional papers through the War Office, Foreign Office and Colonial Office. An inquiry into all possible sources of information had shown that, apart from the intelligence summaries of the naval and military commands abroad, there was no organised system of records. Thus, if the machinations of enemy secret service agents throughout the Empire were to be checked, it was considered vital that there should be an exchange of counter-espionage intelligence.[154] Of note is the fact that the military authorities in the East African Protectorate (later Kenya) deported one L.W. Ritch, who had organised a railway strike and was continuing to preach unrest. He was deported to England, and the colonial governor, Sir Conway Belfield, informed afterwards. Belfield approved this action.[155]

The aim throughout was to promote the same close personal relations with the constituent parts of the Empire as had been established between MO5(g) and the various police forces in the UK.[156] Thus, on 5 August 1915, the aforementioned memorandum was sent semi-officially to the Governors-General of the Self-Governing Dominions, with a covering letter from Andrew Bonar Law, the Secretary of State for the Colonies. On 18 August, copies were also sent to all Governors and Administrators in territories not possessing responsible government.[157] The memorandum, which became the starting point for later developments, pointed to the need for a state organisation for counter-espionage work, having access to every source of intelligence there.[158] Replies to these proposals had been received from nearly all of the Dominions and Colonies by February 1916. By the following month, counter-espionage services had been established in Australia and Malta and, apart from a few exceptions, other Governors or officials had established contact with MI5.[159]

The following episode suggests that this system experienced some early teething problems. On 19 February 1916, Kell wrote to the Colonial Office, in reply to a letter regarding Robert E. Whelan, a suspected German spy who had been arrested in Melbourne, Australia, to ask if the Australian Government could investigate.[160] On 23 February 1916, Hall was informed that a telegram concerning Whelan had been despatched to Australia.[161] On 25 February 1916, Hall acknowledged this letter, adding:

'We would certainly have made these enquiries ourselves and hope to do so in future, but as we have not yet had an acknowledgement of our letter telling the people who we are and what our telegraphic address is, we thought it advisable in this instance to let the enquiry take the established official route.'[162]

The reports sent to MI5 regarding the existing conditions in the Colonies at that time demonstrated that, except for Malta, where a small agency had been set up under the Military Intelligence Department to collect information at the start of the war, no definite counter-espionage organisation had ever existed in any of the Colonies. Since the war, some preventive measures, such as censorship, had come into effect, while in some Colonies Martial Law had been declared; in others the Governor had used his authority under an Order in Council of 26 October 1896 to declare emergency regulations. Wherever military and naval interests were involved, counter-espionage was the domain of military and naval units, usually in cooperation with the civil police. In some cases the arrangement was satisfactory, in others it suffered from an insufficiency of personnel and from the difficulties entailed by the combination of counter-espionage with other duties. In Canada this was being conducted efficiently by the police, but where the work was being handled by a number of different agencies, as in Australia or Egypt, a want of centralization was telling.[163]

By October 1915, correspondence with the Colonies was being undertaken by sections of G Branch. The duty of Imperial Overseas Special Intelligence was first entrusted to G3, to which was already assigned, working with G1, the preliminary investigation of cases of espionage, sedition, treachery, fomentation of strikes and sabotage and dissemination of peace propaganda in Ireland. Cooperation with the police and counter-espionage agencies in India and Egypt on these subjects was the work of G2(b).[164]

When corresponding with the Colonies, MI5 soon learned that the term 'counter-espionage' was misunderstood by many, and in some instances the concern over its connotations with secret service caused them to become reluctant to comply with the proposals to establish a universal system across the Empire. Owing to the memory of the Boer War, South Africa might have feared that the aim was to spy on the Boer community, rather than to counter German espionage. There had also been an Afrikaner rising in September 1914, involving former die-hard bitter-enders like de la Rey and de Wet.[165] Thus, the less threatening term 'special intelligence' was employed instead of counter-espionage and used in all correspondence with the Colonies and Dominions. Hence, MI5, as represented by D Branch, was known by its counterparts throughout the Empire as the Central Special Intelligence Bureau (CSIB).[166]

THE GENERAL ORGANIZATION OF A COUNTER-ESPIONAGE BUREAU

In his covering letter to Colonial Governors, the Secretary of State for the Colonies, Andrew Bonar Law, explained that he was sending them a secret memorandum on counter-espionage that had been drawn up in the War Office, because it was felt that it would be useful 'to take further steps to co-ordinate and focus information on this subject.' Bonar Law asked the Colonial Governors to discuss this with their Prime Minister and then inform him whether the proposals in the War Office Memorandum could be carried out in their colony.

Owing to the 'considerable importance' of the matter and the necessity for 'complete secrecy', the view was that it 'hardly lends itself to ordinary official correspondence. ' This explains why Bonar Law had written to them informally. He added that, 'Pressure of work at the War Office has prevented this question from being dealt with before, by the Bureau concerned.'[167]

The memorandum began by asserting that the global nature of the war had made it necessary to arrange '...for the widest possible interchange of Confidential Intelligence bearing especially upon the activities of hostile secret service agents "throughout the Empire".' It also offered MO5(g)'s analysis of the threat, which reveals much about MO5(g)'s perceptions of the threat in mid-1915:

'At the present juncture greater importance attaches to Naval and Military Counter-Espionage than to enemy activities directed to the capture of British trade or to seditious purposes.'

The memorandum suggested that a number of matters required consideration:

(1) Colonial intelligence reports passed to the War Office, Admiralty and other departments 'do not as a rule deal closely with Counter-Espionage.' It was felt that this was due to 'limited facilities and brief local experience... Moreover owing to the short tenure of local appointments by Service Officers these reports lack the width of view and continuity of purpose which is derived from a stable organization having access to all the sources of Intelligence in the country, which is essential in peace and in war; and for the efficient working of such an organization.'

(2) In the UK, this was done by 'a Central Counter-Espionage Bureau with permanent records and a small permanent staff.'

(3) '... Experience has shown (a) That the co-ordination necessary to obtain effective results cannot be expected if such work is confined to the technical Intelligence Sections either of the Army, or the Navy, or the Criminal Investigation Branches of the Civil Police or Post Office. (b) That the best results can only be obtained by a Central Bureau, under an officer who commands the personal confidence and assistance of all concerned, and brings to a common focus all the intelligence services.'

(4) 'The legislative and administrative side of counter-espionage work requires knowledge of naval, military and police matters,' whilst '...the executive work must be entrusted to selected officers of the civil police and postal services.' This '...points to certain advantages in the selection of a military or naval officer of experience as the head of such a Bureau.'

(5) The memorandum had been prepared because it was '...felt that a free interchange of information about enemy agents, and an effective co-ordination of the means for detecting their activities throughout the Empire, is essential.'

(6) In order to avoid the leakage of information, it was felt that it was best 'to avoid the passage of secret papers through unnecessary hands.' Therefore, correspondence should be '...conducted by direct personal semi-official communications between the officers immediately concerned.' As such, it was proposed that the officer selected for this work should be placed in direct personal communication with Kell, and that letters should be forwarded in the Colonial Office bag.

It also asked for feedback on the points raised and requested that MO5(g) should be provided with copies of existing regulations akin to OSA 1911, DORA and the ARA, with commentary on how these Orders and Regulations were being enforced. The memorandum ended by expressing the hope that it might eventually be possible to arrange an exchange of visits between MO5(g) and their colonial counterparts.[168]

The Colonial Office also enclosed 'Notes on the General Organization of a Counter-Espionage Bureau', which are undated, but which were probably prepared in the summer of 1915. They reveal a great deal about the workings of MO5(g) and are worth quoting at considerable length:

'A Counter-Espionage Bureau should by providing a link between the naval, military and civil authorities enable a Government to decide what concerted measures are necessary to prevent the betrayal to an enemy, whether actual or potential, of vital national interests.

The duties of a Counter-Espionage Bureau comprise:

1. The prevention or at least the obstruction of espionage by precautionary legislation and such other means as can be openly enforced by the uniformed police and other Government officials for facilitating personal identification and for the control of potential suspects in the mass.

2. The detection of espionage by means of the detective police force, supplemented by and co-operating with a small number of agents specially trained for counter-espionage work, who are under the direct control of the Bureau; and the preparation of such evidence and exhibits as can appear in court to enable the law officers to secure the conviction and punishment of offenders without publicly disclosing the processes by which the crime has been detected.

3. The examination of the credentials and the control of travellers passing through the seaports, across the frontiers, or circulating within the country; including the circulation of warnings and descriptions of suspects to the officials at the ports and frontiers.

4. The compilation of records and interchange of information with British and Allied officials.

5. The internal organization and administration of the Bureau, including financial and secretarial duties, and the registration, indexing, filing and custody of documents.'

MO5(g) suggested that where the above duties were to be assigned to two or more officers, then 1 (Prevention), 4 (Records) and 5 (Organization) should be the work of one officer, and 2 (Detection) and 3 (Control) should be the work of the other. It also recommended that, depending on the prevailing conditions in the particular colony, either an official and open, or unofficial and secret, register of aliens should be kept.

MO5(g)'s note paid particular attention to the importance of records, and suggested that a Register of Documents, a name card index, a place card index, a subject card index, personal files, subject files and official files were 'essential'. Plus, as the work increased, classification cards – for example, for classifying the register of aliens under different localities, and books containing photographs and specimens of handwriting.[169]

The Edwin Case

Edward Edwin came to MO5(g)'s attention when the Intelligence Officer at Dover notified the Bureau that he had received independent statements from two wounded soldiers that Edwin 'had asked specific questions as to the number, organization, etc. of British troops in Belgium and France.' He had also 'incited the men to desert and promised to get them out of the country if they did.' Edward Edwin was a Swedish masseur who had been engaged to treat wounded troops at the Duke of York's School at Dover from 27 March 1915. He was arrested on an espionage charge on 5 August of that year. However, the case presented some difficulty as neither of the witnesses against him had a completely clean record. Investigation revealed that Edwin had also been arrested in early April 1915 for examining certain military works near Dover, and it had been reported that at the end of March 'he had put specific questions as to the numbers and training of recruits going to France.' Edwin was tried by court martial on 2 October and found guilty of attempting to elicit information that might be of use to an enemy and sentenced to seven days' hard labour, with deportation at the end of the sentence.[170]

The Hensel Case

Irving Guy Ries landed at Liverpool on 4 July 1915, ostensibly to collect clients for American firms dealing in hay and corn. He claimed that he was heading straight for London. Instead, he passed through Newcastle, Glasgow and Edinburgh before eventually arriving in London on 28 July. On 8 August 1915, he booked a passage from Hull to Copenhagen. He approached the American Consulate for a visa to get his travel permit. The American Consulate discovered that his passport was a forgery and impounded it. Ries was arrested on 10 August 1915.[171] Thomson recalled that Ries,

> '…was a grave and measured person who answered all my questions very deliberately and thoughtfully. On one point he refused altogether to be drawn. He would not tell me his true name, but he explained that this was only because if his real name ever came to be published it would give pain to his relations. About his movements he was frank enough.'[172]

He had also been the object of enquiry by MO5 since 5 August 1915. The GPO reported that Ries had received a £20 telegraphic money order from 'Madame Cleton' of Rotterdam and that the sum was 'suspect'. This was followed by news from Rotterdam that a telephone conversation between the German GHQ at Wesel and the German Consulate in Rotterdam had been tapped and decoded. The conversation carried instructions to pay Cleton of 72 Provenierstraat, Rotterdam, money for the mission of Irwin (not Irving) Guy Ries of the Hotel Cecil. 72 Provenierstraat was a known spy address used by Richard Sanderson (alias Dierks), which had been on check since May

1915. Madame Cleton was a name assumed by Sanderson's wife when he was taken into custody by the Dutch authorities. Ries was charged with committing an act preparatory to collecting information without lawful authority, having been in communication with a spy, being found in possession of a false passport, and having falsely represented himself to be a person to whom a passport had been duly issued. He was found guilty at trial by court martial on 5 October and shot on 27 October 1915.

It was later discovered that the spy's real name was Paul Hensel. He was fifty-five years old, and had been impersonating Ries. The real Irving Guy Ries received a passport from the US Department of State in Washington DC on 10 March 1915 in order to visit the UK to take photographs for the Newspaper Enterprise Association in Chicago.[173]

The De Bournonville Case

Eva de Bournonville was Danish by birth, but had been naturalized as a Swedish citizen. She was a forty-one year old shorthand clerk and typist employed by the Danish Legation in Stockholm who had arrived in London on 24 September 1915 'for recreation'. Between the next day and 1 November 1915, she wrote twelve letters to an address in the Swedish capital which she recorded on the back of her writing block, all signed with fictitious names, the style of the signature changing with every letter, while the names of the addressees varied, but always to the same address – 35/37 Birger Jarlsgatan, Stockholm. The letters were vague and their 'lack of interest' aroused the censor's suspicions. The third letter, of the twelve, dated 30 September, was intercepted and tested, revealing a secret message 'about the falling off of recruiting and a sorrowful admission of failure on the writer's part.'[174] On 12 October, MO5 learned that the address in Sweden that she posted her letters to was that of a German Secret Service Bureau under Baron von Oppel, a former secretary to the German military attaché in London. De Bournonville was identified by the handwriting on a telegram to an address in Stockholm on 20 October. The police kept her under surveillance from 1 to 5 November. An MO5 agent stayed at de Bournonville's hotel, the Whitehall Hotel, and supplied her with 'incorrect information' that she sent to the Stockholm address. De Bournonville was eventually arrested on 5 November. When her hotel room was searched, the writing block (mentioned above) was found, plus tablets of soap impregnated with potassium ferrocyanide, which could be used for secret writing. During interrogation at Scotland Yard on 6 November, she confessed to her activities as soon as she was confronted with her letter and she admitted that she had received money sent from the German Legation through a bank in Stockholm.

De Bournonville was tried in the civil court on 18 and 19 January 1916. She stated that she had been recruited for the German Secret Service by a man named Schmidt, whom she had known since 1912. She had met Schmidt in a restaurant in July 1915 'and being pressed by debt, she accepted work at a remuneration of £1 a day.' Her original letters were presented in court. In defence, she stressed that she had only reported 'what the man in the street could find out unaided.' Nonetheless, the jury found her guilty of attempting to communicate information which might be useful to the enemy with intent to assist him. She was sentenced to death by hanging, but her sentence was later commuted to penal servitude for life on the advice of the Home Secretary.[175] Kell felt that this was a grave mistake. He opposed a reprieve simply because she was a woman, protesting that once the Germans learned that Britain would not execute female spies, they would crowd the country with them.[176] Indeed, female spies were shot in France.[177]

COUNTER-SUBVERSION

It has also been argued that MO5's growth was influenced by the fear of dissent in wartime. Certainly, in October 1915 G Branch was given the additional duties of investigation of all cases of suspected fomentation of strikes and sabotage, and the dissemination of peace propaganda, although available MI5 reports do not explicitly state why this additional duty was taken on. One MI5 report simply states that it was due to 'the increase of certain methods of attack.'[178] However, it seems likely that this happened because MO5 had begun to investigate the infamous Diamond Reign public house and the so-called Communist Club.

As a place known to be frequented by Germans, the Diamond Reign public house at 31 Foubert's Place, Regent Street in London was raided on the outbreak of war, but without result. Scotland Yard kept the pub under observation and observed 'that it had become the resort of Germans whose clubs had been closed.' In August 1915, the Anti-German Union employed an agent, a Czech, to observe what was going on at the Diamond Reign. These reports were passed on to MO5. Then, on 20 September 1915, an unnamed MO5 agent (the agent's name has been redacted out of the report that has been declassified) '…began a series of visits to the Diamond Reign. His reports confirmed those of the Czech; the habitués anticipated revolution in Russia and sent abroad by hand messages and circumstantial reports of the damage done by the Zeppelins here. … [the agent] considered that nearly every man at the place would seize the opportunity to do harm to this country.' MO5 also began 'having the telephone tapped.'

In April 1915, Scotland Yard asked MO5 to send an agent into the Communist Club at 107 Charlotte Street in London. The informers who were watching the Diamond Reign noted that members of the Communist Club frequented the pro-German circle at the house of the landlord of the Diamond Reign.[179] Following the aforementioned closure of numerous German clubs at the outbreak of war, the pub 'became a meeting place for bitterly hostile British citizens of German birth.' Investigation revealed that some of its patrons maintained close contact with members of the Communist Club. The Communist Club 'kept in touch with German Prisoners of War, intrigued with the Labour Party to stop the arrest of "peaceful" alien enemies, fomented strikes on the Clyde and spread revolutionary doctrine among Russian seamen.' Between September 1915 and April 1916, ten Germans and nine naturalized British subjects of German birth who frequented the Diamond Reign were interned.[180]

In November 1916, as a result of G1 investigations, the Communist Club was raided and twenty-two of its members of various nationalities recommended for internment. The Home Secretary agreed to the internment of seventeen. By this time MI5 had its own informant at the Club and Kell grew deeply disturbed by what he and other sources revealed. The purpose of the Club, Kell reported to the Home Office in January 1917, was '…the hampering by all possible means (e.g. by anti-recruiting propaganda, fomentation of strikes etc) of the Execution of the War in the present crisis.' Kell was also concerned by the activities of Chicherin's Russian Political Prisoners and Exiles Relief

Committee and wrote:

> 'Perhaps the greatest immediate danger arises from the instigation of enmity to the British Government on the part of the thousands of immigrants and refugees from Russia (and their offspring) now in the country... That the active enmity thus engendered may be cunningly manipulated at some opportune time by Germany very considerably adds to the danger of the moment.'[181]

At this stage, this was a very small part of MO5's work. MO5's investigations into these cases were strictly limited to looking for any evidence of a German 'hidden hand' behind these activities. And, at this time, this had little impact on MO5's development.

BCI

The Bureau Centrale Inter-Allie (BCI) was a clearing house formed on 27 September 1915 with a headquarters in Paris and used by the Allied countries to share intelligence other than that which dealt with military operations. The British mission comprised the following four sections:

    I War intelligence (excluding operations)
    II Counter-espionage
    III Commerce and contraband of war
    IV Press control and censorship.[182]

INDIAN SUBVERSIVES – 1915

The subversion strategy deployed by Germany was directed at Britain's imperial interests as well as the events taking place in Ireland. The Empire was paramount to Britain's war effort, contributing three million men, half of them in the Indian Army. Thus, the threat from German subversion in India was significant. The Germans created an Intelligence Bureau in the East, which was tasked with calculating how to foment unrest in India and Egypt that would wear Britain down. German hopes of creating disaffection within the British Empire's Muslim community were raised considerably when, on 5 November 1914, the Ottoman Empire entered the war as an ally to Germany.

MO5(g)'s main 'Indian expert' for much of the First World War was Mr (later Sir) Robert Nathan. Having qualified as a barrister, Nathan spent twenty-six years in the Indian civil service, becoming vice chancellor of Calcutta University, but he had been forced to come back to England in early 1914 owing to health problems. He joined MO5(g) on 4 November 1914.

Intercepted correspondence revealed that Indian revolutionaries were plotting an assassination campaign in England, France and Italy during 1915. Although the assassination campaign failed to materialize, Nathan had good reason to take it seriously:

'The last political assassination in Britain had been the killing in London of Sir William Curzon Wyllie, the political aide-de-camp of the Secretary of State for India, by an Indian student, Madan Lal Dhingra, in the summer of 1909.'[183]

On 29 November 1915, Nathan requested through the Foreign Office that the Italian government should stop all Indians arriving from Switzerland at the border and, if possible, deport them to the UK. In October 1915, under interrogation by Nathan and Thomson, Harish Chandra, an Indian revolutionary, confessed that he had been working for a so-called Indian Committee in Berlin, intending to subvert the loyalty of Indian POWs. He further betrayed German efforts to persuade the Amir of Afghanistan to join a Muslim *jihad* against the British Raj. Nathan and Thomson managed to turn Chandra to become a double agent for the British. In early-1916, Nathan left MI5 to take charge of a department that the Indian Directorate of Criminal Intelligence (DCI) had set up in the USA to investigate Indian revolutionary activity there.[184]

MO5's monthly report for September 1915 showed that MO5 investigated nineteen 'Eastern suspects' during that month. A number of Indian revolutionaries were found, or suspected, to be in touch with Indian revolutionary leaders who were acting as German agents in Switzerland. One of them had been interned. The others remained under investigation.[185]

The Triest Case

Amidst the myriad of ludicrous accusations born of spy mania, MO5(g) occasionally received useful tip-offs from members of the public. In May 1915, a private citizen in Cardiff received information from a friend in America that a German, using the name Lathom Mahon, was serving in the Royal Naval Division at Crystal Palace. Lathom Ramsey Mahon was discovered to be the alias of Kenneth Gustav Triest, the nineteen-year old son of an American of German origin. He was arrested, interrogated and released. He then wrote to Baron Bruno von Schroeder, a well-known philanthropist among the German community in Britain, in September 1915, offering his services to Germany. The Baron handed this letter in to the British authorities. The available documentation does not, however, provide any indications of his motivation for doing so. Triest was arrested once again and it was proposed to try him by Naval court martial in October.[186] His father was a wealthy and influential businessman, who knew former US President, Theodore Roosevelt, who took a keen interest in Triest's case. Probably as a result of these connections, the US Ambassador in London requested that Triest should be freed. Initially, the British Government was inclined to ignore this appeal, because it felt that the trial of an American would deter other German-Americans from becoming agents.[187] However, British nurse Edith Cavell's execution for spying by a German firing squad in Belgium on 15 October 1915 had shocked the world. Kell and others thus recognised an opportunity to contrast British and German behaviour by releasing Triest to the custody of his father in an act of clemency calculated to win favour in American eyes.[188]

The Greite Case

Thanks to a warning from one of Tinsley's agents, MO5 was expecting a ship's captain called Theodore Greitl to come to England via Rotterdam while in transit to the USA, and that he would endorse his telegrams 'Frank Greitl'. On 9 October 1915, the vice consul at Le Havre reported that Frank L.T. Griebe, an American travelling salesman in the oil-cake business, had crossed on 8 October bound for Hull.

On 13 October, Frank Greite applied for a permit to go to Holland. At MO5's suggestion, he was delayed for a few days whilst it was arranged to have him arrested and interrogated at Scotland Yard. On 23 October, he was questioned by Sir Basil Thomson, the Assistant Commissioner. Greite's answers were convincing and he was issued with the permit. He made a number of return trips to Holland in the months that followed.

On 18 March 1916, the censor, whose suspicions had been aroused, submitted a 'curious' telegram in which Greite was recalled to Holland on business. On 22 March, the port officer at Tilbury submitted a report about Greite's frequent travels. The next day, the Consul General at Rotterdam telegraphed the Foreign Office that Frank Theodore Greitl, who had been reported as a German agent in October 1915, was returning to England. Thus, G Branch decided that he was to be 'well searched' every time he travelled and detained if he was unable to produce proof of having conducted genuine business. On 27 March, the port officer detained Greitl and sent him to Scotland Yard. During interrogation Greite could not give an adequate explanation of the amount of money in his bank account or where certain cheques paid to him came from. He was arrested. Search revealed that he possessed the address of Mulder, a known German agent who had been in communication with Fernando Buschman (see earlier). The case 'depended' upon proving that Mulder was a spy and that his address was a spy address. Mulder's communications with Buschman could be used as evidence of this.

Greite claimed US citizenship, stating that he had been born in Brooklyn to a Dutch father and a Danish mother, but the American Embassy in London denied this. Investigation revealed that had been in Germany at the outbreak of war, and had registered with the police as a Prussian subject. Under interrogation, Greite eventually admitted that he had spent five years at school in Berlin and then served as a ship's boy, and afterwards as a steward. He had obtained an emergency passport as a US citizen in Berlin and returned to the USA in April 1915. In May 1916, he promised a fellow prisoner 'a large sum of money to procure his escape.' The prisoner informed the authorities about this.

On 12 July 1916, Greite was sentenced to ten years' imprisonment for 'doing an act preparatory to collecting information calculated to be useful to the enemy' and 'for being in communication with a spy.' The Germans believed that Greite had been executed and paid a pension to his reputed widow.[189]

PREVENTIVE MEASURES – 1915

DRR/ARO 1915

The Preventive Branch also brought forward three proposals in 1915. First, that marriage between male British subjects and enemy alien women was to be prohibited throughout the war. Secondly, that all subsequent spy cases should be tried in camera. Thirdly, it recommended an inland pass that was to be used by particular approved officials and officers of Allied countries working for their governments in the UK. A local control system was also begun at Harwich, out of which the system for the protection of areas known as 'special military areas' eventually came, which was further developed in 1916.[190]

The main changes to the ARA during 1915 were in respect of passports for all aliens embarking or disembarking at British ports, passports for prohibited areas, hotel registration, and the Aliens Restriction (Seamen's) Order 1915. On 13 April 1915, 12A was added to the ARA, requiring that all aliens landing or embarking in the UK as a passenger had to possess a valid passport, or similar document, not more than two years old and, importantly, bearing the alien's photograph. ARO 12A eventually became inoperative, when it was superseded by DRR 14C. ARO 18B was also issued on 13 April 1915, under which aliens not already living in prohibited areas were not allowed to enter them without a passport.

On 13 April 1915, the ARA introduced a system of hotel and lodging house registration throughout the UK, which had long been employed in Germany as a regular police measure. According to an F Branch report of 1921: 'The particulars contained in this register were only asked for in the case of aliens, but in order to make its compilation practicable, it was necessary to include a provision requiring all persons to furnish a signed statement giving the information (as to nationality, etc) that was needed for the preliminary classification in to aliens and British subjects; and this was the sole provision in the A.R.O. which imposed any duty on anyone other than aliens.'

The Aliens Restriction (Seamen's) Order of 28 August 1915 comprised two sections. Article 1 provided that no alien seaman or master could land at a port unless he possessed a valid passport. Article 2 provided that if a ship stayed at a port for twenty-four hours or more, any aliens on the ship were considered to be residing in the area (ARO19) and were therefore required to register with the police.[191]

The chief improvements to DORA during 1915 can be split into four groups. Firstly, in terms of censorship regulations, 24A strengthened 24 by prohibiting the conveying of letters for any other person, thereby stopping letter-carrying. It also made secret writing an offence against these regulations. Related to 24A, 22A was passed on 10 June 1915, forbidding the possession or use of any code, cipher or other method for the secret communication of military or naval information without the authority to do so, and guilt was to be assumed unless innocence could be proved. The introduction of DRR22B in late 1915, aimed at accommodation addresses, further strengthened the censorship regulations. Anyone whose business was to be paid to receive letters, etc was compelled to register his business with the police, and to maintain a register of all the letters received that could be inspected by the police. Secondly, espionage regulations. During 1915, DRR18 was brought into line with OSA 1911, by changing the words *any other information intended to be communicated to the enemy or* in favour of '*any information.*' This made it an offence 'to collect, record, publish, communicate or attempt to elicit any information of such a nature as to be directly or indirectly useful to the enemy.'[192] The burden of proof was thrown on to the accused, as for OSA 1911. DRR18A was added, making it an offence to communicate, or attempt to communicate, with a spy. The term spy was also expanded to include '…any person who has committed or attempted to commit an offence under Regulation 18, and who is reasonably suspected of having done so with the intention of assisting the enemy.'[193] It also encompassed any individual outside the UK who was, or was reasonably suspected of being, an individual to whom information had been, or attempted to be, passed on to in breach of DRR18. Thirdly, personal restrictions. DRR14B, one of the most useful paragraphs of the DORA, was also introduced in 1915.[194] It applied to people of hostile origin or association, who could thereby be interned or otherwise restricted at the behest of the Secretary of State. F Branch had a key role in this, because the details of all cases for internment under 14B submitted by the CMAs were sent to MO5(g) and dealt with by F3, a new sub-section formed during the summer of 1915. Under 14C, added on 30 November 1915, passports became mandatory for all passengers leaving or entering the UK, including British subjects. Fourth, miscellaneous. DRR41 was improved to counter those wrongly claiming to serve in the armed forces. DRR45 made obtaining or abusing military, naval or police permits much more difficult. Regulation 51A conferred powers to JPs, moving on information from CMAs, CNAs or the police, to authorise the searching of premises and seizure of papers. All of the above alterations to the legislation were made on F Branch's recommendation.[195]

STATISTICS – 1915

It has not been possible to find statistics covering January through March 1915. However, the following data give some indication of the work performed by MO5(g) in the first half of 1915:

	April 1915	May 1915	June 1915
General suspects	128	251	449
The figures given above included the following suspects abroad and coming to the UK.	39	105	124
Letters submitted	[not given]	730	1,006
Telegrams submitted	[not given]	273	376[196]

The following statistics cover MO5(g)'s work from 1 July 1915 to 31 December 1915:

Personal dossiers	7,543
Telegrams	3,559
Letters	7,690
Suspects circulated	2,980
Internments sanctioned	70

Between 28 September and 31 December 1915, MO5 also dealt with 4,874 permit applications.[197]

★ ★ ★

Towards the end of 1915, MO5 began to develop an interest in counter-subversion, as shown by its investigations of the Diamond Reign pub and the Communist Club. However, at this time counter-subversion was a very minor part of MO5's work.

The additions that were made to the ARR and DRR throughout 1915 reveal a great deal about how the perceived threat changed and how MO5 reacted to plug gaps in its defences, such as how, once it was felt that the threat from passengers travelling to and from Britain had been brought under control, MO5 began to pay more attention to the threat posed by alien seamen.

The organizational changes that took place throughout 1915 also reveal much about MO5's development and the forces that drove it: the change of name from MO5(g) to MO5 reveals an increase in status; MO5 began to assume wider responsibilities for coordinating counter-espionage throughout the British Empire as a whole; its growing role in port control showed that it was ready to step in wherever it felt that other departments were not up to the task; however, it is also telling that MO5 assumed an advisory role rather than an executive one; also the creation of a separate branch for port control demonstrates that MO5 saw that its core work was divided into investigative, preventive and records functions, and that any other role that it assumed was to be handled by a separate branch.

The 'Notes on the General Organization of a Counter-espionage Bureau' that MO5 sent to Colonial Governors is one of the key documents for an understanding of MO5's development during the First World War. MO5's conviction that counter-espionage work could be divided into the duties of Prevention, Detection, Control, Records, and Organization had a profound impact on 'how' MO5 developed.

The way in which MO5 handled the spy cases of 1915 also says much about its development. MO5 seemed to be very good at catching spies – as shown by how quickly German agents were caught and by the number of German agents shot in the summer of 1915, albeit that the quality of the agents the Germans chose to employ was generally very poor. Kell clearly did not feel comfortable using live spies for deception operations. Thus, a First World War double-cross system was not on the cards. The types of agents employed by the Germans also showed that the threat was evolving – from Germans (often using false US passport) to genuine neutrals. As 1915 came to an end, MO5 had to be alert to how the threat would further evolve.

CHAPTER FIVE

New Threats
1916

THE year 1916 was arguably the key stage in the development of MI5's role from a narrow remit concerning counter–espionage to a wider one concerning security intelligence.

COUNTER-ESPIONAGE

MI5's detractors claim that the main reason for its success was the poor quality of its opponent. It is therefore of relevance to assess the German espionage attack in 1916, and to consider how competent or incompetent MI5 was at this stage in the war.

Named MI5
In December 1915, a separate Directorate of Military Intelligence was formed in addition to the Directorate of Military Operations, and the intelligence departments that had previously been placed under the Directorate of Military Operations became part of this new Directorate. As part of these changes, MO5 changed its name to MI5 on 3 January 1916.[1]

German espionage attack during 1916
By mid-July 1915, it was clear that MO5(g) '…had smashed the German organization painfully built up by the Admiralty Zweigstelle and their system of employing bogus commercial travellers had failed.' However, between July 1915 and May 1916 three new types of travelling agents appeared: artistes, better educated people with business experience and social backing, and genuine businessmen. Between June and December 1916, a fourth type of agent was employed in the form of American journalists.[2]

British counter-espionage methods
The cases seemed isolated, especially so since there was no connecting link of spy addresses to help MI5.[3]

The Guerrero Case

On 30 January 1916, the Admiralty warned MI5 that there was a strong likelihood that Spanish journalists would be despatched to the UK to act as German spies. On 1 February, the port officer at Folkestone notified MI5 of the arrival of Adolfo Guerrero, a correspondent for *El Literal*, and that he was heading for the Regent Palace Hotel in London. Checks were placed on all letters and telegrams to and from Guerrrero and the police were tasked to keep him under close observation. Guerrero's letters were tested for secret ink without results, but certain marks before certain initials were noticed. Investigation revealed that Guerrero was the son of a Spanish father 'of good position' and a Philippino mother. He had been brought up by an uncle and educated in Switzerland where he was described as having 'imbibed German sympathies'. He qualified as a barrister, but never practiced, and 'soon dissipated his fortune in riotous living'. He taught dancing in Paris and also attempted some journalism before leaving for the UK, landing at Folkestone on 1 February 1916. A Spanish-speaking detective from the Metropolitan Police, Detective Sergeant Tausley, was sent to Spain to verify facts and people related to Guerrero's case. His report was damning. Guerrero had never had associations with *El Literal* and he had forged his identification card himself. He was arrested on 16 February. Amongst his possessions was found a piece of paper inscribed '*Norvege, Frederick Skjellas, Minde, Bergensbanen*'; Frederick Skjellas, a German ex-consul, was a known spy. Guerrero was tried on 13 July 1916 with having come to the UK to collect information that might be of use to an enemy and of having communicated with a known spy. He had come to the UK unable to speak a word of English: 'a hindrance indeed to a foreign correspondent but also to a spy'. He was found guilty and sentenced to death. This was later commuted to ten years' penal servitude. On 9 September 1916, Guerrero confessed and gave information about German codes and secret ink. He also claimed that the Germans were aiming to recruit North Americans as spies.[4]

The Bright Case

Curiously, as the case of Albert Bright demonstrates, MI5 was clearly not involved in every espionage case that occurred in the UK during the war. Bright was a British subject born in Sheffield, residing in Rotherham, and an engineer by trade, although he had no place of business and was known to be in financial difficulties. On 28 March 1916, he was remanded in custody by the Sheffield police, charged under DRR18 with attempting to elicit information regarding the manufacture of war materials. He had tried to obtain details of the exact ingredients used in the manufacture of the steel made by Vickers Limited for the production of war materials which was strictly confidential.[5] Bright pleaded guilty at the Leeds Assizes on 5 May 1916, being sentenced to penal servitude for life.[6] Later, on 11 May 1916, Major John Carter, at this time assistant to Reginald Drake, the head of G Branch, (he would succeed Drake on 15 January 1917) wrote to the Director of Public Prosecutions (DPP) asking if he could provide MI5 with a report of Bright's trial.[7] This strongly suggests that MI5 had nothing to do with this seemingly straightforward case.

The Casement Case

It is accepted that the crucial intelligence used to track support for the infamous

Sir Roger Casement originated from the Admiralty SIGINT unit, Room 40. Between the start of the First World War and the Republican Easter Rising in Ireland in April 1916, Room 40 decoded over thirty telegrams passed between the Foreign Ministry in Berlin and the German Embassy in Washington concerning German aid to Irish nationalists. These intercepts alerted the British that Germany intended to ship weapons to Ireland to be used in the Rising, and that Casement would follow this shipment in a submarine.[8]

Sir Roger Casement was born in Dublin on 1 September 1864, the son of a protestant retired captain of The King's Own Regiment of Dragoons. Although he was brought up as a protestant, Casement later converted to Roman Catholicism. He served in the Consular Service in West Africa, East Africa and Brazil from 1895-1913, being knighted in 1911, and ending his career as consul general in Rio de Janeiro, Brazil. Casement should not be dismissed as a consul. His report on the atrocities by Belgians in the Congo, produced in 1906, was of great importance and influential in the ending of the Belgian King Leopold II's personal rule. His investigation into the Belgian atrocities led Casement to develop strong anti-imperialist, Irish republican and separatist political opinions. He also reported on the Peruvians' oppression of the Putumayo people. After his retirement, he returned to Ireland where he took an active part in organising the Irish National Volunteers. As war broke out, Casement was in New York espousing Sinn Fein propaganda and soliciting money to procure arms for the Irish National Volunteers. He soon travelled to Germany in the hope of gaining support for a rebellion in Ireland and where he endeavoured to enlist POWs from Irish regiments to form an Irish Brigade – a military force envisaged as being formed by the German Government to fight against Britain.[9] Casement's attempt was a dismal failure: he only managed to recruit fifty-five men and the Germans did not provide anything like the support he had been hoping for.[10] The ship carrying arms to Ireland, the *Aud*, was intercepted by the Royal Navy and scuttled by its crew before it could be taken. Subsequently, a British diver was sent to search the wreck and it was discovered that there were Russian marks on the rifles that had been carried on the vessel. Basil Thomson recalled that, 'We sent for the Russian military attaché, and then it was found that even this grudging service to the cause of Ireland had been done on the cheap, for the rifles were all Russian, captured at Tannenberg, and very much the worse for wear.'[11] Casement returned to Ireland in a German submarine at the time of the Easter Rising, landing ashore in a collapsible boat. However, it seems that he travelled there not so much to join in the Rising, but to try to stop events that he thought would be futile.[12] He was arrested immediately near Ardfert on 21 April 1916 and was tried at the High Court on 15 June. He was found guilty of high treason and sentenced to death. The 'Black Diaries' covering 1903, 1910 and 1911 found amongst Casement's papers portrayed him as a promiscuous homosexual sex tourist with a fondness for young men. After his conviction for treason, photographs of the 'Black Diaries' were circulated by the British Government to individuals urging commutation of Casement's death sentence. At a time of strong social conservatism, including among Irish Catholics, the Diaries undermined support for Casement and he was hanged at Pentonville in August 1916.[13] The degree of MI5's involvement in the Casement case is not clear, apart from a role in the preparation for his prosecution. Certainly, MI5 was responsible for investigating cases of suspected espionage, sedition or treachery in Ireland. However, it has been suggested that the intelligence chief most interested in the political situation in Ireland was Rear-Admiral Sir Reginald 'Blinker' Hall, Director of Naval Intelligence (DNI).[14]

The Vieyra Case

On 27 April 1916, the censor submitted to MI5 a letter from a Leo Pickard enclosing three photos that he had sent to Mrs Anny Pickard Fletcher requesting that she should endorse them to certify that they were pictures of him and then return them to Rotterdam adding 'that his name was VIEYRA as well as PICKARD'. On 4 May 1916, Commander Richard Tinsley, head of MI1c's Rotterdam station (see Chapter Four), wired that Leopold Vieyra, alias Pickard, was coming to the UK and suggested that his statements should be verified. He landed on 6 May, was searched, interrogated, and sent to Scotland Yard. There, he provided a convincing explanation that he had come to England to buy films for resale and was subsequently released. A police (CID) report of 10 May into Vieyra's history revealed that he first came to England in 1904

Admiral Sir William Reginald 'Blinker' Hall, Director of Naval Intelligence (DNI), 1914-1919. Hall was responsible for the Royal Navy's codebreaking organisation (Room 40), which decrypted the Zimmermann telegram which was a key factor in the USA's decision to enter the war in 1917.

and from then until 1911 he managed a band known as 'The Midgets'. Since 1909, he had been on 'intimate terms' with a widow, a Mrs Fletcher, who passed as his wife and who managed a boarding house in Acton, west London that Vieyra owned. In a report of 22 May, Tinsley added that Vieyra '...had been denounced by LOGEHER, brother-in-law to ELTE, who was engaged in recruiting spies for the Germans'. He was also reputed to have a mistress called Josephine Jensen. 'Pickard's' correspondence was placed under check and he was found to be communicating with Josephine Jensen of Hemonystraat, Amsterdam, Holland, and also with S. Blom of 28 Pretorierstraat also in Amsterdam. On 17 July, MI5 asked Tinsley for information about Blom. He reported on 24 July that there was no such person at 28 Pretorierstraat, but that Sophia, wife of Simon Dikker and sister-in-law to Philip Dikker of the Greite case, might be the intended recipient because Blom was her maiden name. Shortly afterwards on 26 July, Blom wrote to warn Vieyra that 'some mysterious person' had made enquiries about the film business. Several of his letters were tested for secret writing without result. On 21 July, 'Pickard' applied for a permit to leave the UK. It was then decided that he might be worth searching and he was arrested on 24 August. At search, secret writing equipment was found among his possessions including ammonia, cotton wool, a bottle of an unknown liquid, and ballpointed pens. At interrogation he claimed that since coming to England he had brought £164 of films and sold them for a profit of £80. However, he could give no reasonable account of his business dealings. Exhaustive analysis of the bottle of unknown liquid that had been found amongst Vieyra's effects led eventually, on 13 September, to a secret message on one of his letters being successfully developed which concerned the calling up of Belgian soldiers, munitions and the transport of troops. Until then the case against Vieyra had been 'singularly weak'. Vieyra's trial by court martial started on 14 November 1916 and the following day he confessed. He was sentenced to be shot, but the sentence was commuted to imprisonment for life.[15]

Double Agent Como

In April 1916, MI5 recruited its 'most successful double agent' of the First World War – an American living in Holland who was given the codename 'COMO'. COMO is not mentioned in any of the MI5 records that have been released to the UK's National Archives. Knowledge of COMO comes from Christopher Andrew's book *The Defence of the Realm* in which the author cites his sources as 'Security Service archives' which have not yet been declassified. COMO is described in his file as 'working in Holland as a German Agent, but double-crossing for us'. In May 1916, the German Secret Service sent COMO to Britain to track down German agents who had not contacted them for a while. COMO informed MI5 that the first of the agents he contacted, Fritz Haas, was 'harmless and probably never an agent, if so unknowingly.' In July, the Germans sent COMO on a second mission to collect information on Canadian troops stationed in England and to ascertain when it was likely that they were going to be deployed in France, plus to gather intelligence on the Royal Navy's losses during the battle of Jutland. Andrew quotes an MI5 note that illustrates the kind of disinformation that COMO fed to the Germans:

> 'We gave "COMO" information about our Canadian Divisions – their numbers and positions, etc – at places not obviously incorrect, and gave particulars of their numbers etc, as would make them plausible. Also, fictitious information of Naval, Industrial and Political situation, most convincingly written. Also sent information regarding the effects of Zeppelin raids on London.'

In September, COMO fed the Germans more misleading information about the military situation in the UK and probable developments on the Western Front. He informed them that Britain was planning an attack against the Belgian coast on 15 September and '…continued to pass on at irregular intervals details of the intelligence missions entrusted to him by the Kriegsnachrichtenstelle, and MI5 continued to channel disinformation through him.' A post-war MI5 report on COMO's usefulness noted that he '…was always quite honest and trustworthy and did some v[ery] valuable work for us at the same time as holding the German's confidence.' Andrew concludes that it was 'nervousness' on the part of the War Office that prevented the development of a full-blown Double-Cross System:

> 'On at least one occasion, the Director of Military Intelligence described the questions put to COMO by the Kriegsnachrichtenstelle as "extremely dangerous", and instructed that "no answers could be given".'[16]

The van Zurk Case

Jacobus Johannes van Zurk (alias Johann Zurmuehlen) was a German agent who came to the UK with his British mistress, Elsie Scott, and who also offered information to the British. In reports of 31 May 1916 and 3 June, Tinsley informed MI5 that he had interviewed van Zurk who had disclosed that he had been recruited by the German Secret Service to visit Glasgow, Newcastle and Cardiff. He was to post his reports to a 'van der Hucht' and a 'Meisner-Denis' at 68 Rokin in Amsterdam. He carried secret ink, purporting to be toilet water, in a silver-mounted scent bottle and his *en clair* communications were to concern the insurance business. He also provided the British with a sample of his secret ink. He 'was made use of [by MI5] to write to van der HUCHT', but not to Denis. The Germans paid £77 into his bank account for this. However, van Zurk's usefulness for deception operations was limited. 'He proved not only unsatisfactory but dangerous …' Scott soon quarreled with him and went to live with her mother in Barry Dock. Scott and her mother even denounced van Zurk to the local police. MI5 had him shipped back to Holland with a 'no return' permit on 23 August. A check on van Zurk's correspondence showed that the quarrel with Scott had been contrived. Van Zurk kept up 'affectionate relations' with Scott and she hoped to rejoin him in Holland. However she was denied permission to leave the UK and van Zurk was not allowed to come over and fetch her. In March 1917, Tinsley 'was warned to have nothing more to do with van ZURK'.

In December 1918, MI5 discovered the Antwerp Roll of spies for 8 October 1916, a list of spies employed by the German Secret Service's *Kriegsnachrichtenstelle* in Antwerp, on which van Zurk was listed as spy A40. After he was shipped back to Holland, he again applied for work with the Germans. He was tasked to report on conditions in the Bristol Channel, Edinburgh, Glasgow and Ireland. The Antwerp Centre was also expecting a report from Scott on her return from the UK.[17]

The Stanaway Case

The check on the Meisner-Denis address resulted in the interception of a letter from a Mrs Stanaway of 63 Sandgate Road, Folkestone on 13 July 1916. Albertine Stanaway (née Regnier) was a French-born dressmaker married to Frederick Stanaway of Folkestone. Frederick Stanaway had joined the Kent Cyclists Corps in September 1914 and was serving in India, while Albertine Stanaway became acquainted with Pierre Rotheudt, a wounded corporal in the Belgian Army then convalescing in England and a Belgian grain merchant of German parentage. In early February 1915, Rotheudt 'went to her house for three nights' then returned to the front. On his next trip to England, in July 1915, Rotheudt went to Folkestone and 'again put up with Mrs. STANAWAY'.[18] He also rented another room in a house situated opposite the French Consulate, positioned so that he would be able to see everyone who went in and out of the building. Shortly after this, the Germans apprehended a number of French agents as soon as they set foot on German territory: 'It was supposed that ROTHEUDT had furnished information leading to such action for, by the 26th July, the French Intelligence Service had evidence that ROTHEUDT was in communication' with Haasbroeck, a sub-agent of Dierks. The Belgians kept Rotheudt under surveillance and collected enough evidence of espionage to bring him to trial. He was tried by court martial in France, found guilty and sentenced to death on 11 December 1916, but his sentence was commuted to penal servitude for life. Stanaway wrote to Rotheudt in prison many times. The case against

Stanaway 'rested solely upon three letters in themselves innocent, although addressed to DENIS'. Therefore, Archibald Bodkin, lead prosecutor in every spy trial instigated by MI5 during the war (see Chapter Three), advised against prosecution and recommended internment. Thus, Stanaway was interned under DRR14B in March 1917, 'on the grounds of her association with the spy ROTHEUDT and of her correspondence with another German agent.'[19]

The Bacon Case

George Vaux Bacon, an American journalist, was a correspondent of the Central Press Association. He landed at Liverpool from New York and claimed that he had come to Britain to write articles on behalf of the Association. He went straight to London, arriving there on 5 September 1916. On 20 September, he wrote to 'Denis' the known spy address in The Netherlands', advising that he would soon be coming to Holland on business. His letter was intercepted by the censor on 29 September. Enquiries revealed that Bacon had left for Holland on or about 22 September, while further enquiries through Scotland Yard confirmed that he had been occupying a flat in Jermyn Street, and was regarded as 'a loose liver.' On 10 October, Tinsley was tasked to make enquiries about him. Tinsley's agent approached Bacon in a somewhat clumsy manner in Holland. Bacon admitted knowing Denis, but made no further statement and 'avoided further intercourse with the agent'. He also knew that Denis had not received his later of 20 September and therefore suspected that the British authorities were on to him. On 21 October, orders were issued that he was to be searched upon his return to the UK. Meanwhile, Tinsley had reported Bacon's departure and that he was seen off by a US journalist named Rutherford. He was searched on his arrival on 2 November 1916, but although nothing suspicious was detected, he was kept under surveillance.

Meanwhile, a Frederick Graff, a metal merchant, had been placed on the British Black List and had lost business because of this. In order to get himself removed from the List, he gave Tinsley information about his mission to a branch that the Antwerp KNSt had set up in the USA and with which it communicated via messengers. Tinsley reported this to MI5 on 14 November advising that the couriers carried orders in secret writing on what looked to be blank pieces of paper. Graff also handed over two sheets of paper that he was supposed to deliver to an 'A.A. Sander' of 876 East 15th Street in Brooklyn, and the War Film Office at 115 Nassauer Street in New York. They mentioned payments to be made to a Mrs Rutl, and that all 'Charlie's' letters were to be addressed to Rutl at 47 Pieber Bothstraat, The Hague. Tinsley was further tasked to identify Rutl, and British agents in New York were asked to investigate Sander. Enquiries in the USA revealed that Sander, a contributor to the *New York American*, was the manager of the Central Powers War Film Exchange. His associate was Charles Wunnenberg who was the 'Charlie' referred to in the secret instructions.

As a journalist, Sander had formerly been employed by Hearst on a German newspaper, while Wunnenberg was a naturalized American of German birth and an engineer by profession. Sander and Wunnenberg operated under the cover of the film company. It was later reported that, 'At the address of the company they set up the German American Literary Defence Committee with the object of fomenting sedition in Ireland and India.'

On 30 November 1916, MI5 decided to have Bacon interviewed at Scotland Yard and 'frightened out of the country'. On 1 December, European ports and capitals were warned that New York had become a German spy centre and that special attention should be devoted to those individuals, particularly neutrals, who travelled from the USA to the UK by indirect routes. Sir Basil Thomson interviewed Bacon at Scotland Yard on 9 December during which Bacon admitted his connection with Denis and was detained awaiting further search.

A key informant, whose name has been redacted out of the relevant MI5 reports released to The National Archives in the UK was interviewed at Scotland Yard on 11 December. He explained that he had been approached by Sander in New York in November 1916. He informed the British Military Control Office in New York of this, 'and at their bidding had carried on'. He had arrived in England on 2 December. He also gave an account of his recruitment and the instruction that he received. His story bore out what had been learned from Graff and also provided many other details, such as that the latest German tactic was to send US journalists to work in pairs – one to collect information in the UK and forward it in secret writing to the other in Holland; the other was sent to Holland to supply the cover address and to forward German instructions to the spy in the UK. The informant's correspondent was to be Charles Hastings at the Maas Hotel in Rotterdam. Hastings was 'a disreputable American journalist' who had been employed on publicity work for the Germans and was in almost daily contact with Sander. Sander had recruited Hastings to work as a German agent in Europe in November 1916. He had arrived in Rotterdam on 9 December. The informant also advised that another US journalist, whose name began with R., had been operating in the UK for some time. Of course, Rutherford had been known to MI5 to be a friend of Bacon's since 11 November. In a report dated 29 December, Tinsley identified Rutl with Rutherford. This was corroborated by a letter in which Mrs Rutherford informed her husband that she had received $200 'on a particular date'. Thus, by the end of 1916, MI5 knew that the Germans had a spy centre in New York under Sander, which was subordinate to the Antwerp spy centre. Bacon's letters would go through Rutherford. Hastings' letters would go through the informant; 'Moreover all this gang of American spies used the same arbitrary code and secret ink.'

Search of Bacon's possessions revealed secret writing equipment: ballpointed pens, a bottle of Argyrol and a pair of socks impregnated with Argyrol. When soaked in water the socks produced an invisible ink. They also found a notebook containing the addresses of Denis and van der Kolk, who had been known to be a spy address since 25 September 1915. Bacon's possessions also included letters from Rutherford. On 9 February 1917, confronted with this incriminating evidence, he made a 'full confession' that he had been engaged by Wunnenberg and Sander of the German spy centre in New York to spy in the UK.

Bacon was found guilty at trial by court martial and sentenced to death on 26 February 1917. The sentence was subsequently commuted to penal servitude for life. However, at the request of the Americans he was returned to the USA to give evidence in the trial of Sander and Wunnenberg. After the trial, Bacon was sentenced to one year's imprisonment in the USA.

A draconian bill against espionage was passed by the US Senate on 20 February 1917. Sander and Wunnenberg received two years' penal servitude and a fine 'for conspiring to spy upon a government with which the United States was at peace'. After they had arrested Sander and Wunnenberg, the Americans tried to apprehend Hastings and Rutherford. Hastings, who had lost the confidence of the Germans, willingly left Holland with an American emissary who took him to Scotland Yard where he was interrogated on 14 and 15 March 1917. He returned to America on 31 March and was tried and sentenced to one years' imprisonment. Rutherford was 'deeply compromised' and returned to Germany where he worked for the *Continental Times* in Hamburg.[20]

The ensuing G Branch Report highlights the importance of MI5's success in the Bacon case:

> '*This period between June and December 1916, includes perhaps the highest achievement of G. Branch, if the importance of results rather than the number of spies arrested be considered. And these results are due partly to some carelessness and lack of judgement on the part of the Germans, and partly to ill-luck.*'

After the Dierks episode, it was careless to let one spy address run on from early June to late September. It was also 'ill-judged' to recruit the agent who turned double-agent without more precaution. It was also a mistake to recruit Graff, whose business relied upon his good standing with the British:

> '*But it was genuine ill-luck that just the information given almost simultaneously by [the informant] and GRAFF should bear directly and in the most illuminating fashion upon the spy who was making use of that cover-address; and the spy-habit of giving information when in a really tight place did the rest.*'

As a result, not only did the German spy centre in New York stand revealed, but the Bacon case also revealed a new type of spy: the American journalist. New methods of spying and spy communication were also laid bare: from a spy in England to the cover address of his partner in Holland, plus new forms of code. Ultimately, the US authorities took 'drastic action' and the German spy centre in New York was destroyed.[21]

Double agent Whytock

Professor Christopher Andrew eventually unmasked the unnamed double agent in the Bacon case as Captain Roslyn Whytock, an American journalist with a 'colourful background'. Prior to the First World War, Whytock had been a newspaper editor in St. Louis, Missouri and a captain in the Missouri National Guard. However, he was forced to resign his commission after revelations about his affair with a married woman, Mrs Irma Jones, a fashion model. The affair became public knowledge after Mrs Jones' husband cited Whytock as co-respondent when he applied for a divorce. Mrs Whytock, who also sued for divorce, gave an interview to the *New York Times*, in which she claimed that when Mr Jones came to St. Louis with the intention of killing Whytock, Whytock talked him out of it and they soon became good friends. Whytock's experiences with MI5 certainly came in useful as, following the USA's entry into the war in April 1917, he went on to serve as a captain in the US Army Intelligence Service.[22]

The Spalding Case

In a report of 1921, G Branch recorded that,

'It was alleged that Rutledge RUTHERFORD had become a member of the London Press Club. The report was neither contradicted nor corroborated, but the fact remains that he satisfied the Germans and the case of Anthony SPALDING affords a good illustration of how this could be achieved.'

Anthony Spalding was a journalist of twenty years' standing 'and some position'. He had been the chief sub-editor of the *Daily News* in Manchester and at the end of August 1914 he joined the Press Bureau as an assistant censor. He was engaged in the cable room and it was his duty to enter in a note book all decisions taken by the Presiding Chairman of Censors with regard to the circulation or stopping of specific items of information and to guide the other censors in their work by the light of these notes. Between March 1915 and February 1917, Spalding wrote some twenty-five letters to Charles Stead, a colour merchant of Manchester. Spalding's letters to Stead contained specific news relating to naval and military movements, 'new inventions', damage done by air raids, foreign alliances, and the private and public affairs of 'Government officials in high places'. Spalding and Stead were described as 'intimate friends' and the letters were apparently written for the information of Stead only. However, Stead communicated them to other persons, in particular to Charles Way, a Traffic Assistant for the Manchester Ship Canal Company. On 23 February 1917, Way showed the letters to William Goodman, an agent and merchant of Manchester. Goodman was also a special constable and he informed the police about the correspondence. Way subsequently told the police about Stead, who then admitted that Spalding had written the letters to him and the Chief Constable of Manchester Police reported the case to MI5. Way, Stead and Spalding were arrested and charged under DRR18 and from their statements it became clear that they were aware that it was dangerous to be in possession of such letters. At the Director of Public Prosecutions' (DPP) suggestion, it was decided that there was no evidence of hostile intent or corruption against any of the accused and that Stead and Way 'had been merely receivers of information'. They were therefore dealt with in a court of summary jurisdiction, Clerkenwell Police Court, on 19 April, and fined for breaching DRR18. Spalding was committed for trial in the Civil Court. Spalding's case was heard on 26 April. His defence counsel had counted on being able to meet a charge of collecting and communicating information likely to be useful to an enemy. Initially he pleaded not guilty, but the indictment was so drawn that of the seventeen counts of receiving, collecting and communicating information, only four were coupled with the clause alleging utility to the enemy, and in the face of the documentary evidence it was not possible to deny the more general charge. At trial, Spalding claimed that he had obtained his information either from gossip in the Press Club, or in conversation with other members of the Press Bureau, and not directly from the cables and other documents to which his work gave him access. But because of the very reason for which a Press Censorship was established such a defense was inadmissible. Therefore, at his defence counsel's suggestion, Spalding changed his plea to guilty. He was sentenced to three years' penal servitude, but upon appeal his sentence was reduced to twelve months' hard labour.

During the case, the judge, Mr Justice Low, 'laid down the principle that disclosure of any information whether significant or insignificant obtained in the course of duty was a breach of faith and should be punished severely as such.'[23]

The Earle Case

On 7 November 1914, the police informed MI5 that a Mrs Martha Earle was the German-born sister of Baroness von Bothner. Mrs Earle would have been registered as being of German birth under the compulsory wartime registration of aliens carried out by the police who passed on details of such individuals to MI5. Although surviving records do not state precisely how the police found out this information, it is most likely that Earle came forward at the outbreak of war and informed the police that she was of German birth, as the Aliens Restriction Act required her to do, and that the police then undertook standard vetting checks which revealed that she was the sister of the Baroness. In 1910, she had married Francis Earle, a teacher of modern languages and went to live in Bristol, although the couple later moved to London.

In July 1916, the censor informed MI5 that one of Mrs Earle's letters contained 'hostile sentiments'. In October of that year, the censor further discovered that she was communicating with suspects in Spain. In June 1917, it was noted that she received a coded warning from Baroness von Bothner. On 31 July, orders were issued prohibiting the use of private intermediaries and commanding all those writing to enemy or enemy occupied territory to send their letters via Messrs Thomas Cook and Son. In November, the censor detected that Mrs Earle was using a code in a letter that she had sent to the Baroness through a private intermediary in which she 'gave some account of air-raids in a kind of code'. Earle's letter of 30 April 1918 showed that she suspected that her letters were being held and thus MI5 felt that it was time to arrest her and search her possessions. She was arrested on 14 May. Earle was 'somewhat of an invalid' and considered as 'not in a position to acquire information of value'. But there was no doubt that, at age sixty-four at her trial in 1918, she 'favoured Germany'. She was tried in September 1918 and was sentenced to one year's imprisonment for breaching the following DRRs: DRR18 (information that might be of value to an enemy); DRR22A (possession of a code) and DRR24A (secret communication).[24]

Organisational Changes: 1916

By June 1916, MI5 had fifty-two officers at headquarters and 150 administrative staff.[25] D Branch was added on 21 September 1916, to further the connection of MI5's work overseas.[26]

The Standing Advisory Committee

On 25 September 1916, a Standing Advisory Committee was formed to assist the Director of MI5 in questions of policy and administration, to form a channel of inter-communication between the various branches of MI5, and to enable officers to bring forward matters for discussion which affected other branches of MI5 as well as their own.[27]

As well as advising on matters concerning their own particular branch, the committee's members were to act as advisers on general matters of policy and administration. The committee consisted of the branch heads plus two extra members nominated by Kell – Mr Moresby, the legal adviser, and Captain Maxwell, who edited the Black List – and met weekly in his office. Any MI5 officer who wished to bring up an issue for discussion was invited to do so by submitting a note to his branch head who would then put it forward at the next committee meeting. This suggests that Kell ran MI5 rather like a managing director running a large and diverse organisation through a board of directors. The committee's decisions that affected office procedure were circulated to MI5's staff as 'Office Instructions' and decisions where policy was laid down were circulated as 'Important Decisions'.[28]

D (OVERSEAS SPECIAL INTELLIGENCE) BRANCH

Frank Hall

The head of D Branch, was Major (later Lieutenant-Colonel) Frank Hall, of the General Staff, who had joined MI5 on 7 December 1914, having served in the Royal Garrison Artillery (RGA).[29] An Old Harrovian landowner from County Down in Ireland, before the war Hall had been the military secretary of the Ulster Volunteer Force.[30] Prior to heading D Branch, he had served as a section officer with G3.[31] He was considered MI5's 'main Irish expert'.[32]

D Branch during the First World War

G3 was eventually made into a separate branch, known as D Branch, in September 1916, because the colonial work had grown to such an extent that it warranted the formation of a specialised branch to handle it. The work remained the same as before, but in addition included correspondence with the Eastern Mediterranean Special Intelligence Bureau (EMSIB) which had been set up at Alexandria in March 1916 by Holt-Wilson who had conducted a tour of the region the previous month.[33] Its task was to undertake counter-espionage work in Egypt in cooperation with MI5.[34]

As an example of MI5's advisory role, in December 1915, Frank Hall went to Malta to assess the situation there. Having consulted the senior officials concerned, he prepared a plan of organisation in which he stressed the importance of keeping all branches under a single roof, and of setting up a direct telephone link via cable lines between the central bureau and its sources of information. Soon after his return to the UK, Hall sent his secretary, Miss Hodgson, to Malta to organise the working of the new bureau. She arrived on 17 January 1916 and succeeded in putting the clerical, secretarial and registry work on similar lines to MI5.[35]

The principles of D Branch's organisation were that the 'duties of the several Branch sections had from the first been apportioned according to geographical areas and race divisions. These principles were followed in the formation and development of D. Branch.'[36] MI5's list of staff for 11 December 1916 shows that D Branch had eight members, including three officers and five secretaries,[37] while its distribution of duties of February 1917 gave the Branch's duties as a whole as 'the co-ordination of Imperial Counter-Espionage'. This included both Colonial and Irish affairs.[38]

Following the discovery of the aid that Germany had given to Ireland in connection with the rebellion of April 1916, the Irish work of MI5 had assumed greater importance.

By February 1917, as well as working with G Branch in the investigation of cases of espionage and sedition in Ireland, D Branch had also become concerned with the examination of intercepted correspondence related to Colonial or Irish-American affairs. It worked with the Home Office and other Government Departments on subjects linked to German-Irish-American intrigues; it also handled Irish intelligence reports, in cooperation with GHQ Home Forces.[39]

An MI5 file on Eamon de Valera provides an example of D Branch's role in the censorship of Irish correspondence. The postal censorship (MI9) intercepted a letter from A. Ginnell, the honorary secretary of the Pearse memorial committee in Dublin to de Valera, at the time imprisoned in Lincoln for his leading role in the Easter Rising, asking for de Valera's permission to add his name to an appeal for funds for a Pearse memorial. The deputy assistant censor (DAC) felt that this appeal was undesirable and on 27 August 1918, MI9A requested D Branch's advice whether the letter should proceed. Hall's reply to MI9A was pragmatic:

> 'I should be inclined to let the letter go on – so as to obviate a 'grievance' and let Irish Govt. know through H.O. One more name on the list of patrons wont hurt and they will put De Valera's name on anyhow.'[40]

The short-lived B Branch, which dealt with questions affecting natives of India and other Oriental races, was absorbed by D Branch on 1 September 1917, thereby increasing the scope of D Branch's work.[41] In the distribution of duties of October 1917 D Branch was divided into three sections, each with one or more officers, subordinate to the Head of the Branch, and with its own secretary and clerical staff. Besides the general duties performed by B and D Branches the work apportioned to the Branch as a whole and to each section individually was as follows:

D.   Coordination of Imperial Special Intelligence services in the Overseas Dominions, India and the Colonies; Correspondence with the Dominions, India and the Colonies by letter and cable; Collection and communication of Special Intelligence affecting the Dominions, India and the Colonies. Cooperation with Colonial Office. Investigation of cases of espionage and sedition in Ireland in consultation with G. Cooperation with Home Office and other Government Departments on matters connected with German-Irish-American intrigues. Ciphers.

D1.   Irish-American Affairs. Examination of censored letters or intercepted correspondence dealing therewith. Irish Intelligence Reports and co-operation with G.H.Q., H.F. thereon. Questions affecting Ireland.

D2.   Colonial Affairs, general correspondence with the Colonies. Questions affecting the Dominions and Colonies except Wei-Hai-Wei, Hong Kong, Sarawak, North Borneo, Labuan, Straits Settlements, Ceylon, Aden and Egypt.

D3.   Oriental Affairs. Investigation (in consultation with G) and all correspondence regarding suspected espionage, sedition and treachery among Asiatics and

Egyptians. Co-operation with India Office. Questions affecting India, the Middle East and the Colonies excepted from D.2.[42]

Two further sections, D4 and D5, were added in October 1918, because MI5 had established direct communication with the Special Intelligence Missions in Allied countries, such as those at Washington and in Rome. D4 was given the duty of the coordination of these missions. D5 assumed responsibility for codes and ciphers, despatching telegrams, apart from those to MCOs in neutral countries (sent through MI1c) and inland telegrams sent *en clair*, and for the receipt and distribution of code and cipher telegrams. This code and cipher work had always formed part of D Branch's duties.[43]

The Near East and Far East sections were also rearranged, with the transfer of work concerning suspects or seditious movements in, or connected with, the Near East from D3 to D2. This comprised the former Ottoman Empire (save Mesopotamia) and the countries of North Africa and the Eastern Mediterranean. The Far East sub-section, dealing with the activities of Japanese, Chinese and Siamese worldwide, remained with D3.[44] Japan was an ally, but may well have been regarded with growing reservations.

Until autumn 1918, the CSIB functioned as the clearing house. However, as the work grew, the more important Colonial links frequently requested that they should also be able to correspond directly with each other. Having overcome the difficulty of finding a suitable cipher which could be used by all, on 19 September 1918 some of D Branch's correspondents were put, with their agreement, in direct communication with each other, thereby enabling an interchange of information about suspects. MI5 equipped them with a special cipher and code, and they were to send copies of the reports that they exchanged to MI5 for its records. Australia, South Africa, Canada, New Zealand, Malta, Egypt, India, Singapore, Trinidad and Nairobi were included in these new arrangements, as well as the MCOs in charge of passport and travel control at Tokyo and New York, and the British Military Missions in Rome and Washington. This scheme was named the 'A' circulation, and unanimously approved by those involved.[45]

By November 1918, D Branch had nineteen members of staff, comprising seven officers and twelve secretaries. The branch's growth illustrates the development of both preventive and detective work from a concern solely with Ireland to all external matters.[46]

As each sub-section of D Branch was formed a separate section of MI5's central Registry was also created to handle its papers. Every section had its own card index, as well as the Registry's own general indices, and a specially selected H2 worker was given responsibility for these files. By November 1918, D Branch's subject files were grouped into Indian and Oriental matters, Far East, and Near East.[47] Indeed, several of D Branch's officers were chosen because they had experience in India and the Colonies and thus were thought to understand the local conditions there and 'the peculiarities of race and nomenclature'.[48] Mr S. Newby, of D3, joined MI5 on 28 January 1916, having served with the Indian police.[49] By February 1917, he was working in B Branch, moving to D Branch when it absorbed B Branch.[50]

By degrees, the objects set forth in the Colonial Office circular memorandum came to be achieved. In all of the Self-Governing Dominions and Colonies, means for collecting intelligence and passing it on were provided '...so that it was hardly possible for the movements of an enemy agent to escape observation.' Measures for the prevention of espionage were implemented, particularly for the control of ports, and much benefit was gained from comparing Colonial wartime legislation with the DORA and ARA. Connections were instituted between D Branch and all parts of the Empire, even the remotest ones, and the benefit of establishing cordial personal relations with the overseas authorities was proven.[51] An official report from October 1917 outlined how the branch served as a central clearing house for the interchange of all information regarding enemy activities outside the area of military operations:

> 'The head of M.I.5. corresponds unofficially with all the Departments of the Home Government and has established direct personal relations with some official in each of the Dominions charged with duties of an analogous character. All these, at home and abroad, exchange information with the central office, while the officials in the Dominions to some extent model their local policy and procedure upon that adopted in the United Kingdom.'[52]

The Colonial Governors or their representatives were invited to visit MI5 whenever they had the opportunity, and those who did were shown the work done and the office system was fully explained to them.[53] Acting upon Kell's suggestion, the DMI wrote to the Chief of the General Staff (CGS) India on 18 January 1918, inviting consideration of the question of counter-espionage in India. The DMI proposed that a carefully selected officer should be attached to MI5 for three months to gain an understanding of counter-espionage work in the UK, before moving on to take charge of the new counter-espionage section in India. Lieutenant-Colonel S.F. Muspratt DSO, of the 12th Cavalry, at that time serving as the Assistant Adjutant and Quartermaster General with the Cavalry Corps in France, was chosen, reporting for duty at MI5 on 22 June 1918.[54]

The constant exchange of information led to useful results. All of the Self-Governing Dominions, apart from Newfoundland, and India, Egypt and the more important Colonies were given MI5's Black List and the circulars amending it. Warnings about forged passports and such general subjects, as well as the activities of Indian seditionists and of particular missionary and other societies which MI5 was convinced were German agencies, were passed on whenever necessary.[55] On 8 January 1916, Andrew Bonar Law, Secretary of State for the Colonies, transmitted a memorandum concerning the activities of German agents in the UK, which had been prepared by Drake, warning that:

> 'It has come to notice that German Agents coming to this country, many of whom are of neutral nationality, have now adopted the method of pretending to give information [particularly in connection with explosives and inventions] to various Government Departments about enemy trade or kindred subjects. By this means they hope to obtain some official letter from an officer of the Department concerned which, it is anticipated, will serve as some sort of laissez-passer to them in their visits to the various centres which are of interest to them…'[56]

As an example of the links established, on 6 March 1917, Sir Ronald Munro Ferguson, the Governor-General of Australia sent a telegram, through the Colonial Office, suggesting that the bona fides of Miss Emilie L.C.D. Rundle should be investigated.

On 12 April that year, section G2 of MI5 replied to the Colonial Office that:

> '…the bona fides of Miss Rundle may be regarded as sufficiently established, and that the suspicious acts mentioned in the telegram of the Governor-General of Australia would appear to be capable of explanation from Miss Rundle's eccentricity and want of balance, of which both her solicitor and banker speak.'[57]

The available evidence suggests that D Branch succeeded in managing to run such a worldwide system. When there were no direct links, it was arranged for information to be passed on to MI5 via other War Office Departments or the Foreign Office. Therefore, MI5 was in a position to obtain information about German activities in even the most remote corners of the globe, 'from Peru to the Dutch East Indies and the Islands of the Pacific', and a watch was kept on German propaganda through missionaries or otherwise 'in every continent'.[58] On 10 August 1918, Munro Ferguson forwarded a copy of a letter from the native king of the Loyalty Islands concerning a suspected German spy to the Secretary of State for the Colonies.[59] Similarly, in January 1917, an intercepted letter, which MI5 forwarded to SIB Melbourne, led to the Australian SIB's discovery that an Irish organisation, the Irish National Association, with revolutionary and pro-German aims, whose leaders were members of the Irish Republican Brotherhood, had existed in Australia since the beginning of 1916. Established in Melbourne, Sydney and Brisbane, the Irish National Association's object was the establishment of an independent Irish Republic, to be achieved by force with German assistance. It was discovered that money was being collected in Australia to assist armed rebellion in Ireland and sent to America to be transmitted to Germany for the purchase of war material. Intercepted letters showed that a request had been made from America that Germany should be provided with the names of Irish enemy sympathisers in Australia. The Australian SIB prepared a report on seditious Irish societies in the Commonwealth for the Government, resulting in the internment of seven of the leaders of the Irish seditionary movement on 19 June 1918.[60]

D Branch's worldwide role demonstrates just how far MI5 had evolved by the end of the war from its humble beginnings in 1909. As Eric Holt-Wilson told his audience in a lecture delivered in 1934:

> 'Our Security Service is more than national, it is Imperial. We have official agencies cooperating with us, under the direct instructions of the Dominion and Colonial Offices and the supervision of the local Governors, and their chiefs of police, for enforcing local Security Laws in every British community overseas.'[61]

D Branch's function also says much about MI5's role, particularly its lack of executive powers, such that much of its work was in directing the actions of other agencies. In this sense, D Branch was the brain that stored information and coordinated the other parts of the imperial counter-espionage body which served as the eyes, ears, arms and legs to provide the brain with information and execute its directives. D Branch's work thus set the pattern of MI5's interest and concern in the colonial Empire until decolonisation in the 1950s and 1960s, with MI5's overseas representatives, known as Defence Security Officers (DSO) where there were British garrisons and Security Liaison Officers (SLO) elsewhere, being posted throughout much of the Empire and in some allied states.[62] MI5's work in the colonial Empire continued for long into the 1960s, even after independence in some countries. MI5 officers also worked in the Cold War CENTO (Central Treaty Organisation) and SEATO (Southeast Asia Treaty Organisation) organisations.

COUNTER-SUBVERSION

MI5's harshest critics focus on its role in counter-subversion and suggest that it was beginning to develop into a political police. Here, I will question whether MI5 was developing into a political police, or whether the scope of counter-espionage was widening in response to new threats from German espionage? It has often been claimed that MI5's development was heavily influenced by Kell's loss in a turf battle with Thomson. This section will examine the foundations upon which this claim is built, by looking at what kind of role Kell wished for MI5 to take on regarding counter-subversion. In short, to see if Kell really had coveted the role that Thomson was given.

Counter-Subversion

Unlike counter-espionage, at first Kell viewed the need for counter-subversion as a low priority. It was MO5(g)'s view that pacifism and labour unrest posed little threat to the war effort. In August 1914, the Trades Union Congress (TUC) declared an 'industrial truce' for the length of the war. Although six of the forty Labour MPs opposed the war, Arthur Henderson, wartime leader of the parliamentary party, joined a coalition government formed in May 1915 and such opposition to the war as there was came from the small Independent Labour Party (ILP). MO5(g) was also authorized to check the correspondence of the 'Stop-the-War Committee', that had been established by C.H. Norman, 'one of the most militant ILP leaders', the results of which 'were reassuring'.[63] An MO5(g) report to the Home Office of July 1915 concluded that:

> 'No letter has been seen which would appear to indicate that the writer has anti-British sentiments or that the Committee is in any way inspired or assisted from enemy sources ... It appears therefore that the members of the Committee are obtaining very small results from their propaganda and the harm they are causing at the present time is practically negligible.'[64]

This also shows that MO5(g) was clearly only interested in organisations such as the Stop-the-War Committee to discover if they were in any way inspired or assisted from enemy sources. MO5(g) was not being used by the government as a political police and its assessment of the risk was accurate and measured; there was no attempt to over-hype the threat.

However, as German espionage efforts in Britain began to wane, the main task of MI5 in 1916 passed from counter-espionage to counter-subversion. MI5 was justified in anticipating the Germans to instigate subversion operations in an attempt to weaken the war effort. Right from the outbreak of war, the German high command adopted a strategy of fomenting revolution by sponsoring subversive elements in friendly countries.[65] German agents funded or supported French pacifists, American labour organisations, Indian nationalists, Russian revolutionaries, Muslim *jihadists* and Irish republicans.[66] Although MI5 and Whitehall did not recognize it, the fact that the Germans never launched a serious subversion campaign in the UK was down to their sense that Britain was a much more difficult target for such activities compared to its allies, especially in view of the arrests of the main German agents in 1914.[67] Subversion on the British mainland did not become a serious concern for MI5 until 1916.[68] As Thomson later observed, 'It was not until 1916 that the Pacifist became active'.[69] The cause of the revival of pacifism was conscription for men between the ages of eighteen and forty-one, initially for unmarried men as of February 1916, followed by married men in April.[70]

Between the middle of 1916 and the end of 1917, MI5 investigated over 5,200 suspected pacifists. Christopher Andrew puts this issue into perspective, noting that:

'Little came of the protest against conscription. About 7,000 conscientious objectors agreed to non-combatant service, usually with field ambulances; another 3,000 were sent to labour camps run by the Home Office; 1,500 'absolutists' who refused all compulsory service were called up and then imprisoned for refusing to obey orders. These figures paled into statistical insignificance by comparison with the numbers of conscripts. By the end of 1916 conscription had increased the size of the armed services from 2½ million to 3½ million. During 1917-18 their size stabilized at between 4 and 4½ million – one in two men of 'military age'.'[71]

As already explained in Chapter Four, in early 1916, MI5 uncovered links between the Communist Club and the Diamond Reign pub, which was 'a meeting place for bitterly hostile British citizens of German birth'.[72] MI5 concluded wrongly that the Communist Club 'fomented' the strikes at munitions factories on Clydeside in early 1916, but although the Club 'waved the red flag', it is unlikely to have had any major impact on the industrial action. However, Whitehall nevertheless remained concerned that subversive elements were at large.

Dr Christopher Addison MP, Parliamentary Under Secretary to the Minister of Munitions, suspected that the Germans were involved in 'a systematic and sinister plan' to sabotage production of the most important munitions in the Clyde district so as to hinder Britain's ability to conduct offensive warfare on the Western Front. Addison's fears arose from questionable reports emanating from a small intelligence group organised on Clydeside by Sir Lynden Macassey KC, the chairman of the Clyde Dilution Commissioners, who monitored the 'dilution' of skilled by unskilled labour.[73] Addison, who was soon to succeed Lloyd George as Minister of Munitions, wrote in his diary after receiving Macassey's reports:

'He has traced direct payments from Germany to three workers and also discovered that ... the man who is financing the Clyde workers ... has a daughter married in Germany, a son married to a German and his chief business is in Germany. He is evidently on the track of a very successful revelation.'[74]

PMS2

The work of munitions factories was vital to the war effort and when accidents hindered production, suspicion fell on the Belgian refugees and other aliens working there.

As it was deemed advisable to take precautions to prevent enemy agents masquerading as imported foreign workers, on 15 December 1915 a conference was convened where it was proposed to transfer the Belgian staff employed by MI5 to the Ministry of Munitions. This was done by the beginning of March 1916 and the new organisation was labeled MMLI (Ministry of Munitions Labour Intelligence). As the initials 'MMLI' were thought to give too much away they were afterwards 'camouflaged' and it acquired the new name PMS2 (Parliamentary Military Secretary, Section Number 2).[75]

On 30 March 1916, an Order in Council establishing conditions under which alien workers could be engaged was produced. The Aliens Restriction (Consolidation) Order 1916, contained Article 22A regarding aliens engaged on munitions work. In effect, it meant that an alien could not perform munitions work unless permission had been obtained from the Minister of Munitions and he possessed an identity book attesting to this. Firms were not to employ an alien on munitions if this Order prohibited him from doing so. Employers were also duty bound to bring these provisions to the notice of any aliens they employed.[76]

The Commission of Enquiry into Industrial Unrest later reported that the main cause of discontent was that the cost of living had increased disproportionately to the advance in wages, and that the distribution of food supplies was unequal. There was no evidence of any German influence behind industrial unrest in the UK.[77]

Basil Thomson

Sir Basil Thomson, Assistant Commissioner (Crime) of the Metropolitan Police, 1913-1919. Thomson was in charge of the Criminal Investigation Department (CID), which included the Special Branch.
(Jay Robert Nash Collection)

Basil Thomson was the son of the late William Thomson, Archbishop of York. After Eton and Oxford he trained as a barrister and then embarked on a remarkable and varied career beginning in the Colonial Service. He was Prime Minister of Tonga at only twenty-eight years old and then private tutor to the Crown Prince of Siam, after which came very different work as the Governor of Dartmoor Prison. In June 1913, at the age of fifty-two, Thomson became the Assistant Commissioner of the Metropolitan Police in charge of the Criminal Investigation Department (CID) of which the Special Branch was a part.[78] After his dismissal from his post as Director of Intelligence in 1921, Thomson wrote volumes of his memoirs and detective stories with titles such as *Mr Pepper, Investigator*. In December 1925, at the age of sixty-four, Thomson and one Miss Thelma de Lava were arrested in Hyde Park for committing an act that violated public decency. He was found guilty and fined five pounds.[79]

The Special Branch had been formed in 1883, as the Special Irish Branch, 'to cope with the Irish dynamite outrages in London and elsewhere'. Under Thomson, its role was 'to foresee and to prevent political agitators from committing crime in order to terrorise the community into granting them what they want.'[80] The Special Branch had 114 staff in November 1914, rising to 700 by the end of the war.[81] As Thomson wrote after the war, the 'War Office had none of the machinery for arresting and keeping men in custody: the Metropolitan Police had; and so we found ourselves playing the role of general servant to the Admiralty and the War Office'.[82] As Andrew observes, the Special Branch arrested suspected spies at MI5's behest:

> '…but Kell seems to have resented the way Basil Thomson sought to monopolise the interrogation of spies once taken into custody at Scotland Yard. As a secret organisation MI5 could not publicly claim credit for its part in the capture of German spies. The more flamboyant Thomson, already well used to publicising his achievements, could and did. In the process he earned the collective enmity of most of MI5.'[83]

This enmity was forcefully expressed by Drake in a letter to Rear-Admiral Sir William Reginald 'Blinker' Hall, Director of Naval Intelligence (DNI) during the First World War: '*you know B.T. did not know of the existence, name or activity of any convicted spy until I told him; but being the dirty dog he was he twisted the facts to claim that he alone did it.*'[84] Holt-Wilson summed up the relative roles of MI5 and Special Branch in a post-war lecture:

> 'Contrary to popular fiction and journalism, "Scotland Yard" never had any concern with "spies", unless or until information happened to be passed to them by the Defence Security Service for keeping them under observation or affecting their arrest.'[85]

Compared to the problems with Thomson, MI5's relations with the chief constables of the UK's other police forces seem generally to have been very good indeed.

DRR/ARO 1916

A further series of amendments to legislation also resulted from the Irish rebellion. On 8 June 1916, DRR14B was amended to give power to deal with those interned under DRR14B as if they were prisoners of war. This was needed so as to be able to guard the considerable number of Irish rebels interned in England under DRR14B. In autumn 1916, DRR14, concerning local restrictions on suspects, was strengthened. Due to the distribution and number of munitions works, it had become dangerous to remove suspects to inland areas as had been the practice. Therefore an amendment was prepared empowering CMAs to give orders restricting the movements of suspects within their district. It was deemed sensible that these restriction orders from CMAs should, unless really urgent, be put to F Branch before being put into effect, so as to centralise the administration of these new regulations.[86]

Owing to the trouble caused by an English woman, Miss Emily Hobhouse, a new regulation DRR14F was added in November 1916: she had been permitted, against MI5's advice, to enter Switzerland and had conducted a tour of Ruhleben civilian detention camp, six miles to the west of Berlin. DRR14F made it an offence for any British subject to voluntarily enter into an enemy country or any foreign territory occupied by the enemy, unless they possessed a special permit issued on the authority of the Secretary of State, except during military operations.[87] Hobhouse was an avid opponent of the War and protested vigorously against it. She organized the writing, signing and publishing of the Open Christmas Letter addressed to the women of Germany and Austria in January 1915. It was a public message for peace signed by a group of 101 British women suffragists at the end of 1914 as the first Christmas of the First World War approached. It was a written acknowledgment of the mounting horror of modern war and a direct response to letters written to US feminist, Carrie Chapman Catt, President of the International Women Suffrage Alliance (IWSA), by a small group of German women's rights activists. It was answered two months later by a group of 155 prominent pacifist German and Austrian women. The exchange of letters between women of nations at war helped to promote the aims of peace, and also helped prevent the fracturing of the unity which lay in the common goal they shared: suffrage for women. Hobhouse, who had been born in 1860 and died in 1926, was a British welfare campaigner primarily remembered for bringing to the British public's attention, and working to change, the deprived conditions inside the British concentration camps in South Africa built for Boer women and children during the Second Boer War of 1899–1902. Hobhouse was the sister of Leonard Trelawny Hobhouse, the noted social liberal, and the second cousin of the important British peace activist, Stephen Henry Hobhouse.[88] The Ruhleben camp held between 4,000–5,500 male citizens of the Allied powers, who had been living, studying, working or on holiday in Germany at the outbreak of the War. The detainees included John Cecil (later Sir John) Masterman. A Tutor of Modern History at Christ Church College, Oxford, Masterman was in Germany as an Exchange Lecturer at the University of Freiburg at the outbreak of war. During the Second World War, he served as Chairman of the Twenty Committee (XX in Latin), which ran the Double Cross System, the scheme that controlled double agents in Britain and the misinformation they fed to the Germans as part of strategic deception operations. Masterman went on to become the Vice-Chancellor of Oxford in 1957 and was knighted in 1959.[89] Also at Ruhleben were the crews of civilian ships stranded in German harbours or captured at sea, and fishermen from captured trawlers sunk in the North Sea during the first days of the war.[90]

Similarly, during 1916, two additions were made to DORA, which improved that portion dealing with espionage. Firstly, a paragraph was inserted at the end of DRR18 forbidding the communication or publication of any information concerning any ship's passage along any part of the UK coast. Secondly, 19A was added to stop the loss or misuse of plans, confidential documents, models, photographs, etc. F Branch felt that these additions completed the regulations needed for the purpose of counter-espionage in the narrower sense.[91] Two important amendments were also added to the censorship legislation regarding hidden communication. DRR24A was replaced by another regulation that was framed to include, in the prohibition against invisible ink and other such items, any mechanical method of secret communication, such as conveying a letter between two pages of a pamphlet stuck together. DRR24B prohibited the carrying of any written or printed material from the UK to any neutral or enemy country; apart from ships papers and similar items sent with special permission.[92]

Similarly, in January 1916, four important changes were made to the ARA. Firstly, prohibited areas were expanded to encompass all places within ten miles of the coast.

Secondly, aliens found in prohibited areas where they did not reside without an identity book and passport could be expelled. Thirdly, registered aliens who wished to enter a prohibited area had to be provided with an identity book. Fourth, all hotels had to keep a register of visitors. However, possessing an identity book did not mean immunity from police supervision, or provide right of entry to prohibited areas; it was a formality devised by MI5 to provide greater certainty and convenience in controlling aliens.[93] The available evidence does not explain why these decisions were reached at this particular time. However, it seems fairly clear that they were driven by a conviction that the threat came from aliens rather than British subjects.

During June 1916, an official Army Council letter, drafted by F Branch, drew the Home Office's attention to the number of enemy aliens who had up to that point been exempt from internment – recent official figures had been 22,249. The Home Office created a special commission to consider the situation, and after four months it found considerable differences in chief constables' actions, and that CMAs had exhibited differences in policy. The commission prompted a number of chief constables to confer with CMAs when they were in doubt, which led to the withdrawal of residence permits in some cases that, plus voluntary removals, added up to 126 men and 333 women. Twelve of those the commission called attention to were interned, four were removed and four others were repatriated.[94]

The registration of aliens was extended in early 1916. After 14 February all aliens (not just enemy aliens) were required to register everywhere, except in London. After 7 July all male aliens over eighteen years of French, Russian, Italian or Serbian nationality who had been living in London prior to 14 February 1916 also had to register with the police.[95]

Identity books were improved and changes were made to the categories of people required to possess them. Aliens working in munitions or desiring to enter the new special military areas were added. Whenever possible, aliens were generally issued with identity books rather than registration certificates. The police were reminded that identity books were not a guarantee of an alien's bona fides, but simply a standardised and convenient identification document. Chief constables were asked to make sure that the issuing of an identity book was noted on the alien's passport. The importance of paying particular attention to photographs in identity books was also emphasised. An exception to this rule was made for Belgian soldiers on leave in uniform and in possession of an official furlough pass.[96]

After 16 December 1916, all male aliens in the Metropolitan Police district had to register: Romanians, Montenegrins, Portuguese and Japanese by 23 December, and all other nationalities by 6 January 1917. Henceforth, the only aliens not registered were single females who were resident in London prior to 14 January 1916 and who had not left London after that day.[97]

The new regulation DRR29B had probably the greatest value of any of the changes made in 1916, authorising the creation of special military areas. The first of these was created on 28 July 1916, when all of Scotland north of the Caledonian Canal was designated an area of supreme naval importance. This was later followed by the Isle of Sheppey, because of the naval port of Chatham and its anti-aircraft defences, and also Newhaven, Harwich and Dover. It was an extension of DRR29 and DRR29A's provisions for the restriction of admission to camps, defence works, munitions factories and other places of military importance. Its purpose was the general control of all people entering such a place.[98]

F Branch was also involved in the following three minor amendments to DORA in 1916. Firstly, a paragraph was added to DRR55 to enable fingerprints and photographs to be taken of individuals arrested under this regulation. Secondly, DRR27, which forbade the spreading of prejudicial or false statements and acts prejudicial to the recruiting, training, discipline or administration of the armed forces in order to check the work of enemy agents and enemy sympathisers, was amended to also include films and stage performances of this nature in May 1916. Thirdly, for the same purpose, in July, an addition was made to DRR27 to prohibit sending reports or making statements intended to undermine public confidence in currency or bank notes.[99]

Statistics for work done during 1916

Personal dossiers	10,657
Letters (not including Irish-American or peace letters)	33,257
Irish-American letters	5,551
Peace letters	2,737
Cases of disloyalty	1,966
Suspects circulated	3,174
Internments sanctioned	3
Permit applications	24,919
Convictions under DRR/ARO	1,410
Credentials examined of applications for employment in:-	
Postal censorship	5,160
Red Cross and St John of Jerusalem	3,081
Anglo-French hospitals	1,682
Ministry of Munitions	1,890
Intelligence Department	544[100]

Spies caught 5 August 1914 to 31 December 1916

Sentenced to death (included 1 commuted to penal servitude)	14
Suicide	1
Penal servitude	7
Imprisonment	1
Interned DRR14B etc	157
Detained pending deportation	124
Removed from or forbidden to enter UK	268
Prevented from leaving UK or placed under 'special supervision'	110
Restricted under DRR14 or DRR14B	22
Removed or excluded from certain areas under DRR14	554[101]

By mid-1916, the German espionage attack on the UK had reached a high level of sophistication: as shown by the use of American journalists operating in pairs. Nonetheless, MI5 defeated its adversary quite comfortably. Of course, the Germans made a few small mistakes. However, MI5 skillfully exploited every German slip to the full. During 1916, MI5 also showed that it was capable of rudimentary, and effective, double agent operations. It never approached anything like the sophistication attained during the Second World War. Nonetheless, MI5 made good use of the opportunities presented by COMO and by Whytock.

The threat continued to evolve throughout 1916, as demonstrated by the DRR and ARO issued during 1916 to plug gaps that MI5 had learned existed in its counter-espionage defences. These included measures to counter Irish nationalism, measures to make it harder to evade the postal censorship, and tighter control over neutral and Allied aliens.

The formation of D Branch says much about MI5's development. It marks a key stage in MI5's assumption of an Empire-wide role. The fact that D Branch was formed as a separate branch in its own right, rather than remaining as a part of G Branch, illustrates one of the key assumptions behind MI5's developmental ethos. Any duties that did not belong strictly to the Investigative, Preventive or Records Branch, were to be hived off and assigned to their own branch. The scope of D Branch's work also shows that the German espionage and subversion attack on the British war effort had assumed worldwide dimensions – most notably, German attempts to encourage sedition in Ireland and India.

The acquisition of the name 'MI5' was further acknowledgement of this transformation, from a small sub-department of the War Office to a great department of state in its own right. The formation of a Standing Advisory Committee emphasized that MI5 had grown beyond a small bureau that Kell could direct entirely on his own. In the early days, Kell personally selected all those who joined MI5. By this stage, MI5 was too large to be run like a close-knit family business.

MI5 begins to take an interest in counter-subversion in 1916. It is abundantly clear that MI5 had not become a political police. MI5 began to look into the Diamond Reign pub and the Communist Club because the police asked MI5 to do so. MI5's role within counter-subversion was strictly limited to looking for any evidence of a German hidden hand. Indeed, whenever organisations deemed subversive were raided by MI5, MI5's main interest was in obtaining membership lists and, particularly, financial records to look for German involvement and, especially, financial backing. Indeed, there is plenty of evidence that Kell only desired MI5 to take on this very limited role in counter-subversion. Kell patently did not want to take on the wider labour intelligence role that Thomson so obviously coveted. Indeed, throughout the British Army's history, the military authorities have always stuck to the view that there was something inherently wrong in ordering soldiers to spy on workers. This was firmly in the Home Office and Police's domain. Part of the problem with this issue seems to have arisen because commentators have looked at Kell's post-war turf war with Thomson, and then extrapolated these issues back to 1916. It is clear that Kell was indeed disappointed when Thomson was given the lead role in post-war civilian counter-espionage, and MI5 was limited to counter-espionage within the armed forces. However, this does not mean that

Kell had coveted the wider counter-subversion role that was also given to Thomson at this time, or that back in 1916, Kell had coveted the Labour Intelligence role that was later given to Thomson, and marked the beginning of Thomson's move into counter-subversion.

It has often been suggested that MI5 broke the back of German espionage in 1915, such that during 1916 it began to look for other work to do in order to justify its continued existence, which explains MI5's move in to counter-subversion during 1916. The statistics for work done by MI5 during 1916 shed much light on this issue. Clearly, MI5 did not have as many German spies shot during 1916 as during 1915. However, other statistics for work done, show that MI5 was even busier in 1916 than it had been during 1915. In short, MI5 had plenty of counter-espionage work to do during 1916; it did not need to move into counter-subversion in order to find work to keep itself busy.

From Counter-Espionage to Security Intelligence
1 January 1917 To 11 November 1918

S PY cases from 1916 had convinced MI5 that the main remaining threat posed by German espionage came from neutral seamen, whose work enabled them to make frequent trips to and from the UK. MI5's response was to tighten the control at ports.

Control of Ports and Frontiers, 1917-1918

Control at ports was tightened in early 1917 by increasing the aliens officers' powers under DRR14G and ARO articles 4 and 10A. The permission of an aliens officer was necessary for the landing of any alien in the UK and for the embarkation of anyone, British or alien. Aliens officers were empowered not only to refuse any alien permission to disembark, but also to add conditions to their permission to land. Extra powers were soon granted to the MCOs who were also authorised to grant permission to embark, like the aliens officers. However, the permission to land continued to be exclusively the prerogative of the aliens officers, although in doing so they often followed the advice of the MCOs, with whom they worked on excellent terms.[1]

The discovery and seizure of letters, photographs and other documents under DRR54 was an important part of an MCO's duties at the ports. An effective search was essential for this. This had two objectives: to hinder enemy agents as well as being of great importance to the War Trade Intelligence Department and the Ministry of Blockade that business papers that could refer to enemy trading should not enter or leave the UK without censorship.[2]

During the first six months of 1917 a number of the controls were reorganised and the precise powers of the MCOs and consular authorities at every location were defined. The permit office system was set up in almost all Allied and neutral countries throughout the world by the end of July 1917.[3] The main aim of the passport and permit offices was to deter undesirables by checking the credentials of those wishing to travel. This control aided the aliens officers and others at the ports, not just because it eliminated some potential travellers, particularly the most suspect ones, but it also allowed greater time to search for concealed papers. Enquiring into bona fides also had a detective role, leading to the discovery of much intelligence relevant to counter-espionage.[4]

It is important to look at the restrictions that were gradually imposed on seamen before the advent of the Neutral European Port (NEP) Scheme. In the early days of the war there was a want of restriction. The reach of the German espionage system was not fully appreciated, such that the necessity for precautions concerning seamen was then little understood. While the Germans were able to disguise their agents as passengers, there was less concern with the threat posed by seamen. It was also vitally important, because of supplies, that alien crewmen of neutral traders should not be pushed away from the UK. Therefore, means of control akin to those applied to passengers were only introduced very slowly.[5] The main dangers remained the gathering and passing on of intelligence and the conveying of German agents in and out of the UK disguised as British or alien seamen. Other dangers included letter-carrying, sabotage, smuggling and hostile propaganda. Seamen on short-sea traders between Scandinavia, Holland, Spain and the UK were regarded with great suspicion and revelations about the methods of German agents emphasised that it was this class of seamen that posed the greatest danger.[6]

In March 1917 the censorship of letters to seamen on out-going short-voyage ships was assigned to the MCOs at the principal ports. This proved not only a defence against the leakage of information, but also a way of discovering suspects.[7] In the autumn of that year, the authorities reviewed the situation regarding neutral short-voyage ships and concluded that it was still unsatisfactory. Indeed, because of the successful controls over passenger traffic and the strictness of censorship, the enemy then appeared to be focusing on the opportunities offered by the short-sea trader, as had been evinced by the Bergen spy trial of June 1917 and other discoveries.[8] The German espionage bureau at Bergen in Norway was formed to report on the movement of ships trading with Allied countries and came to the notice of the Norwegian Police in May 1917. Following a trial in Bergen on 7 June, three Germans and seven Norwegians were found guilty of conducting espionage on behalf of Germany and sentenced to terms ranging from thirty days to nine months' imprisonment.[9] With these revelations, it was felt that the threat from enemy espionage was more serious than the risk of reducing neutral trade and that only the strictest controls would thwart it. Thus, the NEP Scheme was designed, so that ships from neutral European countries could be prohibited from any contact with the shore while lying in UK ports.[10] Once MI5 had explained the scheme to all concerned, and gained broad agreement, steps to implement the scheme could be begun by the spring of 1918.[11]

The control of ports and frontiers was helped by the great decrease in passenger traffic during 1916 and 1917, particularly that between England and France. This was partly due to the submarine menace and also because of the strengthening of the control in every direction.[12]

The NEP Scheme was put into force in June 1918. This decreed that the landing of all alien seamen, including masters and officers, was prohibited; exceptions were made only in very exceptional cases. All business was to be transacted on board ship and guards were placed to prevent all exits from ships. The new regulations first took effect at certain ports only from 15 June 1918, but they were then extended to the UK's other principal ports in the months that followed.[13] In order to prevent any communication between NEP ships and the shore, stringent control over all visitors to subject vessels was needed.

From October 1918 only officials and ships' brokers were allowed to board short-voyage ships, and when personnel were allowed on board, the port authorities reserved the right to attend meetings. NEP ships were also segregated to prevent them from communicating with each other.[14]

Under the NEP Scheme the main measures for the control of docks were patrols, closing gates or, if there were none, erecting barriers, segregating NEP ships, and regulating access to the docks and to ships alongside and in a river or harbour.[15] Thereby, admission to docks became much more strictly controlled. Previous schemes to exclude undesirable persons from docks, such as they were, had not been overly successful. Under NEP policy, permits to docks and ships were only to be given to British subjects and, when employed by an alien firm, only to those of British birth. Full particulars regarding the applicants' nationality, occupation, reason for requesting a permit, and photographs had to be provided. These applications were scrutinised by the chief constable, senior aliens officer, MCO and dock representatives.[16] In order to control access to NEP ships, the local commands were required to provide guards from the Royal Defence Corps, and by July 1918 up to 2,000 were deployed.[17]

An MI5 report written in 1921 assessed the NEP scheme as having severed any possible contacts between Germany and Britain through neutral seamen. Other advantages had also been gained. The control had been made effective with the minimum disturbance to shipping, as ships from neutral European ports formed the smallest percentage of total shipping, and it also had been possible to withdraw, to a great extent, former restrictions upon neutral and Allied seamen in Allied and extra-European traffic.[18]

E Branch's main contribution was to 'protective security'. As the case of Captain Hans Boehm, a German saboteur, demonstrated (see below), Britain was a hard target. The 'most sinister' type of sabotage practised by *Sektion* P of *Abteilung* IIIB was biological warfare. In April 1915, *Sektion* P posted Dr Anton Dilger, an American citizen of German parentage who had trained as a medical doctor in Heidelberg to the USA. In a laboratory in Washington DC, Dilger produced cultures of *bacillus anthracis* and *pseudomonas mallei*, the instrumental agents of anthrax and glanders and German agents gave anthrax and glanders to mules and horses being held in pens at docks in the USA while waiting to be exported to Europe. Dilger returned to Germany in autumn 1916 and *Sektion* P's biological warfare programme in the USA came to an end. On 30 March 1917, MI5 issued a warning circular to other government departments notifying them that evidence had been obtained that German saboteurs were plotting to administer glanders and anthrax to mules and horses in the UK. The following month there were four outbreaks on the Isle of Man which were most probably as a result of German biological warfare. It is likely that without the level of protective security there would have been further outbreaks.[19]

The Boehm Case

On 9 January 1917, the S.S. *Zeelandia* arrived in Falmouth and the next day Captain Hans Boehm, a German sabotage agent, was apprehended on board the vessel while on route from Spain to Holland using the American passport of Jelks Leroy Thrasher. He subsequently broke under interrogation at Scotland Yard and confessed to his true identity. He had been working under Captain Franz von Papen, the German Military Attaché in

Washington, on sabotage operations in the USA and Canada and also associating with
Irish extremists there. He was detained as a prisoner of war, because in order to secure a
conviction the Admiralty would have had to disclose information that they felt inadvisable
so to do.[20] In light of the Admiralty's success in decoding the Zimmermann telegram it
seems most likely that the Admiralty was reading telegrams from the German Embassy
in Washington to Berlin, which alerted them to Boehm's travels, but it did not want to
risk compromising this prize source.

Organisational changes, 1917

On 15 January 1917, G5 was made into a separate branch for Oriental Affairs
(B Branch),[21] but it was absorbed by D Branch on 1 September 1917.[22] In February
1917, the duties of G1 were restricted to the 'investigation of cases of sedition and peace
propaganda arising from enemy activities …'[23] By March 1917, MI5 increased to eighty
officers.[24] Whilst Kell was on sick leave in early 1917 (he suffered from chronic asthma),
he appears to have suspected Drake of plotting to replace him. Though details of any
tensions do not survive, Kell later commented that he became 'convinced that [Drake]
was not playing the game'. This may explain why Drake left MI5 in March 1917 to take
over as head of secret service work for the BEF's GHQ in France, his job being to
organise intelligence gathering behind enemy lines.[25] Following the USA's declaration
of war against Germany, Arthur Balfour, then Foreign Secretary, led a diplomatic mission
to the USA, arriving in Washington for top-level talks on 22 April 1917. Balfour's twenty-
five strong team included the recently promoted Lieutenant-Colonel Dansey representing
the intelligence services.[26] Only a single copy of MI5's Black List was ever given to a
foreign official, and this was restricted to volumes 1–3, which were issued to Colonel Van
Deman, head of the US General Staff's intelligence department, by Dansey when he
went to Washington accompanying Balfour's mission.[27] Lastly, a sixth branch, A Branch,
was formed on 23 April 1917 to deal with work related to the registration and control
of aliens employed on war work in the UK.[28] Thus, the complete organisation of
MI5 was:

M.I.5.	Special Intelligence – General
M.I.5.A.	Aliens on War Service
M.I.5.D.	Overseas Special Intelligence
M.I.5.E.	Control of Ports and Frontiers
M.I.5.F.	Preventive Branch
M.I.5.G.	Detective Branch
M.I.5.H.	Administrative Branch (Office & Records).[29]

MI5 did not have branches named B or C at this stage. Lieutenant-Colonel Sywnfen
Jervis, whose work superintending the production of the MI5 Historical Branch Reports
gave him an intimate knowledge of the workings of MI5, explained how the branches
were interrelated:

'F. being the branch that deals with "The Prevention of Espionage" and the policy
thereof all the others are obviously off-shoots from its stem. D. is the continuation of

Kell and the heads of MI5's branches, 1918. (Front row, left to right) Lieutenant-Colonel Eric Holt-Wilson (Deputy-Director and head of F Branch), Colonel Vernon Kell (Director), and Lieutenant-Colonel Maldwyn Haldane (H Branch). (Back Row, left to right) Major Sidney Welchman (A Branch), Major James Sealy Clarke (G Branch), Major Frank Hall (D Branch), and Major Herbert Spencer (E Branch). (Security Service Archive)

F. overseas and completes our net-work over the world. G. is the method of carrying out the work and examples of cases and methods will show how our end is obtained. E. is the corollary of F. preventing people coming in to the country and enabling G. to carry out its work in preventing them getting out. A. is a further offshoot of F. enabling control to be kept over certain alien people who, may be of interest or a possible danger. H. has to do with all the foregoing and would be descriptive of the expansion of M.I.5 generally and in detail as the various branches sprang up and grew under the enforced increase due to the exigencies of War.'[30]

By October 1917, MI5's strength had risen to 701 personnel, comprising ninety-one officers, 360 administrative staff, twenty-three police at headquarters and 227 ports police.[31]

The Chakravarty Case

Dr Chandra Kanta Chakravarty, a Bengali, and Ernst Sekunna, a close German friend of his, were arrested by the New York Police in New York in March 1917 and charged with conspiring to make an attack on India through China, and using false passports. They admitted receiving $60,000 from Germany through Wolf von Igel, secretary to Captain von Papen, the German Military Attaché in the USA. Their arrests led to great developments, and in July 1917 ninety-seven people were indicted in connection with the case by the Grand Jury at San Francisco. On 30 April 1918 sentences from thirty days to two years, with substantial fines in many cases, were passed on thirty-two of them. The judge spoke of the inadequacy of these sentences, two years being the maximum that the law would allow. The evidence had been prepared by D3 in connection with the India Office, and two MI5 officials went to America to assist Nathan with the case.[32]

The Smith Case

Following Mrs Luise ('Lizi') Mathilde Smith's arrival in England in October 1915, her German origins were reported to the chief constable of Cheshire. She had been born in 1867 into the aristocratic von Zastrow family of Neider Heidesdorf who were 'well-known to King Edward'. In February 1913 she married Dr John Henry Smith, a photographic chemist. They lived in Italy and then Switzerland before coming to the UK in October 1915. They first settled at Romiley in Cheshire and then moved on to Manchester where Dr Smith worked as a lecturer. The chief constable informed MI5 and her address was put on check. Various harmless letters passed and the check was cancelled in May 1916. Dr Smith died in March 1917, the same month that the chief censor at Cape Town in South Africa informed MI5 that Mrs Smith had tried to smuggle cuttings from pro-German Swiss newspapers which were hidden inside parcels of tea and of calico, and which were prohibited in South Africa to a member of the von Zastrow family at Grootfontein. The letters that reached South Africa before July 1917 did not contravene the DRR at that time. However, on 17 July 1917 DRR24B (version 3) was issued which made it an offence to 'transmit through the post any written or printed matter by any indirect route or method involving evasion of the censorship.' On 20 July 1917, Mrs Smith sent another such parcel which breached the new regulation. While MI5 was considering what action to take, on 5 October 1917 a letter that she wrote to her mother was intercepted: it contained coded answers to questions about the results of the U-boat and Zeppelin campaigns. Mrs Smith was interrogated at Scotland Yard on 17 October 1917. She admitted using a code, 'but declared that her intention was to discourage the Germans'. She was arrested on suspicion of having conveyed information to the enemy. Whilst she was on remand in prison awaiting trial, Smith admitted to a fellow inmate that she had communicated with her brother Werner, a German U-boat captain, via an intermediary. Mrs Smith was tried in camera, and on 4 March 1918 she was sentenced to ten years' penal servitude.[33]

Regarding the issue of the importation into the UK of literature of a 'dangerous' character, the censor and the India Office had been urging for legislation owing to the dangerous spread of Indian seditious or revolutionary publications coming to the UK from the USA, Holland, Sweden and Switzerland. The Lizzie Smith case served to highlight two such gaps in the DRR. Smith had been caught smuggling pro-German literature to a POW in a colony (South Africa) that was prohibited in that colony. When questioned, she noted that the newspapers from which she had sent cuttings had been passed into the UK through the press censorship. Thus, on 30 June 1917, DRR27B was issued prohibiting the import of publications containing 'dangerous matter' of which the publication or circulation in the UK was forbidden under DRR27. That day, DRR24 was re-drafted adding a clause forbidding evasion of the censorship through the use of letter carriers. DRR24B was also re-drafted that day, adding a clause making it an offence 'to evade censorship through the post by sending letters by devious routes through countries where mails were not usually censored.'[34]

The Hagn Case

Alfred Hagn was a Norwegian journalist who applied to come to the UK as a representative of two Norwegian newspapers. He had been born in 1882 and was a jeweller's engraver by trade. He then took up painting and studied art in Paris, and also published a book and wrote articles for a Norwegian newspaper. Hagn landed at Hull on 11 April 1917 on his second wartime visit to the UK, but on 7 May, MI5 received a report from MI1c that he was a German agent. Their source of information was the Christiania police. After verifying Hagn's address as being at 39 Tavistock Square, London, William Melville was sent to investigate. He befriended Hagn at his hotel. Then, on 12 May, Melville broke into the Norwegian's room and obtained some secret ink which Hagn kept in a bottle there. A number of his letters were tested for secret writing, but none of them was successfully developed. As it was thought that Hagn might be using some medium unknown to MI5, it was considered dangerous to leave him at large any longer and he was arrested on 24 May 1917.[35] Thomson remembered Hagn as the 'most curious and ineffective of the German spies during the war'. Hagn was:

> 'One of those young people who write novels, paint futurist pictures, compose startling poetry and prose for the magazines, and fail to arrive anywhere. He had gone to America in the hope of selling his pictures, and had returned penniless in 1916.'[36]

Hagn was interrogated three times, eventually confessing that on his first visit to England in 1916 he came only for the purposes of journalism. However, his articles on England attracted the Germans' attention and after some resistance on his part they engaged him to work for them. He was tried on 27 and 28 August 1917 under DRR's 48, 18A and 22A with having committed a preparatory act in coming to England, being in communication with a spy address, and unlawful possession of a medium for secret writing. He was found guilty on all counts and sentenced to death. However, as an act of friendship to the Norwegian Government, Hagn's sentence was commuted to penal servitude for life.[37]

The van der Goten Case

In Thomson's words, Leon François van der Goten 'touched' the 'bottom rung of the ladder of infamy'.[38] Van der Goten was a Belgian diamond cutter, who fled Belgium with his family in September 1914 and went to Breda where he found work as a waiter. Together with J. Ven, he established a courier service to smuggle news out of Belgium on behalf of MI1c. The pair also helped Frenchmen and Belgians to escape into Holland, being paid £4 for each person brought across. Van der Goten also sold four plans of strategic points to the British but he was dissatisfied with the payment he received. He quarrelled with Ven, whose share of the profits he kept. Owing to his quarrel, the Belgian consul refused to pay van der Goten the 200 francs that he was owed for the latest group of Belgian refugees. Theunissen, an agent of the French Secret Service, 'wormed' his way into van der Goten's confidence and became his business partner. In a rage over the Belgian consul's refused to pay him the money he was owed, van der Goten vowed to betray the Allied secret services to the Germans. Theunissen convinced van der Goten that he was a German agent at which van der Goten then asked Theunissen to introduce him to the German Secret Service. A French agent, named Gremling, was put up to play the part of 'Lieutenant Krichel' of the German Secret Service and a trap was set for van der Goten. Greed was the Belgian's dominating passion and he hated the British. Exploiting these two aspects of his personality, he was persuaded to go to England as a courier, but was arrested upon his arrival at Hull in June 1917.

British law did not permit van der Goten to be tried for any offences committed in Holland. However, he had accepted a definite mission for someone he thought was a German agent. Thus, he was tried under DRR48 and found guilty of committing an act preparatory to a breach of DRR18 with intent to assist an enemy. He was found guilty and sentenced to death by firing squad. At the Belgian Government's behest, his sentence was commuted to penal servitude for life. Van der Goten's wife 'cast him off' and eventually went to live with Theunissen.[39]

The Patrocinio Case

Jose de Patrocinio was a Brazilian journalist, whose journalist father had achieved fame by procuring the abolition of slavery in Brazil. In 1912 Patrocinio met Josephine Conqui, a French dressmaker, in Santos and they became lovers. The following year the couple moved to France. In 1914 Patrocinio found employment as a courier with the Brazilian Consulate in Antwerp and the next year he was posted to the Brazilian Consulate in Amsterdam. In 1917, the Brazilian Government reduced the salaries of all of its officials and Patrocinio found it hard to make ends meet; he repeatedly applied for a pay increase or funds to enable him to return to Brazil. By July, he was £50 in debt. At the end of the month, he applied for passports for himself and for Conqui to return to Brazil. He stated that he wished to travel via the UK and France, where he intended to marry Conqui. This revealed Patrocinio's real motive for the journey.

An unnamed pro-German Brazilian journalist had introduced Patrocinio to a recruiter or agent for the German Secret Service in Holland in 1915. Hearing of Patrocinio's financial difficulties, Loebel suggested that there was an easy way of making money and introduced him to a German agent named Rene Levy in Amsterdam. Initially, Levy offered Patrocinio £1,000 to obtain a false Brazilian Passport and then engaged the Brazilian to go to England and France to ascertain when the next military offensive would take place. Loebel instructed Patrocinio in the use of secret inks and provided him with cover addresses to report to. Patrocinio was tasked to spend six to seven weeks in France, to collect military information only, and then to go to Switzerland from where he was to write to Frankfurt for his pay.

Whilst Patrocinio and Conqui were embarking at Rotterdam for the journey to England, they were seen by two witnesses 'taking affectionate leave' of a suspect Belgian named Hertogs. The couple became extremely confused when a young Frenchwoman happened to ask them if the knew a Rene Levy; Patrocinio rashly mentioned Levy's name to a Belgian courier named Roels, who already suspected the Brazilian. Roels then forced Patrocinio to confess.

Roels warned the ship's captain to keep watch over Patrocinio and then went ashore to inform the British Vice Consul. Later that evening, Roels made Patrocinio write a signed statement about his dealings with Levy and Loebel. Patrocinio then sought protection in what seemed honesty and told the usual story that he had accepted the mission in order to inform the British authorities and protect other young men.

Upon landing at Gravesend Patrocinio made a voluntary statement to the Port Officer, but his declaration differed from the written statement made under pressure from Roels. Meanwhile, the British Consulate had submitted a summary of the information provided by Roels, and a report from a Russian source, that Patrocinio had received 2,000 francs on presenting his passport and a further 3,000 francs on embarking. It was supposed that Hertogs had brought the money to him. At Gravesend, Conqui was found to be carrying 2,995 francs and Patrocinio claimed that this was his savings, but this did not tally with the reason he had given for his journey to Brazil. When questioned about his relationship with Hertogs, Patrocinio stated that he had met him only the day before embarking at Rotterdam. However, enquiry revealed that from 21 to 31 August, Patrocinio had frequently been seen in Hertog's company at Coomans Hotel. The Belgian Secret Service had no proof that Hertogs was a German agent, but certain facts indicated that he had had 'suspicious dealings' with German officers.

Commander Richard Tinsley, head of MI1c's Rotterdam station, procured a mass of correspondence that Patrocinio had left behind at his lodgings in Amsterdam. This revealed that, with the connivance of the Brazilian Consulate in Amsterdam and the Brazilian Legation in Berlin, Patrocinio had acted as an intermediary for correspondence passing between Berlin and Brazil. Patrocinio had probably employed stewards on one of the Dutch liners to carry these letters. It also established his contact with many suspects, the most important of these being Suzanne van Damme, a known German agent, who supplied Patrocinio with money.

On 14 September, Lieutenant Curtis Bennett of G3 was instructed to prepare a case against Patrocinio under DRR18, DRR18A and DRR48. On 26 October 1917, the leading lawyer, Archibald Bodkin, wrote informing MI5 that these DRRs only applied to offences committed in the UK, or 'perhaps on board British ships on the High Seas', and that even preparatory acts committed abroad 'were chargeable here only in so far as they were relevant and explanatory of actions committed in this country.'

There were a number of legal points in Patrocinio's favour. He had not committed an offence in any place within British jurisdiction and there was no evidence that he had come over with the intention of spying. The possession of Suzanne van Damme's address was not incriminating, because he had not made any attempt to communicate with her whilst in the UK. It was also questionable whether van Damme was a spy as defined under DRR18A since her activities were confined to countries outside British jurisdiction. Furthermore the circumstances in which the address was found gave no reasonable ground for suspecting Patrocinio of communicating or attempted communication with a spy.

Bodkin recommended that DRR18A needed to be simplified to include as offenders '... persons who before their arrival in this country had been visiting or in communication with an enemy agent abroad unless they could prove that they came to this country on legitimate business and did not know or suspect that the agent was a spy'. Bodkin also proposed enlarging the definition of 'spy' 'to include a person reasonably suspected of acting as an enemy agent, thus abolishing the need for proving actual or attempted communications.'

On 29 November, Patrocinio was interned under DRR14B, on the grounds of his hostile associations and suspicion that he was a German agent. He was eventually deported on 23 January 1919. There was considerable doubt about Conqui, but it was felt that she 'was too stupid to be dangerous', so she was released from custody on 18 September 1917 and allowed to return to Brazil under a 'no return' permit.

Patrocinio was, without doubt, an enemy agent against whom no offence could be charged. After the Patrocinio case, on 31 January 1918, DRR18A was redrafted to include as an offence 'communication with an enemy agent within or without the United Kingdom' and 'previous to coming to this Kingdom.' The definitions of 'communication' and 'address' were enlarged to cover activities and places within and without the United Kingdom and the definition of 'spy' was altered to include a person reasonably suspected of acting as an enemy agent. The expression 'enemy agent' included:

> Any person who is, or has been, or is reasonably suspected of being or having been employed by the enemy either directly or indirectly for the purpose of committing an act either within or without the United Kingdom which if done within the United Kingdom would be a contravention of these regulations, or who has, or is reasonably suspected of being, either within or without the United Kingdom, committed or attempted to commit such an act with the intention of assisting the enemy.[40]

DRR/ARO, 1917

An MI5 report notes that in 1917: 'Many times the head of G Branch had called attention to the difficulty in dealing adequately with neutral undesirables who could not be convicted of hostile origin or association.' By early 1917, the preventive system as a whole had achieved its final, definitive form. Further changes, although making improvements in detail, did not really alter or add to the fundamental system. Nonetheless, F Branch's work did not decrease. On the contrary, its administration of ARA and DORA actually increased. As time progressed, the growing likelihood of an end to the war provided F Branch's head, and particularly the legal section, much work in developing post-war legislation for the anticipated time of reconstruction and for the permanent peacetime protection of the British Empire. This included proposals for post-war aliens' restriction. During 1917-1918, the frontier controls carried out by E Branch were completed, the legislation for this being the work of F Branch.[41]

The legislative and administrative changes made throughout 1917 were mostly concerned with frontier control and the control of aliens on war service. The arrival of the German wife of a British subject interned in the Ruhleben camp in Berlin in March 1917 opened the issue of restricting, in some cases, the return of such people to the UK. The Home Office agreed with the proposal that prior to granting visas to such individuals, MI5 should be consulted.[42] However, some relaxations were made for British-born wives of aliens.[43] Turning to powers of deportation, the Court of Appeal held that the ARA empowered the Home Secretary to deport any alien, even a political refugee.[44]

The changes to the legislation and administration of DORA during 1917 can be analysed under five sections. Firstly, regulations for local protection. In April 1917, DRR35C was issued, empowering the Admiralty, Army Council, or Minister of

Munitions to make rules to preserve 'order and good behaviour' in areas where HM troops were located or munitions being manufactured. Under DRR35C any person convicted of any breach of the DRR could be banned from living in or entering such areas. Under 29C, if they were not British-born subjects or if their father had been at any time the subject of an enemy state, shipowners, brokers, surveyors, and similar maritime businessmen were forbidden to enter shipbuilding yards unless they had the written permission of the Admiralty or the Army Council. Secondly, owing to the increased number of vulnerable points, regulations conferring power to impose personal restrictions were introduced. It became possible to substitute local restrictions for removal orders under DRR14, and other minor changes completed F Branch's powers to impose restrictions on individuals. Thirdly, a new regulation, 51C, offered valuable powers to close and deal with premises where undesirable aliens, or other suspects, were known to frequent. Power was given to CMAs, under DRR53, to delegate their authority in cases where it was better that they should not carry out a specified duty themselves. Fourth, the censorship regulations were strengthened in a number of ways.[45]

As it was not possible to check all outward parcels thoroughly, it was arranged that they should only be sent by persons holding permits to do so, and 24C was therefore made. 24B was altered to stop the sending of any prohibited material to a neutral or enemy country independent of the need to prove that it was being sent to a hostile person. DRR24 was also amended to stop the censorship being evaded by (a) transmission by a privileged bag and (b) addressing to a country, whose post was not censored, to be forwarded to another country, which would normally have involved censorship. Two new regulations, 24D and 27B, dealt with the export and import of undesirable printed matter respectively.[46]

Fifth, looking at the espionage regulations, the scope of 18A, which prohibited communication with spies, was increased to cover consorting with a spy or visiting him at his home. This made it dangerous to make verbal reports to agents. It was further amended to encompass the case of someone who was found in the UK after having consorted with an enemy agent abroad.[47]

Statistics for 1917

Personal dossiers made	16,817
Telegrams submitted by censor	9,411
Letters submitted by censor	31,731
Peace letters	3,801
Anti-military cases	5,279
Suspects circulated	3,529
Internments sanctioned	43
Permit applications examined	24,188
Passport applications examined	14,084
Credentials examined for Ministry of Munitions	8,030
Missing aliens	2,159
Persons seen at Scotland Yard on behalf of MI5	262[48]

Review of spy cases from 1917

In 1917, MI5 reported that with regard to spy cases of that year, '…it is evident that British counter-espionage had broken the German military and naval organisations.' Indeed, during 1917, the German spy centres in New York and Norway were destroyed, but, 'on the other hand, the weight of the German attack was transferred to attacks upon the political and social fabric of the British Empire. Peace Propaganda, strikes, sedition and revolution take the first place in their effort.' This was demonstrated by the general enquiries undertaken by MI5 throughout 1917.

The spies who MI5 caught during 1917 seemed to be 'isolated units', except when they travelled in couples and not linked as parts of a wider network. MI5's experience showed that:

> 'Communication of information by word of mouth was on the increase … and after the discovery of their latest writing, when it became too dangerous to use that method, spies were sent out carrying addresses and instructions in their heads, and returned similarly without recording a syllable of the information they had acquired.'

The Patrocinio case had raised considerable difficulties for the prosecuting authorities, because the only wrongful acts that he had committed had taken place outside British jurisdiction, such that he could not be charged under the DRR. DRR18A was further amended 'so as to include as an offence, certain actions that had taken place outside the Kingdom.'[49]

End of PMS2

Dr Christopher Addison, then parliamentary Under-Secretary at the Ministry of Munitions and later Minister of Munitions, was dissatisfied with PMS2's investigations into labour unrest. In December 1916, in what was a clear snub to Kell, Addison asked Thomson 'to undertake the whole of the intelligence service on labour matters for the whole country' and gave him an £8,000 a year budget for the task. Thomson seconded twelve Detective Sergeants from the CID to the Ministry of Munitions to undertake this work.[50] The Home Office outlined this division of labour between MI5 and the Special Branch in a circular to chief constables:

> 'M.I.5A will not however deal with certain matters hitherto dealt with by P.M.S.2, viz. (1) strikes, (2) labour unrest generally or (3) sabotage, except in so far as questions of enemy agency may be involved. Any suggestion of enemy agency should be carefully investigated by the Police, and if there appears to be evidence of such agency, M.I.5A should be communicated with. All reports with regard to (1) strikes, (2) impending strikes and labour unrest generally and (3) sabotage should in future be sent to the Home Office who will forward them to the Department or Departments concerned.'[51]

This transfer of PMS2's labour intelligence work to Special Branch, rather than to MI5, has been viewed as a victory for Thomson and a defeat for Kell.[52] However, declassified MI5 records suggest an alternative interpretation: that actually Kell did not want MI5 to be involved in gathering labour intelligence. On 18 January 1917, Kell wrote a letter to his direct superior, Brigadier-General George Kynaston Cockerill (DSI), concerning the future of PMS2 following the transfer of its labour intelligence role to Thomson. Kell showed no desire for MI5 to assume a role in labour intelligence regarding British workers:

'*Now that this organization has rightly shed their investigations regarding strikes and Labour troubles to Scotland Yard, they now confine their activities to Counter-Espionage, sabotage and the investigation generally of the bona fides of aliens employed in Munition Works (controlled).*'

Nor, at this point, did Kell even wish for MI5 to take over what remained of PMS2:

'*As regards the question of whether we should take over P.M.S.2., I am of opinion that it is better to leave it under the Ministry of Munitions owing to the necessarily intimate relations it must have with all the various branches of the Ministry, provided it continues, as in the past, to keep in close touch with this section.*'[53]

Kell's letter accompanied Major Sealy Clarke's 'Comprehensive Report of PMS2'. Sealy Clarke had joined MI5 on 18 March 1915, leaving on 1 February 1919.[54] He worked in F Branch, before being appointed head of A Branch, which he left to become head of G Branch on 15 April 1918.[55] He explained that PMS2 had been divided into two branches: A Branch was the 'Aliens Branch' '*...which deals exclusively with aliens about to be employed, or already working in Munitions Factories... examining for acceptance or rejection such aliens as are notified by firms as being about to be or actually employed.*' By the beginning of November 1916, A Branch had handled the following volumes of cases:

Allies	24,926
Neutrals	2,649
Alien enemies	302

B Branch dealt with 'Labour Intelligence in connection with British Labour'. Sealy Clarke noted that: '*As this matter has now been handed over to Scotland Yard, P.M.S.2. are confining their energies to the detection of espionage inside works, and for precautions for preventing sabotage.*'[56]

The most well-known case investigated by PMS2 was that of an alleged plot to kill the Prime Minister, David Lloyd George. Mrs Alice Wheeldon, a second-hand clothes dealer from Derby, her daughters, Harriet and Winnie, and Winnie's husband, Alfred Mason, a chemist who had made a special study of poisons, were suspected of planning to fire a poisoned dart from an air rifle at Lloyd George while he played golf on Walton Heath. They were arrested on 17 January 1917, tried and jailed the following March. However, much of the evidence was 'flimsy as well as farcical'. The PMS2 case officer had used two questionable agents provocateurs to entrap the plotters and in April, soon after the trial, the out-of-favour PMS2 was formally reabsorbed by MI5 as A Branch.[57]

The Ministry of Labour made representations that PMS2's interest in general labour unrest might lead to the possibility of friction and was not a legitimate role for the

Ministry of Munitions, whereupon the question arose about MI5 re-assuming some of PMS2's duties and taking on some of the personnel.[58] However, MI5's role was not to go beyond the initial investigation and decision about the bona fides of alien workers. It was not to assume responsibility for the later actions of these aliens, or the general safety of munitions factories. Crucially, all cases suggesting direct or indirect enemy influence were to be handed to MI5, as previously.[59]

It was suggested that only subordinate officials who had been solely employed in administering ARO22A were to be taken on by MI5, along with all existing records of aliens. It was also deemed necessary for an officer of the Ministry of Munitions to be attached as a liaison officer to MI5 to help with enquiries concerning the credentials of aliens as set out in ARO22A.[60] If the transfer was decided upon, there would be a requirement that offices should be taken as near to Waterloo House as possible so that MI5 could take suitable control.[61] A memorandum setting out these suggestions was put to Dr Addison. On 3 April 1917, he informed Colonel Labouchere of PMS2 that he was going to invite MI5 to take on the part of the work concerning the organisation of controlled establishments for checking the bona fides of alien workers plus the administration of ARO22A in partnership with the Ministry of Munitions, and to ask Scotland Yard to carry out the rest.[62] The same day Kell wrote a 'Memorandum concerning a proposed transfer of certain duties from the Ministry of Munitions (P.M.S.2) to M.I.5.', which the Army Council submitted to Addison on 5 May:

'*The question now arises:*

(I) As to whether it is expedient that M.I.5. should re-assume any and which of the duties and personnel of P.M.S.2.
(II) What arrangements should be made as regards other protective duties of the Ministry of Munitions not so taken over.

'*The first question is the only one in which M.I.5. is directly concerned and it is evident that that section would merely be re-assuming a portion of its original functions in taking over the administration in conjunction with the Ministry of Munitions of Article 22A of the Aliens Restriction Order. It is therefore recommended that this course would be proper for adoption subject to the working out of certain financial and other details.*

'*It must, however, be stated definitely that M.I.5.'s functions with regard to Article 22A would not extend beyond the first examination and opinion of the credentials of alien workmen, and no responsibility would be accepted by M.I.5. for the subsequent acts of such alien workmen or for the general safety of munitions works.*

'*It should, however, be understood that whatever changes are made in the distribution of the above duties as hitherto carried out by the Ministry of Munitions, or by P.M.S.2. in particular, all cases disclosing evidence relating to any possibility of enemy influence direct or indirect must be referred for consideration to M.I.5. as heretofore…*

'It is suggested that only those subordinate officials who have hitherto been engaged exclusively in administering the provisions of Article 22A of the Aliens Restriction Order should be taken over with all the existing records of aliens and that the officers who have hitherto been concerned with labour unrest and strikes should not be included.'[63]

On 21 April 1917, Mr Wolff of the Ministry of Munitions informed Kell of the Minister's decision and, accordingly, the transfer was to take place from 23 April 1917.[64] This required an Order in Council to amend ARO22A to provide the Admiralty and the Army Council with similar powers to the Ministry of Munitions.[65] A memorandum was put to the Home Secretary by Order of the Army Council:

'It was made clear that the proposed amendment was not to be restricted to aliens working on munitions of war but was intended to cover many other forms of auxiliary and non-combatant war service, such as were open to aliens serving under voluntary war organisations officially subject to supervision by the Army Council. In short the general intention of the proposed amendment was to extend the system of formal approval to all aliens seeking employment in any kind of war service which might offer them special opportunities for espionage or mischief if evilly disposed.'[66]

The new Order in Council was issued on 22 April 1917. It allowed the powers granted to the Ministry of Munitions to be exercised on the Minister's behalf by any individual or individuals he deputed for the purpose, and made the alterations needed to make the Principal Order apply to the various types of work set out in the memorandum.[67] The administration of this Order was undertaken by MI5 (War Office) as of 23 April 1917 and a special branch (A Branch) was founded to deal with this new Order and the existing control of munitions work being undertaken by aliens.[68]

A Branch

A Branch took over PMS2's offices at Durham House, 16 John's Street in the Adelphi district of London. PMS2 had worked in conjunction with F Branch, of which A Branch can be considered an offshoot. Some of PMS2's staff were taken on by A Branch,[69] of which Captain F.H.L. Stevenson was placed in charge. Formerly of the Highland Light Infantry, Stevenson joined MI5 on 16 March 1917 but left shortly afterwards on 23 July.[70] His duties were general supervision, interdepartmental correspondence and decisions over questions of control. A Branch's distribution of duties for June 1917 was as follows:

(1). Inspection of the proofs of nationality of all aliens employed or desirous of being employed in the manufacture of munitions of war, with a view to granting or withholding permission to work on munitions.

(2). Registration of all aliens so employed and of their movements from one factory to another.

(3). Examination of all applications by alien munition workers for permits to leave the United Kingdom.[71]

A Branch took on forty-four members of staff from PMS2 from 23 April 1917, comprising four officers, four male clerks and thirty-six women clerks. Two of the officers, Baron Sadoine and *Monsieur* Beer, both Belgians, were taken over by A Branch specifically to deal with their countrymen. Captain Stevenson was also one of the four officers taken over from PMS2.[72]

The procedure up to 1917 had been as follows: the identity papers that aliens carried when they arrived in the UK were confiscated. They were then replaced with Provisional Certificates of Nationality. These were endorsed with the 'PWM' (Permission to Work on Munitions) stamp if the holder had permission to work on munitions.[73]

Although aliens could be employed by firms performing confidential and vital work, they were not engaged on secret work, such as on tanks 'or anything that was to be sprung on the Enemy as a surprise.' Nor were aliens allowed to work in Admiralty shipyards. However, they were sometimes engaged on confidential work such as assembling fuses and work involved with glass-blowing, because there was a shortage of workers with these skills.[74]

The PWM stamp was cancelled when permission to leave the UK was given.[75] Control was enforced at the ports, where aliens whose PWM stamp was discovered not to have been properly cancelled were held and their certificates forwarded to MI5 for cancellation.[76]

The system in use in A Branch's Registry, which had been inherited from PMS2, was unsatisfactory. Therefore, Miss Harrison of H2 inaugurated a new system that was approved by Kell on 7 June 1917.[77] On 16 July, Major H.E. Spencer took over A Branch from Captain Stevenson[78] and on the 28th, the branch moved from Durham House to 5 Cork Street off Burlington Gardens.[79]

The amendments to the Aliens Restriction Bill, suggested by MI5, caused A Branch's work to intensify. The increasing demand to import alien workers necessitated extra provisions. Visas were still given when permits were granted to prospective employers. However all aliens from neutral countries were made to sign a declaration to stay in the UK for the war's duration. This encompassed virtually all imported alien workers. The attention of employers, and social and benevolent organisations that worked closely with the army and navy, was brought to the point that no alien could be employed on any kind of auxiliary war service without the Army Council's authorization.[80]

On 26 August 1917, Major Sealy Clarke took over A Branch from Major Spencer who returned to E Branch as its head.[81] Throughout September 1917, much preparation was undertaken in anticipation of the Order of the Home Secretary, widening the scope of Article 22A of the Aliens Restriction Bill, and transferring its administration to the Army Council.[82] On 9 October 1917, the Order was issued and a Home Office circular was sent to chief constables.[83] At MI5's instance it included a request for the police to inform MI5 of any breaches of the Order that they came across.[84] In addition, a circular letter was sent to all firms involved with munitions, informing them of the alterations to the administration of the Order.[85] It was then found necessary to re-draft the memorandum concerning the conditions allowing aliens to work on munitions, to make firms employ aliens only through the employment exchanges, so reducing the volume of necessary correspondence with A Branch. The conditions regarding the importing of alien labour started to become stricter when the Interdepartmental

Committee decided to deny permission to import an alien unless their services were of national importance.[86]

The need for the PWM stamp to be officially cancelled before an alien was permitted to leave the UK was demonstrated in the case of some Dutch glass-blowers who had been recruited in Holland. Two of them worked at the Sheraton Glass Works and were persuaded to leave their employers by Madame Bolderman, a Russian woman, who paid each of them £20 to do so; her professed intention was to recruit them for private work in South Africa. When they attempted to embark at Liverpool, the men were stopped by the port control and passed to A Branch who did not allow them to leave the UK. This example also shows how A Branch worked with, and relied upon, E Branch. Another case, which illustrates the danger of private recruiting, was that of four Dutch glass-blowers for whom Strachan, Osmell and Co. Ltd., London, acting for the Department of Mines and Industries, South Africa, asked the Colonial Office to provide help in getting permission for the four to go to South Africa. In concert with the Ministry of Munitions, A Branch withheld permission due to the want of glass-blowers in the UK. It would also establish an unwanted practice if private recruiting of skilled workers for commercial work abroad, who were still needed for important work, was permitted.[87]

As their departures were obviously hurried, it was decided not to require the cancellation of the PWM stamp of recalled Belgian soldiers and alien civilians called up to serve in the armed forces. Therefore, their identity books were taken at the ports and passed on to A Branch to complete its records.[88]

The new national service or internment scheme appeared to provide chances for enemy aliens to find employment with companies undertaking secret and important work. The case of August Espenschied, a German, revealed an obvious defect in this scheme to make alien enemies productive. Espenschied was sent to Romford by the Sub-Area Substitution Officer as a substitution volunteer for an English worker at the Thames Haven Oil Works. This firm was not on the list of controlled firms or contractors given to A Branch and its workers thus escaped the branch's watchful eye. Meanwhile, Espenschied had seen much at the works that he should not have before it was realised that he was an un-naturalised German.[89]

The Admiralty's policy regarding the checking of the bona fides of aliens working for firms where Admiralty interests predominated was unclear. An instance of non-compliance at the Rolls Royce works gave, with the Espenschied case, the chance to broach this issue. Mr Evans of the Admiralty Law Branch was written to semi-officially, to ascertain if the Admiralty would take A Branch's endorsement of an alien's identity book to be an acceptable guarantee of his suitability for employment. In December 1917, the Admiralty made its policy clear. Evans stated that, as well as A Branch's endorsement, whenever Admiralty interests dominated, firms also had to gain the Admiralty's agreement to employ aliens.[90]

A Branch also made representations to the Air Board about the employment of aliens connected with aircraft construction. The Air Board proposed to submit a list to A Branch of the companies where aliens or individuals of enemy origin should not work, and it was suggested to the Board that their contracts for certain types of work should have a clause that these individuals should not be engaged on those jobs.[91]

An MI5 report provides an example of the policy adopted in a weak case: the police commenced the prosecution of a firm that had contravened ARO22A, having not referred to the War Office. As this case was not strong the chief constable concerned was urged to drop it and the Home Office was asked to notify all chief constables that it was undesirable for prosecutions to occur without consulting the War Office as it could easily happen that a firm's production might suffer, and also that it was desirable that the Ministry of Munitions should always be consulted regarding the policy of prosecuting a particular company.[92] This demonstrates how compromises had to be reached between the often conflicting demands of providing jobs for aliens, so that they would not be left to eat the bread of idleness, the need to find workers for munitions factories, so that essential production would not suffer, and counter-espionage.

The Ministry of National Service, assisted by the police, attempted to put Austrian Jews on munitions work without the approval of the War Office or Ministry of Labour. A Branch pursued this matter and they were moved to rubber factories doing unimportant work, with their identity books being marked for these specific factories only.[93] This renewed the issue of releasing alien enemies for employment in munitions, and the Home Office was told that it was deemed very unwise for such releases to occur without prior consultation with the War Office.[94]

There are indications that MI5 had already begun to develop a concern with Bolshevism by this time. On 19 January 1918, Sealy Clarke wrote to John Moylan of the Home Office, requesting information regarding any change of attitude noticed in Russians employed on munitions work. He further suggested that a circular should be sent to the police asking them to report any changes of attitudes among Russian workers which might be denoted by 'pacifist or anti-war propaganda, a disinclination to continue to help in the production of Munitions, or any active tendency towards holding up supplies, either by restriction of out-put, or destruction of out-put of factories.'[95] However, nothing came of this at the time, because Moylan did not think that the police would be of much use '...in the way of obtaining information as to the attitude of Russians employed on munitions. People inside the works in which they are employed are more likely to know of any special activities on their part.'[96]

On 15 April 1918, Major S.C. Welchman, MBE took over A Branch.[97] Formerly with Kell's old regiment, the South Staffordshires, Welchman had joined MI5 on 2 August 1915.[98] He had served with G Branch, before his new appointment.[99] The work of A Branch had now increased further due to the many cases of aliens working on munitions, whose records were checked by the branch and details provided to the Director General of Labour Supply. Applications for auxiliary war service in the Young Men's Christian Association (YMCA) now also required A Branch's endorsement, and YMCA headquarters submitted a great many names.[100] In agreement with the Harbour Department of the Board of Trade, A Branch circularised approximately 325 ports, asking them to pass on the identity books and nationality papers of all aliens working there, to be endorsed by A Branch.[101] A considerable number of the names of those applying for employment with the Ministry of Munitions and Air Board, plus firms to whom the grant of government contracts was being considered were received.[102] The Air Board made the decision not to engage enemy aliens at aeronautical works and presented a list of thirteen firms where aliens were not to be taken on unless they had the Air Board's permission.[103] Nonetheless, the Ministry of National Service decided to engage 180 enemy aliens at Bramham Moor and 300 at Netheravon for the Air Board. However, they were only to work as land-labourers, and because there appeared little chance of them getting in a position to acquire information of military or naval use, the decision was reached that their identity books should not have the PWM stamp. A list of all those to be engaged was to be provided and their details checked by A Branch prior to their employment.[104]

On 30 July 1918, A Branch moved to Greener House in Haymarket, London.[105] Two months later, the branch prepared a full list of enemy aliens employed on munitions, including their age, nationality and the name and address of the firms where they worked. There were roughly 900 names on this list, and it was submitted to Lord Cheylesmore of the Aliens Advisory Committee.[106] As well, all government employees were made to provide details of their own and their parent's nationality and these were sent to A Branch for vetting, causing a notable increase in work. October 1918 brought further work.[107] Over 2,000 names of the staff of the Ministry of Munitions were submitted, and another list of enemy aliens working in munitions was prepared for the Aliens Advisory Committee. Following the Belgian Government's request for a complete list of all their nationals working in munitions for census purposes, a specialist staff was taken on, with the Belgian Government agreeing to pay the costs incurred. However, when the Belgians received the bill for this, they argued that governments provided each other with this kind of information for free. The bill for about £100 was dropped.[108]

A Branch's scope at this time also included reaching the decision that, after 5 October 1918, no Dutch workers who travelled from Rotterdam were to work in munitions except for glass-blowing.[109] Russian Jews of eighteen and nineteen years of age holding exemption certificates, and who were not included in existing Anglo-Russian arrangements, were no longer granted permission to work on munitions.[110] One can only speculate that this may have been over concern with Bolshevism, held by some at the time as being inspired by Jews.[111]

The decision was made in agreement with E Branch that in all forthcoming emergency cases, it would not be necessary for aliens with identity books endorsed for auxiliary war service and who wished to depart the UK, to send their papers to A Branch for cancellation. The decision regarding permission to leave the UK was devolved to the port officer involved, who subsequently notified A Branch of his action.[112]

In November 1918, the umbrella sub-title of Alien War Service hitherto used to cover A Branch's duties was changed to Auxiliary War Service, and several sub-sections were added.[113] As historian J.C. Bird explains:

'Apart from the munitions industry, a number of other sensitive areas of employment were subjected to special scrutiny by MI5, including military and naval establishments, telegraph, telephone and railway companies involved in the transmission of official messages or carriage of members of the armed forces; hospitals dealing with military personnel; canteens, clubs or organisations of a social, benevolent or religious nature conducted wholly or partly for the benefit of or used by members of the armed forces.'[114]

This illustrates how the scope, and scale, of A Branch's work had increased from being concerned only with aliens employed on munitions work to all aliens in jobs that brought them into contact with the armed forces. This is also demonstrated by the growth in A Branch's staff. In November 1917, the branch had forty-six members of staff, including five officers and forty-one clerks, consisting three British officers, two Belgian officers, two male clerks and thirty-nine female clerks.[115] By November 1918, the staff had increased by the addition of eight clerks to a total of fifty-four members, consisting as before of five officers, but now with forty-nine clerks, including one GSO2 as head of branch, two British officers, two Belgian officers, two male clerks but with now forty-seven women clerks.[116]

The following figures compiled by MI5 give some idea of the scale of A Branch's work. Slightly more than 40,000 aliens, of whom approximately 900 were enemy aliens, had been accepted for work in munitions or other sensitive jobs by the end of January 1918, discounting individuals who were later permitted to leave the UK.[117] Owing to the repatriation of aliens who had been employed in munitions or auxiliary war service, A Branch received approximately 18,393 identity books of which 6,949 names were checked against its records by the end of March 1919. The A.E. (Aliens Enquiry) cards were completed and the identity books were passed on to their office of origin; twenty-seven of them were discovered to be undesirables. Their names were passed to E Branch, in order to prevent them returning to the UK.[118]

There was very little, if any, sabotage at British munitions factories during the First World War. It seems that practically all reported accidents were indeed accidents, and not successful acts of sabotage. Equally, it seems that Germany did not make any really concerted attempts to sabotage British munitions factories. In S.T. Felstead's well-informed words:

'It is one of the great mysteries of the war that with 32,000 Germans in this country no attempts at sabotage took place. Perhaps our vulnerable points were too well guarded; perhaps the certainty of detection was too great; whatever the reason it is beyond all doubt that we were never subjected to sabotage of the kind so common in America in 1915 and 1916. I can state without fear of contradiction that there was not a single explosion which occurred in this country which was not ascribable to accident. Our casualties from this aspect of warfare were confined entirely to explosions which were inevitable in the manufacture of munitions on an immense scale. And even the number of fires which took place was much less than in normal times.'[119]

Enough aliens were permitted to perform auxiliary war service. As such, A Branch did not hinder essential production. However, J.C. Bird concludes that ultimately '…the contribution of enemy alien civilian labour to Britain's war effort was negligible. The majority of enemy men of working age spent most of the war in internment doing little or no nationally useful work.'[120] A Branch did not receive anything like the same official censure that PMS2 did. By these measures A Branch was very successful.

Russian Revolution

The Spring of 1917 witnessed two 'major events' that profoundly shocked the British Government. The failure of Nivelle's offensive on the Western Front precipitated a 'full-scale mutiny' by the French Army. And, on the Eastern Front, the Russian Revolution that ousted the Tsar in March 1917 caused the British Government to become fearful that revolutionary agitators were out to undermine the British war effort. It is important to note that when the War Cabinet wanted an assessment of the threat posed, it turned to Thomson rather than to Kell. Thus Thomson gained the ears of powerful backers in Whitehall, while Kell did not. On 5 April 1917, Thomson was ordered to draft up intelligence reports on 'the growth of anarchist and socialist movements and their influence on the strike'. In view of the importance the Germans were attaching to rendering support to the Bolsheviks as a means of undermining the Russian war effort, it was not unreasonable, if incorrect, for MI5 to assume that support was also being given to British Bolshevik sympathizers. In May 1917, the director of a left–wing French newspaper, the pages of which espoused defeatism, was caught returning from Switzerland carrying a large cheque from a German banker. He was subsequently found guilty of treason and executed. This heightened concerns that Germany was also financing opposition to the war in Britain. Although it was later learned that Clemenceau had grossly over–hyped the level of German-financed subversion in France British observers accepted it as fact. The complete triumph of subversion in Russia as a result of the Bolshevik Revolution of October 1917, ratched up the War Cabinet's worries about subversion in the UK to even greater levels, with some ministers believing that British subversives had accepted German money too.[121]

On 12 November 1917, the Home Secretary and the Minister for War appointed a joint committee to investigate the activities of pacifist societies in Great Britain and to enquire if any of them were being financed by enemy money. Throughout November 1917, the work snowballed. From 12 to 23 November 1917, five pacifist centres were raided for the purpose of discovering how they received and disbursed their funds, though official reports do not record what happened as a result of these raids.[122] The available documentation does suggest that when these organisations had material confiscated in police raids, MI5 was most concerned with their accounts, in order to check if they were being financed by Germany, and also their membership lists in order to ascertain if any of their members had links to that country.[123]

The case of Nicholas Klishko demonstrates that MI5's investigations of Bolsheviks during the war were most concerned with detecting signs of links to Germany. Klishko was a Russian engineer and revolutionary who had come to England as a political refugee in 1907, eventually gaining employment as a technical translator with Vickers, the armaments manufacturer.[124] In September 1915 the British military attaché in Petrograd informed the War Office that the Russians were concerned that Klishko was in a position to provide information about Russian munitions produced at Vickers to a suspected German agent, Litvinov, who was known to be a close friend of his.[125] MI5 was certainly worried about Klishko's Bolshevik views, that he was in touch with leading pacifists, and that he had influential friends who kept him well informed about what was going on in official circles. However, MI5 was primarily concerned with his pro-German views, his association with a suspected German agent and the danger that the knowledge he had gained at Vickers might fall into enemy hands.[126] After a long investigation and much pressure from MI5, the authorities eventually agreed to Klishko's internment under DRR 14B in September 1918, shortly after which he was included in a party sent back to Russia.[127]

Preventive intelligence duties in war

In April 1918, F Branch produced some notes on 'Preventive Intelligence Duties in War'. These notes are absolutely essential to an understanding of MI5's strategy for countering German espionage during the First World War. Unfortunately, nothing is known about the genesis of these notes and it would be intriguing to know if any earlier editions of them had been produced. This would help to determine at what point these preventive principles were developed. As already examined in Chapter Four, in the summer of 1915 MO5(g) produced notes on the work of counter-espionage for officials in the Colonies. It can be speculated that the notes on preventive intelligence duties were part of an on-going process to educate counter-espionage officials in the Colonies. They outlined the policy, general principles and powers underlying the *Preventive* as distinct from the *Detective* Intelligence Work of the Central Special Intelligence Bureau for purposes of military security against enemy agencies in war. In order to appreciate these principles, it is necessary to consider the duties included under Preventive Intelligence. The general functions of preventive intelligence were seen as threefold. Firstly, preventing an enemy from acquiring the information he required to enable him to subordinate British interests to those of his own country. Secondly, neutralising all enemy intelligence services. Thirdly, capturing or rendering harmless all intelligence officers and agents employed by the enemy's intelligence services. In order to obtain this information, an enemy had to mount 'intelligence attacks' upon organisations concerned with: foreign policy; imperial and colonial policy; domestic policy, including national welfare and public safety; commerce; and naval and military policy, and technical information affecting all military and naval operations.

MI5 was the 'British Service of Military Security'. However, although devoted primarily to countering attacks by the enemy's intelligence services upon departments involved in naval and military policy, and technical information affecting all operations of war, it also protected and acted in close liaison with the other organisations covered above. Under normal war conditions the service operated *strategically* throughout the British Empire as regards policy for preventive intelligence purposes, and *tactically* within the United Kingdom as regards general administrative procedure. Normal war conditions prevailed in the area in which the military power remained subordinated or auxiliary to the civil power. Emergency war conditions arose in the area of military operations in which the civil power became subordinated or auxiliary to the requirements of the military power.

The 'cardinal principles for preventive intelligence' (common to both normal and emergency conditions) were: Information, Communication, Records, Counter-action, Examination, Identification, Classification, Control, Censorship, and Protection.

Information: Early and accurate information concerning the intentions, instructions, movements and personal characteristics of hostile agents and persons.

Communication: The direct and immediate transmission of information to the particular officer best situated for taking effective counter-action.

Records: The classified, indexed and centralised records of all information bearing on persons, subjects and places of interest to the preventive intelligence service, which provided a fund of material to assist in making correct deductions as to the meaning of and proper action to take on the latest information received.

Counter-Action: The action taken to defeat a hostile agent or agency.

Examination: A system of preventive intelligence 'examining posts' through which all travellers had to pass, or at which all persons who sought facilities which were restricted or controlled for reasons of military security had to call or pass under examination in person or by correspondence to receive permission or qualified permission to pursue their affairs.

S.I. (Special Intelligence) examination posts and agencies were categorised as follows. Firstly, people who sought to enter the UK were examined at: (a) posts abroad (British authorities in foreign countries who were empowered to issue passports or grant visas to enter the UK); and, (b) posts at home (ports open to passenger or commercial traffic). Secondly, people who resided, travelled or sought general facilities within the UK would be examined at: police stations; hotels and lodging house, etc; the War Office and other government departments at which people applied for war facilities; and, at munitions works for munitions facilities. Thirdly, people who sought to leave the UK were examined at: the Government Passport Office in London; and, the Military Permit Office (for people who desired to travel to theatres of British military operations abroad). Fourth, people who sought local war facilities only were examined by the CMA, CNA, or Ministry of Munitions.

Examination posts referred doubtful cases to MI5. The work of checking the bona fides of such applicants was one of the duties of F Branch (particularly F1), apart from applications for munitions work (A Branch) and travel (E Branch).

Identification: Physical and personal identification was the essential preliminary to the examination of a person and the classification of his credentials for preventive intelligence purposes. The process only ended when it identified that person to a degree at which he was definitely precluded from impersonating another.

It was one of F Branch's roles to persuade the relevant authorities to make sure that a document that was as secure against forgery or transfer as possible was possessed by every individual who could be legitimately required to have one in the interests of national security. This included passports, identity books and permit books.

Classification: Classification for preventive intelligence purposes in war was the process which decided first whether a given person was actually a friend or a foe, and secondly, if a foe, in what particular forms and to what degree his hostility was likely to be translated into action prejudicial to military security.

During wartime, the Civil Government, acting via the police and immigration authorities, was responsible for 'a general classification *by nationality* of all inhabitants and of all immigrants upon arrival, into those who, according to national and international laws, treaties and customs, owe or do not owe allegiance *in theory* to the British Crown'. The Civil Classifications were 'British', 'Allied', 'Neutral', or 'Enemy'.

However, this was unimportant from the preventive aspect, because one of the gravest and most subtle problems that preventive intelligence faced came from the easy process of naturalisation, which provided a cover for the potential betrayer of his adopted country. S.I. took up the classification at this point and carried it 'to the practical point which decides how *in actual fact* each person should be classified and treated from the point of view of military security, in accordance with personal realities and apart from the legal technicalities of nationality'. There were two degrees of Military (S.I.) classification. Firstly, General Military (S.I.) classifications:

> '"AA": true personal sympathies are believed to be "Absolutely Anglicized", or allied and undoubtedly friendly.

> "A": "Anglicized", or allied and friendly.

> "AB": "Anglo-Boche", friendly.

> "BA": doubtful, probably hostile.

> "B": "Boche", and hostile.

> 'BB': 'Bad Boche', and undoubtedly hostile.'

A person may have received any military classification no matter what their civil classification was. For example, a civil British subject could be classed BB if a naturalised enemy subject who retained their enemy sympathies. Anyone classified as BA, B or BB was liable to be subjected to some kind of control, like (a) internment for BB or B, (b) close restrictions for B or BA, and (c) ordinary restrictions regarding BA.

Secondly, if they were classed as an enemy or suspected enemy, then they would also have received Special S.I. sub-classifications. These twelve categories were lettered from A to K with catchwords that were easy to remember:

> '"A", "Antecedents": in a civil, police or judicial sense so bad that patriotism may not be the dominant factor, and sympathies not incorruptible.

> "B", "Banished": during the war from or forbidden to enter one or more of the Allied States.

> "C", "Courier": letter carrier, intermediary or auxiliary to enemy agents.

> "D", "Detained": interned or prevented from leaving an Allied State for security intelligence reasons.

"E", "Espion": enemy spy or agent engaged in active mischief (not necessarily confined to espionage).

"F", "False": or irregular papers of identity or credential.

"G", "Guarded": suspected, under special surveillance and not yet otherwise classified.

"H", "Hawker": hostile by reason of trade or commerce with or for the enemy.

"I", "Instigator": of hostile, pacifist, seditious or dangerous propaganda.

"J", "Junction": wanted. The person, or information concerning him wanted urgently by MI5 or an Allied security intelligence service.

"K", "Kaiser's man": Enemy officer or official or ex-officer or official.'

An actively hostile person may have fallen under several of the above special classifications. General use of the term 'suspect' was to be avoided – unless with qualification or a proper foundation in fact. The term 'suspect' had no precise meaning to S.I. Just because an individual's name was on the black list was not normally enough to enable MI5 to decide the kind of control to be imposed on a suspect. It needed to know what the suspect was suspected of, in order to decide on the appropriate action.

Control: The minimum of personal supervision, interference with ordinary activities or restriction of liberty by the civil or military power which was necessary for the purposes of military security in war.

The civil power exercised its control powers for military security and public safety in two ways. Firstly, standing controls. They were exercised in accordance with predetermined principles, such as the application of certain provisions of the ARA to all people who owed no allegiance to the British crown regardless of their personal sympathies. Standing controls were designed to be applied to all people, or all aliens, or all enemy aliens.

Secondly, optional controls. They were usually exercised at the behest of bodies qualified to advise on military security or public safety, such as the Aliens Advisory Committees, police, or naval and military authorities. Optional controls were designed to apply to individuals, or individual aliens, or individual enemy aliens, all according to selective classification.

S.I. concentrated its routine attention upon securing the application of the appropriate degree of supervision and control (by whatever power exercisable) over all persons of two particular categories. (1) The Special S.I. ('Black List') categories; and, the General Military categories, which consisted of people classified as hostile or probably hostile (BB, B, and BA). The appropriate degree of supervision was 'the minimum control of each person in the above categories which is necessary and adequate to preserve military security...'

Censorship: For military purposes censorship was defined as 'the functions involved in the defence of all British information and propaganda necessary for military security, and of their means of communication, and the attack of all hostile information and propaganda prejudicial to military security, and of the means of their communication'. The censorship was comprised of three types of control. Firstly, controls designed for defensive censorship – for the defence of British information. For example, prohibitions on communicating with an enemy agent. Secondly, controls designed for offensive censorship – to attack enemy information in transit. For example, control of the use of wireless telegraphy. Thirdly, controls designed for both offensive and defensive censorship. For example, control of personal conveyance of communications into or out of the UK.

Protection: Routine measures that protected all vulnerable objects of military value from damage or prejudicial activities by all persons regardless of personal classification or credentials. There were two degrees of protection. Firstly, cooperative or general protection: required where the vulnerable objects were situated on a relatively large area of ground not entirely devoted to military or naval purposes, such as an inhabited and fortified island. Decision over the necessity for control over a given area was a matter of military operations policy. It was S.I.'s role to ensure the cooperation of the civil authorities, police, or the public in the establishment of an area under general protection, and for the central supervision of all of these areas after they had been established.

These powers provided for the protection of areas of three degrees of importance according to the extent, as measured not in area, but in terms of the number and importance of public rights which would be restricted, and the amount of cooperative assistance required from the civil authority, police, or the public. (1) Large protected areas: power to constitute any area as a special military area, to which the admission of all people was controlled by a commandant, apart from some standing exceptions for public servants. The exercise of this power for military purposes in the UK was vested in the Army Council, and required authorisation by a Secretary of State under DRR29B. (2) Medium protected areas: power to constitute as a protected area land or premises that was already in government use, docks, and certain adjacent land or premises to which the admission of all people was controlled by a CNA or CMA under DRR28A. (3) Small protected areas: power to constitute as a protected area any work of defence, factory, road, etc that belonged to the government, or was being used by the government. This power could be exercised either by the central or local service authority concerned under DRR29 and DRR29A.

Secondly, technical or local protection: of a small vulnerable object that did not involve general cooperation by the civil authorities, police, or the public was entirely a matter of concern for the department interested in the protection of the vulnerable point, such as the local naval, military, air, or munitions authorities concerned.

These controls could be simplistically classified under five headings. Firstly, personal identification and restriction on movement, such as registration and reporting. Secondly, local protection, for example trespassing, entering or residing. Thirdly, frontier protection, such as landing or leaving. Fourth, dangerous articles, for example weapons or explosives. Fifth, general controls, such as replies to questions.

The relative roles of these cardinal preventive principles can be illustrated with an example of a normal defence against a typical form of intelligence attack by the enemy:

'INFORMATION is obtained by a British S.I. agent in enemy or neutral territory that an enemy agent vaguely identified as to name, description and possible mission, is setting out for some British area. Immediate COMMUNICATION to the proper S.I. officer in the British Area enables him to consult the S.I. RECORDS and to prepare for suitable S.I. COUNTER-ACTION. On passing through the first S.I. EXAMINATION post, the stranger, owing to the approximate correspondence of the particulars of his personal IDENTIFICATION with the reported description of the enemy agents, receives an S.I. CLASSIFICATION leading to his selection for a degree of S.I. CONTROL and supervision supplementary to that appropriate to the general public, or to persons of certain categories, such as aliens. Unaware that his actions or movements are of special interest to S.I. he despatches disguised messages to the enemy by post, telegraph or messenger. One of his messages, taken from the messenger or intercepted by the S.I. CENSORSHIP discloses that although personally he has done no mischief directed against specified vulnerable objectives, and involving the services of other persons not yet identified, some of whom appear to be his superiors in the enemy intelligence system. The Military and Civil measures for routine standing PROTECTION (against *all* unauthorised persons regardless of personal classification or credentials) of all vulnerable objectives of the nature specified are then tuned up at the instance of S.I. In due course some person is arrested by an ordinary military or civil guard or person, either on suspicion of acting or preparing to act in an unauthorised manner in the vicinity of a vulnerable objective, or because his personal papers of identity or credential are not in order. His personality is probably unknown and of no significance to the Guard. Investigation by S.I. with the aid of previous and collateral information and evidence may lead in a favourable instance to the destruction of an important enemy system or agency in which the enemy persons above mentioned occupied positions of subordinate importance only.'

This example showed, 'That the hasty or immediate arrest or alarm of the enemy agent first mentioned might have been gravely to the disadvantage of the protective system as a whole, but it must not be deduced that it is always advisable to accept the risk of reliance upon the last line of defence before closing with a suspected enemy agent. Under the emergency conditions of active field operations it will generally be advisable to close matters instantly with all such persons.'

Regarding 'Executive Action and Civil Questions', the notes advised that where a special exercise of civil or military power that involved *personal* control or restriction was required to achieve any of the purposes outlined above, the duty of all preventive intelligence services were confined to advising on policy, and providing the best information on which the appropriate executive authority, whether civil or military, could take action. The notes also explained that civil questions that arose out of domestic politics, labour unrest, or strikes were matters in which political considerations predominated over military ones, and were thus not dealt with by the exercise of military powers, except in cases of grave emergency within a zone of military operations.[128]

The Dowling Case

Lance-Corporal Joseph Dowling, a British subject, joined the Connaught Rangers in 1904. He had been born in Queen's County, Ireland in 1885, the son of John Dowling, a prominent member of Sinn Fein. He went to France with the BEF and was taken prisoner by the Germans on 26 August 1914. On 8 July 1915, a report had been received from a Major Furness of the Royal Army Medical Corps (RAMC), a POW repatriated from Germany, that Dowling had joined Casement's Irish Brigade and that he also acted as a recruiting agent amongst Irish POWs.[129] On 13 April 1918, the Naval Intelligence Department (NID) informed MI5 that a man had reportedly landed on the Galway coast on the morning of 12 April 1918, stating to be the sole survivor of the S.S. *Mississippi* which had been torpedoed off Arran Island, Galway the previous night.[130] Enquiry by NID revealed that the *Mississippi* had not yet left the Clyde and NID requested that the prisoner should be brought over to London for immediate interrogation. Under interrogation by NID, Dowling admitted that he had been brought over by a German submarine and landed in a collapsible boat and that he had instructions to get in touch with the leaders of Sinn Fein. He spoke of a German expedition to Ireland.

Dowling was tried by court martial on 8 July 1918 and charged with having joined the Irish Brigade, trying to persuade other POWs to join, and landing in Ireland from a German submarine with the object of aiding Britain's enemies. He was found guilty and sentenced to death, but the sentence was subsequently commuted to penal servitude for life.[131]

Organisational changes, 1918

MI5's main growth during 1918 was in the continued expansion of the ports police who kept a lookout for Bolshevik and German sympathizers, the opening of an office in Rome and in a substantial increase in MI5's representation in the USA. MI5's office in Rome was opened on 1 January 1918, in response to German and Austro-Hungarian success at the Battle of Caporetto which had led to the deployment of six Anglo-French divisions to shore up the Italian Front. The head of MI5's Rome station, Sir Samuel Hoare MP, who would go on to become Foreign Secretary, was the only serving MP to become an MI5 officer. During 1918, MI5 posted thirty staff to its offices in Washington and New York. As already explained, following America's entry into the First World War in April 1917, the British intelligence services began to liaise with their US counterparts when the head of E Branch, Lieutenant-Colonel Claude Dansey was sent to brief US military intelligence.[132]

At the end of the First World War, on 11 November 1918, at its most developed state during the whole 1909-1918 era, MI5 had 844 members of staff. Of these, 490 members were at headquarters, including eighty-four officers and civilian officials, fifteen male clerks, 291 women clerks, twenty-three police and seventy-seven subordinate staff. The other 354 members of staff were based at controlled home ports, or at permit offices and missions in Allied countries, including forty-nine officers and civilian officials, seven male clerks, thirty-four women clerks, 255 ports police and nine subordinate staff.[133]

By the Armistice in 1918, over 40 per cent of staff were based outside the capital at home ports, at permit offices and in missions in Allied countries.[134] But if MI5's wartime expansion seems excessive, it should be compared with the exponential growth of the Postal Censorship from a single censor at the beginning of the war, to a staff of 4,861 by the end.[135] Indeed, MI5's wartime growth was not dramatically different to that of the War Office as a whole. The intelligence historian, Nicholas Hiley has calculated that although MI5 grew at an average of 9.8% per month during the first three years of war, compared to 6.2% for the War Office overall, this rate dropped to only 1.4% a month for the war's last year, which was similar to the War Office's overall rate of expansion for that period.[136]

ARO/DRR, 1918

No completely new ARA or DORA regulations of particular interest to MI5 were introduced during 1918 – just a few small changes. Post-war issues took up much of F Branch's time. By May 1918, the draft for a National Security Bill had been prepared: its key points were that it became a penal offence to approach certain prohibited places, or to communicate with an enemy spy, trials were to take place in camera, and impersonation, forging credentials, and harbouring spies were also prohibited.

In May 1918, F Branch took part in an inter-departmental conference concerning the powers to be given to the Air Ministry under the DORA. MI5 was particularly interested in the question of the appointment of Competent Air Authorities. The UK was divided into areas controlled either by a CMA or CNA and the intrusion of a third authority threatened misunderstanding. A satisfactory solution was reached, with the Army Council nominating three members of the Air Council as CMAs.

During May 1918, the power under DRR14B, which had been invaluable to F Branch, to intern or impose restrictions, was granted to the Chief Secretary for Ireland. Other amendments were introduced to deal with dangerous Sinn Fein members in Ireland.

Two further minor amendments of interest to MI5 were introduced. DRR43A made it an offence for anyone to obstruct, impede or interfere with any member of the armed forces carrying out his duties. A new article added to the ARA in February 1918 provided that Poles were to be classed as alien friends. The available evidence does not explain why Poles were reclassified as such.[137] However, it can be speculated, with some confidence, that it was part of a political strategy to win Polish allegiance for the Entente, which had seen the Allied powers formally recognise Poland as 'an allied belligerent nation' on 3 June 1917, the French raise a Polish army in June 1917, and British recognition of a Polish National Committee in October 1917 in the hope of raising Polish forces to continue the war in the east after the evident collapse of the Provisional Government in Russia.[138]

Towards the end of summer 1918, F Branch was involved in a new review of all cases of enemy aliens who had up until then been exempted from internment or repatriation undertaken by the Aliens Advisory Committee. By October, the committee had reviewed approximately 3,200 cases; about 300 decisions were for internment, about 220 were for repatriation, and the other 2,680 people were again discharged to police supervision under the ARA.

Three days prior to the armistice, DRR46A, which covered the supervision of POWs in camps, was amended to make the regulations regarding helping POWs to escape, sending letters for them and parcels to them, and similar acts, much stricter.[139]

Statistics, January-November 1918

Personal dossiers	21,180
Anti-British cases	4,364
Suspects circulated	2,291
Internments under DRR14B	14
Permit and passport applications	29,216
Credentials censorship examined	16,704
For munitions work and Auxiliary War Services	3,156
Missing aliens searched for	4,057[140]

Competition with Thomson over post-war roles

As victory approached in the summer of 1918, pacifism and fears of German-sponsored subversion evaporated. As Christopher Andrew observes, Kell's '…lack of powerful backers in Whitehall left him ill equipped to compete with Thomson for the post-war control of British domestic intelligence.' Whilst Kell was on sick leave away in Northumberland, Thomson was busy in London lobbying Government ministers to give him the leading role in post-war domestic intelligence.[141] As a secret agency, MI5 was unable to publicly stake its claim for recognition of its role in the defeat of German espionage, whereas Thomson, who was experienced in self-promotion, did. Andrew concludes that:

'Kell's bureau became a victim of its own successes. Had German espionage remained a serious apparent threat throughout the war or Germany succeeded in launching a major sabotage campaign in Britain, Kell would have found it much easier to retain the lead domestic intelligence role. But during the second half of the war, with government now more concerned with subversion than with espionage, it was easier for Thomson than for Kell to gain the ear of ministers.'[142]

Declassified MI5 records for this period contain very little about Kell's thoughts about the post-war role of MI5. An undated report by an unnamed author, probably prepared in late-1918 or early-1919 by a senior MI5 officer, entitled *Proposals as to the Future of the Service of Security Bureau*' recommended a unified Secret Service handling both espionage and counter-espionage. It would be comprised of five branches, one of which would be a Counter-Espionage Branch:

'This would be responsible for the detection of all cases of espionage and for considering what measures legislative or otherwise, were necessary in time of peace and war for the prevention of espionage. To this branch would also fall the compilation and revision of regulations for purely war organisations, including censorship in all its branches, importation of alien labour, traffic in arms, war trade intelligence and cryptography.'[143]

The key point here is that this report envisaged the post-war MI5 retaining responsibility for 'all' cases of espionage – both military and civil.

Post-war Reorganisation

Recent research has shown how MI5 continued to have only this limited role in counter-subversion up to the end of the war. Indeed, when the Secret Service Committee (SSC) began to meet in February 1919 to consider reform of the intelligence services, MI5 maintained that its responsibility was for counter-espionage and 'declared its scrupulous adherence to a policy of non-investigation of political and labour unrest, except in cases of clear-cut enemy activity'.[144]

As a result, MI5's role was limited to military counter-espionage and preventing the spread of Bolshevism within the armed forces, and Kell's budget was reduced from £100,000 per annum to £30,000.[145] However, MI5 survived into the post-war period, which intelligence specialist, Michael Smith, credits to its files about undesirable aliens:

'Despite seeing his staff slashed by more than 800 to just 30, Kell fought a rearguard action to keep MI5 alive. He centred his activities on his registry of undesirable aliens, now renamed the Precautionary Index, using this to monitor the activities of all Russians and their sympathisers in Britain. MI5 expanded the list to include anyone who held or was suspected of having held left-wing views and might therefore pass them on to unsuspecting soldiers, sailors and airmen.'[146]

E Branch disappeared on 1 August 1919 when military control at home ports ceased and missions abroad were re-tasked to keep Bolshevik agents out of Britain. Called the Passport Control Department, it was given, with its MI5 personnel, to MI1c,[147] while A Branch was absorbed by F Branch on 1 September 1919. The changes of the immediate post-war era were completed on 31 March 1920, when MI5 was reorganised back into three branches, very much as it had been in the early stages of the First World War. The Preventive (F) Branch was renamed MI5(A), the Investigative (G) Branch was re-titled MI5(B), and the Organisation and Administration (H) Branch absorbed D Branch and became MI5(O).[148] In May 1920, the Defence Security Intelligence Service, as MI5 had also come to be known by then, produced a distribution of duties, with the following main features:

Director of Security Intelligence (D.S.I.):
Counter Espionage. Defence Security Policy in dealing with the Police Authorities and the Civil Population (including Aliens) in the United Kingdom and British Possessions Overseas.

A. Branch: Prevention of Activities prejudicial to Defence Security.

A.1.: Defence Security Control within the United Kingdom. Co-operation with the Naval, Military, Air Force, Munitions, Police and Civil Authorities in the routine application of Security Intelligence Precautionary Measures.

A.2.: Defence Security Control of Ports and Frontiers. Policy and Measures for the control of civilian passenger traffic to and from overseas territory in occupation by British Armed Forces.

A.3.: Legal procedure and advice concerning the duties of the Security Intelligence Service.

B. Branch: Organisation of the Detective Branch and supervision of measures for detecting espionage or sabotage by agents of foreign powers.

B.1.: European Powers group.

B.2.: America and Far Eastern Powers group.

B.3.: Scandinavia and Russian group.

B.4.: Administrative and Liaison.

B.5.: Intelligence Police Section.

B.6.: Scientific Section.

O. Branch: Organisation and Administration.

O.1.: Secretariat.

O.2.: Personnel.

O.3.: Interior Economy.

O.4.: Financial.

Records Section

R.1.: Registry.

R.2.: Personal Records.

R.3.: Subject Records.

R.4.: Trade Records.[149]

★ ★ ★

During the last two years of the war, MI5 perceived that the main threat from German espionage came from neutral seamen. Thus, much of its work during 1917-1918 was devoted to tightening the control at ports, particularly increasing the control over neutral seamen, which culminated in the NEP Scheme.

MI5 was also convinced that the German Secret Service had switched the main focus of its attack on the British Empire from espionage to subversion. Kell was not an inveterate empire-builder and he moved into counter-subversion with reservations. In February 1917, MI5's investigations of cases of sedition and peace propaganda were limited to those that arose from enemy activities. MI5's investigations into organisations deemed subversive were restricted to looking for evidence of a German 'hidden hand'. Indeed, whenever these organisations were raided, MI5 was most interested in their financial records in order to see if they were being financed by Germany.

It is abundantly clear that Kell did not covet the labour intelligence role that was given to Thomson. When PMS2 was disbanded, Kell explicitly told his superiors that he did not want MI5 to have anything to do with labour intelligence. Indeed, he only took on the role of vetting aliens applying to work on munitions under sufferance. Kell would have preferred that this work remained with the Ministry of Munitions.

Kell's distaste for labour intelligence coupled with Thomson's great appetite for it helps to explain why Thomson secured the leading role in post-war British domestic intelligence and why Kell was limited to military counter-espionage and preventing the spread of Bolshevism within the armed forces.

i

CHAPTER SEVEN

Settling Accounts

Conclusion and MI5 and the Historiography

THIS book has examined how MI5 foiled the spies of the Kaiser in the era of the First World War, paying particular attention to the preventive measures the organisation instituted to 'frustrate' espionage and how investigations to 'cure' espionage were conducted. This focus has also enabled a detailed examination of how well MI5 performed in the battle against the spies of the Kaiser. The research has also shown that an appreciation of how MI5 saw its work as being divided between preventive measures and investigative work provides valuable insights into the evolution of the organisation's role and structure during its first ten years. Before moving on to address these issues, it is useful to set out the gold standard by which espionage during the First World War era should be judged. Arguably, the challenge was for German espionage to recruit agents like TR16 and for MI5 to prevent them from doing so.

In his memoirs published in 1934, Henry Landau, an MI1c officer during the First World War, described MI1c's agent TR16 as 'the greatest of the Allied war-time spies'. TR16 was the code name for Dr Karl Kruger, a naval engineer working in the German shipbuilding industry. Aged about forty years-old at the start of the First World War, Kruger offered his services to the British Legation in The Hague in November 1914. He was motivated by greed and resentment, having been court-martialled from the German Navy for insulting a relative of the Kaiser. Surviving MI1c reports noted that Kruger's information on submarine and naval construction 'was always accurate, up to date and of the very greatest possible value'. He made complete tours of the German shipyards approximately every month from May 1915 to January 1919. The Battle of Jutland, on 31 May 1916, was the only wartime engagement between the main British and German fleets, but it was inconclusive, with both sides taking heavy losses. The Admiralty badly needed to know how much damage the German fleet had suffered at the battle of Jutland and how soon it might be able to fight again. On 2 June, MI1c's headquarters in London informed Commander Richard Tinsley, MI1c's head of station in Rotterdam, that the Admiralty urgently required reliable intelligence on this.

Later that same day, Tinsley instructed to Kruger to find out this information. Kruger duly provided MI1c with first-class intelligence on this. Intelligence historian Keith Jeffrey provides a post-mission summary which shows just how valuable Kruger was as an agent:

'Between 3 and 20 June he visited ten German dockyards, including Kiel, Bremen, Rostock and Danzig and on 27 June delivered a comprehensive five-page report which the Admiralty Director of the Intelligence Division praised as "100%".'

Kruger confirmed that the Germans had suffered more serious damage than they had admitted, reporting that eight capital ships would be out of service for at least three months. Jeffrey, noted: 'The principal result of Jutland, indeed, was that for the rest of the war the German fleet never again ventures out to battle.'

Kruger continued to work for SIS throughout the inter-war years. He met his case officer in Rotterdam every month, reporting on naval matters and coastal defences. When he failed to report for his monthly debriefing on 20 August 1939, SIS headquarters presumed that he had been caught by the Germans. However, after the Second World War, SIS learned that Kruger had been betrayed by a member of staff at SIS's station in The Hague, Folkert von Koutrik, who had been recruited by the *Abwehr* in October 1938.[1]

It is instructive to divide the practice of espionage into four distinct stages, and to outline how MI5 tried to stop the German espionage organisation at each of these stages. Firstly, agents have to be recruited and trained. Punitive regulations, such as the OSA 1911 and DORA, were designed to deter people from becoming spies. Secondly, if they do not live there already, spies have to be infiltrated into the country where they are to conduct their activities. Wartime control of ports and frontiers erected the necessary barriers. Thirdly, agents must collect the required intelligence and perform other activities, such as sabotage. Schemes were designed to protect vulnerable points against sabotage. Measures were enacted to control access to sensitive areas. Legislation was also introduced to control people, especially enemy aliens, such as the ARA and DORA. Finally, spies must pass intelligence back to the intelligence organisation; which must be done in time for the intelligence to still be of use, rather than out-of-date. A number of measures were put into place to block likely channels of communication with the enemy such as control of ports and frontiers, cable and postal censorship and regulations forbidding illicit signalling at night.

Moreover, there are important questions for the study of intelligence generally. How can the level of effectiveness of a counter-intelligence organisation be measured? Against what criteria can MI5's performance be evaluated? The outcome of the war? Intelligence does not decide wars on its own. Other factors are much more important. The records of what intelligence the Germans managed to collect in spite of MI5? The level of payment Germany's agents demanded for this work, and the danger that they felt was involved in facing MI5? Tallies of how many agents were caught, against those who were not caught? How pleased, or displeased, the British government and armed forces were with MI5's performance? What MI5 achieved in terms of counter-attacking German intelligence, such as with deception or double agents?

Counter-intelligence aims to do more than just defensively protect its own side's information and neutralise enemy agents. At a deeper level, counter-intelligence also aims to gather intelligence on enemy intelligence organisations and their methods, and to thwart them by misleading them through deception and the use of double agents. The ultimate goal of counter-intelligence is to confuse the enemy intelligence organisation with deception, penetrate it with double agents, and recruit enemy intelligence officers as one's own agents to such an extent that the enemy's intelligence organisation can almost be controlled for the benefit of one's own side. This includes making sure that the enemy fails to collect intelligence of any real value, that their assessment of intelligence collected is inaccurate and that one's own side's intelligence collection succeeds, because the enemy counter-intelligence has failed to prevent it. Indeed, recruiting enemy intelligence officers and agents as spies is one of the best ways of gaining access to intelligence about the enemy's intelligence operations against one's own side, particularly to discover who their agents spying against one's own side are.

Between 1911 and 1914 MI5 brought ten German agents to account: six received prison sentences, two were cautioned, one was discharged from the Royal Navy and another was declared insane. As part of a deliberate policy to roll up the German espionage network in the UK in one knockout blow, MI5 had also been keeping a further twenty-two spies under surveillance ready to be rounded up on the outbreak of war.

Eric E.B. Holt-Wilson, by this time Deputy-Director of MI5, provided the following summary of the fate of the German spies caught by MI5 during the First World War, which illustrates MI5's wartime work:

'During the war we settled accounts with thirty-three more bona-fide enemy agents. Of these, 21 were sentenced to death. [of whom] 14 were executed. [and] 7 sentenced to death, but sentence commuted to penal servitude. 10 imprisoned – one for life, others for 10 years and under. 2 were discharged for various reasons.

'In addition we caught and handed over spies who were found not to have broken British laws but to have acted against our allies, such as MATA HARI the Dutch spy, who was shot by the French.'[2]

Colonel Walther Nicolai, head of the German General Staff's military intelligence department (*Sektion* IIIb) during the First World War, concluded that the '...number of spies captured is no proof of the efficiency of the defence-service; that is only proved if state interests are successfully kept secret.'[3] Therefore, if the principal aim of espionage is to collect information of real value, then the *raison d'être* for counter-espionage is to deny the enemy's espionage organisation information of real value. By this criterion MI5 appears to have been exceptionally successful because Germany's spies in the UK provided very little information of any real value, particularly during wartime. No claims have ever been made that German intelligence achieved any scoops of note in the UK that might have had an impact on the War. As an example on an issue of very real importance, Germany did not learn of the BEF's despatch to France until about two weeks after it had happened.

MI5 also succeeded in its role of destroying the German espionage organisation in the UK, capturing almost all of its spies and denying Germany any really useful intelligence. The pre-war policy of tracking the known German spies, but not actually arresting them ntil the outbreak of the war, was a far-sighted and well-organised policy which delivered ne Germans a knockout blow from which they never properly recovered throughout the var. However, the German intelligence specialist, Thomas Boghardt, contends that ssessing German intelligence 'purely on the basis of evidence relating to captured agents ..is like judging a business community by its bankrupts'. Thus, he suggests that the npression that MI5 successfully stifled German espionage has been created because there as been a greater focus on the agents who were caught, rather than those who got back o Germany safely.

Yet MI5 could never be absolutely certain that it had caught all of Germany's spies n the UK. It had to be wary that there might be other spies who had not been caught. ndeed, they could well have been Germany's best spies, which would explain why MI5 ad not caught them so easily. It was MI5's job to be wary, because it was most responsible f spies were not caught. Equally, it was also MI5's job to provide accurate assessments of he nature of the espionage threat – and not to scaremonger or to become too omplacent about its successes. Of course the pre-war belief in the consummate efficiency of the German intelligence services made it harder to accept how poorly they actually performed during the war.

MI5 concluded that the increase in the wages being demanded by German spies was evidence of its success, because it showed that spies were becoming increasingly afraid of being caught and therefore in need of greater inducement to brave these risks. This is exactly the deterrent effect that counter-espionage aims for. Of course, some of the ncreasing wage demands may also have been due to wartime inflation, or the fact that Germany would pay agents more money.

The following items must be set against this in the debit column of an account of MI5's performance. Firstly, although useful, intelligence from, and sabotage conducted in, the UK was only of secondary importance to Germany. Germany's real need, and main effort, was for intelligence from the main battle-zone of France, Belgium and Russia. Indeed, it is striking how much of the German effort against the UK was concerned with either, and particularly, the Royal Navy, defence works or harbours in the UK. Thus, the targeting of German intelligence regarding Britain in 1914 appears to have been driven by naval requirements, which is understandable given that Germany's strategy against Britain was to hope for a victorious naval *der Tag*.

It is worth speculating what the Germans expected to achieve. Details of ships' guns and similar details were all pretty much common knowledge. Gaps in this knowledge could have been filled when the Royal Navy visited Kiel during Navy Weeks and other such events. Peacetime movements and concentration of ships were well known. Acquiring technical details, such as the superior fire control system being developed and installed a little later in HMS *Queen Mary*, would have required skilled and well-placed agents. Yet there is no evidence of this. Indeed, the one piece of naval intelligence that could have been of enormous use to Germany was a piece they never got – the strategy of a distant blockade with the Grand Fleet at Scapa Flow. If they had had prior knowledge of this, they could have harassed Scapa Flow, which was not defended in any way in the early days of the war.

Thomson recalled that it became clear throughout the war that the only type of espionage that is really worth conducting during wartime 'is the gathering of intelligence just behind the enemy lines and on the lines of communication'. This was because,

'To be of real value in an enemy country a spy must be highly placed. The ener
must, in fact, buy someone who is in naval and military secrets, for even the ordina
citizen of the country is very rarely in a position to give useful information.'[4]

The foreigner, 'who dared not ask questions', had even less chance of gatheri
useful information.[5]

While the German strategy of 1914 hinged on the Schlieffen Plan, Germany wou
have most obviously needed to discover if, and where, the BEF was to land, its plans a
its equipment. The inability to spot the BEF's move to France was a significant failure
German Intelligence. However, it is questionable how far this can be credited to M
because it seems that Germany's agents in Britain were not even targeted to gather t
relevant intelligence, their concern being naval intelligence. Similarly, this failure
forecast the BEF's crucial arrival for the opening was more the fault of German battlefie
intelligence than its agents in Britain. Once landed, the BEF should have been spott
by German reconnaissance aircraft or cavalry patrols. One reason for this shortcomi
appears to be that noted by Nicolai who observes that the German General Staff,
opposed to the Navy, was only provided with a secret service against France and Russ
Time and means had not sufficed for Britain. Nicolai was responsible for relations wi
the press as well as intelligence. This must also have affected the time he could devote
intelligence. However, it is possible to speculate that the German Army's absence
interest was in part Clausewitzian; Clausewitz had little faith in intelligence. Clausewi
wrote that: 'Many intelligence reports in war are contradictory; even more are false, an
most are uncertain.'[6] This no doubt moulded the attitudes and priorities of the Gener
Staff. Related to this, money was short; the army left Britain to the navy; and no or
coordinated German Intelligence, the various agencies just being left to get on with
It was also partly a serious underestimation of the British Army's capabilities.

The Germans rather contemptuously discounted the relatively small BEF as unlike
to make any difference to the defence of France. In a lecture delivered in 1934, Hol
Wilson remarked that Germany had taken,

'...no interest in our army, and probably still remembered the famous remark, mad
I think by Bismarck, who upon being asked if he had contemplated the possibility c
the British army coming to the aid of France in 1870, replied "Yes I have, and if the
do I shall most certainly ring the bell and send for the police".'[7]

Edmonds concluded in his memoirs, 'I doubt whether the Germans in 1906-14 seriousl
contemplated invasion. The intention was intimidation.' In which case, '...the mai
purpose of the spying was to learn all about our navy, and to frighten any Governmen
from sending troops out of England to the Continent should a war break out betwee
France and Germany.'[8]

Secondly, it must also be entered into the equation that the fact that Britain is a
island provides it with natural counter-espionage defences and gave MI5 an obviou
advantage over the Germans. Nonetheless, MI5 still did well to exploit this to the full
such as with the eventual formation of E Branch. Thirdly, the quality of the agent
employed by the Germans was decidedly third-rate. Thus, MI5 was never fully tested by

a first-class adversary. Before the war, Germany's agents generally passed on gossip or items from openly available sources such as local newspapers. Indeed, the Germans often berated their agents that they only wanted them to pass on material marked secret, not from open sources. There were a few very minor exceptions to this rule. George Parrott, for example, provided confidential material of a type that would be available to most petty officers in the Royal Navy, but nothing of exceptional value. The Germans did not have any well-placed spies, with access to material of real consequence.

German sources also concur that the vast majority of spies that Germany sent to Britain were of laughably poor calibre. However, they also show that Germany was not too concerned with intelligence on what was happening in Britain itself, which was only a secondary target. Germany's primary target was the theatre of actual fighting. Boghardt concludes that undoubtedly 'the balance sheet' of the Admiralty Staff's naval intelligence department (*Nachrichtenabteilung im Admiralstab* or 'N') is 'overall negative'. It had failed to establish an effective intelligence organisation in the UK prior to the war. At the start of the war it had been unable to provide any material on British mobilisation and strategic plans. Reports on British convoys and merchant shipping did not render unrestricted submarine warfare a success. Sabotage did very little to prevent US goods from reaching Western Europe and actually provided the Allies with opportunities for propaganda. 'In other words,' as Boghardt opines, 'in this arena naval intelligence proved not only to be inefficient but outright counter-productive.'

Boghardt questions why, if MI5 did not put up an impenetrable defence, did German naval intelligence fail in the UK? This seems particularly intriguing given that Germany had managed to score some notable intelligence successes in other theatres, such as the attempts to incite unrest in Persia, the activities of Agent 17 (Baron August Schluga) in France, and Nicolai's *Abteilung* IIIb's part in introducing the Bolshevik revolution to Russia. He suggests that some of the reasons were clearly 'home made'. Steinhauer and the German naval attaché in London were not good candidates to establish an efficient intelligence system. The naval attaché did as much as he could to stay out of things, while Steinhauer did much to wreck things. The German naval intelligence department also, especially before the war, recruited numerous individuals who proved failures as naval agents. Inter-service rivalry presented another obstacle.

'More damaging to Germany's overall war effort was the lack of civilian control over the services.' Boghardt feels that a civilian authority would not have condoned sabotage in neutral states. The outlook of naval staff was governed by narrow-minded tactical considerations that prevented them from appreciating the political consequences of military acts. For example, the UK understood the political benefits of being seen to treat female spies mercifully, whereas Germany affirmed its prerogative to kill Edith Cavell, which, although legal under martial law, proved disastrous in the eyes of the world.

Notwithstanding, Boghardt feels that circumstances beyond N's control should take even more of the blame for its failure than these 'inherent defects'. The technical means that proved crucial to intelligence during the Second World War were not available in 1914-1918. Unlike the Second World War, for example, German agents could not use the parachute to infiltrate enemy territory or the radio to transmit intelligence to Germany. Additionally, Britain's defences as an island denied any comprehensive intelligence collection there during the era of the First World War. Finally Boghardt suggests that, fundamentally, even if spies had been able to pass intelligence to Germany in good time, it would hardly have made a difference. In the early stages of the war, German naval intelligence hoped to wear the Royal Navy down until the German fleet could meet the British on approximately equal terms. This never happened. And, even if spies had provided intelligence on Allied convoys, it is unlikely that submarines would have risked attacking them. Destroyers were plainly superior to submarines and the Germans realised this. Lastly, although spies did report on the failure of unrestricted submarine warfare, at that stage of the war such disclosures no longer mattered. This leads Boghardt to conclude that 'N would have failed regardless of the existence or non-existence of MI5'. He adds that the laments over the UK's formidable counter-espionage defences penned by former members of the German Secret Service were 'more often than not defensive lies to disguise one's own impotence.'[9]

The research I have undertaken for this study reinforces the standard interpretation that MI5 did comprehensively win the battle against its German foe, albeit that this opposition was decidedly third-rate, which does detract somewhat from the sense of achievement, and defends it against the recent revisionist claims of Boghardt, whose evidence that MI5 did not detect all of the German spies in Britain appears questionable to say the least.

Perhaps MI5 could have built on its successes and done even more to aid the war effort, such as in double-agent or deception operations to mislead the enemy, as it did so successfully during the Second World War. This charge against MI5 does not stand up to scrutiny, because it was arguably much easier to do this during the Second World War, than it would have been during the First World War. Firstly, during the Second World War, signals intelligence (SIGINT) enabled the British to read Germany's communications to check if Germany had swallowed the bait dangled before it by deception and double-agents. Secondly, it was easier to control double-agents when they were communicating with Germany via radio during the Second World War than during the First World War when other methods of communication were used which were harder to supervise in order to make to make sure the messages were being passed on. Thirdly, during the Second World War, many of MI5's most successful double-agents were anti-Nazis who had really come to Britain posing as spies for Germany, but in reality it was so that they could join the British in the fight against Germany. Therefore MI5 could be much more confident of their loyalties.

The vast majority of German agents in Britain during the First World War were only spying for the money it paid and could not be trusted not to betray MI5 to the highest bidder if taken on as double-agents. Nonetheless, perhaps MI5 was more imaginative during the Second World War than it had been in the First World War. During the First World War, spies were generally seen as traitors who would sell out their own country for money and despised as such. Nevertheless, MI5 did have some successes at deception during the First World War, such as in the cases of Muller, COMO, and Whytock. They were inconsequential, however, because they had little impact on the course of the war. Notwithstanding, convicted spies were usually imprisoned or shot. Very little thought was given as to whether they could be of any use to the British, or not. By contrast, during the Second World War, there was a greater willingness to at least consider if any use could have been made of captured spies.

The assessments of MI5's performance have been varied, but its degree of success can be well summed up by using a cricketing analogy: MI5 clearly beat Germany very convincingly. MI5 was never really truly tested by its third-rate German opponent. MI5 did not play a faultless, perfect game. It did not bowl all German batsmen first ball for nought. Of course, no team has ever played such a perfect game. Although it played a poor opponent, this does not detract from the fact that MI5 still acquitted itself admirably and showed that it knew the game very well, as it developed a sound organisational structure and evolved a good strategy. MI5 also demonstrated some impressive moves, such as the round-up of German agents following the outbreak of hostilities. The scorecard would read that some German agents were bowled first ball for a duck. Most German agents were bowled without having scored any runs, but survived for a few balls. Some German agents lasted for a few overs, but made meaningless scores of only one or two runs. A couple of German agents stayed at the crease for a long time and scored twenty or thirty runs, albeit in ones and twos, but no spectacular sixes, without ever really threatening to score a decent century or a potentially match-winning double-hundred.

It is instructive to look at how MI5 initially detected the spies that it caught during the First World War era. The spies caught before the outbreak of war were detected owing to informants, and intercepted letters. Max Schultz offered two British men money to provide him with confidential information, and they immediately reported him to the authorities. Similarly, Heinrich Grosse offered a naval pensioner money to provide him with confidential information, and the naval pensioner immediately reported him to the authorities. Ireland, Klare, and Schroeder were all detected by the HOW on Gustav Steinhauer. Hentschel, Parrott, and Graves were all detected by the HOW on Otto Kruger. Hattrick was detected when a letter he wrote to The Head, Intelligence Department, War Office, Germany, was intercepted. Maddick was detected by the HOW on Alberto Rosso. The vast majority of spies rounded up in August 1914 were detected owing to intercepted letters; the others were reported to the authorities for suspicious behavior. In a good example of the preventive principle of posting guards to protect confidential information, Franz Heinrich Lozel was arrested by a soldier for carrying a camera on the sea wall at Sheerness. Kruger was detected by the HOW on Reimers. Heinrich Schutte was detected by the HOW on the similar address of Reimann. Karl Gustave Ernst was detected by the HOW on Croner. Engel was detected by the HOW on Kruger. August Klunder was detected by the HOW on Croner. Walter Rimann was detected by the HOW on Steinhauer. Marie Croner was detected by the HOW on Steinhauer. Heinrich Schmidt was detected by the HOW on Klunder. Frederick Fowler was detected by the HOW on Steinhauer. Fredrik Apel was detected by the HOW on Hugo Munschied. It is instructive to note that the spy address of Munschied had been discovered by the HOW on Schmidt. Kurd von Weller was arrested following the outbreak of war and searched as a known retired officer of the German Army. The available records do not state how Adolf Schneider was detected. However, they do mention that a HOW was taken out on him. It seems most likely that he was detected by a HOW on one of Steinhauer's intermediaries. W.F.Brown was reported to the police by former work colleagues who felt that he had behaved suspiciously. Rosso was detected when he wired to the well-known spy agency, 'Mr Adams' in Brussels, whose clients included the German Secret Service. Lina Mary Heine was detected by the HOW on

Schneider. Robert Blackburn was detected by the HOW on Klunder. Friederich von Diederichs was detected by the HOW on the known spy address of Streckel. Enrico Bernstein was arrested when he approached the Admiralty with intelligence to sell. Harold Dutton was discovered to have copied classified documents whilst working as an army clerk. The majority of the spies caught during the First World War were first detected by the preventive measures enacted by the postal and cable censorship, or by investigations carried out by agents working for MI1c. Carl Hans Lody was detected in the first winter of the war when he telegraphed to a known spy address in Stockholm. 1915 was arguably the year of the censorship. Kupferle, Muller, and Hahn were detected by the HOW on Leibacher and associated spy addresses, such as Lybecq. Melin was detected after an unknown informant informed MI5 that Melin was a spy. Buschmann was detected when he telegraphed to Flores, Dierks' partner. Janssen and Roos were detected by telegrams to Dierks and Co. George Breckow was detected by a telegram to Dierks and Co. Louise Wertheim was detected when search of Breckow's possessions revealed the receipt for a registered letter to L. Wertheim. Ludovic Zender was detected when suspicious telegrams that he sent attracted the attention of code experts. Alfredo Roggen was detected by postcards to Flores and Grund, known associates of Dierks. David Stad and Cornelis den Braber were detected by information supplied by the British Consul-General at Rotterdam. Josef Marks was detected after the American Minister at The Hague warned the British Consulate there that Marks' American passport was a forgery. Albert Meyer was detected when the censor took exception to one of his letters and uncovered a secret message. Kurt de Rysbach was detected by the HOW on J. Cords, a spy address that had been used by Zender. Edward Edwin was detected when two wounded soldiers he had attempted to solicit sensitive information from reported him to the authorities. Paul Hensel was detected when he received a suspect telegraphic money order. Eva de Bournonville was detected when the censor took exception to a letter that she had written and uncovered a secret message. Frank Greite was detected by an MI1c agent. MI1c played a particularly important role during 1916, most notably in collecting further evidence against Bacon and the German spy centre based in New York. Adolfo Guerrero was detected after the Admiralty warned MI5 that Spanish journalists would be coming to the UK to act as spies, and checks were thus placed on letters and telegrams to and from him. SIGINT alerted the authorities that Casement would be coming to Ireland in a submarine. Leopold Vieyra was detected by MI1c. Albertine Stanaway was detected by the HOW on Denis. Bacon was detected by the HOW on Denis. Anthony Spalding was detected when his breach of confidentiality was reported to the police. Earle was detected by the censorship. 1917 showed that MI5 relied on a variety of sources of detection. Boehm was detected by SIGINT. Smith was detected by the censorship. Hagn was detected by MI1c. Jose de Patrocinio was detected by a Belgian courier who witnessed Patrocinio taking affectionate leave of a suspect and forced him to confess. In 1918, Joseph Dowling was detected by investigations co-ordinated by the NID. Once spies had been initially detected, MI5 could deploy a range of investigative techniques in order to gather enough information for prosecution or other action to be taken. The most important methods were the interception of communications, agents, informants, and directed surveillance either by MI5's own detectives or local police forces. MI5 learned much from captured spies they searched and interrogated, particularly about

German espionage methods and spy addresses. Indeed, one of the head of the Investigative Branch's main duties was to learn about the German espionage system and the methods used by its agents, and apply this knowledge to MI5's methods. Preventive measures, such as censorship, port control, the creation of prohibited areas, and the control of aliens, turned Britain into a hard target for German espionage. Once spies were detected, investigative measures were brought into play to gather the evidence necessary to secure a conviction or other form of control. Both the ARO and DRR constantly evolved throughout the First World War in order to plug in gaps that had been revealed in Britain's counter-espionage defences. Of course, MI5's task was also made easier by weaknesses in the German's use of intermediaries and spy addresses, the incompetence of most German agents sent to Britain, and Britain's natural defences as an island.

The quotation below, taken from an MI5 report written in 1921, sets out the guiding principle behind the development of MI5 from 1909 to 1918:

> 'The work, and consequently the organisation, of such a Bureau is naturally divided into two main Branches, (1) the investigation of particular cases involving a definite suspicion of espionage and (2) the construction of legal and administrative machinery calculated to embarrass and, if possible, frustrate such attempts in general and for the future. The first Branch deals, in a word, with the cure of hostile espionage, the second with its prevention.'[10]

The original mission was seen in terms of investigative measures to 'cure' espionage, and preventive measures to 'frustrate' it. Thus, on the eve of the First World War, MI5 had two branches: one investigative and the other preventive, with a sub-section of the latter being concerned with records. By the end of the war MI5 had six branches, which had all clearly grown out of the investigative and preventive branches.

Instructively, MI5's methods stood the test of time. In 1910 Kell wrote that the investigative side of counter-espionage work should be divided between active and passive measures. In 1991, Abram N Shulsky, whose *Silent Warfare: Understanding the World of Intelligence* is the standard US textbook on the subject, also made the same distinction between active and passive measures.[11] Similarly, writing an in-house history of MI5 in 1946, John Court Curry observed that MI5's functions were 'naturally divided into':

1. detection or investigation
2. prevention or security
3. intelligence including records, and −
4. active deception of the enemy.[12]

It is immediately striking how much this reads like analogous passages in MI5's historical branch reports produced in 1921 to capture the experiences of the First World War. The only important difference is in the far greater emphasis placed on deception during the Second World War.

In terms of MI5's developmental ethos, it would be interesting to test how MI5's procedures compared with like organisations serving Britain's allies and enemies, particularly France, Russia, USA, Austria-Hungary, Germany and Turkey. Unfortunately, although there is a considerable literature concerning counter-espionage in these countries, there does not seem to be any relevant material available regarding the method adopted in them.

It is also instructive to question what motivated these men and women to become spies, especially when they knew that Britain had formidable counter-espionage defence and that if they were caught they were likely to be shot. Traditionally, as mentioned, the main motivations for becoming a spy have been seen as money, ideology, compromise, an ego (easily remembered by the acronym 'MICE'). Since the end of the Cold War, spite has also been recognised as an important motivating factor, particularly for embittere government officials with an axe to grind against their employers. The spies that MI5 too action against in the pre-war period were motivated to spy for Germany by a range o different motives. Helm was motivated by a sense of patriotic duty as a German office and by a desire for adventure. Schultz was a criminal adventurer, with a willingness to tak risks in the pursuit of what he felt would be a lucrative venture. Grosse was another such criminal adventurer. Ireland was clearly pressured into working for Steinhauer by hi beloved uncle, Otto Kruger. Klare felt that espionage offered him easy money. Schroede was an experienced professional spy, who went into the 'business' with both eyes wid open. Hentschel was another who felt that espionage offered him easy money Parrott betrayed his country having been compromised by Patricia Hentschel. As hi demands for more and more money showed, he was also motivated by greed. Graves wa another of the criminal adventurers much favoured by the Germans in the pre-war year Hattrick was bored with his mundane job and felt that espionage would be much mor lucrative. Maddick also felt that he could make easy money from the Germans, but he wa also not of sound mind, and this may well have influenced his decision to approach the German Secret Service. The vast majority of the German agents rounded up in Augus 1914 were motivated by pure greed. Lozel found that espionage was a lucrative sideline to his photographic business; Kruger became involved in espionage to supplement hi earnings from his hairdressing business; Schutte gave up working as the manager of a coaling hulk and became involved in espionage as it was more lucrative; Ernst was also motivated by pure greed; Engel found that espionage added a nice supplement to hi pension from the German Navy. He may well also have been motivated by a patriotic desire to continue to serve his country. Klunder was clearly motivated by money However, Croner may also have pressured Klunder into working for Steinhauer. Rimann was also motivated by money. Croner was motivated by greed. However, he may have been pressured into working for Steinhauer by Kruger. Mrs Croner approached Steinhauer out of pure desperation. Indeed, she may not have been of fully sound mind when she offered to continue her late husband's work. Schmidt was another motivated by the lure of what he perceived as easy money. Fowler was clearly motivated by money However, Kruger may have pressured Fowler into offering his services to the German Secret Service. Apel wanted money. Von Weller was driven by patriotism. Schneider wanted to supplement his income as a clerk. Brown remains an enigma! He appears to have been a professional spy, much like Schroeder. Rosso wanted money. Hine could earn more money as a spy than as a language teacher. Her husband, Herinert, was simply in the wrong company at the wrong time. Gregory was greedy to supplement his income as a ship-fitter. Nedjib was doing his duty as a Turkish officer. Blackburn was motivated by a desire for adventure, which had been fired up by spy stories. Von Diederichs was another patriotic retired German officer. Bernstein was a mercenary, willing to sell his services to the highest bidder. Dutton felt that he could make some money from taking copies of official documents. Sampson was motivated by a desire to make easy money from the Germans, and also probably by a spiteful desire to avenge having been reduced in rank. Lody, the first German spy caught spying in Britain during the war, was motivated by a sense of patriotic duty as a German officer.

1915 was arguably the high watermark of German espionage against Britain during the First World War. Kupferle was motivated by patriotism as a German soldier. Muller spied for the money it paid him, not out of any allegiance to the German cause. However, he was also a victim of circumstances that had made it much more difficult for him to make an 'honest' living. Hahn was in it for the money, but he was also a victim of circumstances and he may have been pressured into it by Muller. Melin was motivated purely by money. He was also another victim of circumstances, who turned to espionage out of desperation. Buschmann was motivated by pure greed. Rosenthal was a criminal adventurer. Jappe was greedy to earn more money than he could as an 'honest' electrician. Janssen and Roos were snared by the Germans' offer of easy money. Breckow, Wertheim, Zender, Roggen, Stad, den Braber, Marks, Meyer, Slager, Ulrich, Edwin, Hensel, de Bournonville, and Greite were all motivated by money. Breckow may have been lured into espionage by a desire to earn enough money to return to the USA. Wertheim may have been pushed when her ex-husband's financial difficulties resulted in her alimony payments being cut. De Bournonville may have been preyed upon by a recruiter for the German Secret Service who exploited her financial difficulties. De Rysbach was motivated by money, but also by a desire to secure his release from internment as an enemy alien in Germany. Triest was driven by loyalty to the German cause, although he was also not of sound mind.

Throughout 1916, the Germans struggled to recruit agents willing to risk going to Britain. The motives of those who did so were more varied than in 1915. Guerrero was simply greedy. Bright saw selling secrets as a way to solve his money problems. Casement was motivated by a desire to gain Ireland's freedom, although he also had a colossal ego as a result of which he felt that he alone was capable of gaining Ireland's freedom from British rule. Vieyra, van Zurk, and Bacon were all motivated by money. Stanaway was motivated by adulterous love for an imprisoned spy. Spalding seems to have been motivated by an egotistical desire to impress his friend with his knowledge of current affairs. Mrs Earle was motivated by loyalty to the land of her birth.

The German espionage attack upon Britain fizzled out in 1917 and 1918. Boehm was a patriotic German officer. Chakravarty was motivated by Indian nationalism. Mrs Smith was motivated by a desire to serve the country of her birth. However, the recent death of her British husband may have had an impact on her decision. Hagn was another spy motivated purely by money. Van der Goten was motivated by exceptional greed and also by a spiteful desire for revenge against the Allies whom he felt had cheated him out of money that he had rightfully earned for working for them. Patrocinio was also motivated by greed. Dowling was motivated by Irish nationalism. Thus, the vast majority of those who spied for Germany against Britain during the First World War era were motivated by money alone. In Felstead's words, they were 'hirelings' – 'men and women who spied for what it would bring.'[13]

Today, MI5 (or the Security Service as it is also now known) is the UK's security intelligence agency, countering threats to national security. Most of MI5's resources are now devoted to countering international terrorism, but it also works in counter espionage and countering the proliferation of Weapons of Mass Destruction (WMD) MI5 began in 1909 with a narrow remit to investigate German espionage activities in the UK. By 1918, the scope of counter-espionage had widened to encompass any activities undertaken or backed by the enemy that served to hinder the British war effort. In the process, MI5 developed into Britain's security intelligence agency and assumed responsibility for developing military policy regarding the control of the civilian population, particularly aliens. MI5's main focus was on counter-espionage, although as the threat evolved, it also assumed an increasing interest in countering sabotage and enemy-sponsored attempts to subvert the British war effort. At that time, MI5 did not have any role in counter-terrorism at all. The Metropolitan Police Special Branch had originally been formed as the Special Irish Branch to combat Fenian terror attacks on London. The Special Branch's remit soon widened to combatting all kinds of terrorism in the UK, such as anarchists and Indian revolutionaries. However, by the end of the First World War, MI5 had begun to acquire the capabilities that would later see it move into counter-terrorism, expertise in the preventive side of security intelligence work and most importantly, the ability to deploy agents to infiltrate groups under surveillance This capability would be further developed in the 1920s and 1930s, when long-term penetration agents were infiltrated into communist and fascist groups in Britain.

Today, MI5's work can be classed as to investigate, act, advise, or assist. MI5 has had an investigative role ever since its inception in 1909. Early on, it was established that was also to act to combat espionage, such as persuading the Royal Navy to move suspected individuals away from work that gave them access to information that would be of use to an enemy and into other less sensitive work areas. However, the principle that MI5 should not have any executive powers was also enshrined in these formative days During the First World War, MI5 advised the Army Council on policy matters regarding counter-espionage and military policy concerning the control of the civilian population especially aliens. This was arguably the beginning of a process that today sees it directly advising Government, not just the military, on dealing with threats to national security Today, MI5 assists a number of other government departments and agencies, and works with a wide range of intelligence and security agencies worldwide. From the very beginning, MI5 appreciated that its work relied on close co-operation with other government departments and agencies in order to operate the preventive controls and conduct investigations. As the war progressed, MI5 developed similarly close relations with intelligence and security agencies throughout the British Empire and in Allied countries.

Today, MI5 collects secret intelligence using undercover agents (covert human intelligence sources or CHIS in modern jargon), the interception of communications directed surveillance, and intrusive surveillance. Despite the obvious advances in technology, it is striking how similar these are to the collection methods employed by MI5 in the First World War era. Intrusive surveillance was employed as a last resort, when no less intrusive means could provide the intelligence sought – such as when Melville broke into Hagn's hotel room to procure a sample of his secret ink. MI5 had its own team of specialist detectives (later known as 'Watchers') to keep suspects under directed surveillance. Interception of communications, particularly letters, was arguably its key weapon in its pre-war contest with Steinhauer's network in the UK. During the First World War, most of MI5's leads came from agents, particularly those working for Tinsley's organisation in Rotterdam.

MI5 began quite humbly with a solitary member of staff, tasked with the limited remit of ascertaining the extent of German espionage in Britain and an uncertain future. By the armistice its role had expanded considerably and it had begun to develop into an established security intelligence agency with 844 personnel spread over six branches covering the investigation of espionage, prevention, records, ports and travellers, overseas, and alien workers. It was to function as the link between the civil, military and naval authorities to enable the Government to decide what was required to prevent the betrayal of key national interests to the enemy. In pursuance of this aim, MI5's duties lay in five key directions: prevention, detection, control, records, and organisation. It had assumed the following four key roles: first, it was the central clearing house for all counter-espionage information, which eventually functioned as the hub of a network spreading throughout the British Empire and also liaised with allied states. Secondly, it coordinated, directed and oversaw all of the various activities and organisations involved in counter-espionage. Thirdly, it was the Government's expert on counter-espionage and security intelligence matters. Fourth, it provided training or personnel trained in counter-espionage and security intelligence matters. This development was aptly summed up by MI5 towards the end of the First World War, when it tended to describe its role no longer simply as counter-espionage, but in wider terms as defence security intelligence.

The key stages in the development of MI5's role can be further summarised as follows. In 1909 Kell was appointed to look into the question of German espionage in Britain. Having discovered a German espionage network operating in the UK, MI5 developed so as to be able to also undertake the investigative work to counter this network, work which later became the province of G Branch. As MI5's interests developed from counter-espionage into the wider arena of defence security intelligence, G Branch broadened the scope of its investigations into Bolshevism, pacifist groups and industrial unrest, but only to check if these groups were under German influence and as such another part of the German Secret Service's attack on Britain. MI5 became the central clearing house for all counter-espionage information, developed its own investigative staff, and assumed the role of directing and coordinating the other organisations involved in counter-espionage, such as the police. Its early frustrations with its investigative work revealed the weaknesses in Britain's counter-espionage defences and prompted MI5 to act to have the situation improved, such as with the OSA 1911, HOW and the unofficial Register of Aliens. These legislative and administrative measures, as well as the desire to develop security schemes to protect vulnerable points from potential saboteurs, would become the work of F Branch. As well as producing papers on the methods employed by German agents to help the police and other government departments to defend against them, these preventive duties would see MI5 become the UK's specialist on counter-espionage and security intelligence matters.

Both successful investigations and preventive measures depended upon records, and MI5's position as the central clearing house for all counter espionage information, which developed into H Branch. The control of ports and frontiers was an essential wartime counter-espionage measure, such that E Branch was soon formed to deal with this in its own right. The fact that MI5 played a part in port control, but was not solely responsible for all aspects of it, is quite telling. It shows how MI5's expertise in counter-espionage matters was recognised and used to help with port control. It also illustrates how MI5 had to work with other well-established government departments, and demonstrates the power and influence that MI5 had and also what it did not have. It could not simply dictate policy and control everything on its own. Representatives of E Branch were posted to a number of Allied and neutral countries to scrutinise the applications of those who wished to travel from these countries to Britain. It would be a mistake, however, to describe them as liaison officers, or to suggest that MI5 had liaison relationships with allies worldwide at that time. Their role was limited to controlling who could travel from these countries to Britain. With the eventual formation of D Branch, MI5 became an Imperial counter-espionage and security agency at the centre of an Empire-wide network.

Finally, the creation of A Branch illustrated a number of key points about MI5's place. It demonstrated how MI5's knowledge of dealing with aliens, its records of aliens and its expertise in organising such a system of records could help in a vetting process. The fact that it absorbed the parts of PMS2 that were concerned with vetting aliens employed, or applying to work on munitions work, but did not take on PMS2's other work in gathering labour intelligence, which was passed on to the Special Branch, illustrates that its role was in counter-espionage and security intelligence, not in collecting intelligence on domestic democratic opposition to the British Government. A Branch's concern expanded from aliens employed in munitions to dealing with the wider issue of aliens employed on auxiliary war service, which provides a good example of how MI5's role expanded generally, particularly once it was shown that its expertise could be of use in such related areas.

It is more difficult to relate the success of MI5 to the organisational changes. It is abundantly clear that the organisation underwent considerable restructuring between 1909-1918, and that these changes were guided by a desire to plug gaps that had become apparent in MI5's defences and to thereby improve efficiency. Such measures usually succeeded in doing so. The development of E Branch offers the prime example of this. Indeed, this does show that MI5 was a dynamic organisation, always alive to the need for change, which was probably one of the key factors in its success. However, it remained on top of the game and was never truly tested by its third-rate opponent throughout this period. Therefore, it is more difficult to gauge how much of a difference these organisational changes actually made, because MI5 was always winning the battle.

This study suggests that the main driver of these developments – if one key factor can be singled out – was the changing perception of the nature of the threat posed by German espionage. This perception was largely created by public hysteria over spy mania and the dangers posed by enemy aliens, rather than actual evidence. Nonetheless, although the German threat was largely illusory, MI5's work was driven by continuing fears of potential spies and changes in wartime legislation arose from a perception of the need to plug particular gaps in Britain's counter-espionage defences. Fear of dissent and from 1917 onwards, Bolshevism, became increasingly important drivers of MI5's development towards the end of the war, precisely because of the perception that these activities were being directed by a German hidden hand. Other factors should also be noted as being of particular importance. In terms of grand strategy, it seems that Kell was very much implementing a programme that had been designed by his superiors, particularly in the early years. The way in which MI5 assumed the role as the axle to the wheel of counter-espionage was influenced by an appreciation that the best way to provide a quick and direct interchange of information was with a centralised counter-espionage bureau. Understanding that MI5 saw the fundamental principle behind its work as being that counter-espionage was naturally divided into the two halves of investigation and prevention helps to explain why MI5 developed the organisational structure that it did. Between 1909 and 1918 the organisation developed on these lines. Thus, on the eve of the First World War, MI5 had two branches: one investigative and the other preventive, with a sub-section of the latter being concerned with records. By the end of the war MI5 had six branches, which had all clearly grown out of the investigative and preventive Branches. G Branch handled the investigation of espionage, while F Branch dealt with its prevention. Both were united by their dependence upon records, hence the centrality of H Branch and the rationale behind MI5's *raison d'être* as the central clearing house for all counter-espionage information. A, D and E were preventive branches under Holt-Wilson which grew as off-shoots from F Branch and G Branch. The scale of MI5's wartime expansion clearly reflected the general wartime growth of government.

Beyond these general principles, evolving operational procedures also guided developments alongside the impact of changing threat perceptions. The best example of this is in the evolution of E Branch's work. E Branch's methods and activities developed as it sought to plug gaps in its defences that it learned the Germans had been exploiting. In so doing it learned from these experiences, which in turn informed the evolution of its operational procedures. Thus, in the sense that MI5 picked up its operational procedures as it went along, this process was pragmatic rather than doctrinal. In short, MI5 learned by doing.

In about 350BC, the Chinese warrior-philosopher Sun Tzu penned *The Art of War*, a highly influential treatise on military strategy, which is still taught in military academies and staff colleges around the world today. The final chapter, '*On the Use of Spies*', offers many lessons for espionage and counter-espionage, both for the study of MI5 during the First World War era and MI5 today, and it is worth, in context, quoting at length:

'*A major military operation is a severe drain on the nation, and may be kept up for years in the struggle for one day's victory. So to fail to know the conditions of opponents because of reluctance to give rewards for intelligence is extremely inhumane, uncharacteristic of a true military leader, uncharacteristic of an assistant of the government, uncharacteristic of a victorious chief. So what enables an intelligent government and a wise military leadership to overcome others and achieve extraordinary accomplishments is foreknowledge.*

'*Foreknowledge cannot be gotten from ghosts and spirits, cannot be had by analogy, cannot be found out by calculation. It must be obtained from people, people who know the conditions of the enemy.*

'*There are five kinds of spy: the local spy, the inside spy, the reverse spy, the dead spy, and the living spy. When the five kinds of spies are all active, no one knows their routes – this is called organizational genius, and is valuable to the leadership.*

'*Local spies are hired from among the people of a locality. Inside spies are hired from among enemy officials. Reverse spies are hired from among enemy spies. Dead spies transmit false intelligence to enemy spies. Living spies come back to report…*

'*Therefore, no on in the armed forces is treated as familiarly as are spies, no one is given rewards as rich as those given to spies, and no matter is more secret than espionage…*

'*One cannot use spies without sagacity and knowledge, one cannot use spies without humanity and justice, one cannot get the truth from spies without subtlety. This is a very delicate matter indeed. Spies are useful everywhere…*

'*If an item of intelligence is heard before a spy reports it, then both the spy and the one who told about it die…*

'*Whenever you want to attack an army, besiege a city, or kill a person, first you must know the identities of their defending generals, their associates, their visitors, their gatekeepers, and their chamberlains, so have your spies find out…*

'*You must seek out enemy agents who have come to spy on you, bribe them and induce them to stay with you, so you can use them as reverse spies. By intelligence thus obtained, you can find local spies and inside spies to employ. By intelligence thus obtained, you can cause the misinformation of dead spies to be conveyed to the enemy. By intelligence thus obtained, you can get living spies to work as planned…*

'*It is essential for a leader to know about the five kinds of espionage, and this knowledge depends on reverse spies, so reverse spies must be treated well…*

'*So only a brilliant ruler or a wise general who can use the highly intelligent for espionage is sure of great success. This is essential for military operations, and the armies depend on this in their actions.*'[14]

Sun Tzu believed that foreknowledge was the key to victory and that this could only be obtained by spies. Intelligence was a wise and humane investment that enabled wars to be won as quickly and as cheaply as possible. Therefore, espionage was a top secret matter requiring delicate handling, and successful spies deserved considerable rewards. Gustav Steinhauer and the other officials involved in running the German intelligence effort against the UK clearly lacked this wisdom. If Sun Tzu was going to attack an army, he wanted to first gain intelligence about his enemy, such as the identities of the defending generals. He knew what kinds of intelligence needed to be collected. This implies a process of setting intelligence requirements and then tasking agents to provide the intelligence required. For much of the First World War, the Germans were reduced to simply instructing their agents to get whatever naval or military information out of Britain they could, rather than more specific tasking in the hope of meeting specific requirements. Sun Tzu stressed the importance of only using highly capable people as spies. Although the Germans invested considerable time and resources into training their agents who were to be sent to Britain, they did not seem to take anything like as much care with their recruitment. Most agents were so obviously incompetent and unsuited to intelligence work, that it seems remarkable that they were ever taken on in the first place. If intelligence has already been heard before a spy reports it, then both the spy and the person who provided the information first 'must die'. This suggests a ruthlessness and desire to check the quality of intelligence reports, for accuracy and for deception operations, which the Germans lacked. Even when they berated agents that they were not producing what was required, they continued to persevere with incompetent agents and exhort them that large sums of money were available for reports that met their requirements. Sun Tzu also stressed the importance of recruiting enemy officials as spies. As the Karl Kruger case has shown, they were most likely to have access to sensitive information. Although the German recruitment of American journalists as agents in the second-half of the First World War was a step in the right direction, the Germans never seemed to appreciate that the quality of the agents engaged was more important than the quantity of the agents taken on. Sun Tzu felt that the key to successful espionage was to recruit enemy spies as double agents. Although MI5 only recruited a few double agents during the First World War era, it clearly embraced Sun Tzu's greater point that the key to defeating an enemy's espionage system is to learn about it, and the best way to do this is to induce enemy spies to tell you what they know about the enemy's intelligence system. As MI5 demonstrated with double agent COMO, double agents could help to transmit misinformation to deceive the enemy's intelligence service. Double agents also had the potential to help in the recruitment of well-placed enemy officials as spies, as well as to pick out suitable resident spies. Double agents could also disable the enemy intelligence system from the inside, thereby preventing the enemy from catching one's own agents and thus facilitating the success of one's own spies.

In addition to Sun Tzu's analysis, this research suggests that the interception of communications has arguably been the key weapon in the counter-espionage arsenal since MI5's formation in 1909. It poses much less risk of alerting the target that MI5 has them on its radar, than following them in order to keep them under surveillance, with the risk that the surveillance team will be exposed, or burgling and bugging, with the risk that bugs will be discovered. It is also relatively cheap and does not require many resources, compared with round-the-clock surveillance, or paying agents. For intelligence to be useful, it has to be received by headquarters before it has passed its use-by date. Thus, measures such as delaying all post to certain countries for a certain amount of time were useful and easy to institute preventive measures. Intercepted correspondence enabled MI5 to uncover Steinhauer's whole pre-war espionage network in Britain. Intercepted letters also revealed much about the German intelligence system: its intelligence requirements, methods, and what it had succeeded in collecting. When the time was right, the whole network could be rounded up in one paralyzing blow. Of course, if the pre-war German espionage network in Britain had used two intermediaries per agent (one for incoming and another for outgoing letters), and the wartime system had employed separate cover addresses for each agent to communicate with, then the process of exploiting captures of individual agents to uncover further agents and thus to round up whole groups of agents, would have been much harder.

Thus, MI5 began as a one-man affair. By the end of the First World War it had developed into an effective and necessary arm of the state. Although it was understandably cut back to a skeleton staff of only about thirty by 1920, it had still survived into peacetime as a specialist nucleus ready for expansion on the eve of another war, unlike previous intelligence organisations that had been hastily improvised in time of war and then abolished just as quickly as peace returned. In this sense, MI5 marks the development of counter-espionage as a permanent institution. The years 1909 to 1918 can thus be regarded as the formative years of MI5, as it developed from a small counter-espionage bureau into an established security intelligence agency.

i

Appendix

The Nomenclature and Organisation of MI5

MI5 was formed on 9 October 1909, as the Counter-Espionage Section of the Secret Service Bureau. (Although it has been variously referred to as the Home Section or Military Section of the Secret Service Bureau or as MO(t) in its early years to August 1914, in his official reports, Kell always called his organisation the Counter-Espionage Section of the Secret Service Bureau.)

By October 1913 the Counter-Espionage Section of the Secret Service Bureau had divided into two main branches:

A Branch: 'the investigation of cases of espionage and preparations for mobilisation'.

B Branch: 'aliens registration, the selection of possible suspects and the upkeep of the Special War and other lists, with the "Observer Scheme" and the protection of vulnerable points'.

The first nucleus of the organisation, administration and records branch can be found in a sub-division of B Branch at that time concerned with:

'the translation, filing and custody of intercepted letters[;] the preparation[,] filing and custody of Secretary of State warrants[;] the arrangement and comparison of handwritings and photographic records[;] the scheduling and filing of correspondence and the indexing and carding of information.'

On 4 August 1914 the Counter-Espionage Section of the Secret Service Bureau became known as MO5(g).

On 1 October 1914 MO5(g) was re-organised into three branches; with a third, C, Branch having grown out of the sub-section of B Branch that had been concerned with records:

A Branch: 'investigation of espionage and cases of suspected persons'.

B Branch: 'co-ordination of general policy of Government Departments in dealing with aliens; questions arising out of the Defence of the Realm Regulations and Aliens Restriction Act'.

C Branch: 'records, personnel, administration and port control'.

A fourth branch, later to be labelled E, was formed in May 1915 to take over the fast developing work of organising and administering the control of ports and frontiers.

Following the formation of this new sub-division, it was decided to reorganise MO5(g), so that on 11 August it became known as MO5, with four branches labelled E, F, G and H. The branch concerned with the control of ports and frontiers was designated

E Branch, the preventive (B) branch became known as F Branch, the investigative (A) branch was thenceforth called G Branch, and the administration and records (C) branch acquired the title H Branch.

On 3 January 1916 MO5 changed its name to MI5.

D Branch was added on 21 September 1916 to further the connection of MI5's work overseas.

Lastly, A Branch was formed on 23 April 1917 to deal with work related to the registration and control of aliens employed on war work in the UK.

Thus, the complete organisation of MI5 was:

MI5:	Special Intelligence – General.
A Branch:	Aliens War Service.
D Branch:	Overseas Special Intelligence.
E Branch:	Control of Ports & Frontiers.
F Branch:	Preventive Branch.
G Branch:	Detective Branch.
H Branch:	Administrative Branch (Office & Records).

CHAPTER NOTES

INTRODUCTION

1 'Role and Organisation', www.mi5.gov.uk.
2 'How the Service Does its Work', www.mi5.gov.uk.
3 Ibid.
4 This definition is based upon A. Shulsky, *Silent Warfare: Understanding the World of Intelligence* (Washington DC, USA: Brassey's (US), 1991), p.99.
5 KV1/57, p.7.
6 N. Hiley, 'Counter-Espionage and Security in Great Britain during the First World War', *English Hostorical Review*, Vol.CI (July 1986); N. Hiley, 'The Failure of British Counter-Espionage Against Germany, 1907-1914', *The Historical Journal*, Vol.28, No.4 (1985).
7 C. Andrew, *Secret Service: the Making of the British Intelligence Community* (London: Heinemann, 1985).
8 B. Porter, *Plots and Paranoia: A History of Political Espionage in Britain 1790-1988* (London: Unwin Hyman, 1989); R. Thurlow, *The Secret State: British Internal Security in the Twentieth Century* (Oxford: Blackwell, 1994).
9 J. Bulloch, *M.I.5: The Origin and History of the British Counter-Espionage Service* (London: Arthur Barker, 1963); S. Felstead, *German Spies at Bay* (London: Hutchinson & Co., 1920); L. Sellers, *Shot in the Tower: the Story of the Spies Executed in the Tower of London During the First World War* (Barnsley: Leo Cooper/Pen & Sword Books, 1997); N. West, *MI5: British Security Service operations 1909-1945* (New York, USA: Stein & Day, 1982).
10 Hiley, 'Counter-Espionage and Security in Great Britain during the First World War'; Hiley, 'The Failure of British Counter-Espionage Against Germany, 1907-1914'.
11 B. Thomson, *Queer People* (London: Hodder & Stoughton, 1922), p.194.
12 H. Fitch, *Traitors Within: the Adventures of Detective Inspector Herbert T. Fitch* (London: Hurst & Blackett, 1933), p.104.
13 Felstead, *German Spies at Bay*, p.135.
14 LHCMA, Edmonds MSS, VIII/35, unattributed newspaper article, 'German Espionage During the War'.
15 Bulloch, M.I.5, p.22.
16 S. Rimington, *Open Secret: the Autobiography of the Former Director-General of MI5* (London: Hutchinson, 2001), pp.85-86.

17 D. Cameron Watt, 'Intelligence Studies: the Emergence of the British School', *Intelligence and National Security*, Vol.3, No.2 (April 1988), passim.
18 Andrew, *Secret Service*, passim.
19 Ibid., p.61.
20 Ibid., p.177.
21 Ibid., p.73.
22 Ibid., pp.84-85.
23 Ibid., p.73.
24 Ibid., p.174.
25 Ibid., p.182.
26 C. Andrew, *The Defence of the Realm: the Authorized History of MI5* (London: Allen Lane, 2009), p.52.
27 Ibid., p.52.
28 Ibid., p.52.
29 Ibid., p.52.
30 Ibid., pp.75-76.
31 Ibid., p.76.
32 Hiley, '*The Failure of British Counter-Espionage Against Germany, 1907-1914*', p.857.
33 Ibid., pp.860-861.
34 Hiley, '*Counter-Espionage and Security in Britain during the First World War*', p.660.
35 Ibid., p.661.
36 Porter, *Plots and Paranoia*, passim.
37 Ibid., pp.120-123.
38 Ibid., p.135.
39 Ibid., p.129.
40 Porter, *The Origins of the Vigilant State*, p.173.
41 Thurlow, *The Secret State*, passim.
42 Ibid., pp.45-49 & 66.
43 R. Thurlow, '*The Charm Offensive: the "Coming Out" of MI5*', *Intelligence and National Security*, Vol.15, No.1 (Spring 2000), p.186.
44 Ibid., p.187.
45 T. Boghardt, '*German Naval Intelligence and British Counter-Espionage, 1901-1918*', (D.Phil.: University of Oxford, 2001), pp.164 & 313. Later published as, T. Boghardt, *Spies of the Kaiser: German Covert operations in Great Britain during the First World War Era* (Basingstoke: Palgrave Macmillan, 2004).
46 Boghardt, '*German Naval Intelligence and British Counter-Espionage, 1901-1918*', p.8.
47 Ibid., p.313.
48 Ibid., pp.313-314.
49 Ibid., p.337.
50 Porter, *Plots and Paranoia*, p.120.
51 Ibid., p.129.
52 Ibid., p.133.

[53] Ibid., p.133.

[54] Ibid., pp.133-135.

[55] Thurlow, *The Secret State*, p.41.

[56] Ibid., pp.37-38.

[57] M. Smith, *The Spying Game: The Secret History of British Espionage* (London: Politico's, 2003), p.77.

[58] B. Millman, *Managing Domestic Dissent in First World War Britain* (London: Frank Cass, 2000), passim.

[59] Ibid, p.178.

[60] PRO (ed.), *M.I.5: The First Ten Years, 1909-1919 on CD-Rom* (Kew: PRO, 1998). The PRO (now TNA) has also published an informative booklet to accompany the release of KV1, PRO (ed.), *M.I.5: The First Ten Years, 1909-1919* (Kew: PRO, 1997).

[61] Thurlow, 'The Charm Offensive: the 'Coming Out' of MI5', p.188

[62] Ibid., p.186.

[63] Ibid., p.186.

[64] J. Curry, *The Security Service 1908-1945: the Official History* (Kew: PRO, 1999). Curry's report was in fact written in 1946. The version published by the PRO (now TNA) has an introduction by Christopher Andrew.

[65] Thurlow, '*The Charm Offensive: the "Coming Out" of MI5*', pp.199-189.

[66] Ibid., p.188.

CHAPTER ONE

[1] Andrew, *Secret Service*.

[2] Andrew, *The Defence of the Realm*, p.5.

[3] Ibid., pp5-6.

[4] Ibid., pp.7-8.

[5] M. Smith, *The Spying Game: the Secret History of British Espionage* (London: Politico's, 2003), p.460.

[6] Ibid., pp.57-58.

[7] KV1/8, pp.3-29.

[8] Thurlow, *The Secret State*, pp.37-38.

[9] Ibid., p.39.

[10] Andrew, *Secret Service*, pp.48-49.

[11] Andrew, *The Defence of the Realm*, pp.8-14.

[12] Ibid., pp.10-14 & 25.

[13] A. Green, *Writing the Great War: Sir James Edmonds and the Official Histories 1915-1948* (London: Frank Cass, 2003), passim.

[14] Thurlow, *The Secret State*, p.40.

[15] HD3/131, report by Colonel Davies, 21 November 1905.

[16] WO32/8873, minute by Colonel Gleichen, 3 June 1907.

[17] KV1/1, pp.2-3.

[18] E. Sparrow, *Secret Service: British Agents in France 1792-1815* (Woodbridge: Boydell & Brewer, 1999), passim.

[19] KV1/2, p.6.

[20] Ibid., 18-33.

[21] KV1/4, pp.1-28.

[22] CAB16/8, Terms of Reference, p.2.

[23] Ibid., p.2.

[24] CAB16/8, Report, p.3.

[25] CAB16/8, Appendix I, pp.12-13.

[26] CAB16/8, Report, p.3.

[27] Viscount Esher's diary, cited in Andrew, *Secret Service*, p.56.

[28] CAB16/8, pp.7-8.

[29] Andrew, *The Defence of the Realm*, pp.14-15.

[30] CAB16/8, p.9.

[31] CAB16/232, pp.2-4.

[32] CAB16/8, pp.10-11.

[33] CAB16/8, Appendix II, p.14.

[34] Andrew, *The Defence of the Realm*, p.21.

[35] KV1/3, pp.2-4.

[36] KV1/53, Annexure 2, pp.9-10.

[37] KV1/3, pp.2-4.

[38] KV1/5, letter from Kell to Ewart, p.2.

[39] KV1/59, p.3.; C. Andrew, 'Introduction' in Curry, *The Security Service 1908-1945*, p.6. IWM, Kell MSS, Lady Kell, 'Secret Well Kept: an Account of the Work of Sir Vernon Kell', provides the only biography of her husband.

[40] KV1/5, Kell's CV, pp.3-4.

[41] Andrew, *Secret Service*, p.191.

[42] KV1/5, Kell's CV, pp.3-4.

[43] Andrew, *Secret Service*, p.59.

[44] Bulloch, *M.I.5*, p.18.

[45] Porter, *Plots and Paranoia*, p.127.

[46] Bulloch, *M.I.5*, p.29.

[47] KV1/53, Annexure 2, p.9.

[48] IWM, Kirke MSS, Vol. VII, p.383, Kirke's notes on George Macdonogh, 29 July 1947.

[49] Andrew, *The Defence of the Realm*, p.116.

[50] Andrew, *Secret Service*, p.500.

[51] Sir Austen Chamberlain, cited in Andrew, *Secret Service*, p.500.

[52] Macdonogh, cited in Andrew, *The Defence of the Realm*, p.27.

[53] KV1/9, 2nd progress report, p.9.

[54] Andrew, *The Defence of the Realm*, pp.25-28.

[55] KV1/53, Annexure 2, p.9.

[56] KV1/49, pp.12-13.

[57] Ibid., p.13.

[58] KV1/9, 2nd progress report, p.9.

[59] KV1/9, 1st progress report, pp.2-8.

[60] Andrew, *The Defence of the Realm*, p.31.

[61] KV1/10, p.53.

[62] KV1/59, p.3.

[63] Andrew, *The Defence of the Realm*, p.32.

[64] KV1/39, pp.26-27.

[65] Bulloch, *M.I.5*, p.31.

66 KV1/39, pp.26-27.

67 Andrew, *The Defence of the Realm*, pp.32-33.

68 Ibid., p.870, footnote 26.

69 Ibid.,, p.33.

70 Andrew, *Secret Service*, pp.61-63.

71 KV1/39, pp.26-27.

72 Andrew, *The Defence of the Realm*, p.39.

73 Ibid., pp.32-34.

74 KV1/9, 2nd progress report, pp.9-11.

75 Ibid., pp.11-12.

76 Andrew, *The Defence of the Realm*, p.35.

77 KV1/59, p.3.

78 KV1/9, 3rd progress report, pp.23-24.

79 KV1/10, p.58.

80 Andrew, *The Defence of the Realm*, pp.29-30.

81 Cumming's diary, cited from A. Judd, *The Quest for C: Mansfield Cumming and the Founding of the Secret Service* (London: HarperCollins, 1999), p.174.

82 KV1/49, p.19.

83 KV1/35, pp.58-60.

84 Andrew, *The Defence of the Realm*, p.30.

85 KV1/35, pp.39-40.

86 HO45/10629/199699, folder 1, Return of Alien form, n.d.; HO45/10629/199699, folder 1, Home Office to Kell, expressing the Home Secretary's approval of the proposed from, 1 November 1910.

87 KV1/35, pp.40-43.

88 KV1/49, p.19.

89 HO45/10629/199699, folder 5, Kell to Troup, regarding progress with the unofficial registration of aliens, 11 December 1913.

90 KV1/38, pp.18-19.

91 KV1/39, p.17.

92 KV1/35, pp.49-50.

93 KV1/49, p.10.

94 Ibid., pp.10-11.

95 KV1/63, p.7.

96 KV1/49, pp.20-24.

97 Andrew, *The Defence of the Realm*, pp.48-49.

CHAPTER TWO

1 KV1/39, pp.101-106.

2 KV1/9, 3rd progress report, p.16.

3 KV1/9, 7th progress report, pp.33-34.

4 KV1/9, 8th progress report, pp.69-70.

5 KV1/10, p.75.

6 KV1/59, p.3.

7 Andrew, *The Defence of the Realm*, p.43; KV1/59, p.3.

8 KV1/39, pp.122-142.

9 Andrew, *The Defence of the Realm*, p.38.

10 KV1/39, pp.122-142.

11 Andrew, *The Defence of the Realm*, p.38

12 KV1/39, pp.122-142.

13 Andrew, *The Defence of the Realm*, p.36.

14 KV1/48, pp.32-34.

15 Andrew, *The Defence of the Realm*, p.36.

16 KV1/48, pp.32-34.

17 Andrew, *The Defence of the Realm*, pp.37-38.

18 Andrew, *Secret Service*, pp.60-61.

19 KV1/39, pp.73-75.

20 Boghardt, 'German Naval Intelligence and British Counter-Espionage, 1901-1918', p.227.

21 Ibid., p.248.

22 KV1/39, pp.54-55.

23 KV1/9, Report on Counter Espionage from December, 1911 to 31 July, 1912, pp.49-50.

24 Andrew, *The Defence of the Realm*, p.39.

25 Ibid., p.39.

26 KV1/35, pp.21-38.

27 KV1/9, 6th progress report, p.14.

28 Bulloch, *M.I.5*, p.80.

29 KV1/59, p.3.

30 KV1/39, pp.214-229.

31 KV1/39, pp.109-121.

32 Ibid., pp.152-171 & 181-185.

33 Bulloch, *M.I.5*, p.59.

34 KV1/39, pp.152-171 & 181-185.

35 Bulloch, *M.I.5*, p.39.

36 KV1/39, pp.152-171 & 181-185.

37 KV1/39, pp.190-210.

38 Ibid., pp.202-213.

39 Kell, cited in Andrew, *The Defence of the Realm*, p.49.

40 KV1/40, pp.67-88.

41 KV1/39, pp.81-85.

42 Andrew, *The Defence of the Realm*, pp.38 & 81.

43 KV1/39, pp.145-151.

44 Andrew, *The Defence of the Realm*, p.47.

45 KV1/41, pp.91-162.

46 KV1/40, pp.91-128.

47 Andrew, *The Defence of the Realm*, p.46.

48 KV1/39, pp.86-89.

49 KV1/40, pp.6-18.

50 Ibid., pp.22-55.

51 KV1/39, pp.75-80.

52 KV1/40, pp.191-193.

53 Andrew, *The Defence of the Realm*, p.41.

54 KV1/59, p.3.

55 Lady Kell, 'Secret Well Kept', p.137.

56 Andrew, *The Defence of the Realm*, pp.41-42.

57 Curry, *The Security Service 1908-1945*, p.72; Andrew, *Secret Service*, pp.59-60; KV1/59, p.3; KV1/39, p.39; J.E.E. [Edmonds], 'Brigadier Sir Eric E.B. Holt-Wilson, Kt., C.M.G., D.S.O.' *Royal Engineers Journal*, Vol.LXIV, No.3 (September 1950), pp.343-344.

58 J.E.E., 'Brigadier Sir Eric E.B. Holt-Wilson',
p.344.
59 Lady Kell, 'Secret Well Kept', p.137.
60 Lady Kell, 'Secret Well Kept', p.137; Hiley,
'Counter-Espionage and Security in Great
Britain during the First World War', p.642.
61 Andrew, Secret Service, pp.59-60; Hiley, 'Counter-
Espionage and Security in Great Britain during
the First World War', p.642; J.E.E., 'Brigadier Sir
Eric E.B. Holt-Wilson', p.345.
62 Hiley, 'Counter-Espionage and Security in Great
Britain during the First World War', p.642;
Andrew, Secret Service, pp.59-60.
63 Hiley, 'Counter-Espionage and Security in Great
Britain during the First World War', p.642.
64 KV1/59, p.3.
65 KV1/52, p.69.
66 Sellers, Shot in the Tower, pp.20-21, 57 & 84.
67 KV1/40, pp.241-259.
68 Ibid., pp.210-215.
69 KV1/39, pp.219-228.
70 KV1/37, Appendix C, pp.13-14.
71 KV1/49, pp.18-19.
72 Sellers, Shot in the Tower, p.4.
73 KV1/35, pp.71-72.
74 Ibid., p.16.
75 Ibid., p.19.
76 KV1/46, pp.7-9.
77 KV1/39, pp.9-10; KV1/46, Appendix C, passim.
78 KV1/39, pp.10-11.
79 Ibid., p.11.
80 D. Stafford, Churchill and Secret Service (London:
Abacus, 2000), p.36.
81 KV1/39, pp.11-12.
82 Boghardt, 'German Naval Intelligence and British
Counter-Espionage, 1901-1918', p.6.
83 KV1/39, p.12.
84 Ibid., pp.12-13.
85 Ibid., pp.13-14.
86 KV1/46, Appendix A, p.10.
87 KV1/39, pp.14-15.
88 Ibid., pp.15-16.
89 Ibid., p.16.
90 Ibid., pp.16-17.
91 KV1/19, p.4.
92 HO45/10629/199699, folder 4, R. Muirhead
Collins (Australian High Commission) to Under-
Secretary of State at the Colonial Office,
11 February 1913; KV1/15, p.32.
93 Material discovered by the Kenya historian Dr
Anthony Clayton in a Colonial Office 533 series
file in TNA.
94 Andrew, The Defence of the Realm, p.875;
KV4/112, Von Weller.

95 KV1/39, pp.90-92.
96 Ibid., pp.235-238.
97 KV1/41, pp.32-40.
98 KV1/41, pp.19-31.
99 Ibid., pp.63-67.
100 KV1/59, p.3; KV1/49, pp.19 & 25.
101 Andrew, The Defence of the Realm, p.59.
102 Bulloch, M.I.5, p.20.
103 KV1/41, pp.6-18.
104 KV1/39, pp.93-95.
105 KV1/41, pp.185-190.
106 Ibid., pp.169-173.
107 Andrew, The Defence of the Realm, p.874.
108 KV4/112, Bernstein.
109 Andrew, The Defence of the Realm, p.875.
110 KV1/59, p.4.
111 R. Allason, The Branch: a History of the
Metropolitan Police Special Branch 1883-1983
(London: Secker & Warburg, 1983), p.89.
112 KV1/59, pp.3-4.
113 C. McKay & B. Beckman, Swedish Signal
Intelligence 1900-1945 (London: Frank Cass,
2003), pp.49 & 63. These documents were
published in Germany after the war as Graf
Benckendorffs Diplomatischer Schriftwechsel
herausgeben von B. von Siebert, Band I-III (Berlin &
Leipzig, Germany, 1928).

CHAPTER THREE

1 KV1/35, pp.51-57.
2 Andrew, The Defence of the Realm, p.50.
3 KV1/35, pp.51-57.
3 Andrew, The Defence of the Realm, p.50
4 Ibid., pp.50-51.
5 KV1/35, pp.51-52.
6 A. von Kluck, The March on Paris and the Battle of the
Marne 1914 (London: Edward Arnold, 1920),
pp.10-45. A translated and edited version of von
Kluck's Der Marsch auf Paris, und die Marneschlacht
(Berlin, Germany: Mittler, n.d.) published under
the auspices of the Committee of Imperial
Defence.
7 IWM, Kell MSS, E. Holt-Wilson, 'Security
Intelligence in War', p.17.
8 LHCMA, Edmonds MSS, III/5, 'Memoirs',
Chapter XX, p.3.
9 Bulloch, M.I.5, p.70.
10 D. French, 'Spy Fever in Britain, 1900-1915', The
Historical Journal, Vol.21, No.2 (1978), pp.364-365.
11 Andrew, The Defence of the Realm, p.51.
12 Ibid., pp.51-52.
13 WO32/10776, p.21.
14 See G. Cockerill, What Fools We Were (London:
Hutchinson & Co., 1944), pp.39-42.

[15] Felstead, *German Spies at Bay*, p.16.

[16] WO32/10776, p.14.

[17] INF4/9, p.38.

[18] WO32/10776, pp.24, 26 & 29.

[19] INF4/9, p.41.

[20] KV1/35, pp.78-84.

[21] Ibid., pp.165-197.

[22] Ibid.,, p.53.

[23] Thurlow, *The Secret State*, pp.30-31.

[24] HO45/10881/338498, folder 13, letter from B.B. Cubitt (War Office) to Home Office, 24 October 1917.

[25] Ibid., memorandum by J.F. Moylan, 10 November 1917.

[26] Andrew, *Secret Service*, p.182.

[27] Thurlow, *The Secret State*, pp.30-31.

[28] R. Popplewell, *Intelligence and Imperial Defence: British Intelligence and the Defence of the Indian Empire 1904-1924* (London: Frank Cass, 1995), p.219.

[29] N. West, *MI5: British Security Service operations 1909-1945* (New York, USA: Stein & Day, 1982), pp.16-17.

[30] LHCMA, Edmonds MSS, II/1/65a, Holt-Wilson to Edmonds, 17 July 1942.

[31] Cockerill, *What Fools We Were*, p.41.

[32] Lady Kell, 'Secret Well Kept', pp.111 & 114.

[33] A. Judd, *The Quest for C: Mansfield Cumming and the Founding of the Secret Service* (London: HarperCollins, 1999), pp.94-97.

[34] KV1/35., pp.78-88.

[35] Ibid., p.147.

[36] KV1/38, pp.69-70.

[37] Ibid., pp.71-72.

[38] KV1/35, pp.177-178.

[39] Ibid., p.178.

[40] Ibid., pp174-175.

[41] Ibid., pp.175-176.

[42] KV1/36, pp.41-42.

[43] Ibid., pp.42-60.

[44] Hiley, 'Counter-Espionage and Security in Great Britain during the First World War', p.669.

[45] D. Englander, 'Military Intelligence and the Defence of the Realm: the Surveillance of Soldiers and civilians during the First World War', *Bulletin of the Society for the Study of Labour History*, Vol.52, No.1 (1987), p.25.

[46] KV1/35, p.149.

[47] Ibid., pp.149-150.

[48] Ibid., pp.157-164.

[49] KV1/346, pp.7-37.

[50] Ibid., pp.179-187.

[51] Ibid., pp.61-69.

[52] Ibid., pp.75-93.

[53] KV1/35, pp.33-144.

[54] Ibid., pp.18-19.

[55] Hinchley Cooke had been schooled in Dresden and at Leipzig University, and in early 1914 was working as a clerk at the British legation in Dresden, but on the outbreak of war was expelled to Britain with the rest of the legation staff. Recommended by the former British Consul at Dresden, Hinchley Cooke joined MI5 on 21 August 1914. He went on to become one of only a few MI5 officers to serve in both world wars. He spoke fluent German and sometimes posed as a German officer to obtain intelligence from German POWs.

[56] Andrew, *The Defence of the Realm*, pp.80-81.

[57] Ibid., pp.80-81.

[58] Ibid., p.53.

[59] Ibid., p.53.

[60] Andrew, *Secret Service*, pp.177-182.

[61] Sir B. Thomson, *Queer People* (London: Hodder & Stoughton, 1922), pp.36-37.

[62] Ibid.,, p.39.

[63] J Charteris, *At GHQ* (London: Cassell, 1931), p.43.

[64] 'Spy Organization in England. Germany's Wasted Efforts. Home Office Statement of Precautions. Espionage Punishable by Death', *The Times*, 9 October 1914, p.3.

[65] Bulloch, *M.I.5*, pp.87-93.

[66] See for example, *Parliamentary Debates, Commons*, 9 September 1914, cols. 563-567; *Parliamentary Debates, Commons*, 18 November 1914, cols. 412-413; *Parliamentary Debates, Commons*, 26 November 1914, cols. 1399-1402. See also, W. Le Queux, *German Spies in England: an Exposure* (London: Stanley Paul & Co., 1915) as an example of popular criticism; also critical of the government, rather than MO5(g).

[67] KV1/41, pp.163-167.

[68] KV1/39, pp.15-16.

[69] B. Thomson, *The Story of Scotland Yard* (London: Grayson & Grayson, 1935), p.212.

[70] Bulloch, *M.I.5*, p.52.

[71] KV1/42, pp.30-33.

[72] Felstead, *German Spies at Bay*, p.29.

[73] Ibid., pp.30-33.

[74] KV1/42, pp.30-33.

[75] Sellers, *Shot in the Tower*, pp.30-31.

[76] Ibid., pp.17-19.

[77] KV1/42, pp.30-33.

[78] Sellers, *Shot in the Tower*, pp.38-39.

[79] Lody quoted from Andrew, *The Defence of the Realm*, p.65.

[80] Lody quoted from Sellers, *Shot in the Tower*, p.41.

[81] Felstead, *German Spies at Bay*, p.25.

[82] Lady Kell is quoted in Andrew, *The Defence of the Realm*, p.65.

[83] Thomson, *Queer People*, p.122.

[84] KV1/42, pp.30-33.

[85] Sellers, *Shot in the Tower*, pp.ix-x.

[86] Andrew, *The Defence of the Realm*, p.65.

[87] KV1/42, pp.30-33.

[88] Andrew, *The Defence of the Realm*, p.65.

[89] KV1/20, p.23.

[90] J. Bird, *The Control of Enemy Alien Civilians in Great Britain 1914-18* (New York, USA: Garland Publishing, 1986), p.263.

[91] KV1/20, pp.23-24.

[92] Ibid., p.24.

[93] Felstead, *German Spies at Bay*, p.11.

[94] KV1/20, p.24.

[95] Ibid., pp.24-25.

[96] KV1/49, p.9.

[97] Ibid., pp.30-31.

[98] KV1/20, p.13; KV1/52, p.4.

[99] HO162/28, p.10, Home Office to Under-Secretary of State at the Foreign Office, 1 September 1914.

[100] KV1/20, p.25.

[101] Ibid., p.26.

[102] KV1/13, p.31.

[103] HO45/10737/261921, folder 172, B.B. Cubitt (War Office) to Under-Secretary of State at the Home Office, regarding the security problems posed by Belgian refugees, 18 November 1914.

[104] Sellers, *Shot in the Tower*, p.12.

[105] KV1/13, p.31.

[106] Ibid., p.32.

[107] Ibid., pp.32-33.

[108] Ibid., pp31-32; KV1/14, p.6.

[109] KV1/13, p.33. An analysis of these developments is forced to rely heavily on MI5 and Home Office records. The available material from the Ministry of Munitions regarding this subject is notably disappointing. Indeed, the three most relevant sounding reports catalogued by TNA are described as 'wanting' (lost prior to transfer to TNA): 'Report and Notes on Alien Labour, September 1915' (MUN5/78/327/1), 'Report of Committee Appointed to Consider Reception and Employment of Belgian Refugees, December 1914' (MUN5/78/327/3), and 'Memorandum on Conditions for Aliens Employed on Munitions Work', which is undated (MUN5/78/327/8).

[110] KV1/19, p.4.

[111] Ibid., pp4-5.

[112] The Kaiser is quoted in H. Strachan, *The First World War, Volume 1: to Arms* (Oxford: OUP, 2001), pp.696-697.

[113] M. Foy & B. Barton, *The Easter Rising* (Stroud: Sutton, 1999), pp.41-45.

[114] Andrew, *The Defence of the Realm*, pp.86-87.

[115] KV1/49, p.9.

[116] KV1/59, pp.3-4.

[117] KV1/49, p.13.

[118] Ibid., pp.26-27.

[119] Ibid., pp.51-52.

[120] Ibid., p.52.

[121] Ibid., p.52.

[122] Ibid., p.53.

[123] Ibid., p.72.

[124] Ibid., pp.72-73.

[125] Ibid., p.74; KV1/52, p.3.

[126] Ibid., pp.74-75.

[127] Ibid., p.75.

[128] KV1/36, pp.102-104.

[129] Ibid., pp.135-136.

[130] Ibid., pp.160-161.

[131] Ibid., p.161.

[132] Ibid., p.161.

[133] KV1/35, pp.76-77.

[134] ADM1/8429/221, GOC Southern Command to War Office, 6 August 1915.

[135] Ibid., War Office to Admiralty, 20 September 1915.

[136] KV1/35, pp.78-84.

[137] Ibid., p.14.

[138] Ibid., pp.15-16.

[139] Ibid., pp.93-98.

[140] Ibid., pp.88-92.

[141] Andrew, *Secret Service*, p.181.

[142] Felstead, *German Spies at Bay*, p.18.

[143] Holt-Wilson, 'Security Intelligence in War', p.26.

[144] G. Aston, *Secret Service* (London: Faber & Faber, 1939), p.62.

[145] Bulloch, *M.I.5*, pp.92-93 & 184.

[146] Andrew, *The Defence of the Realm*, p.77.

[147] Sir E. Troup, *The Home Office* (London: G.P. Putnam's Sons ltd., 1925), p.241.

[148] Lord Hankey, *The Supreme Command, 1914-1918, Vol.1* (London: George Allen & Unwin), pp.220-221.

[149] Andrew, *The Defence of the Realm*, p.85.

[150] KV1/39, pp.13-14.

[151] Ibid., p.14.

[152] Felstead, *German Spies at Bay*, pp.159-163.

[153] KV1/42, pp.8-9.

[154] Ibid., pp.39-40.

[155] Ibid., pp.35-38.

[156] Ibid., p.38.

[157] Ibid., pp.43-44.

[158] Ibid., pp.44-45.

[159] KV1/43, pp.6-9.

[160] Sellers, *Shot in the Tower*, p.88.

[161] Ibid., pp.6-9.

[162] Ibid., p.9.

[163] Curry, *The Security Service 1908-1945*, p.74.

[164] KV1/42, p.60.

[165] KV1/43, pp.10-11.

[166] KV1/44, p.6.

[167] Ibid., pp.6-7.

[168] KV1/46, Appendix F, pp.62-63.

[169] KV1/44, pp.7-8.

[170] Ibid., pp.113-118.

[171] Ibid., pp.113-116.

[172] Ibid., pp.116-118.

[173] KV1/46, Appendix F, pp.66-67.

[174] Bulloch, *M.I.5*, pp.122-132.

[175] Boghardt, 'German Naval Intelligence and British Counter-Espionage, 1901-1918', pp.242-243.

[176] KV1/49, p.23.

[177] Ibid., p.23.

[178] Ibid., p.24.

[179] Ibid., p.25.

[180] Hiley, 'Counter-Espionage and Security in Great Britain during the First World War', p.649; INF4/9, p.43.

[181] KV1/49, p.55.

[182] Ibid., pp.55-56.

[183] KV1/61, p.62.

[184] KV1/49, p.56.

[185] Ibid., p.57.

[186] Ibid., p.58.

[187] KV1/43, pp.101-102.

[188] Ibid., pp.102-105.

[189] KV1/49, p.40.

[190] Ibid., p.40.

[191] Ibid., p.41.

[192] R. Jones, *Most Secret War* (London: Wordsworth Editions Ltd., 1998), p.4.

[193] KV1/49, pp.41-42.

[194] Ibid., pp.34-35.

[195] West, *MI5*, p.36.

[196] KV1/54, pp.6 & 8.

[197] KV1/49, pp.35-36.

[198] Ibid., p.36.

[199] KV1/50, p.56.

[200] KV1/49, p.36.

[201] Ibid., pp.36-37.

[202] Ibid., p.37.

[203] Ibid., pp.37-38.

[204] Ibid., p.26.

[205] Ibid., p.28.

[206] Ibid., pp.28-30.

[207] KV1/52, pp.6-8.

[208] Andrew, *Secret Service*, p.59; KV1/59, p.4; Lady Kell, 'Secret Well Kept', p.110.

[209] KV1/52, p.8.

[210] KV1/49, pp.32-33.

[211] KV1/63, p.15.

[212] KV1/49, p.32.

[213] KV1/52, pp.24-25.

[214] Ibid., pp.21-23.

[215] Ibid., p.43.

[216] KV1/49, pp.33-34.

[217] Ibid., p.34.

[218] Ibid., pp.43-44.

[219] Ibid., pp.44-46.

[220] Ibid., pp46-48.

[221] Ibid., p.60.

[222] Ibid., p.60.

[223] Ibid., p.60.

[224] Ibid., p.61.

[225] Ibid., p.48.

[226] Ibid., pp.48-49.

[227] Ibid., pp.49-50.

[228] KV1/52, pp.46-50.

[229] KV1/49, pp.63-64.

[230] Ibid., pp.64-66.

[231] Ibid., p.66.

[232] Ibid., pp.66-67.

[233] KV1/52, pp.59-64.

[234] KV1/49, pp. 72-74.

[235] Ibid., p.75.

[236] Ibid., p.75.

[237] Ibid., p.75.

[238] Ibid., pp.75-76.

[239] Ibid., p.76.

[240] Ibid., p.88.

[241] KV1/50, pp.57-58.

[242] KV1/49, pp.84-85.

[243] Ibid., pp.90-92.

[244] Thurlow, *The Secret State*, p.42.

[245] Sir G. Macdonogh, 'Military Intelligence and Incidents Connected Therewith During the War', *The Journal of the Royal Artillery*, Vol.XLVIII, No.10 (1921/22), p.404.

[246] A. Black & R. Brunt, 'MI5, 1909-1945: an information management perspective', *Journal of Information Science*, Vol.26, No.3 (2000), p.185.

[247] KV1/42, p.10.

CHAPTER FOUR

[1] KV1/20, p.26

[2] WO32/4892, Field Marshal Sir John French to Secretary, War Office, 24 December 1914.

[3] KV1/20, pp.26-27.

[4] Ibid., p.27.

[5] Ibid., p.27.

[6] Ibid., pp.27-28.

[7] Ibid., p.28.

[8] HO45/10774/276355, folder 229, '*Report on the Organization & Working of the Home Office Permit Offices for the Control of Passenger Traffic from Great Britain during the War*', Appendix 15, Table 6: Summary, n.d.

[9]   KV1/42, pp.55-57.
[10] Ibid., p.29.
[11] Ibid., pp.30-31.
[12] Ibid., p.31.
[13] Ibid., p.32.
[14] Ibid., pp.46-47.
[15] Ibid., p.47.
[16] KV1/41, pp.81-182.
[17] Andrew, *The Defence of the Realm*, p.66.
[18] KV1/42, pp.59-62 & 68.
[19] Thomson, *Queer People*, pp.128-129.
[20] KV1/42, pp.61-69.
[21] Thomson, *Queer People*, p.132.
[22] Sellers, *Shot in the Tower*, p.56.
[23] Ibid., p.159.
[24] Ibid., pp.61-69.
[25] Ibid., pp.46-51.
[26] Andrew, *The Defence of the Realm*, pp.68-70.
[27] Aston, *Secret Service*, p.104.
[28] LHCMA, Edmonds MSS, VIII/35, newspaper cutting, '*Anecdotes of Intelligence*', n.d.
[29] KV1/42, pp.118-121.
[30] Sellers, *Shot in the Tower*, pp.80-81.
[31] KV1/42, p.121.
[32] WO71/1237, A. Bodkin's opening for the prosecution, 20 August 1915, pp.5-6.
[33] Boghardt, *Spies of the Kaiser*, pp.80-88.
[34] KV1/42, pp.52-55.
[35] Ibid., pp.70-74.
[36] Ibid., pp.60-68.
[37] Andrew, *The Defence of the Realm*, pp.72-74.
[38] Boghardt, *Spies of the Kaiser*, pp.85-88.
[39] Sellers, *Shot in the Tower*, p.106.
[40] KV1/42, pp.87-92.
[41] Thomson, *Queer People*, p.141.
[42] Ibid., p.38.
[43] KV1/35, p.69.
[44] WO32/10776, p.21.
[45] Andrew, *Secret Service*, p.256; HO45/10779/277334, Kell to Dixon, 10 September 1915.
[46] KV1/43, pp.199-210.
[47] KV1/20, p.13.
[48] Ibid., p.13.
[49] Ibid., pp.14-15.
[50] Ibid., pp.42-44.
[51] Ibid., pp.15-16.
[52] Ibid., pp.19-20.
[53] Nicolai, *The German Secret Service*, p.197.
[54] KV1/20, p.19.
[55] KV1/34, p.42.
[56] Felstead, *German Spies at Bay*, p.137.
[57] KV1/34, p.42.
[58] Ibid., p.46.
[59] Ibid., p.48.
[60] KV1/20, p.30.
[61] See Read & Fisher, *Colonel Z*, a biography of Dansey.
[62] KV1/59, p.4.
[63] Andrew, *Secret Service*, p.357; KV1/59, p.4.
[64] Andrew, *Secret Service*, p.357.
[65] KV1/52, pp.9-10.
[66] MUN4/3588, circular letter from MI5E, 6 December 1917.
[67] KV1/20, p.32.
[68] Ibid., pp.32-33.
[69] Ibid., p.33.
[70] Felstead, *German Spies at Bay*, p.19.
[71] KV1/20, p.47.
[72] HO45/10727/254753, folder 98, letter, and accompanying copy of circular to port officers, from Dansey to Haldane Porter (Home Office), 16 August 1915.
[73] KV1/20, pp.47-48.
[74] KV1/34, p.28.
[75] Ibid., p.38.
[76] KV1/20, p.36.
[77] Ibid., pp.37-38.
[78] KV1/34, p.32.
[79] Ibid., p.32.
[80] KV1/20, pp.38-39.
[81] Ibid., p.39.
[82] Hiley, '*Counter-espionage and Security in Great Britain during the First World War*', p.667.
[83] KV1/20, p.48.
[84] Ibid., pp.48-49.
[85] Ibid., p.49.
[86] KV1/52, p.21.
[87] KV1/59, p.5; KV1/13, pp.44-45.
[88] KV1/52, p.35.
[89] KV1/20, p.22.
[90] KV1/52, pp.43-44.
[91] Ibid., p.46.
[92] KV1/20, pp.16-17.
[93] See KV1/27, regarding illegal methods of obtaining passports.
[94] KV1/43, pp.83-84.
[95] Bird, *The Control of Enemy Alien Civilians in Great Britain 1914-18*, p.279.
[96] Felstead, *German Spies at Bay*, pp.11-12.
[97] KV4/129, Kell to Pedder, 14 November 1918.
[98] Ibid., Pedder to Kell, 16 November 1918.
[99] KV1/42, pp.110-114.
[100] WO141/1/5, MO5 circular letter, 4 May 1915.
[101] Thomson, *Queer People*, p.148.
[102] KV1/42, pp.110-114.
[103] Felstead, *German Spies at Bay*, p.57.
[104] Andrew, *The Defence of the Realm*, p.71.

105 Ibid., p.70.

106 KV1/43, p.34.

107 Andrew, *The Defence of the Realm*, pp.70-71.

108 KV1/73, pp.27-45.

109 KV1/73, pp.27-45.

110 Ibid., pp.27-45.

111 ADM131/120, report on Abdon Jappe by Major W.P. Drury (Intelligence Office, Plymouth Garrison), 10 June 1915.

112 KV1/42, pp.130-131.

113 Sellers, *Shot in the Tower*, pp.65-66.

114 Thomson, *Queer People*, pp.136-137.

115 KV1/42, pp.74-79.

116 Thomson, *Queer People*, pp.136-137.

117 KV1/42, pp.74-79.

118 Sellers, *Shot in the Tower*, pp.76 & 78.

119 KV1/42, pp.74-79.

120 Sellers, *Shot in the Tower*, pp.118-119.

121 KV1/42, pp.79-87.

122 Sellers, *Shot in the Tower*, pp.121-122.

123 KV1/42, pp.79-87.

124 Sellers, *Shot in the Tower*, p.121.

125 KV1/42, pp.79-87.

126 Sellers, *Shot in the Tower*, pp.138-139.

127 Ibid., pp.96-99.

128 Thomson, *Queer People*, p.149.

129 KV1/42, pp.96-99.

130 Sellers, *Shot in the Tower*, p.96.

131 KV1/42, pp.92-96.

132 Ibid., pp.105-107.

133 Ibid., pp.115-117.

134 Thomson, *Queer People*, pp.171-172.

135 IKV1/42, pp.115-117.

136 Ibid., pp.162-163.

137 Ibid., pp.163-165.

138 Ibid., pp121-126.

139 Sellers, *Shot in the Tower*, pp.160-161.

140 KV1/42, pp121-126.

141 Thomson, *Queer People*, pp.160-161.

142 KV1/42, pp121-126.

143 Ibid., pp.99-101.

144 KV1/43, pp.78-83.

145 KV1/19, pp.18-19.

146 Beckett, *The Great War 1914-1918*, p.222.

147 KV1/19, p.19.

148 KV1/43, pp.43-45.

149 KV1/15, p.63.

150 Ibid., p.6.

151 Ibid., pp.9-10.

152 KV1/19, pp.5-6 & 15; KV1/15, p.6.

153 CO694/28, Colonial Office's register of secret correspondence, 1914-1927.

154 KV1/19, p.15.

155 CO533/151, telegram Belfield to the Colonial Office, 22 January 1915.

156 Ibid., pp.21-22.

157 Ibid., pp.16-17.

158 CO854/168, circular letter and accompanying memorandum regarding counter-espionage, from the Colonial Office to Colonial Governors, 18 August 1915.

159 KV1/19, p.17.

160 CO616/63, p.221, letter regarding suspected spy Robert E. Whelan, from Kell to Under-Secretary of State at the Colonial Office, 19 February 1916.

161 Ibid., p.223, letter concerning Whelan, from the Colonial Office to Hall, 23 February 1916.

162 Ibid., p.225, letter about Whelan, from Hall to Tait (Colonial Office), 25 February 1916.

163 KV1/19, pp.17-18.

164 Ibid., p.6.

165 KV1/15, pp.53-54.

166 Ibid., p.7.

167 KV1/16, Appendix B, Covering letter.

168 KV1/16, Appendix B, Memorandum.

169 KV1/16, Appendix A, pp.4-11.

170 KV1/42, pp.132-133.

171 Ibid., pp.101-105.

172 Thomson, *Queer People*, pp.155-156.

173 KV1/42, pp101-105.

174 KV1/43, pp.86-93.

175 Ibid., pp.86-93.

176 Smith, *The Spying Game*, p.74.

177 Aston, *Secret Service*, p.153.

178 KV1/43, pp.6-9.

179 Ibid., pp.76-94.

180 Ibid., pp.62-64.

181 Andrew, *The Defence of the Realm*, pp.95-97.

182 KV1/43, pp.16-18.

183 Andrew, *The Defence of the Realm*, pp.95-97.

184 Ibid., pp.91-92.

185 KV1/43, pp.67-68.

186 KV1/42, p.130.

187 Bulloch, *M.I.5*, pp.89-91.

188 Ibid., p.90.

189 KV1/43, pp.118-126.

190 KV1/36, pp.129-131.

191 Ibid., pp.106-108.

192 Ibid., pp.104-112.

193 Ibid., p.113.

194 Ibid., p.113.

195 Ibid., pp.113-117.

196 KV1/42, p.40.

197 KV1/43, p.70.

CHAPTER FIVE

1 WO32/10776, p.21.

2 KV1/43, pp.181-190.

3 Ibid., pp.199-210.

4   Ibid,, pp.108-117.

5   DPP1/45, Major J. Hall-Dallwood (Chief Constable of Sheffield Police), to DPP, 28 March 1916.

6   DPP1/45, Clegg & Sons (Bright's solicitors) to DPP, 5 May 1916.

7   DPP1/45, Carter to Sir Charles Matthews (DPP), 11 May 1916.

8   Andrew, *The Defence of the Realm*, p.87.

9   KV4/113, defence security case no.66.

10   R. Doerries (ed.), *Prelude to the Easter Rising: Sir Roger Casement in Imperial Germany* (London: Frank Cass, 2000), pp.1-25.

11   Thomson, *Queer People*, pp.84-85.

12   Doerries (ed.), *Prelude to the Easter Rising*, pp.1-25.

13   KV4/113, defence security case no.66.

14   Andrew, *Secret Service*, pp.114-115 & 247-249.

15   KV1/43, pp.127-136.

16   Andrew, *The Defence of the Realm*, pp.72-73.

17   KV1/43, pp.139-140.

18   Ibid., pp.141-154.

19   Ibid., pp.141-154.

20   Ibid., pp.155-174.

21   Ibid,, pp.188-189.

22   Andrew, *The Defence of the Realm*, pp.74-75.

23   KV1/43, pp.174-179.

24   KV1/44, pp.137-148.

25   Hiley, *Counter-Espionage and Security in Great Britain during the First World War*, p.667.

26   KV1/35, p.69.

27   KV1/49, p.50.

28   KV1/53, Appendix 17, pp.86-88.

29   KV1/52, p.46; KV1/59, p.4.

30   Andrew, *The Defence of the Realm*, p.87.

31   KV1/52, pp.2-3.

32   Andrew, *The Defence of the Realm*, p.87.

33   Y. Sheffy, 'British Intelligence and the Middle East, 1900-1918: How Much Do We Know?', *Intelligence and National Security*, Vol.17, No.1 (Spring 2002), p.45.

34   KV1/19, pp.6-7.

35   KV1/15, pp.91-93.

36   KV1/19, p.5.

37   KV1/52, p.21.

38   KV1/19, p.7.

39   Ibid., p.8.

40   KV2/515, MI5 report on intercepted letter from Ginnell to de Valera, 29 August 1918.

41   KV1/19, p.8.

42   Ibid., pp.8-10.

43   Ibid., p.10.

44   Ibid., pp.10-11.

45   KV1/19, pp.20-21; KV1/15, p.19.

46   KV1/19, pp.4 & 11-12.

47   Ibid., pp.12-13.

48   Ibid., pp.14-15.

49   KV1/52, p.60; KV1/59, p.7.

50   KV1/52, p.51.

51   KV1/19, pp.19-20.

52   INF4/9, p.41.

53   KV1/19, p.20.

54   KV1/15, pp.70-72 & 80.

55   KV1/19, p.20.

56   CO854/169, circular letter, and accompanying memorandum concerning the activities of German agents in the UK by Drake, from Andrew Bonar Law to Colonial Governors, 8 January 1916.

57   CO418/166, pp.45-51, letter and accompanying reports regarding an investigation into the bona fides of Miss E.L.C.D. Rundle, from MI5 to Under-Secretary of State at the Colonial Office, 12 April 1917.

58   KV1/19, p.13.

59   CO418/170, pp.108-111, letter forwarding a letter from the native king of the Loyalty Islands, regarding a suspected German spy, 10 August 1918.

60   KV1/15, pp.347-38; CO418/170, pp.138-142, letter regarding the internment of seven members of the Irish Republican Brotherhood, from the Governor-General of Australia to the Secretary of State for the Colonies, 29 August 1918.

61   IWM, Kell MSS, Holt-Wilson, 'Security Intelligence in War', p.12.

62   N. West, *A Matter of Trust: MI5 1945-72* (London: Weidenfeld & Nicolson, 1982), pp.13 & 19.

63   Andrew, *The Defence of the Realm*, pp.65-66.

64   HO45/10741/263275, F.B. Booth, MO5(g), memorandum for Kell, 27 July 1915.

65   Andrew, *The Defence of the Realm*, pp.85-86.

66   Boghardt, *Spies of the Kaiser*, pp.117-118.

67   Andrew, *The Defence of the Realm*, p.86.

68   Ibid., p.94.

69   Thomson, *Queer People*, p.266.

70   Andrew, *The Defence of the Realm*, p.94.

71   Ibid., p.95.

72   KV1/43, pp.62-64.

73   Andrew, *The Defence of the Realm*, pp.95-96.

74   Addison, cited in Andrew, *The Defence of the Realm*, p.96.

75   KV1/13, pp.33-34.

76   KV1/13, Appendix B, p.87.

77   MUN5/49/300/34, 'Commission of Enquiry into Industrial unrest: Summary of the Reports' by the Right Hon. G.N. Barnes, M.P., 17 July 1917, pp.4-7.

78 Andrew, *Secret Service*, p.60; Hiley, *Counter-Espionage and Security in Great Britain during the First World War*, pp.635–636.

79 Andrew, *Secret Service*, p.283.

80 Thomson, *Queer People*, p.47.

81 Porter, *The Origins of the Vigilant State*, p.179.

82 Thomson, *The Scene Changes*, p.227.

83 Andrew, *Secret Service*, p.191.

84 CCAC, Hall MSS, Drake to Hall, 1 November 1932.

85 Holt-Wilson, *Security Intelligence in War*, p.10.

86 KV1/36, pp.147–151; KV1/43, p.213.

87 KV1/36, pp.147–151; KV1/43, p.213.

88 S. Oldfield, *International Woman Suffrage: November 1914-September 1916* (London: Taylor & Francis, 2003), passim.

89 See Andrew, *The Defence of the Realm*.

90 See Matthew Stibbe, *British Civilian Internees in Germany: the Ruhleben Camp, 1914-18* (Manchester: Manchester University Press, 2008).

91 KV1/36, pp.128–131.

92 Ibid., pp.128–131.

93 KV1/38, pp.128–131.

94 Ibid., pp.128–131.

95 Ibid., pp.128–131.

96 Ibid., pp.128–131.

97 Ibid., pp.128–131.

98 KV1/36, pp.151–154.

99 Ibid., pp.151–154.

100 KV1/43, pp.72–73.

101 KV1/44, p.12.

CHAPTER SIX

1 KV1/20, p.40.

2 Ibid., pp.40–41.

3 Ibid., p.38.

4 KV1/34, p.19.

5 KV1/20, p.45.

6 Ibid., pp.45–46.

7 Ibid., p.50.

8 Ibid., pp.50–51.

9 KV1/28, Appendix N, pp.151–157.

10 KV1/20, p.51.

11 Ibid., pp.51–52.

12 Ibid., p.41.

13 Ibid., p.52.

14 Ibid., pp.52–53.

15 KV1/34, p.67.

16 Ibid., pp.68–69.

17 Ibid., p.71.

18 Ibid., pp.72–73.

19 Andrew, *The Defence of the Realm*, pp.78–79.

20 KV4/113, defence security case no.71.

21 KV1/44, pp.6–8.

22 WO32/10776, p.22.

23 KV1/44, pp.6–8.

24 Hiley, 'Counter-Espionage and Security in Great Britain during the First World War', p.667.

25 Andrew, *The Defence of the Realm*, p.98.

26 A. Read & D. Fisher, *Colonel Z: the Secret Life of a Master of Spies* (London: Hodder & Stoughton, 1984), pp.98–99.

27 KV1/49, p.56.

28 KV1/35, pp.69–70.

29 Ibid., p.70.

30 KV1/68, p.69.

31 Hiley, 'Counter-Espionage and Security in Great Britain during the First World War', p.667.

32 KV1/19, pp.13–14; Popplewell, *Intelligence and Imperial Defence*, pp.248–251.

33 KV1/44, pp.82–90.

34 Ibid., pp.20–21.

35 Ibid., pp.55–66.

36 Thomson, *Queer People*, pp.161–162.

37 KV1/44, pp.55–66.

38 Thomson, *Queer People*, p.173.

39 KV1/44, pp.67–72.

40 Ibid., pp.73–81.

41 KV1/36, pp.155–156.

42 Ibid., pp.164–169.

43 HO45/10882/343995, folder 1, Kell to Pedder (Home Office), suggesting that it might be safe to soften the ARO in the particular case of women of British birth who have become by marriage subjects of Britain's allies, 10 July 1917.

44 KV1/36, p.169.

45 Ibid., pp.172–179.

46 Ibid., pp.172–179.

47 Ibid., pp.172–179.

48 KV1/44, pp.110–111.

49 Ibid., pp.92–94.

50 Andrew, *Defence of the Realm*, pp.96–97.

51 HO45/10809/311425, folder 39, Home Office circular to chief constables, 18 May 1917.

52 Smith, *The Spying Game*, p.77.

53 KV1/13, Appendix C, p.89.

54 KV1/59, p.5.

55 KV1/52, pp.3, 11, 59 & 66.

56 KV1/13, Appendix C, pp.92–93.

57 Andrew, *Secret Service*, pp.195–196.

58 KV1/13, p.38.

59 Ibid., pp.38–39.

60 Ibid., p.39.

61 Ibid., p.39.

62 Ibid., pp.39–40.

63 KV1/13, Appendix E, pp.134–136.

64 KV1/13, p.40.

65 Ibid., p.40.

66 Ibid., pp.40–41.

67 Ibid., p.41.

68 Ibid., p.42.

69 Ibid., p.42.

70 KV1/59, p.13.

71 KV1/13, pp.42–43.

72 KV1/13, Appendix H, p.142.

73 KV1/13, p.43.

74 Ibid., p.29.

75 KV1/14, p.11.

76 KV1/13, p.44.

77 Ibid., p.44.

78 Ibid., p.44.

79 Ibid., p.44.

80 Ibid., pp.44–45.

81 Ibid., p.45.

82 KV1/13, p.45.

83 Ibid., p.45.

84 Ibid., pp.45–46.

85 Ibid., p.46.

86 Ibid., p.46.

87 Ibid., p.47.

88 Ibid., p.48.

89 Ibid., p.48.

90 Ibid., pp.48–49 & 51–52.

91 Ibid., p.51.

92 Ibid., p.51.

93 Ibid., p.52.

94 Ibid., p.52.

95 HO45/10809/311425, folder 71, Sealy Clarke to Moylan, regarding the attitude of Russians employed on munitions work, 19 January 1918.

96 HO45/10809/311425, folder 71, minute by Moylan, 22 January 1918.

97 KV1/13, p.53.

98 KV1/59, p.6.

99 KV1/52, pp.17, 37, 52 & 66.

100 KV1/13, p.53.

101 Ibid., p.53.

102 Ibid., p.53.

103 Ibid., p.53.

104 Ibid., pp.53–54.

105 Ibid., p.54.

106 Ibid., p.54.

107 Ibid., p.54.

108 Ibid., p.55.

109 Ibid., p.55.

110 Ibid., p.55.

111 Winter has commented on the prejudice against Russian Jews in terms of the application of conscription. J. Winter, 'Military Fitness and Civilian Health in Britain during the First World War', *Journal of Contemporary History*, Vol.15 (1980), passim.

112 KV1/13, pp.55–56.

113 Ibid., p.57.

114 Bird, *The Control of Enemy Alien Civilians in Great Britain 1914-18*, p.301.

115 KV1/14, p.16.

116 Ibid., pp.19–20.

117 Bird, *The Control of Enemy Alien Civilians in Great Britain 1914-18*, p.301.

118 KV1/13, p.62.

119 Felstead, *German Spies at Bay*, p.12.

120 Bird, *The Control of Enemy Alien Civilians in Great Britain 1914-18*, p.302.

121 Andrew, *The Defence of the Realm*, pp.98–102.

122 KV1/44, pp.34–36.

123 See, for example, MI5 files on the National Council for Civil Liberties (NCCL), KV2/663-667.

124 KV2/1411, Nicholas Klishko, Summary made in H1 from papers filed between 1.9.15 & 9.9.18, n.d.

125 KV2/1410, MI5 copy of report from Military Attaché, Petrograd to War Office, 17 September 1915.

126 KV2/1410, report on Klishko by Captain M.W. Bray of MI5, July 1918.

127 KV2/1411, Nicholas Klishko, Summary made in H1 from papers filed between 1.9.15 & 9.9.18, n.d.

128 KV1/37, Appendix O, pp.58–76.

129 KV4/113, defence security case no.79.

130 DPP1/51, report by MI5D, 13 April 1918.

131 KV4/113, defence security case no.79.

132 Andrew, *The Defence of the Realm*, pp.104–105.

133 WO32/10776, p.22.

134 Andrew, *The Defence of the Realm*, p.85.

135 Andrew, *Secret Service*, p.177.

136 Hiley, '*Counter-Espionage and Security in Great Britain during the First World War*', p.647.

137 KV1/36, p.179.

138 Beckett, *The Great War 1914-1918*, pp.129, 133 & 139–140; O. Halecki [Trans. M. Gardner & M. Corbridge-Patkaniowska], *A History of Poland* (London: J.M. Dent & Sons, 1942), pp.223–224.

139 KV1/36, pp.179–188.

140 KV1/44, p.118.

141 Andrew, *The Defence of the Realm*, p.108.

142 Ibid., pp.82–83.

143 KV1/53, Annexure 19, p.112.

144 V. Madeira, 'No Wishful Thinking Allowed': Secret Service Committee and Intelligence Reform in Great Britain, 1919-23', *Intelligence and National Security*, Vol.18, No.1 (Spring 2003), pp.4–5.

145 Smith, *The Spying Game*, p.77.

146 Ibid., pp.77–78.
147 WO32/10776, p.22; Smith, *The Spying Game*,
    p.77.
148 WO32/10776, p.22.
149 KV1/63, pp.31–32.

CHAPTER SEVEN

1 K. Jeffrey, *MI6: The History of the Secret Intelligence
   Service, 1909-1949* (London: Bloomsbury, 2010),
   pp.83–85 & 300.
2 IWM, Kell MSS, Holt-Wilson, *Security Intelligence
   in War*, p.27.
3 W. Nicolai [Trans. G. Renwick], *The German
   Secret Service* (London: Stanley Paul & Co., 1924),
   pp.216-217.

4 Thomson, *Queer People*, p.150.
5 Ibid., p.120.
6 C. von Clausewitz (M. Howard & P. Paret eds.),
   On War (London: Everyman's Library, 1993),
   p.136.
7 Holt-Wilson, *Security Intelligence in War*, p.12.
8 LHCMA, Edmonds MSS, III/5, 'Memoirs',
   Chapter XX, pp.3-4.
9 Boghardt, *German Naval Intelligence and British
   Counter-Espionage, 1901-1918*, pp.311-316.
10 KV1/35, p.8.
11 Shulsky, *Silent Warfare*, p.99.
12 Curry, *The Security Service 1908-1945*, p.60.
13 Felstead, *German Spies at Bay*, p.2.
14 Sun Tzu [Trans. T. Cleary], *The Art of War*
   (Boston, USA: Shambhala, 1988), pp.168-172.

SOURCES AND BIBLIOGRAPHY

PRIMARY SOURCES
Unpublished Official Papers, The National Archives (TNA), Kew

Admiralty (ADM)
ADM1/8429/221 – Prevention of espionage by persons impersonating officers, 1915.
ADM131/119 – spies and anti-espionage measures, August 1914–July 1918.
ADM131/120 – suspected enemy agents; aliens regulation; censorship; Defence of the Realm Act, 1914–
    September 1918.
ADM137/3856 – Extract from German directions to war intelligence agents and questionnaire given to
    German agents, 1915-1917.
ADM137/4688 – Naval Intelligence: note on duties of I.D. Section 16a, 1915-1918.
ADM178/99 – Gustave K W Triest alias Latham R Mahan RNVR. American citizen of German extraction
    charged with spying, 1915.

Air Ministry (AIR)
AIR1/551/16/15/28 – Home Defence Intelligence Summaries: Aliens, etc., also charts showing pattern of
    reported hostile submarines, April 1915-September 1915.
AIR1/558/16/15/55 – Weekly Intelligence Summary: GHQ Great Britain, December 1917-March 1918.
AIR1/561/16/15/61 – Miscellaneous correspondence and press cuttings: social and industrial matters in
    U.K, May 1918.

Board of Trade (BT)
BT66/7: Ministry of Munitions: optical munitions, glassware and potash: files. Optical munitions and
    glassware branch, c.1915-1920.

Cabinet Office (CAB)
CAB16/8 – Foreign Espionage in the United Kingdom: report and proceedings, 1909.
CAB16/232 – Conclusions of the sub-committee requested to consider the setting up of a secret service
    bureau, 1909.
CAB17/90 – Treatment of aliens in war, 1909-1913.

Colonial Office (CO)

CO418 – Colonial Office: Australia Original Correspondence, 1899-1922.

CO533/151 – Colonial Office: Kenya Original Correspondence, dispatches 1 January 1915-14 February 1915.

CO616/63 – Colonial Office: Dominions (War of 1914 to 1918) original correspondence, January 1916-July 1916.

CO694/28 – Colonies general register of secret correspondence, 1914-1927.

CO706 – Commonwealth of Australia register of correspondence, 1909-1922.

CO707 – Commonwealth of Australia register of out-letters, 1909-1922.

CO854/168-170 – Colonies confidential and secret circulars, 1907-1921.

Central Criminal Court (CRIM)

CRIM1/145/2 – Defendant: GOULD, Frederick Adolphus and GOULD, Maud. Charge: offences against the Official Secrets Act, March 1914.

CRIM1/151/2 – Defendant: ERNST, Karl Gustave. Charge: offences against the Official Secrets Act, November 1914.

CRIM1/160/1 – Defendant: DE BOURNONVILLE, Eva. Charge: attempting to communicate information to the enemy, January 1916.

CRIM1/161/3 – Defendant: MATTOCKS, Charles and MAUDE, Thomas Lupton. Charge: offences against the Official Secrets Act, 1911, May 1916.

CRIM1/176/1 – Defendant: EARLE, Martha Wilehlmina Clara. Charge: offences against the Defence of the Realm Regulations, September 1918.

Ministry Of Defence (DEFE)

DEFE1/130 – 'Report on Cable Censorship, 1914-1919', 1920.

DEFE1/131 – 'Report on Postal Censorship, 1914-1919', 1921.

DEFE1/402 – 'Report on cable censorship during 1914-1919', 1920. (2nd copy of DEFE1/130)

Director of Public Prosecutions (DPP)

DPP1/14 - HELM, S. Offence: Official Secrets Act, 1910.

DPP1/16 – GROSSE, H. Offence: Official Secrets Act, 1911.

DPP1/20 – PARROTT, G C. Offence: Official Secrets Act, 1912.

DPP1/24 – AHLERS, N E H A. Offence: High Treason, 1914.

DPP1/26 – DIEDERICHS, F. Offence: Official Secrets Act, 1914.

DPP1/27 – ERNST, K G. Offence: Official Secrets Act, 1914.

DPP1/28 – GOULD, F A, and another. Offence: Official Secrets Act, 1914.

DPP1/29 – LODY, C H. Offence: Defence of the Realm Regulations, 1914.

DPP1/30 – BRECKOW, G T, and another. Offence: Treason, 1915.

DPP1/31 – BUSCHMANN, F. Offence: Spying, 1915.

DPP1/32 – DE BOURNONVILLE, E. Offence: neutral assisting enemy, 1915.

DPP1/33 – JANSSEN, H M P, and another. Offence: Defence of the Realm Regulations 18 and 48, 1915.

DPP1/34 – MARKS, J. Offence: Defence of the Realm Regulations 18 and 48, 1915.

DPP1/35 – MELIN, E.W. Offence: Spying, 1915.

DPP1/36 – MEYER, A. Offence: Spying, 1915.

DPP1/37 – OLSSON, E G W. Offence: Official Secrets Act, 1915, 1915.

DPP1/38 – MULLER, C F and another. Offence: Spying, 1915.

DPP1/39 – RIES, I G. Offence: Spying, 1915.

DPP1/40 – ROGGEN, A A. Offence: Spying, 1915.

DPP1/41 – ROSENTHAL, R. Offence: Spying, 1915.

DPP1/42 – RYSBACH, K H de. Offence: Spying, 1915.

DPP1/44 – ZENDER, L H Y. Offence: Spying, 1915.

DPP1/45 – BRIGHT, A. Offence: Spying, 1916.

DPP1/47 – VIEYRA, L. Offence: Spying, 1916.

DPP1/48 – HAGN, A. Offence: Spying, 1917.

DPP1/51 – DOWLING, J. Offence: Army Act, Section 4 (5), 1918.

DPP4/46 – CASEMENT, Sir Roger and another. Offence: Treason, 1916.

DPP4/48 – PARROTT, G. Offence: Official Secrets, 1913.

DPP4/49 – OLSSON, E. Offence: Official Secrets, 1915.

DPP4/51 – E DE B [Bournonville], relates to an unidentified Swedish body. Offence: Official Secrets, 1916.

Foreign Office (FO)

FO371/1126 – Foreign Office: Political Departments: General correspondence from 1906: Germany, 1911.

Secret Intelligence Service (HD)

HD3/124 – Memorandum on Secret Service in event of a European War and correspondence about activities of 'A'; proposal for exchange of information with Japanese, 1903-1905.

HD3/127 – Movements of arms; further correspondence about 'A' and correspondence with War Office, 1904.

HD3/128 – Correspondence with various foreign service officials; declarations of money received and expended; comments on 'Secret Service in the event of a European War'; Kaid Maclean; correspondence with HM Embassy in St. Petersburg, 1905-1906.

HD3/131 – Letter from Mr Reddan; employment of agent in German South-West Africa; correspondence about 'A'; accounts; memorandum about smuggling arms into South Africa; correspondence between 'F' and 'I'; correspondence with HM Consul Stevens; Kaid Maclean, 1905-1906.

HD3/133 – Repatriation of unprotected British subjects in Russia; employment of agents; Russian attempts to tamper with secret papers; accounts; vouchers and declarations; 'M'; 'I'; correspondence with HM Consul Stevens; attempt to buy secret German papers; Dr Leyds, 1906.

Home Office (HO)

HO45/10629/199699 – ALIENS: registration of aliens in wartime, 1911-1914.

HO45/10727/254753 – WAR: European war 1914 – activities of enemy agents, 1914-1916.

HO45/10730/255584 – WAR: messages dropped from aeroplanes – circular issued to Chief Constables, 1914.

HO45/10732/255987 – ALIENS: Aliens Restriction Order – administration of, 1914-1917.

HO45/10734/258763 – WAR: Boy Scouts services in guarding public property, 1914.

HO45/10737 & 10738/261921 – ALIENS: Belgian refugees – position under the Aliens Restriction Order, 1914-1919.

HO45/10741/263275 – WAR: anti-recruiting and peace propaganda, 1914-1919.

HO45/10756/267450 – ALIENS: the 'spy peril' and the question of interning all enemy aliens, 1914-1917.

HO45/10757 & 10758/268174 – ALIENS: recruitment of the Belgian army in the United Kingdom, 1914-1919.

HO45/10762/270427 – ALIENS: alien friends travelling between ports in United Kingdom, 1914-1919.

HO45/10765/271164 – WAR: Defence of the Realm Act: Court Martial sentences, 1914-1916.

HO45/10772/276081 – WAR: rewards for information concerning hostile vessels, 1915.

HO45/10773 & 10774/276355 – ALIENS: control of passenger traffic to certain countries – establishment of Permit Office, 1916-1919.

HO45/10776/276521 – ALIENS: restrictions on alien seamen, 1914-1919.

HO45/10779/277334 – WAR: enemy agents causing fires in United Kingdom ships – precautions to be taken, 1915-1919.

HO45/10780/277601 – ALIENS: registration of aliens in hotels, etc, 1915-1919.

HO45/10782/278537 – WAR: military service – anti-conscription agitation, 1915-1916.

HO45/10788/299216 – WAR: Belgian refugee seamen in prohibited areas, 1914-1919.

HO45/10801/307823 – WAR: British subjects of foreign extraction – position under Military Service Act 1916, 1916.

HO45/10807/310716 – ALIENS: approved ports for aliens entering and leaving United Kingdom, 1914-1919.

HO45/10809/311425 – Aliens: employment of aliens in munitions factories, 1916-1918.

HO45/10828/323249 – ALIENS: notice for the guidance of aliens landing in United Kingdom, 1916.

HO45/10831/326287 – ALIENS: central register of aliens in United Kingdom, 1916-1919.

HO45/10831/326555 – ALIENS: scheme for employment of aliens on national service, 1917-1919.

HO45/10839/332271 – ALIENS: issue of identity books to Belgian refugees, 1917-1918.

HO45/10839/333624 – WAR: spread of diseases among animals by enemy agents, 1917-1918.

HO45/10841/335981 – ALIENS: Precautions against enemy agents at British ports, 1917-1918. And WAR: Precautions against enemy agents in British ports, 1917-1918.

HO45/10881/338498 – ALIENS: supervision of enemy aliens at large in United Kingdom, 1917-1918.

HO45/10882/343995 – ALIENS: British women married to Germans – exemption from the Aliens Restriction Order, 1917.

HO45/10882/344019 – ALIENS: repatriation of Belgian refugees, 1917-1919.

HO45/10890/355539 – CRIMINAL: definition of 'enemy agent' in the Defence of the Realm Regulations, 1918.

HO45/10892/357291 – POLICE: appreciation of work done for MI5 by police officers, 1918.

HO45/10898/368063 – ALIENS: registration of persons born in neutral or friendly countries of fathers of enemy origin, 1918.

HO45/22901 – POLICE: national intelligence service: scheme for forming, and for incorporating the police, 1917-1923.

HO144/1250/233717: Parrott, George G. Court: C.C.C. Offence: Communicating information to the enemy. Sentence: 4 years P.S, 7 January 1913.

HO144/1338/258086 – ALIENS: Captain Kurd von Weller acquitted of spying. Repatriated in exchange for Lord De Ramsey, 1914-1915.

HO144/1358/261916 – ALIENS: Aliens Restriction Orders – prohibited areas, 1914-1916.

HO144/1415/277302 – Kupferle, Anthony. Court: C.C.C. Offence: Espionage. SENTENCE: committed suicide before trial took place, 25 March 1915.

HO144/1429/288639 – Rosenthal, R. Court: London Court Martial. Offence: Espionage. Sentence: Death, 6 July 1915.

HO144/1437/298806 – Breckow, George T. Court: C.C.C. Offence: Assisting the enemy. Sentence: Death by shooting, 7 September 1915.

HO144/1484/349684 – DISTURBANCES: Industrial unrest, strikes, sabotage, pacifist organisations, arrangements for police reports, 1917-1918.

HO144/1498/364780 – CRIMINAL: 'The Black Book' mentioned in the criminal libel action against Mr. Pemberton-Billing, M.P., 1918.

HO144/1552/199768 – DISTURBANCES: South-Wales miner's strike (Tonypandy riots), 1910-1920.

HO144/3444 – CRIMINAL CASES: DOWLING, Joseph, 1918-1924.

HO144/11720 – ALIENS: Internment of enemy aliens during 1914-1918 War. Classified list, 1918-1930.

HO144/17485-7 – ALIENS: Peter Michailevitch Petroff, interned under DRR14B, 13 January 1916-13 March 1933.

HO144/23414-509 – TREASON: Sir Roger Casement, 1922-1959.

HO161/1-5 – Diaries of Roger Casement, 1901-1911.

Ministry of Information (INF)

INF4/9: Deposited Papers of Sir Robert Donald: Memoranda and Reports, n.d.

Supreme Court of Judicature (J)

J17/662 – Rex V Sir Roger David Casement and Daniel Julian Bailey, 1916.

J93/3 – Rex V Sir Roger David Casement and Daniel Julian Bailey: shorthand notes of trial, 26 June 1916-19 July 1916.

J130/119 – READING, Lord: Capital Offence (Casement trial), 1916.

Security Service (KV)

KV1/1, 'Organization of Secret Service. (Note prepared for D.M.O. on the 4th Oct. 1908)', 4 October 1908.

KV1/2, 'Espionage in Time of Peace'; War Office branch memorandum, 1908-1909.

KV1/3, 'Memorandum re Formation of a S.S. Bureau', 26 August 1909.

KV1/4, 'Intelligence Methods', 1909.

KV1/5, Copy of Kell's Letter accepting Secret Service Post and CV, 19 September 1909 & 1915.

KV1/6, CID Meeting: Kell's Presentation of Work and Records of Bureau, 3 March 1914.

KV1/7, 'List of persons arrested as Foreign Agents, and of Prosecutions undertaken up to 4th August 1914', 4 August 1914.

KV1/8, 'Memoir by William Melville MVO MBE, ex-Supt of Metropolitan Police who was Kell's first detective', 31 December 1917.

KV1/9, 'Kell's Bureau's six-monthly progress reports 1909-1914', 1909-1914.

KV1/10, 'Kell's Diary 1/6/10-28/7/11', 1 June 1910-28 July 1911.

KV1/11, Analysis of Accounts for February-October 1917, February 1917-October 1917.

KV1/12, Analysis of Accounts for February-September 1919, February 1919-September 1919.

KV1/13, 'Report on the A. Branch of M.I.5.', 1921.

KV1/14, 'A' Branch Report. Summary', 1921.

KV1/15, 'D' Branch Report. Imperial Overseas Intelligence. Vol.I', 1921.

KV1/16, 'D' Branch Report. Imperial Overseas Intelligence. Vol.II. Appendices', 1921.

KV1/17, 'D' Branch Report. Imperial Overseas Intelligence. Vol.III. Eastern Mediterranean Section and Appendices', 1921.

KV1/18, 'D' Branch Report. Imperial Overseas Intelligence. Vol.IV. Cyprus Section and Appendices', 1921.

KV1/19, 'D' Branch Report. Summary', 1921.

KV1/20, 'E' Branch Report. The Control of Ports and Frontiers. Vol.I', 1921.

KV1/21, 'E' Branch Report. The Control of Ports and Frontiers. Vol.II', 1921.

KV1/22, 'E' Branch Report. The Control of Ports and Frontiers. Vol.III', 1921.

KV1/23, 'E' Branch Report. The Control of Ports and Frontiers. Vol.IV', 1921.

KV1/24, 'E' Branch Report. The Control of Ports and Frontiers. Vol.V. First and Second Supplements', 1921.

KV1/25, 'E' Branch Report. The Control of Ports and Frontiers. Vol.VI. Third Supplement. The Military Control Office, New York', 1921.

KV1/26, 'E' Branch Report. The Control of Ports and Frontiers. Vol.VII. Fourth Supplement. History of the Port of Hull', 1921.

KV1/27, 'E' Branch Report. The Control of Ports and Frontiers. Vol.VIII. Fifth Supplement. Illegal Methods of Obtaining Passports', 1921.

KV1/28, 'E' Branch Report. The Control of Ports and Frontiers. Vol.IXA. Appendices', 1921.

KV1/29, 'E' Branch Report. The Control of Ports and Frontiers. Vol.IXB. Appendices', 1921.

KV1/30, 'E' Branch Report. The Control of Ports and Frontiers. Vol.X. Annexures Nos.1-52', 1921.

KV1/31, 'E' Branch Report. The Control of Ports and Frontiers. Vol.XI. Annexures Nos.53-84', 1921.

KV1/32, 'E' Branch Report. The Control of Ports and Frontiers. Vol.XIII. Index. A to N.E.P.', 1921.

KV1/33, 'E' Branch Report. The Control of Ports and Frontiers. Vol.XIV. Index. N.E.P. Ships to Zurich', 1921.

KV1/34, 'E' Branch Report. Vol.XV. Summary', 1921.

KV1/35, 'F' Branch Report. The Prevention of Espionage. Vol.I', 1921.

KV1/36, 'F' Branch Report. The Prevention of Espionage. Vol.II', 1921.

KV1/37, 'F' Branch Report. The Prevention of Espionage. Vol.III. Appendices', 1921.

KV1/38, 'F' Branch Report. Summary', 1921.

KV1/39, 'G' Branch Report. The Investigation of Espionage. Vol.I', 1921.

KV1/40, 'G' Branch Report. The Investigation of Espionage. Vol.II', 1921.

KV1/41, 'G' Branch Report. The Investigation of Espionage. Vol.III', 1921.

KV1/42, 'G' Branch Report. The Investigation of Espionage. Vol.IV', 1921.

KV1/43, 'G' Branch Report. The Investigation of Espionage. Vol.V', 1921.

KV1/44, 'G' Branch Report. The Investigation of Espionage. Vol.VI', 1921.

KV1/45, 'G' Branch Report. The Investigation of Espionage. Vol.VII', 1921.

KV1/46, 'G' Branch Report. The Investigation of Espionage. Vol.III. Appendices and Annexures', 1921.

KV1/47, 'G' Branch Report. The Investigation of Espionage. Vol.IX. Index', 1921.

KV1/48, 'Rough Draft Summary of the G Branch Report', 1921.

KV1/49, 'H' Branch Report. Organisation and Administration. Vol.I. Chapters 1 to 5', 1921.

KV1/50, 'H' Branch Report. Organisation and Administration. Vol.II. First Supplement. Report on Women's Work', 1921.

KV1/51, 'H' Branch Report. Organisation and Administration. Vol. III. Second Supplement. Copy of a Monthly Report (June 1918)', June 1918.

KV1/52, 'H' Branch Report. Organisation and Administration. Vol. IV. Appendices and Annexures', 1921.

KV1/53, 'H' Branch Report. Organisation and Administration. Vol. IVB. Annexures. (Papers.)', 1921.

KV1/54, 'H' Branch Report. Organisation and Administration. Annexures. (Books.) No. 23. Duties of 'H' Branch (Dec. 1917). I-P Book 12', December 1917.

KV1/55, 'Work of the Registry. (M.I.5 H.2.)', October 1917.

KV1/56, 'Office Instructions. June, 1916', June 1916.

KV1/57, 'H' Branch Report. Organisation and Administration. Vol. VI. Annexures. (Books.), MI5 Distribution of Duties, November 1918', November 1918.

KV1/59, 'Chronological List of Staff taken to 31 December 1919', December 1919.

KV1/61, 'H' Branch Report. Organisation and Administration. Vol. VII. Annexures. (Books.) No 30. M.I.5. B.L. – Volume XIV (October 1918)', October 1918.

KV1/63, 'H. Branch Report. Summary', 1921.

KV1/65, 'Control of Aliens in the United Kingdom. Volume II. 1914 to 1915', 1914–1915.

KV1/66, 'Control of Aliens in the United Kingdom. Volume III. 1916 to 1917', 1916–1917 and 1939.

KV1/67, 'Control of Aliens in the United Kingdom. Volume IV. 1918 to 1927', 1918–1927.

KV1/68, 'Contents of Reports', 1921.

KV1/69, Analysis of Accounts for April 1915–January 1916, April 1915–January 1916.

KV1/70, Analysis of Accounts for January 1916–January 1917, January 1916–January 1917.

KV1/71, 'E' Branch Report. The Control of Ports and Frontiers. Annexure No. 84. Aliens Restriction Order. Passenger Traffic. General Instructions to Aliens Officers at Approved Ports (Home Office, 31 January 1918)', 31 January 1918.

KV1/72, 'E' Branch Report. The Control of Ports and Frontiers. Annexure No. 85. The Port Officers' Guide', undated.

KV1/73, 'H.M. Postal Censorship (M.I.9.). The Testing Department (M.I.9.c.). Short Report on work done during the War', Vol. 1, April 1919.

KV1/74, 'H.M. Postal Censorship (M.I.9.). The Testing Department (M.I.9.c.). Short Report on work done during the War', Vol. 2, April 1919.

KV2/1-2 – PERSONAL FILE: MATA HARI: 'Mata Hari' alias MCLEOD, Marguerite Gertrude. German spy executed by the French in 1917, 4 December 1915–14 March 1924.

KV2/3 – PERSONAL FILE: Leopold VIEYRA, 12 May 1916–27 October 1952.

KV2/4-5 – PERSONAL FILE: George Vaux BACON, 7 November 1916–23 March 1917.

KV2/6-10 – PERSONAL FILE: CASEMENT: Roger, 13 November 1914–11 July 1921.

KV2/514-5 – PERSONAL FILE: Eamon DE VALERA: Irish, 2 August 1915–31 March 1949.

KV2/663-667 – National Council for Civil Liberties, 16 June 1916–22 February 1934.

KV2/1410-1416 – PERSONAL FILE: Nicolas Clementievitch KLISHKO & Phyllis KLISHKO, 1 January 1915–31 December 1972.

KV3/1 – COUNTER ESPIONAGE LAWS IN FOREIGN COUNTRIES: other nations' laws regarding the offence of espionage, 1908–1918, 1905–1918.

KV3/2 – INVISIBLE INK AND SECRET WRITING: first volume on World War 1 secret writing, 1917–1919.

KV4/9 – SECTION HISTORIES: report on the operations of B1H in connection with Northern Ireland and Eire during the Second World War, 1 January 1946–31 December 1946.

KV4/112 – MI5 'Game Book'. First of two volumes of MI5 case summaries from the period 1909–1937, 1 January 1909–31 December 1937.

KV4/113 – MI5 'Game Book'. Second of two volumes of MI5 case summaries from the period 1909–1937, 1 January 1909–1 December 1937.

KV4/114 – MI5 'Game Book'. MI5 case summaries from the period 1909–1937, 26 August 1927–20 October 1937.

KV4/127 – Security Service organisation from 1918 to 1939, including staff-lists, 1 November 1918–31 December 1939.

KV4/128 – division of duties between Home Office Director of Intelligence, Scotland House and the Security Service. Papers relating to the period when responsibility for the study of subversion lay with the Metropolitan Police, 1 January 1919–31 January 1919.

KV4/129 – appreciative letters from and to the Security Service. Beginning with letters of thanks exchanged with departments and police forces at the end of the First World War, the file contains other similar letters, as well as those exchanged on postings of individuals, 11 November 1918–8 August 1942.

Commissioner of the Metropolitan Police (MEPO)

MEPO2/10659-74 – Casement Papers, 1914–1921.

MEPO3/243 – William Le Queux: request for personal protection, 1914.

MEPO3/2435 – aliens holding liquor licences or employed in licensed houses in wartime: reports to local authority, 1914–1915.

MEPO3/2444 – MATA HARI: Margaretha Geertruida ZEELE known as MATA HARI: convicted of espionage and executed on 15 October 1917, 1915–1917.

MEPO3/2446 – householder's liability to report aliens living on premises, 1916–1918.

Ministry of Transport (MT)

MT25/2 – Ministry of Shipping, 1917–1921: Correspondence and papers, 1917–1921.

Ministry of Munitions (MUN)

MUN4/3588 – INTELLIGENCE: intelligence service reports, 15 December 1916–15 June 1917.

MUN5/49/300/34 – 'Commission of Enquiry into Industrial Unrest. Summary of the Reports of the Commission', Rt. Hon. G.N. Barnes, M.P., 11 July 1917.

MUN5/78/327/1 – Report and notes on alien labour, September 1915.

MUN5/78/327/3 – Report of committee appointed to consider reception and employment of Belgian refugees, December 1914.

MUN5/78/327/8 – Memorandum on conditions for aliens employed on munitions work, n.d.

Prison Commission (PCOM)

PCOM9/2315-40 – SIR ROGER CASEMENT, c.1916–1969.

Public Record Office (PRO)

PRO30/57/75 – KITCHENER PAPERS [PRIVATE PAPERS NOT PUBLIC RECORDS]: correspondence relating to the discussion of aliens in the CID in 1914, 1914.

War Office (WO)

WO32/4160 – MEMORIALS AND GRAVES: Graves (Code 36 (C)): Place of burial of KARL HANS LODY, 1936.

WO32/4161 – MEMORIALS AND GRAVES: Graves (Code 36 (C)): Request from the German Embassy for the removal of the body of KARL HANS LODY to another burial ground, 1934.

WO32/4892 – SECURITY: General (Code 84 (A)): Conference on control of passenger traffic between England and Continental ports, 1914–1915.

WO32/4898 – SECURITY: General (Code 84 (A)): Observations on imprisoned espionage agents and appeal by F L T Greite for review of sentence, 1920–1921.

WO32/5364 – ALIENS: General (Code 74 (A)): Release of enemy aliens under bond, 1914.

WO32/5368 – ALIENS: General (Code 74 (A)): Question of authority for arrest and internment, 1914.

WO32/5370 – ALIENS: General (Code 74 (A)): Question of authority for arrest and internment. Instructions for carrying out orders for arrest, 1914–1915.

WO32/5372 – ALIENS: General (Code 74 (A)): Liability of aliens for military service on return to homeland despite oath taken to effect release, 1915–1916.

WO32/5553 – INTELLIGENCE: General (Code 69 (A)): Abolition of intelligence organisation for dealing with revolutionary and industrial unrest in United Kingdom, 1919–1920.

WO32/8873 – ALIENS: General (Code 74 (A)): Legal powers necessary to deal with suspicious aliens. Question of amendment to Official Secrets Act, 1907.

WO32/9098 – HOME DEFENCE: General (Code 90 (A)): Memorandum on duties of the Police in the event of War, 1911–1914.

WO32/10776 – ARMY ORGANISATION: General (Code 14 (A)): History of Military Intelligence Directorate, 1920–1921.

WO32/15541-2 & 44 – Prisoner of war, Capt Lt Franz Rintelen, 1915-1918.

WO71/1237 – Melin, E W. Offence: Espionage, 1915.

WO71/1238 – Ries, I G. Offence: Espionage, 1915.

WO71/1239 – Van Der Goten, L F. Offence: Espionage, 1917.

WO71/1312 – Roos, W.J. and Janssen, S.S. Offence: Attempting to communicate information to the enemy, 1915.

WO71/1313 – Buschman, F. Offence: Supplying information to the enemy, 1915.

WO94/103 – Documents concerning prisoners confined in the Tower of London for espionage during the First World War, including those executed, 1914-1918.

WO94/104 – Two papers notifying the Tower authorities of Sir Roger Casement's arrival and departure, April 1916-May 1916.

WO106/262 – Report of the Commission concerning the native rising within the Nyasaland Protectorate, 1916.

WO106/295 – Cable Censor's Handbook, incorporating MI8 list of enemy traders and their agents, 1917.

WO141/1/3 – Espionage charge against Anthony Kupferle, 1915.

WO141/1/5 – Robert Rosenthal. Espionage charges, 1915.

WO141/1/6 – W J Roos. Espionage charges, 1915.

WO141/1/7 – H M P Jannsen. Espionage charges, 1915.

WO141/2/1 – F Buschmann. Espionage charges, 1915.

WO141/2/2 – C F Muller. Espionage charges, 1915.

WO141/2/3 – E W Melin. Espionage charges, 1915.

WO141/2/4 – L H Zender. Espionage charges, 1915.

WO141/3/1 – R Rowland and Mrs L E Wertheim. Espionage charges, 1915.

WO141/3/2 – I Guy Ries. Espionage charges, 1917.

WO141/3/4 – Charges of spying against G V Bacon and trial by Court Martial, 1917.

WO141/3/5 – Charges of spying against Norwegian Alfred Hagn and commutation of sentence, 1917.

WO141/3/6 – Charges of spying against L F Van der Goten, Belgian subject, 1917.

WO141/61 – Auguste Alfredo Roggen: Espionage, 1915.

WO141/82 – Hans Lody or Lodi, alias C Inglis: espionage, 1914-1915.

WO141/83 – Albert Meyer: espionage, 1915-1916. [Formerly classed as: WO32/3903.]

WO158/981 – 'Lecture on Prevention of Leakage of Information', by Lt-Col W. Kirke, GS(I)b, May 1916.

WO158/984 – instructions on the collection and transmission of intelligence in the United Kingdom, March 1916.

WO158/989 – General Headquarters, Home Forces: Intelligence Circulars. No6: alleged enemy signalling in Great Britain, 1 May 1916-31 May 1916.

Unpublished Memoirs and Unofficial Papers

Viscount Cave MSS, British Library, Manuscripts Section.

Brigadier-General Sir James Edmonds MSS, Liddell Hart Centre for Military Archives (LHCMA), King's College, London.

Admiral Sir W. Reginald Hall MSS, Churchill College Archives Centre (CCAC), Cambridge.

Major-General Sir Vernon Kell MSS, Imperial War Museum (IWM), London.

Major-General Sir Walter Kirke MSS, Imperial War Museum (IWM), London.

Reginald McKenna MSS, Churchill College Archives Centre (CCAC), Cambridge.

Published Papers

Blake, R. (ed.), *The Private Papers of Douglas Haig*. London: Eyre & Spottiswoode, 1952.

Brett, Maurice V. & Esher, Oliver, Viscount (eds.), *Journals and Letters of Reginald Viscount Esher*. (4 Vols.) London: Ivor Nicholson & Watson, 1934-1938.

Curry, John Court, *The Security Service 1908-1945: the Official History*. Kew: PRO, 1999. The report was in fact written in 1946. The PRO published version has an introduction by Christopher Andrew.

Doerries, Reinhard R. (ed.), *Prelude to the Easter Rising: Sir Roger Casement in Imperial Germany*. London: Frank Cass, 2000.

Ferris, John (ed.), *The British Army and Signals Intelligence during the First World War*. Stroud: Sutton/Army Records Society, 1992.

Jeffery, Keith (ed.), *The Military Correspondence of Field Marshal Sir Henry Wilson 1918-1922*. London: Army Records Society, 1985.

Kemp, P. (ed.), *The Papers of Admiral Sir John Fisher*. (2 Vols.) London: Navy Records Society, 1960 & 1964.

Marder, A. (ed.), *Fear God and Dread Nought: the Correspondence of Lord Fisher*. London: Jonathan Cape, 1952-9.

Mitrokhin, Vasiliy (ed.), *KGB Lexicon: the Soviet Intelligence Officer's Handbook*. London: Frank Cass, 2002.

Morris, A.J.A. (ed.), *The Letters of Lieutenant-Colonel Charles à Court Repington CMG Military Correspondent of the Times, 1903-1918*. London: Army Records Society, 1999.

O'Halpin, Eunan (ed.), *MI5 and Ireland, 1939-1945: the Official History*. Dublin: Irish Academic Press, 2003.
    Parliamentary Debates, Commons, 1909-1918.

Paterson, A. Temple (ed.), *The Jellicoe Papers*. (2 Vols.) London: Navy Records Society, 1966-68.
    The Times, 1909-1918.

Woodward, David R. (ed.), *The Military Correspondence of Field-Marshal Sir William Robertson, Chief of the Imperial General Staff, December 1915-February 1918*. London: Army Records Society, 1989.

Published Memoirs and Biographies

Ash, Bernard, *The Lost Dictator: a Biography of Field-Marshal Sir Henry Wilson*. London: Cassell, 1968.

The Earl of Oxford and Asquith, K.G., *Memoirs and Reflections, 1852-1927*. (2 Vols.) London: Cassell & Co., 1928.

Aston, G., *Secret Service*. London: Faber & Faber, 1939.

Bonham-Carter, V., *Soldier True: the Life and Times of Field Marshal Sir William Robertson*. London: Frederick Muller, 1963.

Boyle, A., *Trenchard: Man of Vision*. London: Collins, 1962.

Callwell, Charles E., *Experiences of a Dug-out, 1914-1918*. London: Constable & Co., 1920.

Callwell, C. (ed.), *Field-Marshal Sir Henry Wilson Bt.: his Life and Diaries*. (2 Vols.) London: Cassell, 1927.

Callwell, C.E., *Stray Recollections*. (2 Vols.) London: Edward Arnold, 1923.

Charteris, J.A., *At GHQ*. London: Cassell, 1931.

Churchill, Randolph, *Lord Derby: 'King of Lancashire'*. London: Heinemann, 1959.

Churchill, The Right Hon. Winston S, C.H., M.P., *The World Crisis, 1911-1918*. (1 Vol. abridged & revised.) London: Macmillan & Co., 1941.

Cockerill, George K., *What Fools we Were*. London: Hutchinson & Co., 1944.

Cook, Andrew, *M: MI5's First Spymaster*. Stroud: Tempus, 2004.

Dutton, David, *Simon: a Political Biography of Sir John Simon*. London: Aurum Press, 1992.

Felstead, S.T. (ed.), *Steinhauer: the Kaiser's Master Spy. The Story as Told by Himself*. London: John Lane, 1930.

Fisher of Kilverstone, Baron, *Memories*. London: Hodder & Stoughton, 1919.
    – *Records*. London: Hodder & Stoughton, 1919.

Fitch, H., *Traitors Within: the Adventures of Detective Inspector Herbert T. Fitch*. London: Hurst & Blackett, 1933.

Fraser, Peter, *Lord Esher: a Political Biography*. London: Hart-Davis, MacGibbon, 1973.

Grey, Sir Edward, *Twenty-Five Years*. (2 Vols.) London: Hodder & Stoughton, 1925.

Haldane, Richard Burdon, *An Autobiography*. London: Hodder & Stoughton, 1929.

Hankey, Lord, *The Supreme Command, 1914-1918*. (2 Vols.) London: George Allen & Unwin, 1961.

Hardinge, Charles, *Old Diplomacy: the Reminiscences of Lord Hardinge of Penshurst*. London: John Murray, 1947.

Holmes, R., *The Little Field Marshal*. London: Jonathan Cape, 1981.

Hyde, H. Montgomery, *Carson: the Life of Sir Edward Carson, Lord Carson of Duncairn*. London: William Heinemann Ltd., 1953.

Jellicoe, John Rushworth, *The Crisis of the Naval War*. London: Cassell & Co., 1920.

Jenkins, Roy, *Asquith*. London: Collins, 1978.

Jones, R.V., *Most Secret War*. Ware: Wordsworth Editions Ltd., 1998.

Kluck, Alexander von, *The March on Paris and the Battle of the Marne 1914*. London: Edward Arnold, 1920. An edited and translated version of von Kluck's *Der Marsch auf Paris, und die Marneschlacht* (Berlin, Germany: Mittler, c.1920) published under the auspices of the Committee of Imperial Defence in 1920.

Lloyd George, D., *War Memoirs*. (2 Vols.) London: Odhams Press, 1938.

MacKay, R., *Fisher of Kilverstone*. Oxford: Clarendon Press, 1973.

Magnus, Philip, *Kitchener: Portrait of an Imperialist*. London: John Murray, 1958.

Mallet, Charles, *Lord Cave. A Memoir*. London: John Murray, 1931.

   – *Herbert Gladstone: a Memoir*. London: Hutchinson, 1932.

McKenna, Stephen, *Reginald McKenna*. London: Eyre & Spottiswoode, 1948.

Morgan, Kenneth, & Morgan, Jane, *Portrait of a Progressive: the Political Career of Christopher, Viscount Addison*. Oxford: Clarendon Press, 1980.

Naylor, John F., *A Man and an Institution: Sir Maurice Hankey, the Cabinet Secretariat and the Custody of Cabinet Secrecy*. Cambridge: CUP, 1984.

Nicolai, Colonel W. (Translated by G. Renwick), *The German Secret Service*. London: Stanley Paul & Co., 1924.

O'Brien, Terence H., *Milner: Viscount Milner of St James's and Cape Town, 1854-1925*. London: Constable, 1979.

Paterson, A. Temple, *Jellicoe: a Biography*. London: Macmillan, 1969.

Read, A. & Fisher, D., *Colonel Z: the Secret Life of a Master of Spies*. London: Hodder & Stoughton, 1984.

Rimington, Stella, *Open Secret: the Autobiography of the Former Director-General of MI5*. London: Hutchinson, 2001.

Rintelen, Captain von (With an Introduction by Reinhard R. Doerries), *The Dark Invader: Wartime Reminiscences of a German Naval Intelligence Officer*. London: Frank Cass, 1998. First published in 1933.

Robbins, Keith, *Sir Edward Grey: a Biography*. London: Cassell, 1971.

Robertson, Sir William, *From Private to Field-Marshal*. London: Constable, 1921.

   – *Soldiers and Statesmen, 1914-1918*. (2 Vols.) London: Cassell & Co., 1926.

Roskill, S., *Earl Beatty*. London: Collins, 1980.

Roskill, Stephen, *Hankey: Man of Secrets*. (3 Vols.) London: Collins, 1970.

Rowland, John, *The Finger-Print Man: the Story of Sir Edward Henry*. London: Lutterworth Press, 1959.

Rowland, Peter, *Lloyd George*. London: Barrie & Jenkins, 1975.

Seeley, J.E.B., *Adventure*. London: William Heinemann, 1933.

Seth, Ronald Sidney, *The Spy Who Wasn't Caught: the Story of Julius Silber*. London: Hale, 1966.

Silber, Julius C., *The Invisible Weapons*. London: Hutchinson, 1932.

Siebert, B. von, *Graf Benckendorffs Diplomatischer Schriftwechsel herausgeben von B. von Siebert, Band I-III*. Berlin & Leipzig, Germany, 1928.

Sims, Joseph P. (ed.), *Three Wars with Germany: Admiral Sir W. Reginald Hall and Amos J. Peaslee*. New York, USA: G.P. Putnam's Sons, 1944.

Spiers, Edward M., *Haldane: an Army Reformer*. Edinburgh: Edinburgh University Press, 1980.

Terraine, John, *Haig: the Educated Soldier*. London: Cassell & Co., 2000.

Thomson, Sir Basil, *My Experiences at Scotland Yard*. New York, USA: Doubleday, Page & Company, 1923.

Thomson, Sir Basil, *Queer People*. London: Hodder & Stoughton, 1922.

   – *The Story of Scotland Yard*. London: Grayson & Grayson, 1935.

   – *The Scene Changes*. London: Collins, 1939.

Troup, Sir Edward, *The Home Office*. London: G.P. Putnam's Sons Ltd., 1925.

SECONDARY SOURCES

Works of Reference

Beckett, Ian F.W., *The First World War: the Essential Guide to Sources in the UK National Archives*. Kew: PRO, 2002.

Davies, Philip H.J., *The British Secret Services*. Oxford: ABC-Clio, 1996.

Hazlehurst, Cameron, & Woodland, Christine (eds.), *A Guide to the Papers of British Cabinet Ministers 1900-1951*. London: Royal Historical Society, 1974.

Makepeace-Warne, Antony, *Brassey's Companion to the British Army*. London: Brassey's, 1995.

PRO, *M.I.5: the First Ten Years, 1909-1919*. Kew: PRO, 1997.

Roper, Michael, *The Records of the War Office and Related Departments, 1660-1964*. Kew: PRO, 1998.

Monographs

Allason, Rupert, *The Branch: a History of the Metropolitan Police Special Branch 1883-1983*. London: Secker & Warburg, 1983.

Andrew, Christopher, *Secret Service: the Making of the British Intelligence Community*. London: Heinemann, 1985.

– *The Defence of the Realm: The Authorized History of MI5*. London: Allen Lane, 2009.

Andrew, Christopher, & Dilks, David (eds.), *The Missing Dimension: Governments and Intelligence Communities in the Twentieth Century*. London: Macmillan, 1984.

Andrew, Christopher, & Gordievsky, Oleg, *KGB: the Inside Story of its Foreign Operations from Lenin to Gorbachev*. London: Sceptre, 1991.

Andrew, Christopher, & Mitrokhin, Vasili, *The Mitrokhin Archive: the KGB in Europe and the West*. London: Allen Lane, the Penguin Press, 1999.

Andrew, Christopher, & Noakes, Jeremy (eds.), *Intelligence and International Relations 1909-1945*. Exeter: University of Exeter, 1987.

Beckett, Ian F.W., *The Great War 1914-1918*. Harlow: Longman, 2001.

Beesly, P., *Room 40: British Naval Intelligence 1914-18*. London: Hamish Hamilton, 1982.

Bird, J.C., *The Control of Enemy Alien Civilians in Great Britain 1914-18*. New York, USA: Garland Publishing, 1986.

Boghardt, Thomas, *Spies of the Kaiser: German Covert Operations in Great Britain during the First World War Era*. Basingstoke: Palgrave Macmillan, 2004.

Bulloch, John, *M.I.5: the Origin and History of the British Counter-Espionage Service*. London: Arthur Barker, 1963.

Bungert, Heike, Heitman, Jan G., & Wala, Michael (eds.), *Secret Intelligence in the Twentieth Century*. London: Frank Cass, 2003.

Clayton, Anthony, *Forearmed: a History of the Intelligence Corps*. London: Brassey's, 1996.

Clausewitz, Carl von (Howard, Michael, & Paret, Peter (eds.)), *On War*. London: Everyman's Library, 1993. First published in 1832.

Dockrill, Michael, & French, David (eds.), *Strategy and Intelligence: British Policy during the First World War*. London: Hambledon Press, 1996.

Felstead, S.T., *German Spies at Bay*. London: Hutchinson & Co., 1920.

Fergusson, Thomas G., *British Military Intelligence, 1870-1914: the Development of a Modern Intelligence Organization*. Frederick, USA: University Publications of America, 1984.

Fisher, John, *Gentleman Spies: Intelligence Agents in the British Empire and Beyond*. Stroud: Sutton, 2002.

Foy, Michael, & Barton, Brian, *The Easter Rising*. Stroud: Sutton, 1999.

Gilbert, Martin, *First World War*. London: HarperCollins, 1995.

Gill, Peter, *Policing Politics: Security Intelligence and the Liberal Democratic State*. London: Frank Cass, 1994.

Godson, Roy, *Dirty Tricks or Trump Cards: U.S. Covert Action & Counterintelligence*. New Brunswick, USA: Transaction, 2001.

Halecki, O. [Trans. Monica M. Gardner & Mary Corbridge-Patkaniowska], *A History of Poland*. London: J.M. Dent & Sons, 1942.

Herman, Michael, *Intelligence Power in Peace and War*. Cambridge: CUP, 1996.

Hopkirk, Peter, *On Secret Service East of Constantinople: the Plot to Bring Down the British Empire*. Oxford: OUP, 2001.

Judd, Alan, *The Quest for C: Mansfield Cumming and the Founding of the Secret Service*. London: HarperCollins, 1999.

Keegan, John, *The First World War*. London: Pimlico, 1999.

Knightley, Phillip, *The Second Oldest Profession: the Spy as Bureaucrat, Patriot, Fantasist and Whore*. London: Andre Deutsch, 1986.

Le Queux, William, *German Spies in England: an Exposure*. London: Stanley Paul & Co., 1915.

Le Queux, William (With an introduction by Nicholas Hiley), *Spies of the Kaiser: Plotting the Downfall of England*. London: Frank Cass, 1996. First published in 1909.

McKay, C.G., & Beckman, Bengt, *Swedish Signal Intelligence 1900-1945*. London: Frank Cass, 2003.

Millman, Brock, *Managing Domestic Dissent in First World War Britain*. London: Frank Cass, 2000.

Occleshaw, Michael, *Armour Against Fate: British Military Intelligence in the First World War*. London: Columbus, 1989.

Panayi, Panikos, *The Enemy in our Midst: Germans in Britain During the First World War*. Oxford: Berg, 1991.

Parritt, B.A.H., *The Intelligencers: the Story of British Military Intelligence up to 1914*. Ashford: Intelligence Corps Association, 1983.

Popplewell, Richard J., *Intelligence and Imperial Defence: British Intelligence and the Defence of the Indian Empire 1904-1924*. London: Frank Cass, 1995.

Porter, Bernard, *Plots and Paranoia: a History of Political Espionage in Britain 1790-1988*. London: Unwin Hyman, 1989.

Porter, Bernard, *The Origins of the Vigilant State: the London Metropolitan Police Special Branch before the First World War*. London: Weidenfeld & Nicolson, 1987.

Proctor, Tammy M., *Female Intelligence: Women and Espionage in the First World War*. New York, USA: New York University Press, 2003.

Richelson, Jeffrey T., *A Century of Spies*. Oxford: OUP, 1985.

Sellers, Leonard, *Shot in the Tower: the Story of the Spies Executed in the Tower of London During the First World War*. Barnsley: Leo Cooper/Pen & Sword Books, 1997.

Shulsky, Abram N., *Silent Warfare: Understanding the World of Intelligence*. Washington DC, USA: Brassey's (US), 1991.

Smith, Michael, *New Cloak, Old Dagger: How Britain's Spies Came In From the Cold*. London: Victor Gollancz, 1996.

– *The Spying Game: the Secret History of British Espionage*. London: Politico's, 2003.

Sparrow, Elizabeth, *Secret Service: British Agents in France 1792-1815*. Woodbridge: Boydell & Brewer, 1999.

Stafford, David, *The Silent Game: the Real World of Imaginary Spies*. London: Viking, 1989.

– *Churchill and Secret Service*. London: Abacus, 2000.

Strachan, Hew, *The First World War, Volume I: to Arms*. Oxford: OUP, 2001.

– *The First World War*. London: Simon & Schuster, 2003.

Thomas, Rosamund M., *Espionage and Secrecy: the Official Secrets Acts 1911-1989 of the United Kingdom*. London: Routledge, 1991.

Thurlow, Richard, *The Secret State: British Internal Security in the Twentieth Century*. Oxford: Blackwell, 1994.

West, Nigel, *A Matter of Trust: MI5 1945-72*. London: Weidenfeld & Nicolson, 1982.

– *MI5: British Security Service Operations 1909-1945*. New York, USA: Stein & Day, 1982.

Articles

Bennett, Gill, 'Declassification and Release Policies of the UK's Intelligence Agencies', *Intelligence and National Security*, Vol.17, No.1 (Spring 2002), pp.21-32.

Black, Alistair, & Brunt, Rodney, 'Information Management in Business, Libraries and British Military Intelligence: Towards a History of Information Management', *The Journal of Documentation*, Vol.55, No.4 (September 1999), pp.361-374.

– 'Information Management in MI5 Before the Age of the Computer', *Intelligence and National Security*, Vol.16, No.2 (Summer 2001), pp.158-165.

– 'MI5, 1909-1945: an information management perspective', *Journal of Information Science*, Vol.26, No.3 (2000), pp.185-197.

Buse, Dieter K., 'Domestic Intelligence and German Military Leaders, 1914-18', *Intelligence and National Security*, Vol.15, No.4 (Winter 2000), pp.42-59.

J.E.E. [Edmonds], 'Brigadier Sir Eric E.B. Holt-Wilson, Kt., C.M.G., D.S.O.', *Royal Engineers Journal*, Vol.LXIV, No.3, (September 1950), pp.342-345.

Englander, David, 'Military Intelligence and the Defence of the Realm: the Surveillance of Soldiers and Civilians during the First World War', *Bulletin of the Society for the Study of Labour History*, Vol.52, No.1 (1987), pp.24-32.

French, David, 'Spy Fever in Britain, 1900-1915', *The Historical Journal*, Vol. 21, No.2 (1978), pp.355-370.

Hiley, Nicholas, 'The Failure of British Counter-Espionage Against Germany, 1907-1914', *The Historical Journal*, Vol. 28, No.4 (1985), pp.635-670.

– 'Counter-Espionage and Security in Great Britain during the First World War', *English Historical Review*, Vol.CI (July 1986), pp.835-862.

– 'British Internal Security in Wartime: The Rise and Fall of P.M.S.2, 1915-17', *Intelligence and National Security*, Vol.1, No.3 (September 1986), pp.395-415.

– 'Decoding German Spies: British Spy Fiction, 1908-18', *Intelligence and National Security*, Vol.5, No.4 (October 1990), pp.55-79.

Hiley, Nicholas, & Putkowski, Julian, 'A Postscipt on P.M.S.2', *Intelligence and National Security*, Vol.3, No.2 (April 1988), pp.326-331.

Hoare, Oliver, 'Introduction', *Intelligence and National Security*, Vol.17, No.1 (Spring 2002), pp.1-5.

Jelen, George F., 'The Defensive Disciplines of Intelligence', *International Journal of Intelligence and Counterintelligence*, Vol.5, No.4 (Winter 1991-2), pp.381-399.

Kealey, Gregory S., 'The Surveillance State: The Origins of Domestic Intelligence and Counter-Subversion in Canada, 1914-21', *Intelligence and National Security*, Vol.7, No.3 (July 1992), pp.179-210.

Lander, Sir Stephen, 'British Intelligence in the Twentieth Century', *Intelligence and National Security*, Vo.17, No.1 (Spring 2002), pp.7-20.

MacDonogh, Sir G.M., 'Military Intelligence and Incidents Connected Therewith During the War', *The Journal of the Royal Artillery*, Vol.XLVIII, No.10 (1921/22), pp.399-408.

Madeira, Victor, "'No Wishful Thinking Allowed': Secret Service Committee and Intelligence Reform in Great Britain, 1919-23', *Intelligence and National Security*, Vol.18, No.1 (Spring 2003), pp.1-20.

Popplewell, Richard, 'British Intelligence in Mesopotamia, 1914-16', *Intelligence and National Security*, Vol.5, No.2 (April 1990), pp.139-172.

– 'The Surveillance of Indian Revolutionaries in Great Britain and on the Continent, 1903-14', *Intelligence and National Security*, Vol.3, No.1 (January 1988), pp.56-76.

Porter, Bernard, 'The Historiography of the Early Special Branch', *Intelligence and National Security*, Vol.1, No.3 (September 1986), pp.381-394.

Sheffy, Yigal, 'British Intelligence and the Middle East, 1900-1918: How Much Do We Know?', *Intelligence and National Security*, Vol.17, No.1 (Spring 2002), pp.33-52.

Spence, Richard B., 'Englishmen in New York: The SIS American Station, 1915-21', *Intelligence and National Security*, Vol.19, No.3 (Autumn 2004), pp.511-537.

Thurlow, Richard C., 'The Charm Offensive: the 'Coming Out' of MI5', *Intelligence and National Security*, Vol.15, No.1 (Spring 2000), pp.183-190.

Watt, D. Cameron, 'Intelligence Studies: The Emergence of the British School', *Intelligence and National Security*, Vol.3, No.2 (April 1988), pp.338-341.

Wark, Wesley K., 'In Never-Never Land? The British Archives on Intelligence', *The Historical Journal*, Vol. 35, No.1 (1992), pp.195-203.

Winter, Jay, 'Military Fitness and Civilian Health in Britain during the First World War', *Journal of Contemporary History*, Vol.15 (1980), pp.211-244.

Theses and Dissertations

Boghardt, Thomas, 'German Naval Intelligence and British Counter-Espionage, 1901-1918'. D.Phil.: University of Oxford, 2001.

Davies, Philip H.J., 'Organisational Development of Britain's Secret Intelligence Service 1909-1979'. Ph.D.: University of Reading, 1997.

INDEX